D1603606

Pitt Latin American Series

SPORT IN CUBA

THE DIAMOND IN THE ROUGH

*Paula J. Pettavino and
Geralyn Pye*

UNIVERSITY OF PITTSBURGH PRESS

Pittsburgh and London

Published by the University of Pittsburgh Press, Pittsburgh, Pa., 15260
Copyright © 1994, University of Pittsburgh Press
All rights reserved
Manufactured in the United States of America
Printed on acid-free paper

Library of Congress Cataloging-in-Publication Data

Pettavino, Paula J.
    Sport in Cuba : the diamond in the rough / Paula J. Pettavino and
Geralyn Pye.
        p.   cm.—(Pitt Latin American series)
    Includes bibliographical references (p.   ) and index.
    ISBN 0-8229-3764-6 (alk. paper).—ISBN 0-8229-5512-1 (pbk. :
alk. paper)
    1. Sports and state—Cuba—History. I. Pye, Geralyn, 1962–.
II. Title. III. Series.
GV706.35P48   1993
796'.097291—dc20   93-24372
                                                                CIP

A CIP catalogue record for this book is available from the British Library.
Eurospan, London

Contents

Preface

In the streets of Havana today, the *gua guas* (buses) pass in fewer numbers, spewing ever bigger clouds of dark black smoke. Unlit streets in el Centro and Old Havana add to growing problems with assault and prostitution as Cubans seek ways to get material goods and the dollars to buy them. Shortages of food, clothing, gasoline, and electricity have reduced the quality of Cuban life. Even "activists" in government bodies and the Partido Comunista de Cuba (PCC) seek out (or at the very least accept with smiles) gifts from the growing number of tourists. Workers in the tourism services accept tips previously frowned upon and even hand American dollars to visitors willing to purchase in tourist shops goods that are scarce elsewhere on the island. The few cars (mostly Russian Ladas or 40-year-old American models) seem likely to crash into the multiplying numbers of bicycles without lights in the innumerable darkened, uneven, narrow streets in the crowded Cuban capital.

With all these problems and many more, Cuba's sports achievements may seem insignificant, or even irrelevant. Indeed, money spent on sports is likely to be cut. Yet, practicing sports is something the Cubans take pride in, take part in, and may escape into, at very little expense. The Cuban sports system that has been built up since 1959 is indeed impressive, and it is comprehensive in both mass participation and elite performance.

These achievements in sports provide the focus of this book. Yet the scope of Cuban sporting success did not come to pass only with the revolution. Cuba had shown itself to be a fount of athletic talent (although selective) as early as the mid–nineteenth century. This

book, then, will compare sport in Cuba prior to 1959 with what develops afterward, and consider some of the limitations and problems of sports in revolutionary Cuba. The future of sports and the
political uses to which it is put are considered in the light of the des-
perate economic and political isolation in which this tropical island
finds itself.

Acknowledgments

We would like to acknowledge the following people for their assistance in this effort: Howard Wiarda, who suggested the project; Kathy McLaughlin, our editor and unraveler of tables at the University of Pittsburgh Press, who always gave us just a little more time; all of the Cubans at INDER and ICAP for interviews and assistance; Professor Bill Brugger at The Flinders University for help with "trans-Pacific computing"; Dean Robert Draghi and Lynne Kelly of the Arts and Sciences Department, and the staff at the Reinsch Library at Marymount University; the special support and especially the "clipping services" of John and Wilma Pettavino; family and friends, especially Miguel Guzmán Vega, Angie Gillingham, Annette Iafrate, Rob Ruck, and Allen, Sam, and Madeline Farber for support and encouragement.

SPORT IN
CUBA

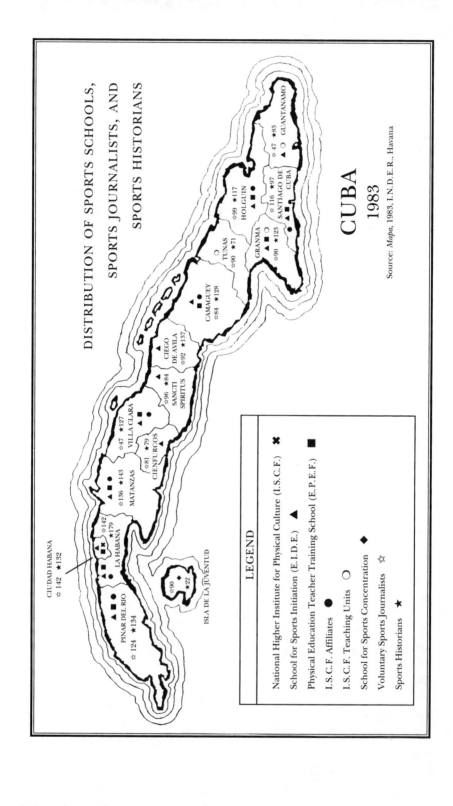

DISTRIBUTION OF SPORTS SCHOOLS,
SPORTS JOURNALISTS, AND
SPORTS HISTORIANS

CUBA
1983

Source: *Mapa*, 1983, I.N.D.E.R., Havana

LEGEND

National Higher Institute for Physical Culture (I.S.C.F.) ✖

School for Sports Initiation (E.I.D.E.) ▲

Physical Education Teacher Training School (E.P.E.F.) ■

I.S.C.F. Affiliates ●

I.S.C.F. Teaching Units ○

School for Sports Concentration ◆

Voluntary Sports Journalists ☆

Sports Historians ★

CIUDAD HABANA
☆ 142 ★ 132

PINAR DEL RIO
☆ 124 ★ 134

LA HABANA
☆ 142 ★ 179

MATANZAS
☆ 136 ★ 143

CIENFUEGOS
☆ 81 ★ 79

VILLA CLARA
☆ 47 ★ 127

SANCTI
SPIRITUS
☆ 96 ★ 84

CIEGO
DE AVILA
☆ 92 ★ 137

CAMAGUEY
☆ 84 ★ 128

TUNAS
☆ 90 ★ 71

HOLGUIN
☆ 99 ★ 117

GRANMA
☆ 90 ★ 123

SANTIAGO DE
CUBA
☆ 116 ★ 97

GUANTANAMO
☆ 47 ★ 83

ISLA DE LA JUVENTUD
☆ 90 ◆ 92

1

The Politics of Sport in Cuba: Foundations

After the 1987 Pan-American Games in Indianapolis, a Cuban newspaper headline read, "CUBA: 7.5 Medals per Million Inhabitants. USA: 0.70."[1] Despite a limited pool of talent and a notorious weakness in certain sports, Cuba has proved itself a sporting powerhouse since the end of the nineteenth century. An island with a population smaller than many U.S. cities has achieved an astounding measure of athletic success.

Before the revolution, such wild success was limited to selected sports such as baseball and boxing. In 1959, however, Fidel Castro pulled the stops on Cuban sports fanaticism, and he has since presided over unprecedented growth and mastery of a long list of international sports. In baseball, for example, Cuba has amassed a record of 71–1 in international tournaments. Cuba also won gold medals in the last two Pan-American Games, in the 1988 and 1990 world championships, and in the 1987, 1989, and 1991 Intercontinental Cup Games. Most significant, perhaps, Cuba won the first Olympic gold medal ever awarded for baseball, at the 1992 Olympics in Barcelona. The Cuban team was called "the other Dream Team."[2]

3

When it came time for the 1991 Pan-American Games held in Havana, Cuba had not been tested in other sports for a decade, because they boycotted the 1984 and 1988 Olympics. Because of the U.S. boycott of the 1980 Moscow Olympics, Cuba had not faced U.S. Olympic athletes since 1976, when Alberto Juantorena had won both the 400– and 800–meter races. In 1991, the United States won the most medals (352 to Cuba's 265), but Cuba took home the most gold (140 to the United States' 130) and did so in the sports that really matter: basketball, baseball, boxing, and track and field. This was the first time the United States had been beaten in the tally of gold medals since 1951, when the Pan-American Games began. In silver medals, the United States recovered some national pride (winning 125 to Cuba's 62), as well as in bronze (97 to Cuba's 63). In the famous national pastime of both Cuba and the United States, sixty thousand Cubans watched their undefeated national team beat the "yanquis," 3–2.[3] Cuba also won 11 of the 12 gold medals in boxing and amassed 29 of the 30 gold medals in weightlifting.

In 1992 came the Summer Olympics in Barcelona. Cuba placed fifth in the tally of gold medals, with a total of fourteen: seven in boxing, one in women's volleyball, one in women's discus, one in men's high jump, one in baseball, two in wrestling, and one in women's judo. In addition, Cuba won six silver and eleven bronze medals.

Yet, despite this glowing success, the Cuban sports system is in jeopardy, and one need look no further for a reason than those same Pan-American Games held in Havana. There is a striking contrast between the relative poverty of ordinary Cubans with their ration books and the relative plenty of the athletes. Cuba has overwhelming economic problems, resulting from the near-cessation of aid from the former Soviet Union and Eastern Europe, but the Cuban government still spent an estimated $24 million (in hard currency) and 100 million pesos ($132 million) to build athletic and residential facilities for the Pan-American Games. The average Cuban has to wait in line for soap, bread, chicken, coffee, and even sugar, and there was understandable resentment throughout the island that seventeen thousand visitors were served all-you-can-eat buffets. Castro was "doing the wave," while ordinary Cubans were lining up for essentials. Although the demonstrations against Castro predicted by some people did not materialize, one U.S. official pointed out that Fidel may still be generally popular, but "you can't eat charisma." One graduate of the University of Havana cited by

Spencer Reiss compared Cuba and the Games to the Roman Empire. "Remember the end of the Roman Empire—bread and circuses? That's the *Panamericanos.* Only soon even the *pan* [bread] will be gone."[4]

According to Gustavo Rolle, an official of the Cuban Institute for Sports, Education, and Recreation, there is no resentment:

> The Olympics are important to our people, especially in these difficult economic times. So our people clearly understand that our athletes need more food than the average person because their energy consumption is very high. They understand that our athletes have to consume what they need.

Yet sports writers covering the Pan-American Games, such as Tom Knott of the *Washington Times,* spoke of the "jarring contrasts: the shiny facilities and the decay; the official pomp and circumstance against the unofficial whispers of discontent. I was jarred by the food lines and grim faces, jarred by the omnipresent police and military." He also wondered if Cuban boxer Teófilo Stevenson, who said "We are all equals in Cuban society," had to wait in bread lines or ride on a bicycle.[5]

The athletes seem to want for nothing. They certainly have all the food they can eat and, instead of the now-typical Cuban bicycle (imported from China), they have cars, drivers, and houses. According to José Fuentes, manager of the Cuban National baseball team, "Our government has a general assistance [policy] for all people who are outstanding. The government tries to give better living conditions to the most outstanding people. I think our resources are distributed in a just way. I think the people who do the greatest effort should be the prized ones."[6]

Has the situation in Cuba deteriorated to such a level, in this "Special Period in Peace Time," that resources from other areas may be used to bail out the economy? The sports system has held a special place of honor in Cuban society since 1959, and this attention has paid off in both domestic and foreign policy. Now it may pay off in the more literal sense. Sport in Cuba now pays for itself. According to Cuban officials, their $120-million-a-year sports and physical education program is self-financed: from prize money won in international competitions, from the export of sports equipment, and from the contracting of Cuban coaches to rival Olympic programs. Further, a new policy permits Cuban athletes, coaches, and sports officials to charge some foreign TV crews for interviews.[7]

In addition, other countries have helped Cuban sports financially. The Italian government financed a large part of the expenses for the Cuban baseball team to go to Barcelona. Host countries pay the way for Cuban athletes to compete.[8] Sport may turn out to be a moneymaker as well as an imagemaker. Clearly, for the last three decades, sport has been used by Fidel Castro to the utmost Cuban advantage. There is little evidence that he will break this record.

UNCONVENTIONAL DIPLOMACY

Cuba is an island country of 44,128 square miles and approximately eleven million people. It seems almost ludicrous to speak of such a small nation—especially one located so much in the shadow of the United States—as conducting a global foreign policy. Yet, Cuba does indeed have a "big country's foreign policy."[9] In fact, since 1959, Cuba has conducted itself as a leading player in the international arena, even without the necessary domestic resources.

Cuban foreign policy as a whole has served clear defensive interests since 1959. These objectives, though specific to the Cuban situation, are not too dissimilar to the initial foreign policy objectives of any new regime. Castro's first priority has been, and continues to be, to insure and enhance his political base within Cuba. His second concern is to assure the security of the regime from hostile outside powers, the United States in particular.

With a realistic eye toward Cuba's economic limitations, Castro has had to seek external economic assistance to insure the continued development of his country, if not its very survival. He also had to solidify and maintain support for his revolution within his own country. To accomplish these goals, it was essential to portray Cuba in the best possible light. Castro's solution to the problem has been the use of unconventional forms of diplomacy, which he wields with phenomenal success.[10]

His unconventional diplomacy encompasses a wide range of methods of disseminating propaganda, both within Cuba and externally. Often denied use of the more conventional modes of political, military, and economic diplomacy, Cuba has turned instead to other means, such as tourism, cultural activities, health systems, the astute use of the media, sports, and the physical culture system. Clearly, the Cuban sports system provides a vivid example of Cuba's most successful diplomatic tools.

The development and use of Cubans' vast athletic talent as a form of foreign policy has served Castro well in many ways. First, Cuba was at least partially able to distance itself from the Soviet Union and to develop an independent, albeit limited, foreign policy. Second, Castro wisely chose forms of unconventional diplomacy (such as sports) that were less likely to place him in direct conflict with his benefactor. Third, since 1961 Castro has taken the role of a leader of the Non-Aligned Movement, and Cuba's sporting successes have reinforced this image. Castro's international successes in unconventional forms of foreign policy have allowed him to increase his maneuvering power with Moscow, to come to terms with the United States, and to project Cuba as a leading model for the developing world.

The choice of sports as a method of diplomacy conveniently fits into Cuba's strong tradition of forceful nationalism and serves domestic purposes as well. Castro, for whom Cuba has never been quite big enough, has been the driving force behind Cuba's attempt at a global foreign policy. Adopting the ideology of socialism has served to enhance his chosen methods of building Cuba's domestic and worldwide image and realizing his own ambitions.

SPORT AS A POLITICAL TOOL IN CUBA AND THE USSR

There is no aspect of Cuban life that more clearly epitomizes the Cuban leadership's emphasis on image-building and egalitarianism than the system of physical culture and competitive athletics. The Cuban record in international athletics is among the most recognized successes of the revolution. The revolutionary government knew from its inception that such a powerful image could serve the regime well. Developed countries are almost forced to admire Cuban athletic prowess. Developing countries are hopeful that emulation of the Cuban system will give them similar results.

Cuba's surge of athletic strength is a consequence of its conversion to socialism. With athletic superiority as a political goal, the Cuban government has imitated the Soviet system of physical culture, modifying it where necessary and expedient. The former Soviet Union discovered the value of sport as a political tool, over time, and formulated sports policy as a consequence of initial successes. Cuba immediately incorporated this tool into its system and ideology after seeing the positive effect of sport in the Soviet Union. The Soviet Union began with victories, which led to policy; Cuba laid down policy, which led to victories.

Cuba approaches the type of system that the Soviet Union was supposed to have had. The differences are of degree rather than substance. The Cuban system is modeled on the Soviet system, emphasizing central control in service to the goals of mass participation and the development of champions. However, the results of the two systems are different. Soviet athletes appeared cold and calculating, machinelike, ruthless. The Cubans are warmer, more human, less regimented. Cuban athletes emerge as more well-rounded individuals than their Soviet counterparts, ironically, closer to the ideal "new communist man."

The Soviet system was older and more established, its policies characterized by science, routine, and no-nonsense regimentation. It produced athletes and personnel who were followers, rewarded for their discipline, obedience, and performance. The Cuban sports system is still emerging, characterized by novelty, creativity, and experimentation. Those involved in sports have a greater degree of efficacy and freedom. They are seen as and see themselves as innovators, discoverers, leaders in a true sense. They work in a system that is still developing, although in recent times there are signs of increased bureaucratization and a greater emphasis on scientific methods.[11]

Sport is even more important for Cuba than for the Soviet Union. At a similar stage of development on economic and military levels, the positive image provided by the Soviet Union's sporting victories was merely a boost; it was already secure in its position as a world power. On the other hand, for Cuba, its positive impact in the international sporting world is a major force whereby Cuba can prove itself of world caliber.

Overall, Cuba provides the world with a clear example of how a communist system can help a developing country move from backwardness to excellence in a single area. The phenomenal success of the sports system is inspirational to all sides of the ideological spectrum. Despite the fact that sports funding now comes from athletes' earnings and other sources,[12] the cost of developing the sports program has been high. Sacrifices have had to be made in other areas of society. For other nations, especially those with different political systems, such sacrifices would have been impossible. But the Cuban government has received what it paid for.

For politicians, the virtue of sport is readily understandable. Sport has tremendous exposure worldwide and, at first glance, is apolitical. It is precisely sport's surface innocence that renders it so well suited to use as a political tool. However, the political motivation behind the system of physical culture in Cuba does not dull Cuba's justified pride in the effectiveness of that system.

ECONOMIC HARDSHIP AND POLITICAL ISOLATION

In an earlier time, Cuba was isolated economically and politically because of its belief in socialism. Sport was one area that allowed this circle of isolation to be broken. Now, in this era of flight from communism in Nicaragua, in Eastern Europe, and in the Soviet Union itself, Cuba stands alone as the bulwark of Marxism-Leninism. As economic aid from the former Soviet Union and other allies dries up, Cuba needs to break the circle of isolation that has arisen anew. Sport may once again be the perfect tool for the job.

However, Cuba is suffering an era of severe austerity. Cars and trucks are being replaced by bicycles and oxen and the sports system may be one area from which Cuba could cut excess. In fact, the Cubans are being forced to do just that; the austerity is affecting even their national obsession. As the island moves to further conserve electricity, for example, night baseball games have been cancelled.[13] Sports coverage in the newspapers has been reduced significantly because of the shortage of newsprint. The main offices of the National Institute for Sports, Education, and Recreation (INDER) have had to move all the computers into one room to save air-conditioning costs. The recent shortage of gasoline caused an annual bicycle race around the island to be canceled. There was not enough fuel to transport the racers, staff, and their equipment during the event. The race will be replaced by an indoor competition.[14]

Yet these examples illustrate the Cuban ability to turn adversity into advantage, a talent called *resolviendo* that has been finely honed for thirty years since the abortive Playa de Girón (Bay of Pigs) invasion and the start of the U.S. embargo. Castro has elevated sacrifice almost to a virtue. Cuban foul balls, for example, are never kept by the fan who catches them, but rather returned to the field with a virtuous flourish. Actually, baseball games have not been completely canceled but are now held during daylight hours and generally just on weekends.[15] The bicycle race was not discontinued but rather was converted into an event that used less of a precious resource. Neither of these changes constitutes great sacrifice. Sporting events play a tremendous role in sustaining the

Cuban morale, especially in a time of austerity. So their complete cancellation would have far-reaching effects.

Although the system of sports in Cuba is distinctively Cuban (as will be seen below), its origins can be found in the system of physical culture that was prevalent in other socialist countries. Before we turn exclusively to Cuba, it is instructive to look at the basis for the socialist approach to sports.

THE THEORETICAL BASIS OF THE SOCIALIST APPROACH TO SPORT

The Cuban system of sports is clearly based on those of the Soviet Union and the formerly socialist countries of Eastern Europe. Unlike in the Soviet Union, however, the Cuban revolutionary leaders did not inherit a highly centralized or a very well-organized sports system. The new organization had to be built basically from the ground up, following and modifying the Soviet example.

The socialist countries adhered to a common philosophy of education and sport that had its roots in the philosophies of Marx and Lenin. Cuba also draws on the ideas of José Martí.[16] In Marxist-Leninist theory, sport is not merely an activity for individuals but, rather, a social phenomenon. Because it is regarded as a part of the social superstructure, sport is inevitably tied to the relations of production, or the socioeconomic structure. Then the nature of sport in a society depends upon its class relationships:

> In good Marxist logic, everything is interrelated. In Marxist conceptualising, since the human organism develops and changes under the influence of external conditions including the social environment, subjection to physical exercise not only develops that part of the body to which it is directed, but also has an effect on the body as a whole—on the personality. A strong bond exists, then, between social and individual development and between the physical and mental development of the individual. The socialist societies seek to shape this development.[17]

Marx and Lenin both shunned the separation of the body from the mind. The combination of a healthy body and a healthy mind produced a completely formed person, capable of contributing a tremendous amount to society. Marx himself felt that the educational combination of "productive labor with instruction and gymnastics" would not only improve "the efficiency of production" but was also the only way to produce fully developed human beings.[18] For Marx, recreation under communism would be a fusion of worklike activities with play.

The socialist view of sport as one of a number of interdependent aspects of society is a major reason for its high place on the list of priorities. The combining of sport and physical culture, for example, is important. The Soviet central committee of the All Union Communist party decreed on 13 July 1925 that:

> Physical culture must be considered not only from the standpoint of physical education and health and as an aspect of the cultural, economic and military training of youth (the sport of rifle marksmanship and others), but also as one of the methods of educating the masses (in as much as physical culture develops willpower and builds up endurance, teamwork, resourcefulness and other valuable qualities), and in addition, as a means of rallying the broad masses of workers and peasants around the various Party, soviet, and trade union organizations, through which the masses of workers and peasants are to be drawn into social and political activity.[19]

Yet physical culture for the socialist countries has almost a mystical, futuristic quality about it. The term defies definition but clearly goes beyond the realm of mere sports: "Sport belongs to the vision of the world we want to create."[20]

Military preparedness and labor productivity are the two most important goals of physical culture and sport. The advent of modern industry required more than physical fitness; it required a healthy mind and a healthy attitude. Strenuous exercise should instill "in young people a love of labor."[21] Such preparation enables the socialist athlete "to be an active builder of communism. Athletes are obliged to raise the productivity of labor by all means at their disposal, to perform exemplary work at their jobs, and at the same time to help their friends achieve victories of production."[22] Labor productivity is inextricably bound to military preparedness in the Soviet mass physical fitness program, *Gotov k trudu i oborone* or GTO (Ready for labor and defense) and its Cuban counterpart, *Listos Para Vencer* or LPV (Ready to win).[23]

At the heart of the philosophy is the ability of physical culture to build strong character. The educational scheme aims to construct a new communist society by creating a new type of socially minded citizen, namely, the "new communist man."[24] He is disciplined, highly motivated, and capable of subordinating his personal requirements to those of the Communist party. Education is the method by which communists can transform society: "Physical culture has become an inseparable part of communist education, an important means of educating the Soviet people for work and the protection of their home-country."[25]

> We speak of a model of sport but we have in mind a model of human personality, a model of society. Therefore, when we try to perceive the emerging outlines of this new model and state what factors are contributing to its creation and implementation, we want, of course, to know what type of man will act under that model and how the latter will affect his personality. . . . We strongly believe that under these new conditions, Man will be able more fully to satisfy his human needs more efficiently, to develop his mental and physical skills. This is the meaning behind all efforts to foresee the future. We strive to penetrate it in order to rationally shape it.[26]

Cuba also uses the term *physical culture* for its program of sports and recreation. According to Raudol Ruíz,

> This name is important conceptually because it is the final stage of our development. It will be how we create the habits and customs, how we will make sports a part of life for all citizens, how sports will form a part of the culture of the people. We still cannot say we have physical culture, but we can say that we are moving very slowly toward that goal.[27]

Physical culture then, like communism, is an ever-present goal. In the socialist countries, the "new man" is the center of the development of society. Physical culture plays a large role in his formation, giving him the mental and physical conditions for increasing productivity and the capability of defending his country.[28]

SPORTS FOR ONE OR FOR ALL?

Within socialist sport, there are two driving, and often competing goals. One is the concept of mass participation in sports: *massovost* in Russian and *masividad* or *participación masiva* in Spanish. The other is mastery of a sport: *masterstvo* in Russian.[29] To critics of either system, these goals are mutually exclusive. To the Cubans, they complement each other.

The question is whether or not the ideal of sport for all is contradicted by the existence of an ability-based elite group of athletes. Certainly, Cuban athletes receive special privileges, such as training, extra food, and better housing (although there are indications that some of these have been reduced).[30] The Cubans argue that the provision of incentives for raising standards during socialism may be necessary in order to build a material and cultural base for communism. In receiving some material benefits, the elite group of athletes may, however, operate in opposition to the development of egalitarian attitudes, despite the greater participation in sports inspired by their international successes.

These athletes cannot function as a class in the Marxist sense, nor can they automatically pass on their privileges to their children. The benefits are necessary for their success in international sports. Their successes, in turn, create prestige for Cuba both inside and outside the country. In addition to encouraging the participation of others in sports, this prestige contributes to the encouragement of Cuban nationalism so crucial to the Cuban identity and to Castro's ambition. Sports victories bring home the message of Cuban independence and progress, as well as send it abroad, thus inspiring support for the revolution.

To the Cubans, both goals mutually support each other in a continual cycle of interdependence. The road from mass participation leads to international competition. Success abroad then inspires more Cubans at home to participate.

The first objective of the Cuban sports system is to make sports available to everyone and to actively promote its development, as written in the Constitution. The second objective is to seek champions. According to Manuel González, former director of the Cuban Olympic Committee, "When we look at our children, we are searching for diamonds. Every child and every adult has a right to participate in athletics. And every diamond has a right to be discovered and polished." Cuba's athletic "diamonds" are found only through *masividad,* or mass participation in sports. However, Castro has warned that "It is very important that we do not be mistaken, that in the search for champions we do not neglect the practice of sports."[31]

Cuban athletes are expected to be revolutionaries, and those who are not involved in mass organizations or political bodies may be excluded from sports schools.[32] Cuba's outstanding athletes are supposed to be examples for others to emulate. They are expected not only to be a vanguard for the development of full human potential in physical culture, but also to be models of the "new man." Consequently, athletes contribute to building socialism.

The international successes of Cuba's top athletes constitute an extremely forceful propaganda weapon. Sport's universal popularity and sheer visibility make it extremely effective:

> Sporting success is seen by some as a measure of national vitality and prestige. . . . By its nature, sport is suited to the task; it excites nationalist instincts and encourages group identification; it is superficially apolitical and readily understandable; and, through modern means of communication, sporting spectacles can be transmitted throughout the world.[33]

By means of this powerful propaganda, socialist countries have been able to utilize sport to (1) weaken the influence of noncommunists upon their citizens and (2) weaken the international prestige of the West by challenging its position as sports leader. Through competition in sports, the other peoples of the world could observe the differences between the socialist and capitalist systems and compare them. The hope, of course, was that such a comparison would show the superiority of communism:

> The Soviet Union has won valuable footholds of influence which have been exploited in every possible way to create a positive image of the Soviet Union and to influence foreigners to seek advantages in the Soviet system. . . . Every Soviet sport triumph is pictured as yet another proof of the superiority of the Soviet system over the decadence of the West.[34]

The goals of Soviet foreign policy have been consistent: (1) commitment to the Marxist-Leninist goal of a worldwide communist social order, and (2) serving the national interests of the Soviet Union. Periods of Soviet weakness—in particular, the advent of nuclear weapons—brought the expedient policy of peaceful coexistence. New methods of continuing the struggle had to be found. Athletic competition is merely one of the methods by which "war without warfare" is waged. Cuba, on the other hand, has never been powerful enough militarily to defeat its primary rival, the United States. Yet in sports, it found a way to do just that.

FOUNDATIONS OF CUBAN SPORTS

Organizing the Sports System

Despite the obvious influences of the other socialist countries on Cuban sports and physical culture, the Cubans have developed a system that, in both practice and results, is all their own. The theoretical base of Cuban sport is simple; it is capitalist versus socialist. Raúl Castro neatly summed up the Cuban viewpoint:

> Sport, like everything, is a reflection, simply, of a country's social system. . . . Sport under socialism is neither restricted nor commercialized. It is mass sport with the participation of the people, all of the people, of all those who want to participate voluntarily. It is a means.
>
> Under capitalism, sport, like almost everything, was an end, and the end was profit. Sport under a socialist regime is a means, before everything else, for the self-improvement of the citizen, for the betterment of his health, constituting also, a type of prophylactic measure. At the same time, it creates the conditions and makes the citizens capable even to the point of increasing production, defending the country, and [providing] a healthy means of recreation.[35]

Statements like this pay obvious lip service to the Soviet Union and other socialist standard bearers. The Cubans freely followed the socialist model in developing their own system of sports, with a sincere admiration for the successful programs they saw in East Germany, the Soviet Union, and other communist countries. It is doubtful, however, that the sports system was so important that all financial aid from the socialist bloc would have been withheld if the Cubans had refused to follow the socialist path. Yet, in following the Soviet example, the Cuban leaders did not blindly take the program found in other countries and superimpose it on their own. Rather, they began with egalitarian goals that later meshed into consistent socialist goals. According to Raudol Ruíz,

> INDER's principal task is to make it possible for the people to engage in physical activity as part of their education, and for their health and recreation. The primary goal of INDER continues to be mass participation in sports, to ensure that every day more men and women, children, young people, and stu-

dents practice sports, physical education, gymnastics, walking, excursions, bicycling; to ensure that they are in contact with nature, enjoy nature and take maximum advantage of our climate.[36]

Fidel Castro concurred when he said that sport

teaches them how to exert themselves, it teaches them how to discipline themselves, it teaches them to work collectively, because precisely the sports they practice in general are team sports, from which they learn to work collectively. . . . Sport [is] a marvelous activity that not only helps the physical health, not only helps to form the character, but it also makes them enthusiastic and it makes them happy.[37]

It is in the paths chosen to reach these goals that the Cubans have shown creativity and independence. The Soviet Union began with victories in sports, which led to policy; Cuba had the luxury of choosing from policies that had already been tested and proven successful. At the same time, the Cubans also exercised their right to reject the policies that had failed, or more importantly, those which produced results that were not consistent with Cuban aspirations.

Both the Cubans and the Russians had to begin building their sports systems out of the chaos of revolution. More than anything, the Cubans wanted a complete break from the past. Shortly after the revolution, Rafael Cambo Arcos wrote that,

The previous sports organization had to be destroyed, the ruling anarchy eliminated, the existing flaws and vices eradicated. On top of this ruin, it was necessary to construct a new organization, one without the smallest link to the past, a completely new system, a product of the radical change in political philosophy which, at this time, leads the destiny of Cuba.[38]

Sports Before the Revolution

This emphasis on sports is not a new phenomenon in Cuba. Although it was hardly the egalitarian system that exists today, the sporting tradition in Cuba has a long prerevolutionary history. Aside from the traditional cockfighting and other gambling "sports," boxing, track, and baseball (a Cuban obsession) were popular in Cuba decades before Fidel Castro allegedly tried out for the Washington Senators.[39]

Baseball has long been the premier sport of the island, even before the American presence there. The Siboney Indians played a game called *batos* that used a bat and ball.[40] The first Cuban baseball stadium was inaugurated in Matanzas in 1874, and by the 1930s, many Cuban baseball players (and boxers) earned a fair wage in the professional realm, with some actually making it big in the lucrative U.S. sports scene.

For the lower classes, baseball and boxing constituted a possible ticket out of poverty as well as steady, reliable entertainment. Yet many prerevolutionary Cuban athletes were "people born into comfort, never touched by misery or want."[41] Cuba's Ramón Fonst won a gold medal in the individual épée event in fencing in the Paris Olympics of 1900. Four years later, he won three individual gold medals and one team gold in the St. Louis Olympics. (For the Cubans, however, this victory was tainted by Fonst's long-time residency in France.) Another Cuban with leisure time, José Raúl Capablanca, held the title of World Champion in chess in 1921 and 1927.

Yet, there was still another Cuban who distinguished himself in St. Louis. Félix Carvajál, known as Andarín, was a postman by trade who hitchhiked to St. Louis to run the marathon. Exhausted by his journey and a bout with some green apples, he won only fourth in the event, having received no support from the Cuban government for his efforts.[42] Like most lower-class prerevolutionary Cuban athletes, Carvajál was unknown until his death in 1948. All of his recognition has come posthumously and after the revolution.

Sport for the Cuban population at large, including Andarín and others of his class, was almost nonexistent. Exclusive clubs denied entry to most Cubans, on racial or economic grounds. U.S. interests dominated some Cuban sports, especially those conducive to gambling, such as boxing.[43] Previous Cuban governments showed little interest in developing the sports system. After the adoption of Marxism-Leninism, the revolutionary government claimed that pre–1959 Cuban athletes were exploited and treated as merchandise. To the revolutionaries, Cuba had few international successes in sports because of the small base of participation in athletics and the lack of public resources available.

Sports After the Revolution

Only after the revolution did Cuba begin to achieve success in sports. Within fifteen years of the revolution, Cuba had changed from a country that had won only a handful of medals to one of the top ten medal-winning nations in the Olympic Games. Western critics claim that this success is due to the technical support that Cuba has received from the socialist bloc, as well as their own specialized training for athletes. These factors are certainly important, but increased participation is also a major force behind the rapid rise in Cuba's success.

At the beginning of the revolutionary transformation, even before the conversion to Marxism-Leninism, Cuban leaders worked to remove legal and socioeconomic barriers to participation in physical culture. They sought a radical change in the social structure of Cuba and moved to break down not only gender and racial barriers but class barriers too, with the aim of extending egalitarianism in all areas, not just in the realm of physical culture. Emphasis was placed on increasing participation in sports and on improving access to physical culture, for health and recreational purposes, and as part of the general process of redistribution and democratization that characterized the early years of the revolutionary process.

In 1961, the year of Castro's conversion to Marxism-Leninism, the revolutionary government institutionalized the Cuban system of sports and physical culture. The administration of sports was transferred to a government body, INDER, which had centralized control for physical culture throughout the island.

The two most important factors for the promotion of egalitarianism in physical culture were the construction of new facilities and the production and distribution of sports equipment. In January 1959, there were just thirteen state-owned sports areas. Private clubs and centers were nationalized, and a program was launched to build new facilities. By 1965, Cuba had established a domestic sports industry to manufacture its own athletic equipment. By 1988, there were more than 9,600 facilities across the island.

The Cuban government also introduced a wide variety of programs aimed at encouraging people to participate in sports. In the 1960s, the emphasis was upon developing programs for young Cubans and in regions other than Havana. In the 1970s, as these programs continued, the Cubans directed their attention to new exercise programs for adults and sports competitions in work centers. In the 1980s, activities for older Cubans received increased emphasis. Since 1959, the vast majority of Cubans participate in sports at some stage in their lives, especially while attending educational institutions. Regular participants number approximately 1.5 million or almost a fifth of the population.[44]

Cuba has in large part reached its goals of mass participation in and the democratization of sports. In the process, Cubans have achieved unprecedented success in international sports competitions. These successes have created the national and international prestige that is so important for Cuban nationalism and in promoting a sense of national unity and pride. In Cuba, this nationalism enhances an already-distinctive Cuban culture and, further, helps to eliminate remaining vestiges of U.S. influence. International success in sports also provides an example to other less-developed countries of the possibilities and achievements of socialism.

Problems do exist, however. Participation in sports is abandoned by many Cubans when they leave school.[45] Although more extensive than in 1959, women's participation—especially in organized sports—is far below that of men. Facilities and coaching are sometimes of lower standards than desired, reflecting at times bureaucratic inefficiencies. There is also the possibility for tension in balancing bureaucratic and funding emphasis between mass programs and elite sports. In the mid–1980s, these and other concerns about overemphasis on top-performance athletes were raised by Cuban sports officials.

Almost all Cubans with ability may aspire to athletic success and receive specialized training in sports schools.[46] Outstanding athletes do not receive salaries above the general wage scales, but they do receive other advantages that may be more highly prized than money in a socialist country with limited goods and devalued currency. And, as in other countries, status from athletic achievement may help an athlete in elections for political positions.

The shifts between emphasizing egalitarianism and emphasizing performance in physical culture reflect many factors, including the attempt to balance democratic ideals with the requirements and benefits of international success. The shifting balance is also linked to variations in the overall revolutionary policy, shifting in response to immediate concerns, which have included redistribution efforts when expanding participation was stressed in the early 1960s; economic problems when there were cuts in sports spending during the late 1960s and late 1970s; security concerns when Cuba joined the Sports Committee of Friendly Armies in 1968 and 1969 and founded military sports clubs in the 1980s; and to the decentralization and institutionalization in the mid–1970s. Policy shifts also arise because decision making is limited mostly to an elite group of administrators and political authorities. Yet, despite these problems, there is an ongoing and determined effort to extend access to physical culture and to prevent the development of a closed elite.

The encouragement of outstanding athletes to behave as communist examples to others means that, in addition to their part in encouraging popular participation, athletes have a role in the socialization of all Cubans to combat old attitudes that may hinder the development of socialism in Cuba. Physical culture, then, is part of social change as well as an agent for social change.

The Limits to Theory

The limits on using sports as an avenue for social control are evident in the antigovernment physical culture organizations that existed before 1959, and in the defection of many Cubans, including some athletes, since 1959. There is no guarantee that participants will adopt the ideology of the revolution. Physical culture is but one of numerous vehicles through which the ideas of the state are promoted. However, the beauty of sport is that even dissidents can participate, without agreeing to ideological compromise, and possibly gain something in the process.

There are also limits on the extension of popular programs in physical culture. Cuba's leaders (and perhaps the population in general) have emphasized international sports victories. The presence of outstanding athletes may, however, inspire others to take up sports. The victories bring prestige to Cuba and demonstrate Cuba's achievements under a socialist system, to both friends and enemies. These victories are claimed as evidence of the benefits of socialism, raising the standard of living and creating a mass base of participation.

There are other more pressing limits as well, however. Achieving Cuban objectives in sports has been limited by the importance of developing the material base in Cuba, which is vital to ensure continuation of the revolution. This necessity is intensified by the limits of Cuban resources, the considerable reliance on imports, and the underdeveloped condition of the economy. With the dissolution of the communist bloc, the breakup of the Soviet Union, and the continued U.S. economic embargo, Cuba has lost its lifeline to the necessary resources to meet even basic human needs, such as food, clothing, and shelter, much less sports equipment. Even Fidel, in an act of socialist anthropomorphic license, has taken to calling the now-ubiquitous bicycles, valuable "daughters of the special period."[47]

The Cuban sports system contains two possibilities that may help ease the situation. First, the system has continued to receive funding, although relatively modest, throughout the period of the revolution. If needed, these resources, including athletes' and coaches' earnings now used to fund sports, can be redirected to more needy areas.[48] Second, participation in sports and physical culture provides, at little cost, one area in which Cubans might temporarily forget their hardships and perhaps make themselves feel a little better.

In order to fully appreciate the accomplishments of the Castro government in the sports arena, it is necessary to look at the system that existed in Cuba before the revolution. In the next chapter, we will look in some detail at Cuban sport before 1959.

2

Cuban Sport Before 1959

The distinguishing features of Cuban sport prior to 1959 were its class and racial divisions and its control by private (often professional) interests. Although there were many outstanding Cuban athletes, most of these were professional baseball players and boxers. In organized amateur sport (which was supposed to be the source of all Olympic champions), only the privileged classes had the necessary requirements for practice—the leisure time and the access to private sports clubs. For those who were less privileged, there was baseball and boxing, two sports that constituted a possible ticket out of poverty and into what seemed to be the "charmed" life of American professional sports. Sports for the general public were not promoted, but gambling was, in the form of horse races, dog races, jai alai or *pelota vasca* (a game of handball), billiards, lotteries, dice, roulette, and slot machines.[1] By the end of World War II, Cuba constituted a playground of sorts for wealthy North Americans.

In November 1935, Law No. 409, which stated that physical education would be obligatory in all schools of the republic, was a typical decree in a developing country, impossible to implement. Sports in the schools were almost nonexistent. What little there were could be found mainly in the private schools. By 1959, there were approximately eight hundred physical education teachers throughout the country. Most of these were from the *classica botella,* that is, they were relatives and friends of officials and politicians and, for the most part, unqualified.[2] According to a trainer for the Cuban national volleyball team:

> Physical education had no importance in the schools. It was not given the attention it deserved. To try to practice sport was a tremendous mess. There was no equipment, no technical preparation, no coaches or instructors. Only a lucky few had the opportunity to develop their sports potential. In the public schools, forget it! It was a disaster.[3]

The abysmal state of Cuban sports before the revolution did not mean that the island was completely undistinguished in sports or in international sports competitions. Before turning to specific sports, it is instructive to study the organization of prerevolutionary Cuban sport.

THE EARLY ORGANIZATION OF CUBAN SPORT

With the exception of baseball (and boxing to a lesser extent), Cuban sport prior to 1959 could be described as elitist; a special skill for non-Hispanics; centered in Havana; and largely lacking in government sponsorship. There is evidence of only limited change over time—after the abolition of slavery, for example and, in the twentieth century, an increase in access of some non-Hispanic male Cubans to a few professional sports. Most sports were practiced by the wealthy—Hispanic Cubans in private schools, at the University of Havana, and in clubs. The majority of the island's population participated in informal recreational activities. Cuban governments took only a limited interest in the recreation of their citizens. Although physical education was nominally compulsory in schools, it was not enforced, and sports were left to private organizations. The exclusive nature of most sports was intensified by the concentration of facilities in or near Havana.

For the vast majority of Cubans, recreation was not organized, although African Cubans and mulattoes did form their own recreational centers. In the nineteenth century, wealthy Cubans began forming their own sports clubs, such as sailing clubs on private beaches. Cuban upper-class youth had access to sports through their private schools and in the University of Havana. In rural

Cuba, similar exclusive clubs were established by U.S.–owned companies, adding to the considerable class and racial discrimination in sports.

Such a separation of facilities existed on a United Fruit sugar plantation in Oriente province. There was a club for U.S. citizens and another for Cubans. Angel Leíba Cabrera, who worked in the mill at Mayarí in the 1920s, described the situation there:

> When the Americans were here, they had these three recreational centers, one just for the Americans, I couldn't put my face in there. In "Brooklyn," there was a club for blacks. The Pan-American Club—the one for Americans—had a swimming pool, but of course it was only for them.[4]

The largely private and U.S.–dominated economy was replicated to a considerable degree in sports. The situation in Cuban physical culture in the years just prior to Castro's accession to power were characterized by limited facilities and limited access to them, especially outside Havana where installations for sports (and other cultural activities) were located. Sports equipment was almost exclusively imported by U.S.–controlled corporations, which also imported equipment for the numerous casinos and nightclubs of Havana, havens for U.S. tourists and rich Cubans. Bingo was held every night in the casinos, with gambling, drinking, and prostitution allegedly protected by the Cuban government.[5]

The Batista government spent very little money on sports activities. In 1958, spending on physical education and sports was around $1 million, plus an additional $75,000 for the Physical Education Institute and Martí Park.[6] This was less than 0.5 percent of the total Cuban budget (see table 1).

Batista's regime also refused to assist in the funding for the 1955 Pan-American Games. A former director of sport invested public funds in professional boxing because it was profitable. Batista was even accused of taking over the offices of the Cuban Olympic Committee. He banned African Cubans from using the swimming pool of the Hotel Nacional during a regional swimming competition.[7] After coming to power, Fidel assessed the status of sport in Cuba under Batista: "Sport . . . what had become of sport? Apart from providing entertainment for the children of the rich families in their aristocratic schools and clubs, sport had become a form of busi-. ness It had been turned into a piece of merchandise, an object of exploitation."[8]

TABLE 1.
Cuban Budget in Millions of Cuban Pesos: 1957–1958

Item	Millions of Pesos
Economic development	45
Social and cultural	98
Sports (incl. Martí Park and PE Institute)	1.75
Military	94
Administration	83
Public debt	40
Other	5
TOTAL	365

Source: *Trimestre de finanzas al día*, no. 1, April 1962, (Ministry of Finance), cited in D. Seers, *Cuba: The Economic and Social Revolution* (Chapel Hill: University of North Carolina Press, 1964), p. 41.

Although Batista claimed to be a supporter of physical activities and did establish the General Directory of Sports (DGD), he failed to challenge or question the exclusive and commercial nature of most sports and recreation. Under his rule some new facilities were constructed, however, especially in Havana, and he spoke of expanding sport.[9] He never made good on his promise. The opening of Martí Park in 1940 appeared to be a step toward improving access to recreation, but only children attending school could use the facilities, and this excluded large numbers of Cuban youngsters who were not in school. Despite some reforms, Batista's own description of the state of sports before he came to power could be applied equally to the situation when he was forced out of power in 1959. Sport was corrupt; would-be athletes were abandoned by Cuban authorities; boxers were exploited; tennis, volleyball, and soccer were left to private sponsors.[10] But baseball, the backbone of Cuban social life, was the nerve center of the island's soul.

THE BEGINNING OF BASEBALL IN CUBA

Before looking at the situation in sports and physical culture throughout the island, it is instructive to view the sport in which Cuba has enjoyed phenomenal success since the mid–nineteenth century. Baseball—the passion of the island—provided the opportunity for the majority of male Cubans to participate in sports. Indeed, more than any other sport, baseball has always enjoyed a unique role in Cuban society. There were the strong winter leagues that drew the best players from North and South America, and there were the leagues that developed around the sugar plantations and the growing season. Baseball deserves a preliminary and in-depth examination, as it provides elements of continuity in Cuban sports over the last century, as well as signs of revolutionary breakthrough.

Before the revolution, Cuban baseball was generally seen by outsiders as an extended talent pool for the U.S. professional leagues, but a closer look at the history of Cuba's national mania reveals that this was hardly the case. From the very moment it was introduced, baseball caught fire in Cuba, and the island soon be-came the epicenter for baseball throughout the Caribbean. Indeed, because of the "color line" in organized North American baseball that prohibited blacks from playing, Cuba was also the focus of U.S. baseball during the winter season.[11] When word spread of the cal-iber of play on the island, many North American players went south for the winter, to hone their skills as well as to supplement their sal-aries (this was before baseball players could negotiate multimillion dollar contracts). African American players from the old Negro leagues regularly played on the Cuban teams during the winter, which enabled them to compete against the stars of organized baseball.

According to the Cubans, long before baseball was "invented" by Abner Doubleday in Cooperstown in 1839, one of the indigenous populations on the island played a game with a ball and stick called *batos*.[12] The first modern bat and ball were brought to Cuba in the 1860s by Nemesio Guillot, an upper-class Cuban who had been studying at Fordham University in New York. Other students studying in the United States, as well as North American business-men and sailors, helped to introduce and spread baseball through-out the island. In 1866, a U.S. ship crew played a team of Cuban stevedores in an exhibition game.[13]

At the same time, another Cuban, Estéban Bellán, became pro-ficient enough to play professional ball in the United States, the first of a long line of Latin Americans to do so. In 1869 he played third base, shortstop, and outfield for the Troy Haymakers, which in 1871 became a charter member of the National Association, the first professional baseball league. Later he moved on to the New York Mutuals and ended a three-year North American professional baseball career with a batting average of .236.[14]

But "Steve" Bellán preferred to play in Cuba, so he returned and helped to organize the first recorded game between two Cuban teams, Matanzas and Havana on 27 December 1874. Catching for El Club Habana, Bellán helped them handily defeat Matanzas, 51–9, hitting three home runs and scoring seven. In left field for Havana and scoring eight runs was Emilio Sabourín, the moving force behind the first Cuban professional league, the Liga de Béisbol Profesional Cubana.[15]

The first organized competition on the island was held between Havana and Matanzas during 1878 and 1879, only four years after the first game. This series, which formed the basis for Cuba's first national professional baseball competition, was held from 1878 until the 1960–1961 season, and play was suspended only in 1881, 1896, and 1897. The first teams (Havana, Almendares, and Matanzas) were made up mostly of university students who initially paid their own expenses. The Havana club, founded by Sabourín, dominated the league. The competition eventually involved sixteen teams in four regions of Cuba.[16]

Other championships emerged after the founding of the national professional baseball competition. These included the Social League of Cuba and the Amateur League of the 1930s; the intercollegiate league of the 1940s; and the Liga Azucarera (Sugar mill league) of the 1950s. The 1940s decade was the "golden age" of amateur baseball in Cuba, with at least fifteen active leagues.[17]

From the very beginning, sports in Cuba played a large role in society, both socially and politically. Early on, the Cubans' growing enthusiasm for the game was directly proportional to Spain's distrust of it. What had begun as leisurely entertainment for rich Cubans quickly spread with a feverish intensity through the lower classes. "By the early 1900s, fans were so fanatic for their teams that those who sympathized with one team often had to be kept separate from those who were rooting for the other side."[18] Yet the colonial authorities remained suspicious of the game the Cubans called *pelota americana,* and practices had to be held in secret.

In December 1895, Spanish officials discovered that revenue from baseball had been diverted to the independence movement of poet and patriot José Martí, and baseball was banned in parts of the colony. Sabourín and others were arrested and shipped to El Castillo del Hacha, the Spanish prison in Morocco (Sabourín died there of pneumonia in 1897). Whatever the extent of the link between baseball clubs and the wagers of the struggle against colonialism, it is clear that baseball was well established in Cuba by the turn of the century; that is, before the introduction of direct U.S. cultural influences in the twentieth century. As early as 1889,

a baseball-player-turned-writer called Wenceslao Gálvez y Delmonte predicted that "baseball would outlast bullfighting and cockfighting, centuries-old pastimes imported from Spain."[19] John
Krich, an American writer with extensive experience traveling
throughout Latin America, has observed that

> A favorite Cuban boast is that their own professional leagues
> were founded before either our National or American leagues.
> The rivalry between Havana and Almendares predates that be-
> tween the Giants and the Dodgers. Most likely, the Cubans
> served as missionaries through the Caribbean—just as today
> they are attempting to teach the sport to their Russian allies.[20]

By the end of the century, as the Spanish retreated, two groups
of Americans landed on Cuban shores to make their lasting marks:
the U.S. Marines and the North American baseball players. The
presence of the United States in Cuba helped to establish baseball
even more firmly as the major sport, while simultaneously ensuring
the introduction of some other modern institutionalized sports. In
1898, shortly after the destruction of the battleship *Maine* in Havana harbor, U.S. league teams toured the island to play against
both Cubans and the squads of black North Americans who were
barred from organized play by segregation. And baseball traffic
flowed in the other direction as well. In 1903, the All Cubans
played in New York, and in 1909 the Cuban Stars toured the United
States to play against African American teams in the old Negro
league. Other Cuban teams soon followed, and the barnstorming of
the early twentieth century had begun.[21]

Cuban Stars in North America, Under the Color Line

In some ways the history of Cuban baseball is a much richer one
than that of early North American baseball, besmirched as that was
by rampant racism. Unlike in the United States, where black ball
players were banned from the major leagues until 1947, the Cuban
version of *pelota americana* had always been an interracial game. In
fact, African American teams often disguised themselves as Cubans
or American Indians so as not to offend the white fans and players.
In 1885, the Cuban Giants were formed from among the waiters at
the Argyle Hotel to entertain the guests. They even attempted to
speak a form of gibberish to further authenticate the charade. It

has been said that a scout told black star Quincy Trouppe that he would have a better chance at the big leagues if he learned to speak Spanish.[22]

As whites became increasingly uncomfortable with free black men and women after the Civil War, sports writers searched for epithets to avoid saying Negro. These included "Cuban, Spanish, Indian, African, Arabian, mulatto, coon, chocolate, dusky, dusky-hued, snow flake, dark object, Ethiopian, simian, son of Africa, darky, colored, nigger, sable, simmenian, Senegambian, cimmenan, colored Ethiopian, Cherokee, Geronimo, gaucho, darkskin, and brunette."[23] But "Cuban" was clearly the epithet of choice for black American baseball players, as it signified both a high caliber of play as well as a place where a black player was also considered a man.[24]

The first Cubans to play in the U.S. major leagues were signed by Cincinnati in 1911. Rafael Almeída and Armando Marsans, formerly of the Cuban Stars, began careers in professional baseball only after the *Cincinnati Enquirer* pronounced them "two of the purest bars of Castilian soap to ever wash up on our shores."[25] Almeída batted .270 in three seasons with the Reds, while Marsans, with a .269 average, played until 1918. Marsans continued to play for Almendares in Cuba in the winter leagues. In 1912, the Havana City Council proclaimed him "Cuba's Greatest Player" and awarded him a $200 gold medal.[26]

Another "white" Cuban, Mike González, signed with the Boston Braves in 1912, thus beginning a seventeen-year career of catching in the National League. He then went on to coach and manage in the National League through the 1930s and 1940s, posting a win with St. Louis in the 1946 World Series. Upon reaching that capstone, González returned to Cuba and purchased the Havana Reds, a club he had managed throughout the winter seasons. He became one of the first local scouts for the U.S. major leagues in Cuba, making famous the assessment of the typical utility infielder, "Good field, no hit."[27]

Other Cubans were also able to break through the barriers before the wall of segregation hardened.[28] Adolfo Luque, "The Pride of Havana," first played for Long Branch, a semipro team in the New York–New Jersey League. At the time, Long Branch was a team of all-white Cubans, but it was later converted into the Long Branch Cubans, a team in the Negro league. Luque played in the minors in the summers and in Cuba in the winters, with a stop on the Boston Braves for the 1914–1915 season. He was finally picked up by Cincinnati in 1918, for whom he threw his first shutout. He went 6–3 in 1918 and 9–3 in 1919, the year he became the first Latin American player in a World Series. He allowed only one hit and no runs in five innings.[29]

Dolf Luque was certainly one of the more enduring players, to be exceeded only decades later by another Cuban, Minnie Minoso. Luque was picked up by the Giants at the age of forty-two and helped them to the National League pennant in 1932. In the 1933 World Series, he pitched four scoreless innings, and called the experience his "greatest thrill as a pitcher."[30] It was after that Series, and Luque's performance in it, that Clark Griffith, owner of the losing Washington Senators, decided to send Joe Cambria on a scouting exhibition to Cuba. Luque's career ended with a 193–179 record, 1,130 strikeouts, 26 shutouts, and two world championships. He also left with a history behind him of macho retaliations for taunts of "nigger" and lesser provocations. He last appeared on the mound in Mexico in 1946 at the age of fifty-six. He then went on to develop other players, such as Sal "The Barber" Maglie, who starred for the Giants, Indians, Dodgers, and Yankees.[31]

In the same era, Cubans Jacinto "Jack" Calvo and José Acosta played for the Washington Senators, with Calvo in the outfield for the Washington Senators in 1913 and 1920 and Acosta pitching from 1920 to 1922, with a 10–10 record. They are the only two men to play in both the segregated majors and the Negro Leagues. Both Calvo and Acosta played for the Long Branch Cubans. In an exhibition game in Cuba in 1920, Acosta struck out Babe Ruth three times.[32]

But for all those Cubans who were light-skinned enough to play in the major leagues, there were even more who were not, and they all realized that skin color—not talent—was the great divide. When Adolfo Luque returned home to Cuba in 1923 after a 27–9 season with Cincinnati, he was met with a parade and a car. He turned to star Negro League pitcher and fellow Cuban José Méndez and said, "You should have gotten this car. You're a better pitcher than I am. This parade should have been for you."[33]

In the first half of this century, interracial teams of Cubans, such as the Cuban Stars, the Stars of Cuba, and the All Cubans, barnstormed throughout the United States, from 1905 to 1911. Other later teams were the Long Branch Cubans (1915), the Cuban Stars of the National League (1923–1938), the New York Cubans (1935–1936, 1939–1950), and the Havana Stars. When the first formal Negro League was established in 1920, the Cuban Stars was one of the nine member teams. Cubans eventually played throughout the black leagues and were instrumental in bringing to Cuba for the winter seasons such stellar talent and future Hall of Famers as Cool Papa Bell, Josh Gibson, Satchel Paige, and Judy Johnson.

It was only in the Cuban winter season that top-ranked white major leaguers met their Negro league counterparts on the field, a fact that, in reality, clouds the record books even as they stand today. It is ironic that, given the preponderance of African Americans in most major sports, blacks were excluded ostensibly because it was feared they would lower the caliber of play. The absurdity of this assumption was obvious early on, for those open-minded enough to notice. In Cuba in 1910, Ty Cobb, then the major league batting champion and a notorious and vicious bigot, was outhit by three black Americans: John Henry Lloyd, Judy Johnson, and Bruce Petway. Cobb also struck out and singled that same trip against José Méndez. A decade later, Babe Ruth was kept to one home run in Cuba and angrily referred to Cristobal Torrienti, the "Cuban Babe Ruth," as "black as a ton and a half of coal in a dark cellar." The Babe considered all Cuban ball players as inferior because of skin color.[34]

The Negro leagues allowed crack Cuban ball players to strut their stuff before North American fans for the price of segregated hotels and restaurants and racist slurs in the stands. One of the very best was José "El Diamante Negro" Méndez, a right-handed pitcher with the Cuban Stars. In the winter of 1908, the fifth-place Cincinnati Reds traveled to Cuba only to be shut out 1–0, with Méndez giving up only one ninth-inning infield single. Using muscles he developed chopping sugarcane, he sent the Reds home with a 4–7 record. He also pitched losses to the Detroit Tigers, the Philadelphia A's, and the Philadelphia Phillies. The last straw came when the New York Giants were beaten by Eustaquio Pedroza and Adolfo Luque. The Giants' manager John McGraw threatened to send his players home, with the warning "I didn't come down here to let a lot of coffee-colored Cubans show me up. You've got to either play ball or go home."[35]

With a 1909 record of 44–2 for the Stars, Méndez would surely have made all the record books had he been "pure Castilian." From 1920 to 1926, he played for the Kansas City Monarchs of the Negro League. In thirteen Cuban winters, he pitched 74 wins to 25 losses (.747). He was inducted into the Cuban Baseball Hall of Fame in 1939. It was the same John McGraw who said that, had Méndez been white, he could have drawn $50,000, a remarkable sum in those days.[36]

Cuba also boasts the only baseball player to be inducted into the Halls of Fame of four countries: the United States, Cuba, Mexico, and Venezuela. Martín Dihigo "was a big man at six feet-three, 225 pounds, he was fast on the bases, he had a strong and accurate arm from the outfield, and he hit the long ball."[37] He is reputed to be the best ball player of all time. He played all nine positions, earning the title "The Team Man" and the "Black Babe Ruth."[38] Buck Leonard, another player from the Negro leagues and a Hall of Famer praised Dihigo:

> Dihigo was the best all-around player I have ever seen. He could run, hit, throw, think, pitch, and manage. He both knew the game and could play it. I was in the game 23 years, and I never saw anyone better than he was. And that includes not only the United States but also Puerto Rico, Venezuela, Colombia, Cuba, and Mexico.[39]

As with many Cuban players, Dihigo was first noticed as he played against the Negro League teams. While still a teenager, he came north to play for the Cuban Stars in 1923. He also played for the New York Cubans, the Homestead Grays, and Hillsdale. He played in Mexico and Venezuela and returned to Cuba for winter ball. It has been estimated that his career record was 256–136, while batting .304.

Dihigo had the distinction of being praised by both Fulgencio Batista and Fidel Castro. His political sympathies, however, were with the latter. In the early 1950s, he was living in Mexico as a political exile from his native Matanzas, Cuba. In 1952, he met Ernesto "Che" Guevara at a restaurant in Mexico City and (reminiscent of Sabourín) was moved to contribute modestly to Castro's assault against Batista, the now-famous Granma exhibition. When Castro came to power in 1959, Dihigo returned to Cuba a national hero and was made a minister of sports. His bust at Estadio Latinoamericano in Havana reads simply, "El Inmortal."[40]

The name of another Cuban stands out from that time and is still familiar today. "Lefty" Tiant (Luís Tiant, Sr.) pitched from 1930 to 1947 for the Cuban Stars and the New York Cubans, defeating Carl Hubbell of the New York Giants in a famous exhibition game. His trademark of twisting and turning on the mound became known to North American fans as it was practiced by his son Luís Tiant, Jr., who pitched with the major leagues from 1964 through 1982 (see also chapter 5).[41]

Branch Rickey, president and general manager of the Brooklyn Dodgers, was the man who reintegrated professional baseball in the

United States. It was a plan he had considered for many years before implementing it. In the 1940s, he had initially considered signing Silvio García, a right-handed Cuban pitcher. Aware of the pressure that the first black in the big leagues would face, Rickey interviewed the prospects to assess their suitability. According to Edel Casas, a Cuban baseball historian, "In the course of the interview, Rickey asked García, 'What would you do if a white American slapped your face?' García's response was simple and sincere. 'I kill him,' he said."[42] Rickey chose Jackie Robinson to do the honors in 1947.

Cuban Stars in North America, After the Color Line

Once the color line was broken, a new wave of Cuban ball players came into the major league (García was not among them). The first dark-skinned Cuban to enter the open door was Saturnino Orestes Arrieta Armas, better known as Minnie Minoso. His stepbrothers, with whom he always played ball, were named Minoso, which naturally gave rise to the nickname Minnie. Minnie Minoso was the name that stuck when he ventured north. Minoso came from a family of cane-cutters in Matanzas and was inspired to play by watching Martín Dihigo. His uniforms were made from cotton-flour sacks and his bats were splintered, but he learned to play every position. As he moved from job to job, he organized baseball teams at every location. He improved at every stage, playing semipro, then professionally, with Club Marianao of the Cuban winter league. In 1944 he hit .301 and was named Rookie of the Year.[43]

The very next year he was signed by the New York Cubans in the Negro League. With the fiery Silvio García as his guide to living, eating, and playing in New York, Minoso hit .294 and made the All-Star team in the Negro League. By 1949, Minnie was at spring training with the Cleveland Indians. After two seasons with San Diego, Minoso became the first black player on the Chicago White Sox. His performance more than justified his signing:

> Within 24 hours of his arrival, Minoso hit a two-run home run in his first at-bat to spark a 4–2 win against Vic Raschi and the hated Yankees. Minoso played third base in that 1951 season, batted .326, scored 112 runs, and led the American League in triples with 14 and stolen bases with 31. Attendance jumped by 500,000 that year, and the White Sox improved by 21 games.[44]

His fans on Chicago's South Side honored him with a Minnie Minoso day and various gifts, including a new Packard. When he returned to Cuba, he received a hero's welcome. He was feted at more ceremonies by all of Cuba's top leaders, including Batista, and showered with more gifts. While playing in the winter league there that year, he gave his stepfather a week off by working for him in the cane fields, just as he had done in the past. "Only this time, his shiny new Packard was parked at the cane field's edge."[45]

Minoso's success continued as he regularly batted .300. He moved from Chicago to Cleveland, to St. Louis, and to Washington, and played in Cuba for the winter season. Unlike his compatriot Martín Dihigo, after Castro came to power in 1959, Minoso never again returned. He played and managed in Mexico for a while. In 1976, he was invited back to help coach the White Sox, where he also played in a few games, becoming the oldest player to hit safely. He played again in 1980, becoming baseball's only five-decade player. Chicago invited him back in 1990, but Baseball Commissioner Fay Vincent refused to allow what he considered a publicity stunt. "Minoso finished with a .298 average, 186 homers, 1,136 runs scored, 1,023 runs batted in, and 1,963 hits. Because he did not become a regular until age 28, he did not post Hall of Fame numbers."[46]

There have been dozens of other Cubans who made it to the big leagues, most of whom were recruited by Joe Cambria, the scout for the Washington Senators. To some, Cuba was considered a "minor league farm club" for the Senators.[47] "Uncle Joe" signed over four hundred Cubans through his twenty-five years of scouting in Cuba. Rather than stay in Havana as the other scouts did, Cambria roamed the island looking for prospects. Although he was criticized by some for signing lots of players who were subsequently released, he is also credited for giving to many Latin Americans an opportunity that no one else was willing to give. In World War II alone, while North American players were fighting overseas, Cambria signed over fifty Cubans to both the Senators and other teams.[48]

Cubans signed by the major leagues included, among others, Pedro "Preston" Gómez, Roberto Estalella, Camilo Pascual, Pedro Ramos, Angel Aragon, Jack Aragon, Julio Becquer, Leo Cardenas, Manuel Cueto, Juan Delis, José Valdivielso, Mike Guerra, Frankie Campos, Orestes Destrade, Connie Marrero, Zoilo Versalles, Sandy Consuegra, Carlos Paul, Angel Scull, Mike Fornieles, Jaime Moreno, and Sandy Amoros.[49] Estalella was signed before the color line was broken, which prompted Red Smith to write, "there was a Senegambian somewhere in the Cuban batpile where Senatorial lumber was seasoned."[50] The more recent Cuban acquisitions have included Tony Pérez, Tony Olíva, Mike Cuellar, Luís Tiant, Jr., Oscar Zamora, Adrian Zabala, and Bert Campaneris. Now come those either born in Cuba but raised in the United States or born to Cuban parents in this country, such as José and Ozzie Canseco, Rafael Palmeíro, and Danny Tartabull (see chapter 5).

Baseball in Cuba in the Mid–Twentieth Century

The decades of the 1940s and 1950s were golden ones for Cuban baseball. Cuban poet Nicolás Guillén provides a colorful description of Cuban baseball in the 1940s and 1950s.[51]

Allá lejos...
Hace cincuenta años
nada menos que en la primera plan de los diários
aperecían las últimas noticias de béisbol
venidas de Nueva York

que bueno El Cincinnáti le ganó al Pittsburgh,
y el San Luis al Detroit!

(Compré la pelota marca "Reich" que es la mejor.)
Cualquier tiempo pasado fue peor
Un club cubano de béisbol
Primera base: Charles Little
Segunda base: Joe Cobb
Catcher: Samuel Benton
Tercera base: Bobby Hog
Short Stop: James Wintergarden
Pitcher: William Bot
Files: Wilson, Baker, Panther.
Sí, señor
Y menos Mal
el cargabates: Juan Guzmán.

(There far away . . .
    Fifty years ago
There appeared, of all places, on the first page of the newspapers,
    the last news of baseball from New York.

How good that Cincinnati beat Pittsburgh,
and that St. Louis beat Detroit!

(I bought the "Reich" brand of ball, which is the best.)
Whatever time in the past was worse
A Cuban baseball club
First base: Charles Little
Second base: Joe Cobb
Catcher: Samuel Benton
Third base: Bobby Hog
Short stop: James Wintergarden
Pitcher: William Bot
Fielders: Wilson, Baker, Panther.
Yes, sir
And thank God
the batboy: Juan Guzman.)

Baseball was so popular that the owners of restaurants, theaters,
and nightclubs petitioned President Prío to cut winter league games
from six nights to three nights per week because attendance at the
games was eating into their business. (The request was refused.)[52]
Pitcher Tommy Lasorda saw just how seriously the Cubans took
their baseball. He approached the home plate umpire to question a
few calls and was subtly shown a handgun stuck in umpire Orlando
Maestri's pants. Lasorda returned to the mound praising Maestri as
"the best damn umpire I've ever seen."[53]

In addition to the exodus of Cuban players to the United States
and the successful winter league, minor league baseball came to
Cuba in the summer. Clark Griffith, owner of the Washington Senators, teamed up with Cuban baseball promoter Roberto Maduro
after World War II to create the Havana Cubans, which became part
of the Class B Florida International League. Although the other
five teams were in Florida, Havana led the league in attendance:

> The Havana Cubans played in Gran Stadium, which was built
> in 1946. This modern stadium presented an impressive setting
> for the momentous merger of Latin [American] baseball into
> U.S. organized ball. The stadium seated 35,000, had an impec-
> cable surface, and boasted a lighting system of major league
> caliber. The large field with prevailing wind from straightaway
> center was a pitcher's paradise. Fans and writers rode elevators
> to upper-level, glassed-in boxes.[54]

In the eight years the Havana Cubans spent in the Florida International League, from 1946 to 1953, they won four regular-season titles and two playoff championships.

This Class B team served as a showcase for prospective talent for the Washington Senators. The youngest recruit ever signed by Joe Cambria was sixteen-year-old Camilo Pascual, and his brother Carlos. In his eighteen-year major league pitching career, Camilo won 174 victories. Sandy Consuegra, Julio Becquer, and Juan Delis were also signed from the Cubans. The team also served as a career extender for some former major league players, such as Bobby Estalella, Sandy Ullrich, and Gil Torres.[55]

With Cuban baseball at its apparent height, Bobby Maduro petitioned the U.S.–based International League to admit the Havana Sugar Kings, which replaced the Havana Cubans. The Sugar Kings competed in the Triple A International League from 1954 to 1960. Until Miami joined the league, the Cubans had to pay the costs of the visiting teams. Maduro also had to agree to clean up the gambling.[56]

Yet, the Sugar Kings had little power over their own administration. After the revolution, the club's franchise was transferred to the United States without the knowledge of the Cuban officials. In 1959, the Sugar Kings were at the top of the International League standings and Castro had pledged to underwrite their debts. He made it clear that he was willing to pitch if necessary. They went on to win the Junior World Series, with stars such as Mike Cuellar, Leo "Chico" Cardenas, and Octavio "Cookie" Rojas. Although Castro assured the Maduro family that their holdings were safe, in 1960 the league moved the team to Jersey City, taking with them Cuba's best ball players. Castro denounced the move as another aggressive act by the United States.[57]

But baseball in Cuba was not focused exclusively on the major leagues in the United States. According to Rob Ruck, an astute observer of baseball throughout the Americas:

> The game was organized on three overlapping levels in its early years. The first was an ad hoc player-organized, self-directed network of teams. The second involved clubs sponsored by businessmen, companies, and politicians who sought the promotional advantages of such patronage. The third level was that of professional (sometimes semi-professional) baseball, which organized championships from 1878 until 1961, with a changing cast of teams and format. In some years, no

tournaments were held, while in others both a summer and winter season took place. Havana, Almendares, Santa Clara, Cienfuegos, and Marianao were the league's mainstays.[58]

The Liga Nacional de Béisbol Amateur, the first amateur competition, ran from 1914 to 1926, with teams representing Vedado Tennis Club, Instituto de La Habana, Club Atlético de Cuba, and Sociedad de Marianao. In addition to clubs from towns in Havana and nearby provinces, there were teams representing the University of Havana, the Havana Yacht Club, and clubs formed in U.S.–owned industries, such as Lawton and American Steel. There were also clubs based on industries, such as Ferroviarios (the railways) and Aduana (the customs), as well as a police club.

Between 1927 and 1930, the Liga Intersocial Amateur (Intersocial amateur league), classified as professional by the Amateur Athletics Union of Cuba in the 1940s, was the strongest outside the major professional league. Teams included the industry-based Telefónicos and Círculos de Artesanos. In 1931, the Liga Nacional was established. In the 1930s, clubs included Regla, Hershey, the YMCA, Cubaneleco, Yara, Club Naval, Stany, Sociedad del Pilar, and Círculo Militar. As in the earlier amateur leagues, several clubs were industry or trade based.[59] The famous Cuban baseball player Miguel Cuevas described the ties between baseball and industry before the revolution: "I would work in the factories and play baseball for the owners."[60] New clubs formed in the 1940s included Cienfuegos Sport Club, Deportívo Matanzas, Atlético de las Vegas, Artemisa, and Rosario.[61]

Cuba dominated (and continues to dominate) the amateur circuit in baseball in the Caribbean. In 1938, the *Mundial,* an amateur international baseball championship, was begun in England and moved to the Caribbean the next year. This tournament was the venue for the closest thing to fair competition that existed in baseball in the region. From 1940 through 1972, Cuba won eleven out of eighteen times.[62]

During the nineteenth century, several baseball stadiums were built in Cuba. As baseball became the most popular sport in the twentieth century, many more were constructed. By 1959, there were two lighted stadiums as well, suitable for night games.[63] Where no stadium existed, baseball was played in the streets or the fields.

Soon after baseball began in Cuba, the Liga Cubana de Béisbol, the foundation league, went professional. After World War II, such professionalism was widespread, and Cuba's best players joined the professional leagues in the United States. By the 1950s, professional baseball had taken over from the once-strong amateur league.

Cuba's amateur and professional competitions were weakened by this "professional drain" to the United States, which had begun in 1911 with the signing of Almeída and Marsans. Before the revolution, ninety-eight Cubans played or managed in the U.S. major leagues. Most of them, however, especially the black Cubans, only played in minor leagues.[64] Early links with the United States probably contributed to the early development of professional baseball in Cuba. Even the sports equipment was imported from the United States.

Since 1949, there has been a Serie del Caribe among the winners of the winter leagues. Cuba, Panama, Venezuela, and Puerto Rico fought for the title of champion of the Caribbean, between 1949 and 1960. In those twelve years, "Cuba won 51 of 71 games for a .718 average, took 7 of the 12 titles, and was undefeated in 3 of the 12 tournaments."[65] When play resumed after 1969, Cuba and Panama had been replaced by Mexico and the Dominican Republic in what is now called the Inter-American Series. The tournament lacks the key players that are necessary for it to be considered a decisive regional competition.

Of the 73 titles in Cuba's main professional baseball competition, Havana won 27 and Almendares 22. Clubs from outside the capital captured only twelve titles.[66] This was indicative of the greater opportunities, the larger numbers of clubs, and the greater availability of equipment and facilities in the capital. As with social services, housing, and education, sports institutions were located predominantly in Havana and a few nearby areas. In addition, much of the wealth, some of which might have been used to sponsor teams, was concentrated (if not earned) in the capital.

Scouts searched for players in rural Cuba to play either on the professional teams in Havana or in the U.S. leagues. Ricardo Hernández, who played school baseball in Guantanamo in eastern Cuba (even though he did not attend school), described how when he was sixteen or seventeen during the late 1940s, a U.S. baseball scout offered players 100 pesos to play in Havana. He claimed that the scouts signed players for 500 pesos and kept 400 for themselves.[67] In the Dominican Republic, baseball scouts have been referred to as "blackcatchers," after the West African slave traders. Before legislation was passed in the mid–1980s to protect young Dominican ball players, scouts were known for unscrupulous behavior, such as lying to prospects and their parents, cheating them, or worse, even sequestering them.[68]

Cuba as the Epicenter of Caribbean Baseball

While trying to solicit money for the Nicaraguan contras, Lt. Col. Oliver North was fond of offering "proof" of Cuban influence over the Sandinistas. He pointed conclusively to the baseball diamonds that were so visible in air reconnaissance photos taken over Nicaragua. His ignorant assumption was that only the Cubans played baseball; the rest of Latin America played soccer. Any baseball played in the region, then, had to be the result of recent Cuban interference. As it turns out, he was right in his assessment of the Cuban influence on the spread of the game; he was just a century too late. Pedro Julio Santana, a former sportswriter and activist in the Dominican Republic, described the phenomenon accurately:

> It is much the same as that which happened with Christianity. Jesus could be compared to the North Americans, but the apostles were the ones that spread the faith, and the apostles of baseball were the Cubans. They went out into the world to preach the gospel of baseball. Even though the Dominican Republic and Puerto Rico were occupied by the North Americans, the Cubans brought baseball here first, and to Mexico and Venezuela, too.[69]

The only thing that preceded baseball throughout the Caribbean was sugarcane, brought by Christopher Columbus in 1493. Cane cultivation languished for several centuries, however. In the 1870s, Cuban émigrés, fleeing the violence of their war for independence from Spain, brought with them their expertise—in both sugar cultivation and baseball.[70]

In Cuba, sugar and baseball developed symbiotically. Leagues developed around the plantations and the growing season:

> Baseball and sugar production fit perfectly. During the six months it took for the cane to grow, baseball was a cheap and easy diversion for the laborers. The slow pace of the game suited the hot Caribbean days, allowing plenty of rest in the shade and only infrequent bursts of exertion. Bodies made strong by slashing the tough, wiry cane in the harvest were per-

fectly suited to action at home plate. In addition, the sugar mill owners wanted to field winning teams, so baseball skills brought a premium to workers who possessed them. The Cubans eventually sold out to U.S. investors, who continued their support of these "sugar leagues" for the next 20 years.[71]

Thanks to the Cubans, cane and baseball spread together throughout the Caribbean as well. Cubans moved west to Mexico's Yucatán peninsula, again fleeing violence and bringing baseball. A Cuban ball player named Emilio Cramer brought baseball to Venezuela in 1895.[72] In Puerto Rico, baseball came with a Spanish diplomat who had been assigned to Cuba. It immediately caught on, and "the first organized game played in front of spectators in Puerto Rico was held on 9 January 1898, six months before the Marines arrived."[73] Clearly, the Cubans—not the U.S. Marines—proselytized the region.

Baseball first came to the Dominican Republic with two Cuban brothers, Ignacio and Ubaldo Aloma, who emigrated there in 1880. Another Cuban, Dr. Samuel Mendoza y Ponce de León brought baseball to the interior of the country. By 1893, two clubs had been formed. By 1891, the first organized game was played on the island, and the dugouts were filled with Cubans, Dominicans, North Americans, and one German.[74] As in Cuba, sugar plantations and baseball diamonds sprang up simultaneously and feverishly. Baseball became more than just entertainment; it became a way of life:

> In the cane fields baseball began as a diversion supplied by refinery managers for their men during the slack harvest period. But the familial, close-knit nature of the communities that grew around the refineries fostered an identification with the baseball players and teams, and this intensified the game.

After the revolution, Cuba withdrew from the circuit in professional baseball, and the Dominicans deservedly accepted the mantle of baseball's apostles:

> There are roughly forty-nine Dominicans in the major leagues, 325 in the minor leagues, and four hundred in Dominican baseball academies. Perhaps 250 play in the Dominican Professional League and are unsigned by American clubs; another

250 are scouts, instructors, and staff members affiliated with the academies. Thus around thirteen hundred Dominicans earn a living through professional baseball.[75]

As of 1989, of the five hundred Latin Americans to ever play in the major leagues, Cuba represented 26 percent, Puerto Rico 25 percent, and the Dominican Republic 23 percent. The rest had come from Venezuela, Mexico, Panama, Nicaragua, Colombia, and Honduras. There is even talk that the Dominican Republic and Venezuela will be included in the North American baseball draft (Puerto Rico already is).[76]

Probably the ultimate irony of Cuban baseball was the alleged rejection of a young pitcher named Fidel Castro by Joe Cambria, scout for the Washington Senators. In an interview just prior to the 1991 Pan-American Games, Fidel Castro neither confirmed nor denied that he was once offered $5,000 to pitch for the Senators; he claimed that he was a mediocre pitcher—dangerous only because his pitch might have hit someone.[77] What might have been had Fidel been seduced by the financial rewards of professional baseball must remain forever a matter of conjecture.

Boxing

Despite the early corruption, boxing was and is one of the more popular sports in Cuba. Yet although it comes close to matching baseball in longevity, on the island, boxing never captured the Cuban soul the way baseball did.

The first professional match was held in 1909 in Havana. The next year, a Chilean named John Budinich established the first boxing academy in Havana. In 1912, boxing was suspended by the government for its brutality and to stop the resulting social disorder that occurred when blacks fought whites. The ban was apparently without effect (the sport merely moved underground), and within the next nine years, there were several other attempts to ban the sport. With each ban, the sport moved further into the interior of the island and spread throughout. Finally, on 13 December 1921, the Cuban government relented and legitimized boxing with the establishment of the National Commission on Boxing and Wrestling, one of whose members was the celebrated fencer Ramón Fonst.[78]

The sport continued to grow in popularity. By 1959, Cuba had six professional world champions, including "Kid Gavilán," "Kid

Chocolate" (Eligio Sardínas), and Benny Paret. Sardínas, the most famous of the early Cuban boxers, won his first fight in 1922 at the age of twelve in the Infantile Championship, sponsored by the newspaper *La Noche*. By 1928, he had turned professional. As with many other Cuban boxers, he adopted an English name and picked up a North American coach. He was a world champion in the 1930s.[79]

Professional boxing, like professional baseball, held the elusive promise of an escape from poverty, although despite earning tremendous sums in the ring, Cuban boxers almost invariably died penniless. Kid Gavilán retired after eleven years, with a world title, but in severe economic difficulties, which were exacerbated by his connections with the mafia. The rumor is that he became a vagabond in Miami, Florida. Jorge Liraldo Leyva, "El Colegia," said that he had worked in a bar all night for 30 pesos a month. In one fight, he won 350 pesos, but he had none left after paying out 33 percent to his manager, 10 percent to his trainer, and the remainder to the medical commission, the sports commission, and the hostel where he was staying.[80]

Cuba's boxing reputation (and probably its gambling and mafia connections) drew foreign boxers as well. From the United States came Jack Johnson, Jess Willard, Jack Dempsey, Joe Louis, Sugar Ray Robinson, and Joe Brown, among others. Then, as with other sports, the revolutionary government banned professional boxing in 1961.[81]

No other sport enjoyed the same degree of success as baseball and boxing before 1959. Sport and related activities merely reflected the divisions within prerevolutionary Cuban society.

OTHER RECREATIONAL ACTIVITIES

Throughout its history, Cuban sport and recreation has been strongly influenced by African, Spanish, and U.S. cultures. In the period prior to and just after 1900, most recreation and sports were loosely organized. This was particularly true in rural areas and for the less well-off non-Hispanic Cubans who made up a large part of the island's population. Pastimes for many Cubans included festivals, music, dancing, drinking, and various gambling activities. Card games, dominoes, checkers, and chess were frequently played in clubs and bars, with "every marble table being in requisition for the purpose of games on Sundays."[82]

Among the Wealthy Cubans

For the wealthier *peninsulares* (born in Spain) and the richest among the Cuban-born Hispanics (*criollos*), informal recreation included billiards (Cuba had a world billiards champion, Alfredo de Oro), fishing, and beachgoing.[83] Other loosely organized "genteel" pastimes for the wealthy included concerts, dancing, and walking or riding in the evening in the squares and avenues (*paséos*) of the capital. In the mid–nineteenth century, wealthy women could often be seen riding at dusk. A traveler through Cuba in the mid–nineteenth century observed, "The ladies do not seem to take the least exercise, except an occasional drive on the Paseo, or public park; they never walk out [except on Holy Thursday]."[84] More formal activities for Havana's upper class included parties (*tertúlias*) which were generally held in the opera house, and concerts given by the governor's band or regimental bands in the Plaza de Armas, the large square overlooking the port entrance. The square and *paséos* surrounding it were popular locations for walking and listening to concerts at dusk, throughout the nineteenth century and to the present day. Music, frequently heard in the clubs of the island's capital, was also a major attraction among less well-off Cubans.[85]

On Plantations

Fiestas, with singing and dancing, feasting and sometimes puppet shows were very popular on the plantations. These fiestas were often based on African traditions, reflecting the presence of slaves.[86] Other activities among Cuban slaves were robust in comparison to the gentrified diversions of Cuba's wealthy. The *maní* dance, for example, was more like a punching match involving forty or fifty men. Some slave masters bet on the dance, while others intervened because of the injuries that often resulted.[87] The Lucumí Africans, the most numerous tribal group among Cuba's slaves, also celebrated El Día de Los Reyes, which incorporated similar games.[88] Among these was the *mayombé*, which was linked to religious beliefs and included playing the drums and singing, in a request for peace and health.

Other games included a version of hide and seek in which the men pursued the women, and a ring game in which young boys would drop a ring in the hand of the girl they liked best.[89] Many of the games had romantic elements to them, but more frequently they focused on gambling activities, such as *tejo* and skittles. Some slave owners tried to prevent the gambling, while others participated in the gambling themselves. (Women were not involved in the tavern games.) For African Cuban youngsters, activities also included marbles and various running games. Girls made and played with rag dolls.

Cuban plantation activities also included horseback riding. The African Cubans and most mulattoes were spectators in these, not having horses. Games highlighting riding skills were held during carnivals. One game involved stuffing a dead duck with grease and hanging it on a rope hung between two poles. The riders would gallop at full speed from ten meters away and then try to pull off the duck's head. The winner was crowned president of the ball.[90] Then, as now, the Cubans were using as recreational objects things that were readily available to them.

In the second half of the nineteenth century, Chinese coolies (approximately 125,000 between 1848 and 1874) gave another dimension to recreational culture in Cuba. The Chinese were often gamblers, adding to the tradition that was already strong in Cuba. They introduced mime and acrobatic shows at festivals, as well as charades, which were later adopted by both black and white Cubans.[91] Like other Cubans, the Chinese were probably involved in leisure activities that were at best loosely organized.

ORGANIZED RECREATION IN THE NINETEENTH CENTURY

Cabildos de Nación and Mutual Aid Societies

Some sports and recreation clubs were, however, established in the second half of the nineteenth century. The foundations for organized sports and recreation were probably laid in the clubs of the wealthiest Cubans, but also in the Cabildo de Nación clubs of Cuba's slave communities.

Cabildos de Nación were based on tribal origins and practiced African rituals, organized festivities, and mutual aid activities. In addition, the cabildos could own property. They were patronized by colonial officials who, during slavery, tolerated these African clubs. Presumably, they were also centers for fiestas, dancing, music, and other recreational activities such as cards and dominoes. In the postemancipation years, there was considerable debate as to whether the cabildos were anti-Cuban separatist organizations.[92] Although they were not formally outlawed, they did gradually disappear. However, the cabildos did influence Cuban culture, and the Mutual Aid Societies that replaced them were similar in some respects.

The main areas of concern for the mutual aid societies were education, recreation, and social welfare, often with political overtones.[93] Unlike the cabildos, they were often divided along ethnic lines rather than along tribal boundaries. This racial division was especially evident in the many Asociaciones de Instrucción y Recréo (Associations for instruction and recreation) that were established in both urban and rural areas.

As with the cabildos, there was considerable debate as to the value of the clubs. Like the slave owners before them, some government officials regarded the mutual aid societies as a useful diversion from political involvement. Others saw them as centers that encouraged politicization. Both were probably true to some extent.

These clubs were important in beginning the institutionalization of leisure time. Despite the earlier tradition of clubs for the less well-off Cubans, in the twentieth century, access to most organized clubs was limited to wealthy Cubans and foreigners. Even in the mid–1940s most Cuban men's leisure activities were unorganized or loosely organized. The most popular of these activities included socializing, music, dancing, listening to the radio, and going to the movies or a cockfight (see table 2). The activities of Cuban women were even more limited. Some of these activities were loosely organized in clubs or trade centers following the earlier pattern of clubs for slaves and agricultural workers and working-class Cubans.

Gambling as Recreation in Cuba

Most Cubans had little or no money to spend on recreational pursuits. A survey in the mid–1940s revealed that, among those surveyed, more money was spent on gambling on the national lotteries than on active recreational activities (see table 3). Indeed, gambling has a long tradition in Cuban society, despite innumerable attempts to stop the practice: Carlos I, King of Spain, tried to ban gambling; in 1771, Carlos II declared gambling to be illegal in all Spanish colonies.[94]

In the late 1820s, the issues of vagrancy and gambling created considerable discussion in Cuba. Prompted by a call in 1829 from the Patriotic Society of Havana to discuss vagrancy, the prolific Cuban chronologist, Saco, wrote on the theme in the journal *Revista Bimestre Cubana*. Saco sought to remove what he considered to be

TABLE 2.
Activities in Trade Centers, Reported by Cuban Families, 1946

Number of Times Activity Mentioned	Male		Female	
	Adult	Youth	Adult	Youth
visiting friends or relatives	380	121	253	70
political meetings	154	59	20	9
listening to radio	106	52	54	34
movies	76	99	44	51
cockfights	75	34	3	2
club meetings	89	15	7	5
dancing	51	110	31	68
baseball	46	44	4	8
drinking	56	37	9	6
dominoes, cards, checkers	48	19	3	1
general amusement	97	149	52	95

Source: L. Nelson, Rural Cuba (New York: Octagon Books, 1970), p. 213.

TABLE 3.
Percentage of Income Spent on Recreation and National Lottery by Region, 1945

Place	Percentage of Income Spent on	
	Recreation	Lottery
Trinidad	4.4	1.6
Manguíto	3.5	2.1
Florida	0.0[a]	5.1
San Juan y Martínez	0.9	0.7
Cabaiguan	1.3	3.9
Sancti Spiritus	4.9	5.3
Bayamo	1.4	2.2
Florencia	4.9	1.9
Guines	2.4	1.5
Average	2.7	2.8

Source: Nelson, p. 217.
[a]The reason for this unlikely zero is unclear. Perhaps no information was available for this region.

the causes of vagrancy. Primary among these, he argued, was the widespread gambling in his country. "There is not a city, town or district in the island of Cuba where this devouring cancer is absent."[95] Saco saw this ever-present gambling as the cause of crime, corruption, and poverty (although one might argue that it was the corruption and poverty that led to the crime and gambling). He called for the closure of gambling centers, the banning of games, and an end to the daytime lotteries. The organizers claimed that these lotteries served only artisans, lawyers, and civil servants, but Saco retorted that the lottery centers (*casas de loterías*) should be opened only in the evening when these clients were not working.

Although Saco claimed that poor people of all ages and ethnicities were gamblers, apparently he stopped calling for the closure of gambling centers because of objections from the wealthy and the military. Perhaps these groups also wished to gamble; they probably had vested interests in the gambling houses. Saco also criticized billiards for the long hours passed in play. Rather than ban it, however, he suggested alternative activities such as museum-going and recreational walking.[96] These activities may have attracted wealthier Cubans, but it is unlikely they would have distracted Cuban workers from the only excitement and diversion to be found in an otherwise drab existence.

In 1895, thirty-seven games were banned in cafés, public houses, and recreational societies. Under U.S. occupation (1898–1902), attempts were also made to ban gambling, but in 1902 the national lottery was reestablished and other forms of gambling were again quite common. In the 1930s, social clubs were described merely as dancing and gambling dens.[97] Thus, despite widespread opposition, gambling continued to be popular with both upper and lower classes. Of course, such activities were, as always, in the economic interests of the gangsters and the government.

For most Cubans, especially those in rural districts, organized sport and physical education were limited. For leisure, men played in the streets with whatever "equipment" was available, while women mainly talked amongst themselves. This is not to say that organized sports and physical education were nonexistent in pre-Castro Cuba, but that these activities were not widely available.

PHYSICAL EDUCATION

Physical education was first included in school curricula in August 1900. However, PE teachers could not train in Cuba until 1916; until then, they had to travel abroad for their studies. At that time, both staff and student numbers were minimal. The 1899 census recorded school attendance as only 5 or 6 percent of those eligible. Indeed, as late as 1956, school attendance for children between the ages of five and thirteen was only 54.2 percent, only a small increase from the 1925 figure of 50.7 percent. Despite some improvement in school attendance at the beginning of the century, public schools often failed to carry out curriculum requirements, partly due to corruption among teachers. Following World War II, a teaching degree could be purchased for between 1,500 and 2,000 pesos, and the salary of a teacher could be collected without actually teaching.[98]

In public schools, there was virtually no physical education, with very little sport introduced at the basic secondary level. Theoretically the schools had specialist teachers, including PE instructors, but there were only about eight hundred actually employed. The contract system for public school teachers granted them life tenure of a class, which allowed them to receive wages, while they could hire a substitute (not necessarily a qualified one) to carry out the actual teaching.[99] Despite the market for PE degrees, the job was one of low prestige, made attractive only by the contract situation.

Cuban governments were generally content to let the private colleges concern themselves with physical education and sports teaching for those who were able to pay for the service. Only 550 PE instructors were employed by the Ministry of Education in 1958. R. J. Pickering claims that a further thousand PE teachers were recorded as unemployed. Some PE teachers criticized the situation in Cuba, but this appeared ineffectual in changing the existing state of affairs.[100]

Access to and the practice of physical education was limited, despite several factors such as the formation of La Dirección General de Deportes (a government agency responsible for sports) in 1938; the organization of PE courses at the Institúto nacional de educación física (National Institute for Physical Education); and the existence of summer courses at the Havana University in the 1940s. In public schools, only 2 percent of the students participated in physical education.[101] Sports were more widely practiced; some were available to many Cubans, especially male Cubans.

SPORTS

Some organized sports had existed in Cuba before 1900. Such activities included cockfighting, bullfighting, jai alai, tennis, baseball, and various water sports. As the twentieth century progressed, sports were institutionalized with competitions between private schools and clubs. By 1950, several professional sports were well established.

Early Jai Alai, Bullfighting, and Cockfighting

The Spaniards had introduced bullfighting and jai alai in an organized form as early as the eighteenth century. In the middle of the nineteenth century, the Plaza de Toros was opened in Havana. There was also a bullring in Matanzas in the 1880s. Bullfights with professional matadors were held every Sunday during the winter season in the capital, and the sport was most popular among Spaniards living in Cuba. By the twentieth century, the practice had ended, although the idea of reintroducing bullfighting was raised (unsuccessfully) in the 1930s. One visitor believed that "the Creoles do not love the sport itself, and they regard its revival as a mere farce."[102]

Jai alai was more popular. The sport was reportedly practiced regularly as early as the eighteenth century. In 1901 the Palácio de los Gritos, a jai alai building, was opened in Havana. The game was introduced by the Spanish and most players were Spaniards even in the 1950s. The United States had some influence on its continued practice in Cuba after the end of Spanish colonial rule. U.S. Military Governor Leonard Wood played jai alai and supported an application to build a stadium for the sport in Havana.[103]

Governor Wood's support was crucial in the establishment of the center, because it contravened the Foraker Law (Article 4) of the Platt Amendment, which banned grants of "any property, franchise, or concession . . . by any military or other authority . . . while Cuba . . . [was] under occupation by the United States."[104] Although the Havana Council and Governor Wood saw no objection to the application, it was rejected by U.S. military officials in 1901. Wood appealed to Washington to allow the Havana Council to rent land for the center. By the time Washington had approved Wood's appeal, the building had already been constructed and operating for two months. In 1902, the Jai Alai Company, which profited from gambling on the sport, was officially recognized, despite controversy as to its legality and criticism by some authorities. By then, the game was well established. The sport had strong ties with gambling and involved professional players in as many as 175 different competitions each year. Managers earned over 11 million pesos per year.[105] Although evidently well patronized in the capital, and perhaps in other major population centers, jai alai lacked the widespread appeal of cockfighting and baseball.

"There, they are fighting. . . . kill! kill! kill!" These were the cries one tourist, W. C. Bryant, reported coming from Valla de Gallos, the main cockpit of the 1840s in Havana. This U.S. visitor declared, "cockfighting is the principal diversion of the island, having entirely supplanted the national (Spanish) spectacle of bullbaiting."[106] Cockpits were in all the towns and villages of Cuba. With the government's approval, this sport was played on Sundays and public holidays, including during Easter when the various fights in towns and villages were recounted in Havana. It was said to be very popular among plantation owners and to a lesser degree among African Cubans. The gambling and consequently the money associated with cockfighting meant that small farmers bred cockerels and sold them at markets to trainers. "The pit is always crowded, and the amount of money which changes hands daily in this cruel mode of gambling is very considerable."[107]

After Cuba's War of Independence against Spain, U.S. occupation authorities banned cockfighting; but its popularity and accessibility were restored after the U.S. withdrawal in 1902. This and other forms of gambling were then not only reinstated, but protected by law. The popularity of cockfighting continued even after the Castro government took over in 1959. The sport was strongly entrenched in Cuban culture and had developed an organized structure for its practice by the mid–1940s when large crowds attended fights.[108]

Soccer

In the early part of this century, soccer rivaled baseball in popularity. In 1909, a soccer club called Hatuey Sport Club was established by some Spaniards and a group of Cubans educated in England. In the early 1920s, a soccer competition began with the involvement of several clubs: Union Racing-Fortuna Sport Club, Iberia, Cataluna, Vigo, and Olimpia. Cuba's soccer association joined the international soccer federation (FIFA). In a 1938 World Cup match, Cuba defeated Rumania by one goal. The famous clubs—Barcelona and Real Madrid (Spain), Colo-Colo (Chile), and Nacional (Uruguay)— all visited Cuba. Although soccer never became the passion that it is in most other Latin American countries, a lighted soccer stadium was built on the outskirts of Havana, at the height of the game's popularity in 1928. It was paid for by the director of one team (the Tígres) and by the president of Club Deportívo Hispano-America, Rafael Armada, a Spaniard who owned a confectionery factory. Soccer, like other sports, was sponsored by the wealthy, with most Cubans playing in the streets with balls made of paper or cloth.[109]

Gymnastics

While boxing, baseball, soccer, and cockfighting were the dominant organized sports, others did exist. Gymnastics began early in Cuban history, and Cuba had some success in regional competitions. In 1839, Doctor Rafael de Castro opened the Gimnasio Normal, the first known gymnasium, at the corner of Consulado and Virtudes in central Havana, and he founded a gymnastics school, the Escuela Gimnastica. The center was promoted by the Real Sociedad Patriotica and by Juan Bernando O'Gaban, one of the earliest PE activists in Cuba. Thirty years later, in 1869, the Casino Español de La Habana, a Spanish recreation club, was set up in the Cuban capital. Similar clubs providing diverse forms of recreation as well as gymnastics were formed in other parts of the country. In 1883, Doctor Castro added two more gymnasiums to his concerns in the capital and established the Círculo Militar de La Habana. Doctor Luís de Aguera joined the push for gymnastics in 1880 by creating a PE school for fire fighters and by following Doctor Castro's example of founding gymnasiums and promoting gymnastics.[110]

The movement continued to expand in the twentieth century. A Clerks Gymnastics Association was established in 1925. In the 1940s, the promotion of gymnastics was continued by a Russian student, Raigorosky. Gymnastics was sufficiently popular by the end of the decade to be included in a public display in Martí Park as part of the 1949 Congress of Physical Education. The strength of gymnastics had been demonstrated two years before that, when Cuba earned eight gold medals in the Pan-American Games and won the gymnastics title.[111]

Water Sports

Water sports were practiced relatively early in Cuba. For example, sailing began, like most sports, in the island's capital with the foundation of the Havana Yacht Club in 1896, the first of several. Limited to wealthy Cubans and U.S. citizens, these clubs took over the beaches and other natural areas for their own private use. African

Cubans, mulattoes, and even the petit bourgeoisie (which probably included Hispanic Cubans) were prohibited from using the best beaches.[112] These clubs monopolized other sports as well, such as deep-sea fishing, archery, fencing, and kayaking.

Water polo emerged at a competitive level during the 1930s and involved many of these sailing associations as well as other existing sports clubs, such as the YMCA and the Havana and Miramar yachting clubs. Later, the water polo competition was expanded by the entry of teams from the Casino Español de La Habana, the Círculo Militar y Naval, the Club Cubanelco, and the Vedado Tennis Club.[113]

Fencing

Fencing was more exclusive than water polo and began much earlier. It was also one of the few sports in which Cuba performed well internationally. It began as an organized activity in the nineteenth century. In 1891, the Club Gimnástico for fencing was founded in Havana.[114] Cuba's international class fencers, however, were generally resident outside Cuba, such as the champion Ramón Fonst, who lived in Paris.

Cycling

Another sport—probably exclusive because of the need for equipment—was cycling. Professional cycling may have enabled some less well-off Cubans to take part, perhaps with the prospect of competing on the strong European circuit. The first national cycling competition was held in 1929. Participants included members of Cuba's first cycling club, the Club Ciclista Azul. There were other clubs by the 1950s, such as Carmelita, Terror, and Veloz.[115] In 1941, Rafael Dopico Marfaing founded a union of Cuban cyclists.

Athletics

Athletics, especially track, was one sport in which poorer Cubans could participate, despite continued discrimination. U.S. influence played a part in the development of athletics. Baptists from the United States set up a school near Santiago de Cuba with a gymnasium. The Baptists apparently played a role in making athletics (and presumably other sports) more popular in this eastern city.

The University of Havana also promoted athletics, along with many other sports. As early as 1905, there was an athletic union at the university and by 1926 an annual university athletics carnival was established.[116]

Tennis

Tennis began in 1914 with the formation of the Yayabo Tennis Club and, like many other sports, was restricted to private clubs. In February 1921, Hispanic Cubans established a tennis club in Artemisa in Havana Province. By 1930, there was also one in Vedado.[117] Tennis was one sport in which women (at least wealthy women) could and did participate.

Basketball

Basketball had been popular in Cuba since the 1920s, and could be played by all (including women), at least socially, if not in organized competition. It came to the island with young Cubans who had studied in the United States. In 1906, the University of Havana defeated a YMCA team from the United States by three points. In 1915, the Liga Nacional de Baloncesto de Cuba (National basketball league of Cuba) was formed. In the late 1920s, tournaments were arranged at the University of Havana. A union basketball club was also formed in the central province of Ciego de Avila, and in the 1930s, teams were formed in the Sociedad Colonia Española (Spanish colony club) and in some schools.[118] Although there is limited information on popular participation in basketball, it is probable that like baseball it was played in the streets and the fields with makeshift equipment.

Other Sports

Other sports introduced into Cuba in the twentieth century included squash, judo (only as self-defense), U.S. football, professional wrestling, professional bodybuilding, swimming, dog racing, volleyball (started in 1906 by soldiers), and horse racing. One of the less widespread sports was weightlifting. Competitions were held in the Clerks Association Gymnasium in 1935, at the same time that a weightlifting federation was formed. The sport was probably practiced only in Havana and nearby. There were clubs in the University of Havana, in the Clerks' Gym, in the Customs Workers Center, and the Club Gran Atlético.[119]

Another sport was wrestling. As early as 1909, Cuban sponsors offered money to any challenger who could last five minutes or defeat the Japanese wrestler, Yamoto Haida. Although amateur wrestling was established in 1929, it was limited to exclusive clubs in the 1930s. The first amateur competition was in 1933 and included such exclusive clubs as the Club Náutico, the Club Atlético, and Miramar Yacht Club. By the 1950s, wrestling like many sports was commercialized with regular professional competitions.[120]

Horse racing was more widespread (among the wealthy) and commercialized and institutionalized in Havana. In the 1950s, races were held at Oriental Park in the wealthy Havana suburb of Marianao, where the Jockey Club also held luncheons for 6 pesos (3.50 to enter the club and 2.50 for the meal).[121]

INTERNATIONAL PERFORMANCE

The limitations on access for many Cubans and racial discrimination in the selection of national teams contributed to Cuba's lack of international success in most sports. "With the exception of a tiny handful of outstanding Cuban athletes . . . Cuba had hardly ever won any medals in competition."[122] Baseball was the major exception: Cuba was champion in five out of seven Central American and Caribbean Games before 1959 (Cuba attended six games); came first in the 1951 Pan-American Games; and won seven of the ten Amateur World Series they attended between 1939 and 1959 (see table 4).

Although only twenty nations competed in the first modern Olympic Games of 1900 in Paris, Cuba won only a few medals, and many of these medalists resided outside Cuba. They were a major force in fencing at the 1900 and 1904 games. Ramón Fonst won three gold medals, two in the épée (in 1900 and 1904) and one in the foil (in 1904). Other Cuban medalists in fencing were Albertson Van Zo Post (silver in the foil and bronze in the épée and the sabre in 1904); Charles Tatham (bronze in the foil and silver in the épée in 1904); and Manuel Díaz (gold in the sabre in 1904). The Cubans won the team title in the foil at the 1904 Olympics. The only other medal won by Cuba in the Olympic arena was a silver in yachting won by Carlos de Cárdenas and his son in the international star class at the 1948 games.[123] None of these successful Cuban athletes lived on the island. The fencers went to Europe, especially France, and the sailors lived in the United States.

The only other highlights in Cuba's Olympic history before 1959 were the feats of Félix Carvajál and the sprinter Rafael For-

TABLE 4.
Cuban Performances in Amateur International Baseball
Competitions, 1926–1953

Year	Am. Games	Pan-Am. Games	World Series
1926	1st		
1930	1st		
1935	1st		
1938	1st		
1939			1st
1940			1st
1941			2nd
1942			1st
1943			1st
1944			3rd
1945			did not compete
1946	3rd		did not compete
1947			did not compete
1948			did not compete
1949			did not compete
1950			1st
1951		1st	3rd
1952	1st		1st
1953			1st
1954	did not compete		
1955		did not compete	

Source: E. A. Wagner, "Baseball in Cuba," *Journal of Popular Culture,* 18,
no. 1 (Summer 1984), p. 116.

tun. Fortun equaled the gold medalist's time in his heat of the 100-
meter event at the 1948 games. That he ran progressively slower
times in the remainder of the meet indicates that he was poorly
trained. He did, however, capture the Pan-American title.[124] The
only other notable international performance by a Cuban athlete
was by Carvajál in the St. Louis Olympics in 1904. Despite several
"distractions," he still finished fourth in the marathon (see chapter
6 for more details about Carvajál).

Cuba was involved in international sports from the very beginning. In addition to attending the first Olympics in 1900, the country was a founding member of the Central American and Caribbean
Games in 1926. In 1930, these games were held in Havana.[125] Cuba's performances were much better in these regional games, which
probably indicated the (worse) problems of the other nations rather
than particularly outstanding performances by Cuba. The island's

only other claims to fame in international competition were in amateur baseball, professional boxing, the famous chess player José Raúl Capablanca, and the billiards champion Alfredo de Oro.

DOMESTIC POLICY IMPLICATIONS

The revolutionaries of 1959—the 26th of July Movement and its leader, Fidel Castro—had traditions to draw upon for their goal of restructuring Cuban PE and sports culture. There were already some facilities, clubs, and competitions with which to begin the process of revolutionizing Cuban sport. Cuban history had always been punctuated by foreign domination and by racial and class divisions, and in sport, this was evident in the differences between the activities of the rich and the poor and in the existence of exclusive private clubs. Cuban governments traditionally took little interest in physical culture, except to use it to reinforce slavery and, later, as a source for revenue. Similarly, despite participation in the first modern Olympic Games, Cuban governments before 1959 tendèd not to regard world-scale competition as important. This was particularly true under Batista, in the period just prior to the revolution. Either international sports victories were not considered political objectives or the financial support to encourage these victories was not perceived to be worth the potential political return, in stark contrast to the policy after 1959.

It was only when there appeared to be a threat to the social order that Cuba's rulers became interested in physical culture: during the War of Independence, for example, or over the role of the Cabildos de Nación, or during the student rebellion of the 1920s. Otherwise physical culture was left primarily to private concerns, open to U.S. influence, corruption, and professionalism. Foreign influence, the neglect and corruption of Cuban governments, and the limitations on access to sports provoked criticism from many Cubans.

Social Control and Resistance in Domestic Policy

The African Clubs   Colonial officials and slaveholders viewed the Cabildos de Nación as valuable diversions for the slaves and during slavery tolerated these African clubs:

> Both slaveholders and the government apparently viewed the cabildos as functional under slavery because they could pro-

vide an outlet for energy and a means of self-expression that might undercut the potential resistance; and at the same time, they isolated Africans from other sectors of society.[126]

After emancipation, the attitude to the cabildos underwent a major alteration. The colonial administration, which had viewed them as "compensatory relaxation, appropriate to slavery," now saw the clubs as a threat.[127] It was feared that their African identity would undermine loyalty to Spain. African Cubans were to be hispanicized and assimilated into Cuban society, and African culture had to be eliminated to accomplish this.

The possibility that a separatist ideology might develop among Africans contributed to the hostility toward the cabildos that was found among the Cuban ruling class. The police inspector in Sagua la Grande pointed to the state-like constitution of the local Cabildo Congo. There was concern about whether freed slaves would work, and there were frequent complaints of their laziness, as they left the plantations to go to *parrands* or parties of musical festivals. Ennobling work was encouraged, cockfighting was labeled a degradation, and African music was attacked.[128]

There were laws prohibiting public gatherings of African Cubans, which presumably included gatherings for recreational purposes, and although the Spanish crown was not prepared to risk unrest by banning the cabildos, it did prohibit the acceptance of new members, which, together with opposition within Cuba, resulted in their gradual decline and the formation, instead, of the seemingly more acceptable mutual aid societies.[129]

Founded in 1878, the society in Remedios was for mulattoes only, and its principal goal was to educate mulatto children. There was a concern that youngsters were spending too much time dancing and not enough time studying. Many of the societies saw education as an avenue for social mobility and were actively involved in the campaign to establish schools for non-Hispanic children and for open access to existing white-only schools. Education was frequently discussed in the journals and newspapers published by these societies (as was the encouragement of legal marriage). The societies reflected ethnic and social divisions within Cuban society. Many of those that were not racially exclusive were based on occupational categories—such as the Recréo de Artesanos (Artisans club) in Trinidad, established in 1892)—or on political beliefs, such as La Fraternidad and the Casinos Españoles de Hombres de Color. La Fraternidad sought unity among all Cubans, whereas the Casinos Españoles supported Spanish colonial rule. The names of the societies demonstrate their varied memberships and goals: El trabajo (Work); El amparro (Protection-charity); Socorros mutuos (Mutual Assistance); Fraternidad (Fraternity); El progreso (Progress); La luz (Light); Las hijas del progreso (Daughters of Progress); Sociedad de instrucción y recréo (Society for Instruction and Recreation); Casinos Españoles de hombres de color (Spanish Club for Colored People); and Sociedad de la raza de color (Society for Colored Races).[130]

Mutual Aid Societies   The mutual aid societies, popular throughout Cuba, represented the Cuban tradition of political discussion and organization. Although some of the societies criticized the Cuban rulers, the divisions evident among them weakened their potential to threaten the status quo. They were allowed to continue, although not without some local opposition and occasional disputes with colonial officials. While these societies were accepted, they were periodically subjected to government scrutiny and harassment. Some—such as the conservative and loyalist Casinos Españoles—served to strengthen the values of Cuba's rulers and were granted concessions in a bid to placate dissension. Some were less acceptable and faced open hostility. The colonial authorities approved of, and even encouraged, the divisions evident between African Cubans and mulattoes and between different occupational groups. For example, the split between African Cubans and mulattoes in the mutual aid society in Santiago de Cuba was aggravated by Commander Camilo Polavieja who arrested black leaders and charged that "the societies of recreations, instituted by persons of color [were] conspiring day and night." Despite attempts to control these societies or to destroy them if they became a threat, some were centers for resistance to the dominant class and to their values. La Fraternidad was very political and published literature calling for reform, independence from Spain, and unity among Cuba's non-Hispanics. The mutual aid societies also played a significant role in pushing for African Cuban children to be educated in white-only schools.[131]

Sports and Politics

The use of leisure to promote the ideological and political hegemony of the dominant forces in Cuba was retained throughout Cuban history, as was the view that leisure activities were acceptable diversions from political activity. This was the opinion of the Baptists, who established schools in Cuba during the twentieth century, claiming that "the Cubans have evinced a growing interest in athletics, and schools have cultivated this interest in honest sports, in order to draw students from objectionable diversions that have previously been offered them."[132]

This application of sport, as well as professionalism, commercialization, and exclusivity was challenged by many Cubans. José Martí, who energetically tried to alert Cubans to the threat of U.S. involvement in their homeland, also warned of the evils of professional sports, while simultaneously calling for participation in physical activities for health benefits. Martí frequently criticized professional boxing, describing it as a modern version of the Roman circus, brutal and ignoble. He also criticized the use of sport for economic gain.[133] His warnings about U.S. interests in Cuba and about professional sport were to no avail, and both of these concerns were to be raised again in Cuba, particularly in the twentieth century.

The use of sport to promote counterhegemonic goals was adopted by followers of Martí's independence movement. Some of the Cubans who fought for Cuba's independence were associated with baseball clubs. One of the founders of baseball in Cuba, Emílio Sabourín, sent money to independence fighters and fought against Spanish attempts to ban baseball. Other players joined as fighters and Club Cuba organized baseball games to raise money for the struggle. "During our wars against the Spanish yoke, so many of our patriots were associated with baseball clubs that the Spanish colonial authorities prohibited the game and some principal organizers were arrested and deported to Spain's prisons in her African territories."[134] In 1895, Sabourín was detained by colonial officials. Two years later, he perished in an African prison.[135] During the war, Cuban exiles in the United States (in Cayo Hueso and Tampa) raised money at baseball games for the independence fighters.

Despite Martí's warnings, growing U.S. influence on Cuban sport was evident in the formation of a scouts association in Cuba. The scouts were first formed by General Carlos García Vélez in February 1913. A banner was donated by José Tarafa, a prominent landowner. Presidential Decree number 871 of 22 June 1927 officially recognized the Asociación Oficial de Scouts de Cuba. After this, the Boy Scouts were supervised by the War Secretary and by the Marines. Public schools were to recommend scouting and it was considered a way to teach youngsters to love their country and obey its laws and authorities.[136]

For Socializing Youngsters

Organized physical culture was praised by various authorities as a means for socializing youngsters. The Boy Scouts were considered a vehicle for creating loyalty and discipline. The dictator Batista saw sports as recreation and as avenues for promoting discipline, patriotism, and civility.[137] The United States saw this potential use of physical activities, and some U.S. citizens viewed Cuban society with such ideas in mind. The idea of establishing playgrounds as a means for control, which had emerged in New York, was suggested for Cuba in a U.S. report on Cuba in 1935:

> In speaking of the need of playgrounds and playground directors in Havana, a Cuban woman told of the children who congregated in a small park near her house. All day . . . the children played at revolution. They lined up and paraded and shot each other with imaginary guns, dragged off the victims.[138]

The report also referred to a playground that had been built by the Rotary Club in Camaguey Province and called for the introduction of other Western forms of physical culture.[139] The United States, with the support of Cuba's upper class, saw physical culture in much the same way as slaveholders had viewed the Cabildos de Nación under slavery. The push for playgrounds, the scout movement, and the earlier attempts to ban gambling, were all seen as useful for socialization to promote social stability. Yet, there were also counterhegemonic uses of physical culture. This use of sporting activities continued into the twentieth century, despite considerable efforts by U.S. and Cuban authorities to prevent it.

In the student rebellions of the 1920s, Julio Antonio Mella, star of the University of Havana basketball team, and other students fought against the exclusive nature of Cuban sports clubs. The clubs had taken over natural lands and beaches and had banned African Cubans and mulattoes from these areas. In 1922, an athletics commission was created at the Havana campus. Mella, who headed the commission, formed the Manicatos Club, so that students might represent the university in sports events, rather than the private clubs, which often formed their teams from the student body. Mella argued that sport under capitalism was escapist and that professional sport was exploitative. While the students' movement was crushed and the exclusive clubs remained, sport continued to be an issue at the university, which was the major sports power in Cuba. On 30 November 1946, the student publication *El Lento* criticized the limitation of sport for the wealthy, its corruption, and the government's indifference to these matters. "Our governments are accomplices of this abandonment and have not supported plans for improving sport, while the majority of our youth vegetates into vice and corruption."[140]

The students were not alone in uniting political activism and criticism of the situation in sport. In the late 1950s, the gymnasiums Chiqui Hernández and Arango y Rosa Enríques were used as contact centers for youths, with the latter serving (among others) the young socialists of the Cuban Workers Confederation. Such centers followed the suggestion of Rubén Martínez Villena in 1927 that the Communist party should establish clubs for young people. A sports association was credited with the goal of attracting youngsters to the Popular Socialist Party. In March 1927, a sports and cultural club was established in the Cerro Municipality in Havana with workers from the railways and from the paper, textile, and transport factories. The Young Communist League was formed the following year, and other sports and cultural centers were opened in Havana, Matanzas, and Cárdenas. The clubs organized sports, cultural activities, recreation, and political activities. The right to practice sports was incorporated into the youth league's political demands. Despite harassment by the police, sports displays in schools and factories were organized by the youth league in 1936. At the 1939 Youth Convention, the right of access to sport and the protection of players was raised. The PSP included these in its program in 1944.[141]

These institutions helped to combat the exclusivity of the private clubs, especially in urban areas, but there were also exclusive clubs in rural Cuba where many of Cuba's poor lived. These clubs, however, also met with opposition.

Such a separation of facilities existed on a United Fruit–owned sugar plantation in Oriente Province. United Fruit had "police" to ensure that these prohibitions were adhered to, and they ruthlessly broke up any meetings among the sugar workers. Recreation, especially baseball, provided the workers with an opportunity to meet. A laborer at Mayarí, Manuel Fernández Chaveco, relates, "You know we couldn't meet in public, so we had to meet during our baseball games. We'd hold a big game and during it hold our planning meetings."[142] Despite this opposition, exclusive clubs persisted as the major centers for organized sport in Cuba.

Government Policy

Prior to 1959, internal Cuban policy on sport was characterized by the lack of government interest in including most Cubans. There was little concern for the benefits of extending sports activities to all Cubans. Health and social participation were apparently not viewed as reasons to encourage widespread participation in sports. Where activities existed in private clubs, Cuban governments valued them as potential sources of social control or nationalism, such as in the case of the various clubs for non-Hispanics or the Boy Scouts Association. Exclusive organizations for wealthier Cubans were favored and occasionally promoted for their role in creating obedience and nationalism, whereas activities for poorer Cubans were in general ignored except when they were considered to be a political threat to Cuba's rulers. Hence, the cabildos and the mutual aid societies were tolerated or harassed according to their perceived political effects. When authorities tried to restrict activities, however, they faced fierce opposition, as when colonial officials attempted to ban baseball during the War of Independence. Thus, sport was used also to resist social control or as an avenue for expressing social dissatisfaction with the marginalization of the majority of Cubans. Sport reflected Cuban social divisions, government disinterest, and occasionally political conflicts. And this parallel between sport and society extended into foreign policy areas as well.

IMPLICATIONS FOR FOREIGN POLICY

Just as Cuba, in its politics, was heavily influenced by foreign powers, so was the development of sport and physical culture. The existence of modern sport was due in large part to the cultural influence of the United States. The Spaniards had introduced some organized sports into Cuba, and African culture had also had an influence on recreational activities and clubs but, although these influences continued into the twentieth century, the commercialization and the professionalism of Cuban sport were signposts of Anglo-Saxon influence, largely through close contact with the United States.

Cuban students who studied in the United States (and some in the United Kingdom) brought sports back to Cuba. U.S. citizens also practiced and promoted modern sports in the Caribbean island state. The appeal of professional boxing and baseball in the United States also helped to attract less well-off Cubans to those sports. The fact that the United States occupied Cuba at the time of the first Modern Olympic Games in 1900 may also explain why Cuba sent a team to these games. Subsequent Cuban governments displayed less enthusiasm for international competitions, and athletes were often forced to raise their own funds to travel abroad for competition.

While there is little doubt that the United States was a major influence on the development of modern sports in Cuba, this is not to say that all U.S. attitudes were integrated easily into Cuban society; cockfighting and gambling proved resistant even in the face of U.S. disapproval, for example. Baseball had spread like wildfire throughout the island, even before the U.S. invasion. And despite the propensity of U.S. governments to use international sport for political benefit, pre–1959 Cuban governments did not adopt a similar approach to international athletics. But Fidel Castro did, possibly in an attempt to beat the United States at its own game.

In part, this previous lack of interest in the potential of sport for foreign policy can be explained by a lack of desire to invest in sports. In organized amateur sport—the source of Olympic champions—only the privileged classes had the necessary opportunities for practicing amateur sports. Either Cuban governments were unwilling to invest the funds to overcome these limitations on international success, or international sports victories were not perceived as politically beneficial. This apparent lack of interest could be explained by the reluctance to expand access and to challenge the racially exclusive schools and clubs of wealthy Cubans.

A lack of desire to fund international competition was evident (in stark contrast to the building frenzy for the Pan-American Games in Havana in August 1991). Batista's regime refused to assist the funding of the 1955 Pan-American Games and was accused of taking over the offices of the Cuban Olympic Committee. Government money was instead directed to professional sports, which could produce profits.[143]

This lack of will to fund amateur sports was particularly restrictive for poor (and usually black) athletes. Track athletes were especially affected and were poorly treated as well. "During the 1948 Olympics, only three runners could be sent to the London Olympics because of lack of financial resources, so Cuba could not even enter the 4x100 meter race."[144]

Similar cases of lack of support can be found for other Cuban athletes, such as Carvajál and Fortun, who suffered from lack of training and (in the case of Carvajál) lack of funding to attend Olympic competition. The experience of Cuba's team for the World Volleyball Championship of 1955 in Paris was not dissimilar. Eugenio George Lafita described how they put the team together: they trained with their one Italian volleyball as much as they could, often well into the morning hours. Acting as their own trainers, they alternated practice with work, and they ended up placing ninth in the championship. Such a poor performance told the world that Cuba knew little about volleyball, about the technical aspects of first class playing, or about the physical preparation needed to excel.[145] For most Cubans, professional boxing and baseball remained more attractive than amateur sports.

Between 1900 and 1956, Cuba participated in six Olympic Games with a total of 107 athletes, only one of whom was a woman. For over half a century, these 107 athletes won only thirteen medals: six gold, four silver, and three bronze.[146] Given such poor performance, Cuban governments were unwilling to support sport at home and preferred to send teams to the less intense competitions of the Central American and Pan-American Games where most participants were faced with problems similar to those of the Cuban athletes. The prestige of sports victories is politically useful; losses are a source of embarrassment. Given the success of some professional Cuban baseball players and boxers and the revenue they generated, it is not surprising that these were the sports sanctioned by the government. The money to be had in professional sports also attracted the poor Cubans, who sought not only the enjoyment of sport but also an escape route from poverty, something amateur sport could not offer them (unlike today).

For Cuba, this meant that the best boxers and baseball players often left the island, and this further weakened the amateur competition. As the United States was the most common destination, this also expanded the existing substantial political, social, economic, and cultural influence of the United States in Cuba. So the United States was, for some, a source of wealth and veneration and, for others, a siphon on Cuban society and its sports.

CONCLUSION

With the exception of baseball, Castro's revolutionary movement inherited a sports system that in many ways reflected Cuban society. Most physical culture imitated the main social divisions of race, class, and gender. Sport was employed to promote the ideology of the dominant sector, in order to aid social control. Government interest in the participation of most Cubans was limited; mass participation was encouraged only where it was perceived as an avenue for social control. Foreign powers also tended to stress recreational activities only when they supported the interests of the foreign power. Under Spanish rule this implied tolerance (as opposed to promotion) of the Cabildos de Nación as a release for the social tensions involved in slavery, but this was followed by concern about the cabildos' potential dangers after the abolition of slavery.

Baseball was the one sport that cut across racial and class (but not gender) lines in Cuba. Although the sport may owe its origin to the United States, baseball on the island developed into a distinctly Cuban hybrid. The century-long Cuban love affair with the sport did not decrease in intensity with the revolution and shows no signs of slowing down even now. Baseball provides a clear link between nineteenth- and twenty-first-century Cuba. It was and is an integral part of Cuban popular culture. For over a century, baseball has gone hand in hand with hardship, whether it was the rigors and grinding poverty of the cane fields or the austerity of the revolution, relieving it if only for a moment.

On the other hand, Cuban physical culture has retained some African traditions, despite Spanish (and later U.S.) attempts to crush them. Popular Cuban activities resisted U.S. cultural values in the twentieth century, although professional baseball and boxing provided evidence of U.S. influence. The situation in sport, however, did not go unchallenged. As with social conditions generally, sport was a target for attacks by Cuba's most prominent rebels. Physical culture was a part of the hegemony of the state—mirroring the elitist structure of society and reflecting the general lack of interest, on the part of Cuban rulers, in promoting either domestic or international amateur sports—but it was also used as a counter-hegemonic force, and especially during times of social unrest.

3

Structure and Administration
Under Fidel

No se concíbe un jóven revolucionario que no sea deportista.
(One cannot conceive of a young revolutionary who is not a
sportsman).

—*Fidel Castro*

Given the results of the Cuban sports system, as measured since
1959, it is clear that the prime minister and his administration have
strongly acted upon the belief expressed above, displayed prominently on billboards in Havana. Before the revolution, Cuba—an
island with a population smaller than New York City—was known
in sports circles mainly for its professional baseball players and boxers, many of whom went to the United States to make it big. By
1976, Cuba ranked eighth overall in the Montreal Olympics, according to the unofficial points table.[1] At the 1992 Olympics in Barcelona, Cuban athletes placed fifth in gold and sixth in total medals,
with fourteen gold, six silver, and eleven bronze medals.

How could a country of almost eleven million people achieve
such extraordinary success in such a short time? There can be no

doubt that the Cubans modeled their sports system after that of the Soviet Union and other socialist countries. However, it is equally true that the Cubans have kept their system uniquely Cuban. In large measure, their unprecedented success is due to this nationalistic fervor.

Before the revolution, the history of sport in Cuba constituted *un mal rato.*[2] In 1959, Fidel—an avid sportsman himself—lamented the almost complete lack of athletic opportunity for the majority of the Cuban people. But before the inexperienced leaders could begin to organize themselves and society to correct this situation, they first had to decide which direction they wanted to follow. In broad terms, the objective was clear. "The revolution must concern itself with physical education and sport as a fundamental question for the country."[3]

THE ADMINISTRATION OF CUBAN SPORTS

The first stage of the planning process has been described by Raudol Ruíz, professor at INDER:

> From 1959 until 1961, we gathered a group of comrades in the sports field and to us fell the honor of founding this institution, INDER. In setting it up, we formulated new criteria for a state apparatus of sports, physical education and recreation. We started from primarily revolutionary criteria, which today we can say were Marxist criteria. In that moment, however, we knew very little about Marxism. Today, looking back on what we did, we launched a whole dialectical process that was truly just.
>
> In a way we wanted everyone to have the conditions of life that the children of the ruling class had. This forced us to think that what we wanted was for all children to have physical education as part of an integrated education. We wanted every citizen to have the right to recreation. We wanted sports to cease being a formal performance to line some people's pockets, to be a way to educate the people and create a new generation. Theoretically this sounds good, but putting it into practice with the weight of our inherited problems, our shortcomings, our ignorance was not easy. We proposed to do some experiments and not define our path until we had analyzed the results. . . .
>
> We also experimented with sports to try to find a method that would permit mass participation in sports, to give every-

one the opportunity to practice and play sports. At the same time, we wanted competition, the climax of sports, to have an ideological foundation while serving as a process of collective, accelerated development.[4]

Unlike in the Soviet Union, the Cuban revolutionary leaders did not inherit a highly centralized nor a very well-organized sports system. The new organization had to be built in large part from the ground up. They did, however, have the Soviet and East European examples to follow.

First Steps from 1959 to 1961

The Castro administration began the process of restructuring sport and physical culture soon after coming to power in January 1959. Their first actions were aimed at expanding access to physical culture. Facilities previously available only to wealthy white Cubans were nationalized and racial restrictions on entry were abolished. Attempts were also made to promote greater participation in sporting activities.

In 1959 and 1960, the administration of sports was shared among private concerns, local government, and the Committees for the Defense of the Revolution (CDRs) and the new central government. The institutionalization of physical culture was to come before most other things, although some remnants of Cuba's pre–1959 administrative structures persisted through 1962. Professional sports such as boxing, baseball, wrestling, and jai alai, with their attendant promoters and contract bosses, were not outlawed until later in 1962. Yet significant steps were taken very early to rectify the inequity that existed in sports and physical culture at the time of the revolution. In March 1959, previously private clubs and beaches were nationalized and opened to the public. Some entry fees were abolished. By 1967, all charges for sporting events had been dropped.[5]

Between March and December 1959, several steps were taken to encourage greater participation in physical culture and recreational activities. These early programs—instituted by the Ministry of Social Welfare, the Havana Council, and probably also in the armed forces—were given a more formal structure on 23 December 1959 in Law 683, which made the Dirección General de Deportes (DGD) the official government body responsible for promoting physical culture in the schools and the community. This new organization, headed by Comandante Guerra Matos, worked in cooperation with the Revolutionary Armed Forces and the CDRs until early 1961. Thus, by the end of 1959, a formal government policy of encouraging open access in physical culture and sports had emerged.

Institúto Nacional de Deportes, Educación, y Recreación (INDER)

In 1961, the Cuban government began to formalize the structure of physical culture, and the institutionalization of sports displayed a quite stable structure relative to many other government agencies and ministries. Law 936, dated 23 February 1961, began the process of developing a single unified administrative structure for Cuban sport and physical culture. This law dissolved the DGD and transferred its funds and rights to the new administrative body, Cuba's National Institute of Sports, Physical Education, and Recreation, or INDER. It was headed by José Llanusa Gobel, the former mayor of Havana, a member of the 1948 Cuban Olympic basketball team, and a crony of Castro's from the University of Havana.[6] At the same time, the Voluntary Sports Councils (CVDs) were established in order to form the grass-roots base of Cuban physical culture.

Under Law 936, INDER has the power to "direct, orient, and plan the development of sports, physical education and recreation as an integrated whole."[7] It is based on the following principles:

1. Exposure of the masses to sports.
2. Selection of the best athletes and maximum development of their skills.
3. Enhancing civil and moral qualities.
4. Dissemination of physical culture and sport throughout the country.
5. Introduction of new forms of sport.[8]

Based upon the model used by other communist countries, INDER is the central authority for sport throughout the island nation. Under the power of the national Cuban government, INDER is responsible for virtually everything connected with sports: physical education, competitive athletics at all levels, as well as recreation and use of free time. It is responsible for the national athletes and their training, as well as further research in the field.

Central INDER offices are located in Ciudad Deportíva (Sports city), a huge complex of sports facilities on the outskirts of Havana. Also located there are the Institúto Superior de Cultura Física, or ISCF (Higher Institute for physical culture), previously the Escuela

Superior de Educación Física, or ESEF (Higher school of physical education), also called Comandante Manuel Fajardo; the Institúto de Medicina Deportíva (Institute of sports medicine); all the facilities available to the National Training Center, some of which are open to the public; and the Industria Deportíva (Sport industry) where most of the athletic equipment for the country is manufactured. Not in the same location but directly under the authority of INDER are all the national coaches and (in combination with the Ministry of Education) all of the sports schools, the voluntary sports councils, and all the provincial branches of INDER.[9]

INDER has from time to time been restructured, to allow for expansion, for new programs, for provincial boundary alterations and, in the early 1970s, for the emergence of the Popular Power Assemblies, which have physical culture sectors at all three levels of government—municipal, provincial, and national. Most of the changes have been for expansions and for the formation of new, smaller provinces and municipalities, as occurred in the reorganization of 1976.[10]

As of 1962, all sports centers, clubs, and teams came under the central administration of INDER. Private entrepreneurs were ousted and sports contracts passed over to INDER.[11] The responsibilities of INDER were progressively expanded to include control of recreational programs such as camping and touring (1962), sports industry (1965), and the Institute of Sports Medicine (1966). Other resolutions included new sports and recreation programs and the appointment of vice-presidents responsible for specific areas (1982–1983). These vice-presidents included those responsible for international relations, legal matters, coaches, technicians, schools, student matters, and for various types and levels of sports and recreation.

Although the basic functions of INDER have remained much the same, the growth of sports participation and the diversification of activities available resulted in the expansion of the sports and physical culture bureaucracy. This bureaucracy is responsible for assessing existing programs and for developing new ones, both for schools and for the general community. While decentralized levels of INDER may make suggestions and recommendations, it is the central bureaucracy of INDER that ultimately decides on physical culture matters, at times in combination with the Ministry for Education (MINED) and other ministries such as those concerned with culture, health, the armed forces, and industry. INDER's capacity to decide is also restrained by the central budget allocations from the Council of Ministers and from the central planning authority (JUCEPLAN); and therefore, in effect, by the Cuban Communist party. Although INDER has discretionary use of funds, it does not control the total budget amount, and provincial INDER offices, local governments, and mass organizations have less control over funds. The investment of resources in Cuban sports and physical culture has been extensive, particularly in comparison with the pre–1959 years. Although the sports system funds itself today (excluding the construction of facilities) through athletes' earnings, the Cuban Communist party and the government can decide to use this money for other things. [12]

THE FINANCING OF SPORT AND PHYSICAL CULTURE

Assessing the expenditure on sport in Cuba is not easy. Little information is available for the years before the revolution, although it is evident that public expenditure was limited and that physical culture activities were dominated by private concerns. It remains difficult to assess government spending from 1959 to 1961, because of the sporadic nature of government programs, and because private funding continued in the major sports.

After 1961, when the state took over much of the Cuban economy, figures became somewhat more reliable and accessible. For the years 1964–1973 and 1976–1983, however, few detailed statistics on funding were published. Other problems have been the changes in classifications over the period of the revolution and that some activities, such as sports schools and recreation, are also funded by other government bodies, such as MINED, the Ministry for Public Health (MINSAP), and the National Institute for Tourism (INTUR).

In addition, state control of rates of currency exchange and of prices causes considerable difficulty in measuring the buying power of these allocations. In the first years of the revolution, prices and currency were not state controlled. Inflation in the mid–1960s, along with the transfer to socialism, motivated the introduction of state control of the peso, of (rationed) distribution, and of many prices. This meant that there was little or no price inflation for many goods until 1980–1981. When demand exceeds supply, it is manifested not in prices but in surplus income. From 1961 to 1981, many retail prices in Cuba remained unchanged. In 1980, wholesale prices were increased. In 1981, wages and retail prices followed suit. The average price increase was 10 percent, but rationed goods were increased by more (from 18 percent for fish to 100 percent for detergents). Wages were also increased by approximately 21 percent from 1979–1982. Budget expenditure (in 1989 prices) was increased in 1980 and 1981, probably reflecting the price reform, but was cut by 15 percent in 1982, probably removing any real increase in spending.[13]

Any assessment of Cuban spending on sports must take these factors into consideration. (The expenditure figures that are available are shown in table 5.) Although there are many gaps in these figures, identifiable trends can be ascertained. Overall, spending on sports increased, except in 1983 when all expenditure was cut. The pattern of budgetary spending and investment was probably one of an initially large growth in spending; there was a fall from 1968 to 1970, during economically troubled years, and a considerable expansion in 1974–1975 when the Cuban economy grew rapidly. In 1983, spending fell, probably reflecting both the price reforms and some economic problems, but by 1988, expenditures had increased again.

Since 1965, Cuba has placed tremendous emphasis both on producing sports equipment and on reducing imports (see detailed section on the Cuban sports industry below). From 1959 to 1965, imports were relatively small, although production in Cuba was limited. Cuba has successfully expanded production of physical culture equipment and has even begun to export some articles. Only in 1981–1982 was there a decrease in production and exports, a problem that was reflected in increased imports of sporting goods (see table 6). The increase of imports in 1982 may be related to the expansion of the military sports clubs, and the fall in production figures may reflect the price reforms of the early 1980s.[14]

Government funding was almost the sole source of finance for sport and physical culture, although now Cuban athletes' appearance money and other earnings support the bulk of the sports system. In 1967, revenue from gate-takings from all sports events was removed. A small amount of money comes from CDR dues. Other sources of revenue are limited, and the practice of free entry to sports events was apparently reconsidered in the 1970s. There were also small charges for some recreational facilities.[15] Some of the labor involved in physical culture is performed voluntarily by mass organizations, which may reduce the cost to the state, although such labor is often inefficient. (Such voluntary labor, particularly in the 1960s, may have served the additional purpose of integrating Cuban workers into the revolutionary process.)

TABLE 5.
Known Data on Cuban Budgetary and Investment Spending on Physical Culture: 1959–1988 (in millions of pesos)

Year	Budgetary Spending			Investment	
	Total	Physical Culture	INDER	Total	Physical Culture
1959	389.6	1.4		—	—
1960	755.9	—		—	—
1961	1,329.6	10.3	15.3	489.0	5.0
1962	1,853.7	12.0		571.6/534	2.5/4.0
1963	2,093.5	16.8		695.9/581	6.1/4.0
1964	2,399.4	24.9		772.4	5.8
1965	—	40.0		841.8	6.3
1966	2,744.8	17.0		893.3	7.5
1967	—	—		—	—
1968	—	45/50		—	—
1969	—	—		800.1	—
1970	—	—		—	—
1971	—	—		—	—
1972	—	—		—	—
1973	—	—		—	—
1974	—	80.4		—	—
1975	—	87.1	43.6	2,304.2	—
1976	—	40.1		—	—
1977	—	40.0		2,765.9	—
1978	—	40.0		2,623.6	—
1979	9,154.0	40.0		2,605.8	—
1980	9,644.0	40.0		2,739.1	—
1981	11,577.0	—		3,386.1/3,205.7	—
1982	12,587.0	—		2,996.4	—
1983	13,183.9	60.5		3,408.5/3,307.1	—
1984	12,413.0	—		3,989.4	—
1985	11,295.4	—		4,289.3	—
1986	11,996.9	—		—	—
1987	11,689.7	—	112.3	—	—
1988	—	110.0		—	—
1989	—	—	116.2	—	—
1990	—	—	117.0	—	—
1991	—	150.0		—	—

Sources: R. J. Pickering, "Cuba," in J. Riordan, ed., Sport Under Communism (Canberra: ANU Press, 1978), p. 157; Gaceta oficial de la Republica de Cuba 63, edición extraordinaria, 31 December 1965, p. 3; Cuba en cifras 1985, p. 56; Anuario estadístico de Cuba, 1985, JUCEPLAN, p. 205; J. Powers, "On a Mission From Havana," Boston Sunday Globe, 16 August 1987, p. 46; R. Ruíz Aguilera, interview, Cuba Review 7, no. 2 (1977), p. 16; United Nations, Economic Survey of Latin America and the Caribbean, 1963 (ECLA), pp. 287–88, and U.N., ECLA, 1982, p. 268; C. P. Roberts and M. Hamour,

TABLE 5.
(continued)

Cuba: 1968 Supplement to the Statistical Abstract of Latin America (Los Angeles: University of California, 1970), pp. 126; Tom Knott, "Medals Won't Help This Tarnished Land," *Washington Times*, 2 August 1991, p. D2. INDER figures come from G. R. González González, L. Robalcaba Ordáz, and G. Díaz Cabrera, *El deporte cubano: Razones de sus exitos* (La Habana: Ediciones ENPES, 1991).
Note: Wide variations exist because some entries are estimates; some are planned expenditure; some are INDER budgets only; and some are actual expenditure. There may also have been variations in the activities included.

In the late 1970s and early 1980s, there were several policies instituted that sought to make more efficient use of spending on sports and physical culture. In 1981, overall funding for housing, health, education, and culture was reduced. In 1984, Castro stressed the importance of making better use of existing facilities, particularly swimming pools (Cuba could not afford new pools), as Cuba was unable to build new sports schools. Cuba's sports school program also suffered a setback when the School for the Initiation of Scholastic Sports (EIDE) in Ciego de Avila was destroyed by Cyclone Kate in 1984.[16] Another example of the drop in government spending on physical culture was the inclusion of physical culture as part of the incentive fund for workers. Two-thirds of these funds were for bonus pay, while one-third went to sociocultural activities, including recreational clubs, gymnasiums, vacation, and housing.

Despite these cutbacks in funding for physical culture, one area escaped the budget ax: spending for basic military training and on military-related sports was expanded. Military sports clubs (SEPMI) were established in January 1980 and expanded rapidly

TABLE 6.
Value of Sports Industry Production, 1978–1989

Years	*Production of Sports Equipment in Thousands of Cuban Pesos*
1978–1980	19,770
1981–1984	370,095
1989	12,000

Source: M. Llaneras Rodríguez et al., "Cuba: 25 años de deporte revolucionario," *Mensaje Deportívo*, special issue (May 1986), p.123; Jean Stubbs, *Cuba: The Test of Time* (London: Latin America Bureau, 1989), p. 60.

for the next several years. "Given that most of the equipment for these sports is expensive and must be imported, the commitment to this program is remarkable." This commitment was related to security concerns that arose not only from the aggressive foreign policy of the Reagan administration in the United States, but also from a number of internal security concerns, such as the Mariel exodus and the occupation of foreign embassies by Cubans wishing to emigrate.[17]

Much of the military equipment was imported from the socialist bloc. Foreign trade and sports aid, both financial and technical, has always been an important part of Cuba's physical culture economy. Technicians and coaches from the socialist bloc aided Cuba, especially during the 1960s, and many Cubans received athletic and technical training in Eastern Europe (see table 7). More recently, Cuba has provided sports aid and training to Third World countries (see table 8).

Cooperation with the socialist bloc is particularly important in military-related sports, and in high performance sports, which has also received considerable funding (see table 9 for a breakdown of four INDER budgets). In 1969, for example, Cuba joined the Sports Committee of Friendly Armies, and in 1972, signed a five-year sports agreement with the USSR. Nevertheless, spending on mass physical culture programs is also significant, and the economic pressures of the early 1980s have seen limits on elite facilities (such as sports schools) as well as on new facilities for the general populace. There was also an attempt to encourage inexpensive mass activities, such as physical culture plans using home articles.[18]

As can be seen from table 9, INDER spends a large part of its funds on wages, despite the contributions of voluntary workers.

TABLE 7.
Physical Culture Technical Assistants Working in Cuba: 1961–1985

	Country of Origin					
Years	USSR	GDR	Bulgaria	Hungary	Others	Total
1961–1965	31	5	3	1	15	55
1966–1970	46	4	2	8	12	72
1971–1975	30	7	20	7	5	69
1976–1980	35	1	3	2	1	42
1981–1985	14	1	0	0	1	16

Source: Llaneras, Rodríguez et al. "Cuba," p. 55.

TABLE 8.
Cuban Physical Culture Technical Assistants in 33 Other Countries,
1971–1985

	Country				
Years	Nicaragua	Angola	Algeria	Others	Total
1971–1975	0	0	1	81	82
1976–1980	19	110	65	127	321
1981–1985	181	84	28	154	447

Source: Llaneras, Rodríguez et al., "Cuba," p. 59.

Wages for workers in the physical culture sector are higher than in other occupations, and slightly above the national average. (This is shown in tables 9, 10, 11, and 12 in the early years from 1962 through 1976.) Yet this has not always been the case, especially for bureaucrats. In 1979, the average wage in the physical culture sector was 1,711 pesos per annum, compared to a national average wage of 1,721. Physical culture workers received increases of 3.9 percent, 10 percent, and 13.4 percent during the next three years, compared to average increases of 3.1 percent, 14.7 percent, and 3.8 percent respectively. By 1982, physical culture workers' wages averaged 2,216 pesos, while the national average was 2,113.[19]

Wages, like spending, have gradually increased over the period of the revolution. Physical culture was clearly considered important, although it tended to suffer cutbacks in times of economic difficulty. After a steep increase in the early years of the revolution, as in all service areas, physical culture funding probably suffered in the economically troubled late 1960s. During the mid–1970s, funding expanded as the economy flourished, but fell again in response to some economic problems late in the decade. Despite these fluc-

TABLE 9.
Average Annual Wage for All of Cuba and for Workers in INDER,
1971–1976

Category	1971	1972	1973	1974	1975	1976
Average for all of Cuba	1,396	1,456	1,514	1,563	1,638	1,688
Workers in INDER	1,466	1,535	1,586	1,636	1,704	1,808

Source: Anuario estadístico de Cuba, 1975, JUCEPLAN, p. 45, and *Anuario estadístico, 1976,* JUCEPLAN, p. 52.

TABLE 10.
Breakdown of Four Physical Culture Budgets
(in millions of pesos)

Item	1958	1961	1974	1975
Salaries, wages	not available	1.9	17.8	21.6
Other expenses	not available	3.4	22.1	22.0
Sports schools	not available		2.4	2.7
Sports	not available		21.0	23.8
Recreation	not available		1.3	1.4
Other activities	not available		15.2	15.8
Total	c. 1.0	5.3	80.5	87.2

Source: Pickering, "Cuba," p. 157.

tuations (including others that may have occurred in years for which no statistics are available), Cuba invested much of its limited resources, including revenue from appearances and prize money for athletes, in sports and physical culture activities. The overall trend has been one of growth in such funding.

Economic Troubles

Despite such clear growth, physical culture is not the primary priority in Cuba, however. Economic development, the supply of basic goods, and the development of health and education are ultimately

TABLE 11.
Average Annual Wage for all of Cuba and for Workers in
Physical Culture, 1962–1965

Category	1962	1963	1964	1965
Average for all of Cuba	1,547	1,564	1,584	1,589
Sports and rec. workers	1,693	1,690	1,747	1,744
Sports instructors	no information		1,830	no info.
PE teachers	973	1,065	1,245	no info.

Source: Compendio estadístico, 1965, JUCEPLAN, p. 16; and *Boletín estadístico, 1965,* p. 26.

TABLE 12.
Scale of Wages per Month for Physical Culture, Instructors and PE
Teachers, 1974

	Level				
Category	1st	2nd	3rd	4th	5th
Sports instructor w/degree	86	100	118	138	163
Bachelor of PE w/degree	210	220	231	231	none
PE teacher w/degree	118	138	163	192	211
PE teachers and instructors w/o degree	86	86	86	100	118

Source: Gaceta oficial de la República de Cuba 72, no. 24, 9 September 1974, p. 1010.

more important than sports, especially with the collapse of socialism in Europe. Yet an emphasis upon sports and physical culture has helped Cuba achieve the government's more important objectives. Clearly, a person who is physically fit is healthier than one who is sedentary. In more concrete terms, perhaps, a reduction in the importation of sporting goods was seen as one way to tackle the hard currency and deficit problems faced by Cuba in 1962.[20] It was also a necessity because of the effective U.S. trade embargo.

From the budget figures that are available, there appears to have been a reduction in spending between 1966 and 1968, and an expansion of spending in 1974–1975, which corresponds to economic decline and growth, respectively. The review of the policy of free entry to sports events in the late 1970s also pointed to economic restraints, as did Castro's 1984 statement on limiting the construction of sports schools. Cutbacks in social services (including physical culture) in 1981, and the inclusion of recreational facilities in labor-incentive funds suggests that there were economic pressures on the growth of Cuba's physical culture system.[21]

Failures in the delivery of materials is another hindrance to the growth of Cuban physical culture, and indeed, of all areas. This problem was reported in 1982 by the CDR in Nicaro. In some years, lack of materials also accounted for not spending the sports equipment allocations. It is also possible that, as in other socialist countries, quota setting for factories leads to poor-quality goods. As with the famous story of the ten-pound nail produced by the Soviet nail factory, which thus fulfilled its weight quota with one item, Cubans may make overweight, undersized, or poor-quality goods if quotas are in weight or numbers of products produced. There has been no evidence that this has been the case. However, there are discrepancies in the quality of goods that are distributed for mass use and those slated for use by the higher-caliber athletes in the sports schools and at the national level.[22]

These economic problems also provide genuine or concocted justification for local and provincial officials to claim inability to control circumstances. Local authorities cannot usually control the delivery of resources, fluctuations in Cuban production and its economy, or the establishment of national priorities. Local officials and mass organizations have limited funds under their control. In 1978, subnational governments controlled only 9 percent of the gross social product and only 20 percent of the national budget. An 18 percent increase in central revenue in 1980–1981 was paralleled by a smaller (14.7 percent) increase in decentralized government revenue. Local delegates of the Poder Popular (National Assembly of Popular Power) often refer to these limits.[23]

Mass organizations depend upon government allocations and on donations and small membership fees for revenue, but these funds are limited, and most workers in these organizations are part-time volunteers. CDR funding, for example, in the late 1970s was increased by membership charges of 25 centavos per month. Hence, on average a CDR received just 200 pesos per annum from this source.[24] These charges remained the same in January 1992. There are also problems of nonpayment of these small fees by as many as 43 percent of members. Money that might be raised from sports events and recreation centers is also limited, and where there are charges, they are small. For example, use of lockers and a beach towel at Marianao, near Havana, cost 20 centavos, that is 22 U.S. cents or 24 Australian cents, at the 1986 official rate of exchange.[25]

These economic constraints give local officials good excuses for not responding effectively to local needs and complaints. It also means that voluntary work and mass mobilization is important for Cuban sports.

THE ROLE OF MASS ORGANIZATIONS

Despite the considerable amount of investment and budget financing, Cuba's physical culture system relies heavily on the efforts of thousands of volunteers in mass organizations. These include the

Committees for the Defense of the Revolution (CDRs), the Fede ation of Cuban Women (FMC), the Confederation of Cuban Workers (CTC), the National Association of Small Landowners (ANAP), the Voluntary Sports Councils (CVDs), and the movement of sports activists. The local and provincial assemblies of Popular Power and the armed forces have also had a role, especially since the late 1970s.

The biggest economic contributions of the various mass groups to physical culture is in voluntary labor, in mobilizing mass involvement, and implementing national policies. These groups also provide avenues for the general populace to voice its views on Cuban sport and physical culture. Centralized decision making in Cuba certainly limits the effectiveness of these avenues. However, the decentralization that accompanied the formation of the Poder Popular (Popular power) enabled Cubans to have a greater input into policy directions, especially at the local level. It remains to be seen whether the democratization efforts at the Fourth Congress in 1991 will lead to greater mass participation in decision making.[26]

In the earliest years of the revolution, sports activities were organized by various groups, including the Havana Council. In 1960 and early 1961, the CTC, the CDRs, and the FMC worked in combination with the Ministry for Social Welfare and the General Directory of Sports to organize physical culture activities. The CDRs, however, were initially concerned with monitoring counterrevolutionary activities. It was only in 1966 that they were given a well-defined role in physical culture and sports. The FMC concentrated on encouraging women to exercise and take part in physical activities. However, it was the CTC (Confederation of Cuban Workers) that played the main role, which in part explains why the CTC is one of the most developed mass organizations in sport and physical culture today. The CTC arranged sports events within and between work centers, and these eventually culminated in the establishment of the National Workers' Sports Games.[27] During the 1960s, the CTC operated with some autonomy from the central government. This was also the case (at least in sports) for the CDRs and ANAP, which worked closely with the CTC in physical culture and sports matters until 1966.

The Role of the CDRs in Cuban Sports

The CDRs (Committees for the defense of the revolution) were founded in September 1960 in response to counterrevolutionary activities. They were organized in small groups and at local levels. During the initial years, the major task of the CDRs was to watch for suspicious activities and to guard against counterrevolutionary sabotage attempts. Such risk subsided to a large degree after the Cuban victory at Playa Girón (Bay of Pigs) in April 1961. Cuba declared itself socialist and began the long process of consolidating and institutionalizing the revolution. This process included a diversification of CDR functions and the formation of mass organizations (the CVDs) specifically concerned with sports and physical culture.

During the remainder of the 1960s, the CDRs were heavily involved in volunteer work, mostly in agriculture, but also in the construction of sports and recreational activities. Although there is no evidence that this labor was forced or paid for, it is possible that pressure to contribute to this work encouraged members to volunteer. Their role in construction continued into the 1970s. The CDRs played a prominent role in renovations to the baseball stadium in Matanzas, and to the expansion of the Latin American baseball stadium in Havana, where the committees salvaged materials, removed unwanted debris, and helped to drain the grounds. They also guarded materials and assisted with the laborers' construction work, with INDER construction, and with the technical brigades. The work on the stadium was completed in eleven months and included light towers, cafés, pizzerias, a novelty shop, a press box, and parking space. Some 500,000 CDR members put in a combined total of 250 days of voluntary labor.[28]

Park construction is also a part of CDR activities. CDRs built a children's recreation park in the Pablo Nuevo neighborhood in Cárdenas, Matanzas Province. These efforts, however, are likely to be hindered by factors that are outside CDR control. A report in 1962 by the CDR in Nicaro reported that work on a playground, park, and sports field was being deferred, largely because of delays in the delivery of equipment, a problem not uncommon in socialist countries. The report also indicated that the CDR had a role in repair work on a swimming pool in the region.[29]

Although these roles were already being performed by many CDRs, they were not specifically defined until 1966. This formalization included an attempt to stabilize CDR leadership and to control membership, which at that time numbered over two million Cubans over the age of fourteen. It was during these reforms of 1966 that the seven main tasks of the CDRs were declared: among them, sports and recreation, urban reform, public health, local administration, education, surveillance, and public information services. The CDRs "are, in fact, groups which assist in all those tasks which are of most immediate interest to the public in each community. Such cooperation bringing into being the efforts of thousands of persons."[30]

CDRs were divided into *frentes* (usually fifteen), and one frente would work on sports and recreation. This frente continued to do the regular committee work, as well as working for the Plan de la Calle (Street plan) and, later, in the LPV Physical Efficiency Programs.[31] The CDRs also continued to work in the construction of stadiums, parks, and recreational centers.

Leadership and membership controls continued to be an issue in the mid–1970s, as they had been in the 1960s. In effect, leadership was taken over by the central committee of the Cuban Communist party. In 1975, a school was established to train CDR leaders. This ran parallel to tighter control of membership, which remained steady after reaching 80 percent of all Cubans over the age of fourteen in the mid–1970s. There was also a successful campaign to encourage members to pay dues, with only 57 percent paid in 1973 compared to 90 percent paid by 1975. Despite these efforts to exert more control over entry to the CDRs, it is unlikely that all members were enthusiastic. Many of the Cubans who fled Cuba in 1980–1981 were registered CDR members, which suggests that they were probably not active. Members of revolutionary organizations do not necessarily behave as revolutionary "new men." As recently as 1988 and early 1992, Cubans belonging to CDRs, the CTC, government bodies, and even the PCC, were involved in such "unsound" activities as direct buying from small farmers, dollar collecting, and soliciting purchases from tourists in tourist shops.[32]

Despite this new stress on organizational and leadership concerns, the CDRs continue to play an important part in sports and recreational programs at the local level. This role, however, is not independent and often involves implementing national programs at the grass-roots level. To a considerable degree, the task of organizing physical culture at this base level has been taken over by the CVDs and the movement of sports activists. Such activists in the sports frentes of the CDRs and in the CTC may also be active (or inactive) members in the CVDs.

Voluntary Sports Councils (CVDs) and Sports Activists

The CVDs gave an institutional form to the activities in physical culture that had begun with the CDRs. Sports activists formed these councils initially as an experiment. The CVDs took an important role in promoting mass participation and in construction and maintenance work. CVDs operated in work centers, in community and recreational centers, in peasant communities and cooperatives, and in the armed forces. They organized local competitions and events, produced films and television clips, and supplied instructors for physical culture activities. Several non-Cuban sources put the council numbers at five thousand (with fifty thousand members) in 1977–78 but these figures are almost double the figures claimed by the Cubans: between eighteen and twenty thousand.[33] Cuban figures also point to a large drop in the number of CVDs and members in the mid–1970s and to a steady growth thereafter (see table 13). The numbers, however, are still well below those of 1961 when the councils were first formed.

This may indicate that there was a trend in the CVDs (similar to the one that occurred in the CDRs and the CTC during the 1970s) to tighten control over membership and possibly leadership. Ostensibly, there was no organized plan for the councils—they were intended to respond to the people's desires—but there is evidence that a tighter definition of the councils' roles was introduced in the mid–1970s. The CTC played a large part in the supervision and control of the CVDs and was responsible for the councils and their constitution. CVDs were selected in a General Assembly of Workers, and each council had a social center in which to meet, show films, practice sports and physical culture, and give awards.[34] The reforms in the CTC in 1970, and the subsequent reduction of CTC independence in sports, may have reduced the related autonomy of work-center CVDs.

TABLE 13.
Number of Physical Culture Activists and Voluntary
Sports Councils, 1961–1985

Year	Sport Activists	Sports Councils
1961	120,000	6,100
1970	53,500	6,107
1975	17,700	900
1980	21,300	1,607
1985	62,350	—

Source: Llaneras, Rodríguez et al., "Cuba," pp. 27, 29.

The CVDs, like other mass organizations, were largely concerned with implementing policies and in mobilizing Cubans. "They are not officials but motivators."[35] The role of the CVDs in deciding upon national physical culture programs and plans was hinted at, in the mid–1970s, by Jorge García Bango, then president of INDER:

> It is significant that the [voluntary sports] councils are themselves a part of the organization and development of the mass nature [of sport], and of the controls that ought to be exercised and in the selection of comrades who should be integrated into the councils, together with the movement of [sports] activists, toward the action of the masses in the impetus of sport.[36]

That the CVDs have limited roles in decision making is made more probable by their hierarchical structure, which is similar to that of other mass bodies. Local sports councils may be overruled by territorial sports councils, which can be overruled by provincial officials who, in turn, can be directed by national authorities of the CVDs or by INDER and government officials. This does not mean that there is no influence from the bottom up, but rather that the top can overrule the base, if so desired. Poder Popular and INDER authorities at the various levels of Cuban administration may also intervene in the CVDs, and all mass organizations, if they wish to. This hierarchical authority structure is perhaps stronger in the Military Sports Clubs (SEPMI), which were established in 1980 in response to security concerns.

The Role of the Military Sports Clubs (SEPMI)

In the initial years of the revolution, the armed forces played an important role in organizing physical culture activities. The first head of the DGD was a commander of the Rebel Army. During the 1960s and 1970s, CVDs operated within military units, with less autonomy within the ranks, given the hierarchical nature of the Cuban armed forces.

In the 1980s, there was evidence of major security concerns in Cuba. Following the Sandinista victory in Nicaragua in 1979, Cuba was watchful of the potential U.S. reaction to a second Marxist regime on its southern flank. Several years later, both Cuba and Nicaragua were on alert, following the U.S. invasion of Grenada in

, convinced that they might be next. Given the history of U.S. relations with Latin America, such fears were not unfounded, and they resulted in an increase in military training and expenditure, as well as in the formation of military sports clubs in January 1980. Activities in these clubs included military-related sports and basic military training. Thus, the military expanded its role in Cuban sports, adding to the already-extensive range of organizations involved in physical culture; the CDRs, the FMC, the CVDs, the armed forces, and Cuban youth groups all had a role in sports and physical culture. Since 1974, voluntary sports historians and journalists also contributed to the efforts to publicize and expand participation in physical culture (see table 14).[37]

The Role of Student and Youth Organizations

There were three major youth organizations in Cuba: the Federation of (High) School Students (FEEM); the Union of Young Communists (UJC), formerly the Association of Revolutionary Youth (AJR); and the Union of Cuban Pioneers (UPC). All of these were involved in promoting sports and physical culture as an arena for developing communist values. These groups reach most youngsters in Cuba, either at school or at university, even though many students drop out before finishing high school level. Sports may even be one way these dropouts become involved in mainstream Cuban society (which they might otherwise escape if they leave school, find themselves unemployed, or avoid regular work by perhaps surviving on the black market). In physical culture and from contact with

TABLE 14.
Number of Sports Historians and Journalists, 1977–1985

Year	Sports Historians	Year	Sports Journalists
1977	466	1974	344
1978	696	1978	1,420
1979	818	—	—
1980	1,090	1980	1,461
1981	1,191	1981	1,318
1982	1,410	1982	1,395
1983	1,713	1983	1,468
1984	1,813	1984	1,186
1985	1,913	1985	1,397

Source: Llaneras, Rodríguez et al., "Cuba," pp. 33, 35.

mass organizations involved in physical culture, these young people may be exposed to socializing influences, especially if the CVDs are not strongly political.[38]

The Union of Young Communists (UJC) and the Union of Cuban Pioneers (UPC) are actively involved in sports and are seen as important in developing anticapitalist attitudes among the youth of Cuba. The UJC has largely replaced the university unions that exhibited considerable independence in the 1960s. One example of the UJC's role in sports was its prominent involvement in the administration of the World Youth Festival of 1978, which was hosted by Cuba.[39] The Pioneers are for younger Cubans and have a large role in organizing recreational programs, such as camps and the Street Plan. Slogans encouraging participation by all ages are painted on buildings and billboards:

> A la escuela iré
> y Pionero seré
> y al plan de la calle
> asistiré.[40]
> ["To school I will go and
> a Pioneer I will be and
> I will assist the street plan."]

The range of mass organizations involved in Cuba's physical culture system, and the high level of involvement, means that these organizations and activities promote the ideology of the revolution and thus socialization, and possibly social control. The hierarchical structure of Cuba's mass organizations—along with the various economic problems in Cuba—combine to restrict the decision-making power of these organizations, and of most Cubans. However, the dominance of the top must not be exaggerated, as the potential does exist for Cubans to influence policy. Criticisms may be voiced, but tolerance of this has varied considerably over the period of the revolution. Such variations may cause Cubans to be wary of the consequences. The essence of this uncertainty is captured in reference to Castro's well-known declaration to Cuban writers and artists: " 'Within the revolution, everything; against the revolution, nothing.' . . . The applauding audience spent the next several years trying to decipher what that meant."[41]

It was not enough merely to mobilize people. For the Cuban sports system to reach the masses, it needed installations, facilities, equipment, and qualified instructors.

PROVIDING THE MEANS: INSTALLATIONS, INSTRUCTORS, EQUIPMENT, AND ACCESS

Installations

On 1 January 1959, there were thirteen state-owned sports installations throughout Cuba. Other sports fields and centers were housed in private sports clubs and schools. One of the revolutionary government's first actions was to outlaw the racial and economic barriers that had restricted entry to these private facilities. One example of this policy was the creation of the Club Obrero Cubanacán (Cubanacán workers' club), in the Havana-Biltmore Yacht and Country Club. Membership in the club before 1959 had cost 2,000 pesos. When the workers' club was established, charges were set at between two and six pesos, depending upon family income.[42]

During 1959, several free sports exhibitions were held, including one by U.S. athletes. But in the early years, major sporting events, still organized by private sponsors, were not free. A game of the Havana Sugar Kings, Cuba's professional baseball team, cost two pesos. Eventually, all charges for sports events were abolished, except those sponsored by an international sports federation to which Cuba belonged. Some charges had already been removed by the time Law 546 was passed in 1967. In 1986, some recreational activities involved a small fee, but sporting events were still free in 1988. Baseball and soccer games in the Latin American Stadium and the Pedro Marrero Stadium (both in Havana) were free of charge in both 1980 and 1988.[43]

It has already been noted that camping and recreational facilities were usually provided at cost. School facilities could be used in return for voluntary labor. "Since sports are part of public entertainment, . . . they should not be considered from an economic view, but rather in their true light, as part of education and recreation."[44] Private clubs and hotel sports facilities, as well as beaches, were open to all. "It makes possible the use of equipment by a much greater number of people. It also . . . combats individualism, egoism, and everything that opposes the rights of the great majority."[45]

The new government made plans to build thousands of sports fields and centers. The new leaders also purchased sports equipment and sent it to the interior of the island. The target set for the end of 1959 was 1,478 state-owned installations and a budget of 250,000 pesos for sports equipment.[46]

Facilities and equipment were improvised to meet needs quickly. Many facilities were built using voluntary labor, especially in the early years. Although use of volunteer labor sometimes de-layed construction—as these workers had to attend their regular jobs or studies—one of the fastest efforts was the remodeling of the Latin American Stadium in Havana for the World Series Amateur Baseball Championships: almost half a million CDR members worked over a period of 250 days to complete the project on time. In another example, 408 playgrounds were built in four days by vol-unteer and construction workers. In the early years of the revolu-tion, shortages of skilled labor and materials were partially overcome by the mass mobilization of volunteers.[47]

By 1964, there were 2,853 state-owned installations. Yet despite these massive early efforts, and later improvements in materials and technical skills, Cubans were not satisfied with the results. In 1971, Castro complained of the lack of sports facilities, especially in urban schools. Quality facilities were not available in all provinces. There was a need for more synthetic athletic tracks, domed baseball sta-diums, pools, cycling ovals, and wooden basketball and volleyball courts. New sports installations and technical developments were needed in the interior.[48]

This goal of increasing the numbers of installations, equipment, and instructors was eventually achieved. There were 951 installa-tions at the end of 1959; 1,893 installations were built between 1977 and 1981; there were 9,609 by 1988; and there were 11,122 facilities in 1990. Of these, 9,091 were open air, 1,765 were covered, and 266 were swimming pools. Nevertheless, problems with the mainte-nance and underuse of facilities, as well as complaints about equip-ment and instructors continued in 1988, indicating at least an ongoing commitment to improvements.[49]

The Sports Industry

In 1971, at the twelfth World Series Amateur Baseball Champion-ships, Cuba scored two victories. One was on the field itself, where for the third year in a row the Cubans became the undisputed world champions in "the game." The second victory was more sub-tle, but perhaps more important. The Cuban-produced Batos base-ball was accepted as the official baseball to be used at this presti-gious international tournament.[50] The Cubans had come a long way.

With 1959 and the revolution came a blockade of the island, which made normal trading and importing impossible. This loss was felt strongly by the Cubans, and perhaps especially in the field of sports. The countries that were willing to help the revolutionary government were already or were soon to be quite advanced technologically, but none of them had a tradition of baseball, either on the playing field or in the manufacturing of equipment. So Cuba, a country of agriculturalists with little manufacturing capacity, had to create a sports industry from scratch.

No time was lost. In 1959, the Zarabozo brothers fashioned a crude machine from pieces of old cash registers and jukeboxes. What emerged, by accident, was a small, almost-round ball; crude, perhaps, but a ball nonetheless. Inspired by this initial success, the inventors set out to develop a machine that would produce better balls more efficiently. After many false starts resulting in a number of balls that either unraveled or that simply were not round, the brothers discovered the solution. "The ball cannot have a fixed center or it will never be round. The center must vary constantly so that the thread distributes itself over the entire periphery and makes a sphere."[51]

Implementing this discovery, the Zarabozos were able to produce 850 balls. In September 1961, with five machines, they established the Industria Deportíva (Sports industry) in the Latin American Stadium. They began with forty workers making poor-quality bats and balls. By 1980, in the Havana plant alone, there were almost 1,300 employees making 623 different types of sports articles.[52] The high-quality, hand-sewn balls are now used in the world championships and the bats are all hand tooled.

> All baseball equipment and clothing is produced by the Cuban sports industry, together with boxing gloves and equipment, football boots, track and field shoes, rowing shells, canoes, sailboats, chess sets, etc. The latest plant to be opened shows production targets of one million balls for various sports each year.[53]

At least 70 percent of the sports equipment in Cuba is manufactured in the Havana plant, now located in La Ciudad Deportíva. Another plant is in operation in Santiago de Cuba, while another is in Las Villas. Future plans project the bulk of the equipment being made in Las Villas, distributed free to schools, colleges, and clubs, wherever there are competitors. The machinery in the plants comes from Spain, Italy, and East Germany. Much of the plastic comes from Japan, England, the Soviet Union, while the fabrics come from China, Bulgaria, Italy, Japan, and Czechoslovakia.[54]

In 1976, specialized training and scientific studies of manufacturing methods were further developed by the establishment of a center for technical development of production, which concentrated on improving design and quality. The State Committee on Science and Technology, established in 1977, dealt with the needs of top-level sports.[55]

Throughout the 1970s, production grew steadily, increasing by 179 percent between 1978 and 1984, with exports growing 25 times in those same years. However, even before the public revelation of serious problems in the industry in 1985, it was evident that difficulties had begun in the 1960s and 1970s, when production had grown so rapidly. Exports of sporting equipment declined, in 1981 and 1982, from the level achieved in 1980. In 1982, imports increased sharply. Costs for 1975 were almost one-sixth of the total value of goods produced between 1965 and 1975 inclusive.[56]

The industry involved high investment costs with limited monetary returns. While that was not necessarily the primary concern, efficiency was considered important. Yet despite these problems, when equipment was available, it was distributed free of charge to anyone who requested it. Interestingly, there are two categories of equipment being made: high quality for competition, equal to 10 percent of the output, and mediocre quality equaling 90 percent for the rest of the population. Once the Las Villas plant is in operation, the Havana plant will produce only the top-quality products.[57]

A more recent non-Cuban source claims that "imports from socialist countries go to supply the sports schools and teams, with some minimal imports from the capitalist area for international contests, while national production supplies the mass sports movement."[58] In addition, it seems that the people making the high-quality equipment and those using it come from different segments of society.[59]

The Cubans are fiercely proud of their Sports Industry. One reason is because it was built from scratch; it was not merely a prior industry that was nationalized. With no help from the United States, the Cubans developed it from one machine turning out not-quite-round balls to an industry of more than eight million pesos' worth of equipment in 1980. The blockade, however, still makes it difficult for the Cubans to improve their methods of manufacture. They are forced to go to Europe or Japan for help. And they are not above copying what they can. When the borders first opened, Cuban émigrés who were returning to visit relatives brought with them some high-quality U.S. sports articles, such as baseball caps, and those same caps are now produced at Industria Deportíva. The Cubans routinely return foul balls during baseball games, which is further evidence of the pride and respect they hold for their native industry. Every time they return a ball, they help break the blockade.[60]

Yet for all of the justified pride the Cubans may have in this achievement, problems remain. Many of the criticisms of the sports equipment related to the distribution of the articles. This was especially true in 1977 after the provincial boundaries were altered. The 1974 review of INDER called for more equipment for the Street Plan.[61]

The highly self-critical 1987 INDER report, requested by the National Assembly of Cuba, gave particular emphasis to problems in Cuba's sports equipment industry. Of the nine thousand manufacturing centers, over 60 percent were classified as average or bad. They were characterized as inefficient and poorly maintained and were accused of ignoring technical recommendations. The distribution of goods was described as inadequate and defective. Repair work was criticized as well. The situation of the entire industry in 1985 was described as disorganized and inefficient. "In 1985, in the collectives within our sports industry system, disorganization and development were predominant, together with the practice of improper habits."[62]

The sports equipment budget for 1975 was 7,800,000 pesos, but shortages of primary materials meant that 2 percent of it was not used. The 1987 INDER report called for better planning, weekly revisions of organization and quality, as well as better distribution of technicians and equipment for competitions. The plan was to remove the unnecessary middle levels in the industry. The report called for continuing investigations into shortages of materials and insisted that the fundamental problems in the industry must be resolved. Although the report offered no specific examples, the difficulties were sufficient to cause major criticisms and a restatement of the need to provide more equipment for the masses: "the growing participation of the people in sport demands the expansion and modernization of the Sports Industry." In response, priority was given to local and provincial ideas, on which workers, sports instructors, and participants were consulted. There was also a call for improved repairs of equipment in local centers.[63]

It was evident that the industry had failed to meet mass demands for equipment, and this was probably a major factor in the development of physical culture programs that did not require equipment or that used articles available in the home or in the workplace.[64] While the problems that occurred after the changes in provincial boundaries were understandable and expected, the fact that they continued remained a source of criticism and concern.

Physical Education Teachers

Shortly after the revolution, Cuban leaders claimed that 70 percent of physical education teachers had left Cuba in the early 1960s. Even if this is an exaggeration, there were not enough sports instructors to meet the needs of the increased numbers of participants in schools and in public programs. In response to this shortage, short courses lasting from one to six months were organized to train or retrain instructors. Between 1959 and 1962, four hundred "healthy and revolutionary youths" were trained. In the 1963–1964 school vacation, four hundred teachers from throughout Cuba took similar courses, and they were encouraged to pass on this training to twenty-six thousand PE teachers through seminars or short courses.[65]

By 1964, short courses were replaced by longer courses, and by extra training for those who were already employed. By 1975, there were 7,280 sports specialists, including 4,374 PE teachers. By 1987, there were approximately 25,000 PE specialists, and by 1986, 17,902 PE teachers, many of whom were college graduates. In 1988, graduates from EPEF reached a total of 17,556, with 6,899 more graduates from ISCF. Between 1967 and 1990, the total number of graduates was 37,133, including 25,375 from Escuela provincial de educación física EPEF and 11,758 from ISCF. In 1983, over 1,000 sports trainers took extra training courses, and 26,124 activists were trained. In addition, twelve postgraduates and forty-two undergraduates were taking courses in the USSR. There were four Doctors in Physical Culture and thirty-four candidates for doctoral degrees. In 1990, there were 37,000 PE technicians, 23,000 professors at the intermediate levels, 11,700 Bachelors of physical education, 50 doctoral candidates, 60 researchers, and 80 sports medicine specialists.[66]

There is no information available on salaries for PE teachers in the 1960s, although workers in INDER were generally paid higher wages than the national average. These figures, however, presumably include the salaries of bureaucrats. In the 1970s, INDER employees continued to receive salaries higher than the national average. By 1974, only PE teachers with college degrees began at salaries above the INDER average. Nevertheless, all PE teachers and sports instructors with a tertiary or pre-tertiary qualification in teaching reached levels above the national and INDER average if they were promoted to the fourth scale of their profession.[67] Presumably, this was an economic incentive to enter the field.

Cuba increased both the quantity and quality of its physical culture instructors. In 1961, only 17.9 percent of school students received PE classes, whereas in the 1985–1986 school year, 76.6

percent of these students (1,651,599 children) had access to formal PE instruction. In primary schools, the (small) shortages were concentrated in grades one through four and in rural areas. The second cycle or upper primary situation is now better, and nearly all students at this level receive PE training. There was no data on physical education in preschools and child-care centers, except that physical culture was not available in all. By 1985–1986, in basic secondary schools, all students received PE instruction.[68]

Despite the claim of universal physical education throughout the school system, the 1987 review of INDER criticized the lack of quality and the irregularity of some courses. The report charged that some school officials did not recognize the importance of physical education and sport. However, most of the criticism was not directed at the PE teachers in general schools, but rather at those in special areas and in the sports schools. The major complaint was that too much emphasis was placed on finding champions, an attitude believed to be harmful to the democratization of physical culture and sport. In keeping with the tradition of antibureaucracy campaigns in Cuba, the report also attacked inefficient technicians and trainers and the bureaucratic tendency to ignore incompetent workers:

> At times, our technical strength is underutilized in problems of organization and within the bureaucracy, or it is a fault in the management of those responsible. . . . On occasions, technicians do not produce any results but they remain in the same position for years, yet the corresponding measures for their removal are not adopted.[69]

The efforts by sports leaders to develop new attitudes and standards in physical culture had not yielded the desired results, despite much effort to publicize physical activities. In 1987, there were still weaknesses in the school system, although by that time formal PE programs were almost universally available. Attitudes toward physical culture and sport were not altered to the extent that the leaders had hoped.

Publicizing Sports and Physical Culture

An important part in the campaign to create a tradition of systematic physical exercise was publicity and the provision of information. In this the media played a crucial role. As early as 1959, special sections on sports in newspapers promoted new attitudes toward physical culture activities. National newspapers carrying sports news included *Revolución, Verde Olivo, Juventud Rebelde, Pioneros, Bohemia, Granma,* and *Mujeres.* Two specialized sports magazines— *Semanario Deportivo: Listos Para Vencer* and *El Deporte: Derecho del Pueblo*—provided information on various forms of physical culture ranging from mass programs, sports schools, and sports science, to sports skills and the results of national and international sporting events. *El Deporte* is a well-produced, colorful, almost glossy, monthly sports magazine. *LPV,* which ceased publication several years ago, was a cheaper, less colorful weekly. Cubans claim that sports coverage emphasizes both team work and individual performance, as well as the techniques involved, rather than individual personalities.[70] However, numerous articles have profiled well-known athletes, clearly adding to the cult of personality.

The Cuban Institute of Cinema Arts (ICAIC) always sends a representative (armed with movie camera) along with the Cuban sports delegates to major events, both national and international. Some of these trips have produced award-winning documentaries: *Cerro Pelado,* directed by Santiago Alvarez; *El Ring,* by Oscar Valdés; and *Nuestra Olimpiada en Habana,* by José Massip. In addition, there have been numerous other films made on sports themes. To the Cubans, ICAIC is merely documenting the way that sports shows people "the truth about the revolution."[71]

CONCLUSION

Today, the infrastructure of the Cuban sports system is in place, to support programs of mass participation. The administrative bodies are well established and functioning with some efficiency, from INDER to the mass organizations. The financing of sports and physical culture is sufficient, at the moment, yet likely to present problems in the future, as the Castro government deals with reduced aid from the rapidly shrinking socialist bloc. The means for implementing programs of popular participation in sport and physical culture—from equipment to facilities to personnel—are also in place. Our next chapter will look at and assess the specific programs for Cuban sport, as well as the system of physical education within the schools.

4

Popular Participation Under Fidel

According to Jorge García Bango, former head of INDER, "our first reform measure was to open to everyone the private sports clubs that abounded on the island."[1] With this act, the revolutionary government began to effect the most important objective of the sports program: mass participation. Sport is seen as a right of the people. In the Cuban Constitution of 1976, sports and physical education are mentioned four times. Under "Political, social and economic principles of the state," Article 8b states that "The socialist state . . . as the power of the people and for the people, guarantees . . . that no one be left without access to studies, culture, and sports." Under "Equality," Article 42 says, "The state consecrates the right achieved by the Revolution that all citizens, regardless of race, color or national origin . . . enjoy the same resorts, beaches, parks, social centers of culture, sports, recreation and rest." Sport merits its own article under "Fundamental rights, duties and guarantees," Article 51, which reads:

> Everyone has the right to physical education, sports and recreation.
>   Enjoyment of this right is assured by including the teaching and practice of physical education and sports in the cur-

ricula of the national education system and means placed at the service of the people, which makes possible the practice of sports and recreation on a mass basis.[2]

Sport is mentioned the fourth time under education.

According to Cuban theory, mass participation was to be the primary concern in Cuba's sports and physical culture system. There was to be a major effort to develop participation programs, both in educational institutions and for the populace in general. Programs ranged from exercises for babies and infants to activities for people over sixty years of age, including recreational activities, physical exercises, and competitive sports and games. Crucial to raising participation in physical activities was the construction of numerous facilities and the development of a national sports industry to provide equipment.

Cuban leaders have encountered a number of problems, however, including poor maintenance of facilities and poor performance by some sports authorities. The dual goals of mass participation in physical culture and high performance in sports at times appeared to conflict, although the two are compatible in many ways. Some officials tend to concentrate on detecting champions rather than on expanding participation. The sports industry sometimes experiences difficulty in meeting demands for both high-performance sports and popular physical culture equipment, and this problem is compounded also by the attempt to produce goods for export too.

Cuba's mass participation program has two prime functions: health and fitness. It also provides a source of top-level athletes, however, and it plays a part in socialization, especially among the young. Critics often label this socialization as indoctrination and control. Certainly, the ideology of the revolution is promoted through physical culture, just as it is through other activities and in other countries. Throughout the world, the dominant ideology is promoted in most social institutions. As for the desire to seek champions, Castro has warned that this goal is second in importance:

It is very important that we do not be mistaken, that in the search for champions we do not neglect the practice of sports. Everyone should practice sports, not only those in primary schools but also adults and the elderly. The elderly need it even more than the young. The youths sometimes need sports to use their excess energy. Moreover, sports is an instrument of discipline, education, health, good manners. Sports is an antidote to vices. Youth needs sports. And the elderly need sports not to use their excess energy but to adequately conserve the energy which they still have and their health which is so important for a full life.

You can have the most complete assurance that whatever we spend on sports and physical education we will save in health and we will gain in the well-being and increased longevity of our citizens.[3]

PROMOTING PARTICIPATION AMONG THE GENERAL POPULATION

From the beginning, the revolutionary government determined that in its move to extend sports, recreation, and physical education throughout the country, no one would be left out. "Nothing fundamental, nothing indispensable for making the principle come true that sport is a right of the people was forgotten by Law 936." The first steps were taken by the new Cuban government in 1959, when previous restrictions on access to beaches, hotel pools, and sports clubs were removed. The doors were opened to all Cubans and entry fees were abolished or drastically reduced.[4] Many of these clubs became workers' recreation centers or *círculos obreros*.

Yet simply opening the doors to the private clubs and increasing the funds allocated for sports did not bring about the mass participation that exists today. In 1963, the total number of Cubans participating in sports activities was 169,134. School students accounted for 39,843, 24 percent of this. By September 1975, the total number had reached 3,504,430, a 2,000 percent increase (of these, 2,136,466 or 61 percent were students).[5]

Employees of the General Directory of Sports (DGD) worked to make existing facilities available to all Cubans and to extend physical education to all schools. Before 1961 and the formation of INDER, programs for popular participation were organized by various groups in a rather uncoordinated manner, perhaps sponsored by a local council, by the DGD, by the Ministry for Public Health, or by the armed forces. The experiences of 1959 and 1960 and of the recreation organized during the 1961 literacy campaign, as well as the results of a survey by the literacy *brigadistas* were used to formulate national plans for physical culture:

> We have studied and become familiar with the systems of sports participation existing in Cuba previously; all of them gravitated around institutions, around the private clubs which were only for the powerful classes, the national bourgeoisie. . . . They were able to attract young people who excelled in sports . . . by promising them jobs or by actually giving them money; by obtaining houses for them; and by offering them membership in an exclusive club.[6]

The Participation Campaign was aimed at destroying this situation. Teams were to be based on regions and would include people of all different social origins. Henceforth, the barriers to popular participation were to be formally removed.

The principal task then was to encourage Cubans to participate in physical activities. In May 1961, 25,000 Cubans participated in a gymnastics parade. In July 1961, 75,000 took part in another parade to publicize sports, and this parade was subsequently held annually on July 25 and included films and awards.[7] On 24 February 1962, 97,000 Cubans took part in a recreation festival that included camping, tours, and physical and intellectual games.

Many other programs were initiated during the 1960s. These included the Listos Para Vencer (LPV) physical efficiency tests, established in 1961; the *fisiminútos*, established in 1962–1963; basic gymnastics for women; and the Plan de la Calle for children.[8] The Plan de la Montaña (Mountain plan) was also instituted in the early 1960s, which sought to extend this mass participation campaign to Cuba's most isolated communities in the island's three major mountain ranges. These and similar programs are the foundations of Cuban initiatives aimed at popularizing physical culture and sports.

These early campaigns aimed to democratize physical culture. (The term *democratization*, in this context, refers to the breadth of access to sports, not to the liberalization of or increased liberty within either sports or the Cuban system as a whole.) In the early 1970s and 1980s, more emphasis was placed upon improving the quality of mass programs, and raising standards in sports performance, although this was not intended to override the aim of increasing the numbers taking part. During the second half of the 1980s, however, there was some evidence of obstacles to extended participation.

THE POPULAR PARTICIPATION PROGRAMS

The Plan de la Montaña

The Mountain Plan began in 1964 in the Escambray Mountains. Areas were selected in which to build facilities for baseball, soccer, basketball, and volleyball. The Plan was later extended to the Sierra Maestra, and in 1967, a similar plan was begun in the Sierra de los Organos in the province of Pinar del Río. As well as providing installations in these relatively remote regions, the Mountain Plan included training local youngsters as sports instructors.[9]

The plan also included competitions between the mountain communities. The first Inter-Montaña Games were held in 1965. Three hundred participants from Escambray, Sierra Maestra, Segunda Frente Oriental, Baracoa, and La Cordillera de Los Organos competed in these games. In the municipality Frank País in the upper Mayarí district, fourteen sports were made available through the Mountain Plan: kayaking, freestyle wrestling, judo, boxing, handball, chess, athletics, baseball, basketball, soccer, table tennis, swimming, weightlifting, and volleyball. By 1978, the region had twenty-one sports centers, but only fourteen trainers.[10]

The extension of sports and physical culture to rural regions was also a major concern of the Association of Small Landowners (ANAP), which organized camps and provided facilities in rural areas. These efforts included building centers, such as the Complejos Deportívos Rústicos (Rustic sports complexes) in agricultural cooperatives and other rural areas. Some sports equipment was produced in these rural centers as well. The first of these complexes was established in April 1982 in Jesús Menéndez municipality, in Las Tunas Province. This center had a shooting range donated by SEPMI, as well as other sports facilities. Thirty-nine similar complexes were planned for July 1983. As with the Mountain Plan, these rural physical culture complexes began in one area (the sugar-producing municipality of Jesús Menéndez) and were later extended to other regions.[11]

While rural regions (where Castro's guerrilla forces had found support and safe haven) were given special attention, many of the programs aimed at increasing participation were instituted on a national scale, and probably the largest and longest lasting of these was the LPV program.

The LPV Ready-to-Win Plan

The Listos Para Vencer (Ready-to-win) programs are direct takeoffs from the Soviet version, GTO (Ready for labor and defense). As in the Soviet Union, the program consists of a series of tests that determine a person's physical condition, including such things as speed, resistance, strength, and ability to jump and throw. Participants compete against themselves, not against each other. Initially, LPV served two purposes: to generate an interest in sports and to see what talent did exist.[12]

In 1961, 15,000 tests were performed with different target standards set according to age and gender. By 1964, at least 380,000 Cubans were tested: in gymnastics skills, broad jumping, 50- and 600–yard runs, rope climbing, and floating abilities. By 1966, the tests also included running, long jump, high jump, and various throwing events. Standards were not intended to be too high, and as the Cubans often state, it was necessary to set their own standards because Cuba was not a developed country.[13]

Throughout the 1960s, many Cubans took the LPV tests (see table 15). The exact number is uncertain; Cuban statistics vary substantially. It is clear that the vast majority of Cubans were not participants in the 1960s, even though the program was by no means conducted on a small scale.

This may be why the LPV program was changed during the 1970s. It was expanded and divided into two programs: the Familia Cederista LPV in November 1975 (for those over forty-five years old) and the LPV physical efficiency tests for those under forty-five. By 1979, one million participants were said to have taken part in the Cederista LPV program.[14]

Also in 1979, the name of the LPV program was changed to Plan de las Pruebas de Eficiencia Física (Plan of physical efficiency tests). The tests were graded according to age and gender and included three levels in each grade. They were intended to promote health and teach basic physical skills. The levels were based upon the number of points earned in each activity. In 1990, there were 4,000,000 tests given.[15]

TABLE 15.
Cuban Statistics on LPV Tests

Year	Schools	Public	Total
	Numbers Taking LPV Tests		
	According to Tapia:		
1962	no information		51,446
1963	no information		95,237
1964	no information		380,994
1965	no information		506,050
	According to *Boletín:*		
1962–1963	134,273		
1963		95,237	229,510
1963–1964	136,118		
1964		388,992	625,110
1964–1965	178,356		
1965		625,326	803,682

Source: O. Tapia, "Fit to Win," *GWR*, 30 October 1966, p. 2; and *Boletín estadístico de la República de Cuba, 1965,* Dirección Central de Estadísticos, JUCEPLAN, p. 148.

A new program was established in 1979: Plan Ponte LPV was coordinated through INDER and the Ministry of Public Health and had the same objectives of raising the standards of health and improving fitness and physical ability. Cubans were encouraged to exercise at least three times a week in order to improve their fitness gradually and thus be able to pass the LPV standards. A doctor at a polyclinic in the Sierra Maestra region between the location of the Second Eastern Front and Santiago de Cuba said that they often recommend certain exercises from the plan for health reasons.[16] Manuel González, former director of the Cuban Olympic Committee, boasted that the greatest achievements of the Cuban government—public health, public education, and public athletics—are all interlocking. "Sports are the greatest of all preventative medicines. We are struggling to build enough hospitals, to train enough doctors. Until we do, and even after, staying well is our biggest goal and athletics are the best pill."[17]

A pamphlet, *Ponte LPV,* produced by INDER and MINSAP, outlined the goals of the plan and advised that exercises be done early in the morning or afternoon and never soon after meals. The pamphlet also included a guide (with diagrams) for a series of one-year exercise programs designed for different age groups. In 1987, several targets were set in mass physical culture: 50 percent of ages 6–65 were to take LPV tests, 40 percent at the first level; 10 percent of adults (women aged 16–55 and men aged 16–69) were to practice physical activities regularly; 10 percent of children aged 8–18 were to take special sports LPV tests, and 5 percent of these had to pass.[18] Each municipality and province was encouraged to strive for these standards, and some of these goals have already been met. Although it is uncertain whether this standard will be maintained, it is clear that the LPV programs were given a position of high priority, and that they helped to increase popular participation in sports and physical activities.

Exercise programs and target setting did not, however, appeal to all Cubans—even if the standards were not overly demanding—and Cuban attempts to expand participation in physical culture were not limited to exercise plans. They also included the development of programs for leisure, recreation, and sports.

Leisure Time and Recreation Programs

The ultimate goal of the Cuban authorities was the development of a "physical culture," that is, regular participation in sports-related activities as an essential part of all-round development. Besides promoting sports and exercises, this goal led to the creation of numerous recreation programs, which included both physical and nonphysical activities. It is possible that these programs were introduced in response to some Cubans preferring less structured or less strenuous activities to occupy their limited leisure time.

The recreation programs were motivated, too, by the Cuban leaders' desire to provide creative activities in people's free time. Recreational activities were regarded as important means to develop communist attitudes, including morality, patriotism, responsibility, discipline, and a collective spirit. Physical recreation was also seen as educational and healthy, and thus beneficial to both the individual and society. It was hoped that free-time recreation might provide young people with constructive activities, instead of petty crime, black marketeering, and dollar trading. Such antisocial activities continue to be a problem, however, especially in Havana.[19]

Recreational programs began with the establishment of social centers and the opening of previously private beaches. Going to the beach is very popular, especially from May through September. In 1988, long lines formed in Havana for a constant stream of buses from Habana Vieja to the beaches at Playa del Este. Hotels are available to the general population, and many Cubans swim in both the sea and the hotel pools. Many play dominoes on the beach. One Cuban remarked how wonderful the crowds were because, before 1959, few of the people there would have been allowed on most of the beaches. After 1992, gas shortages may mean that fewer buses are available for trips to the beach.[20]

In addition, Cubans are able to use school facilities and the abandoned villas of wealthy exiles. The cost of the schools is often merely a few hours of agricultural work in the afternoons. Campgrounds are also popular vacation sites. Previously, there were also tours, although most were too expensive for many Cubans. With the implementation of the "Special Period" in 1992, there are now no interstate buses available.[21]

Separate vacations are available to members of the Young Pioneers (scouts) and to schoolchildren aged from seven to fourteen. A camp at Tarárá Beach near Havana could accommodate more than 5,000 *pioneros* in 1975. There are similar camps in Las Villas and Camaguey. The ultimate goal (according to Fidel) is for Tarárá to accommodate 20,000 children at one time, or 120,000 during the six weeks of summer vacation. The Pioneer Camp in Las Villas, established in 1976, had 184 buildings for nearly 5,000 pioneers and provided areas for sports, horseback riding, canoeing, sailing, and flying model airplanes.[22]

At the end of the first decade after the revolution, studies of recreation and free-time activities pointed to increased organization of recreation. In 1966, surveys of Cubans' use of free time were conducted by a group of researchers from the University of Havana. Other studies of student free-time activities were undertaken by MINED, and by the FMC, the CDRs, the ISCF, and the Center for the Investigation and Orientation of Internal Demand (OCIODE). The late 1960s also witnessed the formation of recreational fishing and hunting groups and the development of legislation to control these activities.[23]

In 1972, Círculos de Recreación Turística (Tourism recreation groups) were established in order to develop plans for excursions and camps, orientation, badminton, and other events such as tug-of-war. During the 1960s and the first half of the 1970s, archery, motorboating, roller hockey, and ice hockey were also included in recreation programs.[24]

After 1976, new programs were developed with a qualitative focus in many areas. Camping has become very popular in Cuba and is inexpensive, only covering costs. Tents, hammocks, and transport are provided by the state, along with communal kitchens and equipment for sports and recreation. In 1980, one campground near Guardalavaca Beach in Holguín Province was filled with people who had even brought animals ready to slaughter for the next picnic.[25]

Recreation was even more strongly promoted in the 1980s, and apparently successfully, as demand for facilities and skilled workers outstripped supply. This strong commitment to recreation may indicate a desire to inspire those Cubans who were not participating in organized sports.[26] This was certainly a motivating factor for recreational programs such as the Plan de la Calle for children. Indeed, reviews of INDER requested by the Poder Popular in the 1980s contributed to the development of new recreation programs.

The Plan de la Calle and *¡A Jugar!*

The Street Plan began on 30 January 1966 under the direction of INDER and was administered by police and militia members as well as by the CDRs and the FMC. On that first day, the plan was initiated in 47 zones in the city of Havana, with reportedly 12,144 children taking part. By early March, 23 zones were established to cater to 5,291 children in the city of Pinar del Río.[27] These recreational programs were later organized each Sunday and during Playa Girón fortnight when many parents were doing volunteer agricultural work.

Similar street plans were also organized during children's week, at Christmas, and on the Día de los Tres Reyes (Epiphany). Sometimes, groups of from one to three hundred children visited other neighboring zones to join with other groups. The plan involved organizing games and sports for children in streets that were closed off to traffic. Modified games, soccer, baseball, basketball, short running races, stilt races, and similar activities were available, with equipment provided either by the Cuban sports industry or by local producers who made makeshift equipment such as paper balls. Facilities for playing chess and for drawing as well as clowns, music, puppet shows, and magicians were also included in the plan.[28]

The Street Plan served several functions. It provided areas and facilities for supervised recreation in a local area and occupied children while their parents were away. Although the revolutionary government built many facilities, the plan provided areas in urban regions where local institutions were not yet available. Later, more permanent facilities were established.

Another significant factor is the local or decentralized focus of the plan. While Cuba, like Latin America as a whole, has major spectator sports, there are also concerted efforts to provide activities that emphasize participation rather than observation. Physical culture is seen as not only a right but also a duty, one that many Cubans fulfill willingly. Indeed, parents' willingness to participate is sometimes an obstacle to the children's participation in the Street Plan, as they want to join in the children's games. "During [the parents'] . . . youth, no one ever brought sports to [their] doorstep. In the past, many of them had to be content to watch others play."[29]

By September 1974, there were 9,144 programs and 978,646 children in the Street Plan. By this stage, permanent zones and areas were established for the plan. Toward the end of the 1960s, parks and recreation centers were built. One such park is in Cardenas, province of Matanzas. Another is the Lenin Park in Havana city. Equipment was still being supplied partly by local producers. Alterations to the Street Plan were formalized in 1977, when it entered a new stage. Before that time, the plan lacked quality and was not systematically organized. With more formal organization came more competitiveness, possibly to increase enthusiasm.[30] Perhaps the Cubans discovered (as the Soviets had in the 1930s) that competition in sports was an attractive feature for many people.

This reorganization was also motivated in part by a tendency to include in the plan any activity played in the street. Baseball, often played in the streets, was a particular cause for concern. Authorities wished to encourage the playing of baseball and other sports in specially designed playing fields, rather than in the streets where the safety of the players and the passers-by was threatened. This new phase sought to bring activists, instructors, and volunteers together to form a CVD in each municipality to organize and plan activities. The children were to be divided into age groups (7–9, 10–11, and 11–14 years), and permanent areas for the plan were to be established. This phase also sought to raise the standards of workers and to make the Street Plan an extension of school physical education.[31]

A new level of sophistication was reached in 1979, when ¡A Jugar! was founded in the city of Havana. This was similar to the Street Plan and concentrated on qualitative development in sports activities and on promoting recreation and conservation in country districts. In addition, there was a weekly television program of the same name that broadcast pictures of school children competing in sports.[32] Competition and sports-oriented muscle development took on a greater importance in the new program, which moved these activities from the streets and into specialized facilities. "Recreation has left the street, but it has taken another route, into physical recreation, which is the art of amusing children healthily, at the same time that they exercise their muscles in sports activities, with the possibility of developing all of their volitional qualities."[33]

Physical Culture for Adults

In Cuba, unlike in the Soviet Union, there is no widespread system of clubs to which athletes (of any level) belong and through which they participate and compete. Cubans participate through three areas: the neighborhood, the school, and the workplace. It is through these that the Cubans find the facilities and equipment needed to practice sport, whether it be a place for a beginning FMC exercise group or coaching and equipment for the provincial champions in the Juegos Deportívos Obreros (Workers' sports games).

The Cuban government is firmly committed to the belief that all people have a right to practice sport, not just the young. To facilitate the development and the integration of all adults, especially workers and peasants, into physical education and sport, the National Board of Physical Culture has these principle objectives:

1. The massive incorporation of all adults into the different types of basic gymnastics.
2. To find a scientific system of tests that determines the level of physical efficiency.
3. To obtain the best result in work through the practice of labor gymnastics (fisiminútos).
4. To provide the material and technical means by which all citizens receive the benefits, and that they achieve health through the practice of sports, gymnastics, and recreation.[34]

Mass organizations such as the FMC, the CTC, and the CDRs work together with the National Board of Physical Culture by sponsoring activities such as basic gymnastics classes for women, the workers' games, and the LPV programs. Efforts are made to include those who live in institutions as well. At Cuba's showcase psychiatric hospital in Havana, there is a clear emphasis on sports. The facilities include a well-tended baseball diamond with bleachers, several basketball courts, and a running track with a large grassy area in the center that is used for field events.[35]

Physical activities for adults are often held as part of celebrations, such as the anniversary of an event in the revolution (26 July, for example), or on special days for sports, such as 19 November, the Day of Physical Culture and Sport. Such commemorative acts include choreographed exercises or "human blackboards," and gymnastics parades with as many as two hundred thousand participants.[36]

One such activity is the Maratón Popular, the annual fun run. Running clubs called Correr Es Vivir (To run is to live) were founded as recently as 6 January 1985. The clubs require members to have medical tests before being admitted. As early as 1980, runners on the streets of Cuba were quite common. Unlike other countries in Central and South America, foreigners running through the streets did not appear an oddity.[37]

Races are held over short distances in many parts of Cuba. In the run in Havana in 1985, for example, the men's was nine kilometers, the women's was five kilometers, and there were 2,658 participants. By 1987, the Maratón in Havana had 9,100 entrants, with a total of 63,222 Cubans taking part in similar runs held all over the island. All ages and levels were represented, with many of Cuba's top athletes taking part. Photos of the event in sports magazines show the variety of participants, few of whom had running footwear. The Day of Physical Culture and Sports, celebrating the formation of the CVDs, also includes a week of physical displays, Pioneer Festivals, and various competitive and noncompetitive activities.[38]

In addition to these annual events, INDER developed programs aimed at encouraging regular exercise by all Cubans. These were aimed principally at those who did not have access to programs in educational or work centers. In various *círculos* held in recreation centers, the Plan Pónte en Forma, developed by INDER and MINSAP, was established. The plan included a published guide, not unlike the LPV pamphlets, to physical activities and exercises that could be done in the home. The objectives of the Plan Pónte en Forma were to improve the health and physical condition of adults over seventeen, in order to increase productivity and to advance mass participation in physical activities.[39] These goals were specified for all organized and unorganized physical activity for adults, as declared at the second congress of the Cuban Communist party in 1980:

> Popular physical culture, known also as physical education for adults, represents the continuing process and its objective is to assure the attainment of [high] levels of physical performance, to maintain an adequate state of health which, at the same time, elevates the capacity of creativity and production, and combats the effects of a sedentary lifestyle.[40]

Organized physical education for adults included workers' gymnastics (*gimnasia laboral*), with 110,000 participants in 1990; gymnastics in education centers (*fisiminútos*); and women's gymnastics (*gimnasia básica*), with 200,000 participants in 1990; and additional groups for older adults. Physical education for adults outside their private homes involved bringing together a group under the supervision of a sports activist or a physical culture instructor. These groups met at least three times a week for sessions of an hour or more. Members were urged to complete a one-year exercise program.[41]

In work centers, this program was a supplement to workers' gymnastics. Also known as *fisiminútos*, this program was supervised by the CTC and was encouraged especially in workshops and factories. It included introductory gymnastics (before work), pause gymnastics, and *fisiminútos individuales* during rest periods from work. These exercises varied according to the type of labor being performed: those with demanding physical work did relaxing exercises, those with repetitive work tasks exercised other muscles, while those in sedentary positions had more physically demanding programs.[42]

By the 1980s, games of physical efficiency were being held, for workers in 1981, and in basic gymnastics for women in 1985. The years from 1972 to 1984 witnessed a large growth in the level of participation in adult physical culture, once structural problems in the development of appropriate programs were solved. Exact figures for participation in popular physical culture are difficult to ascertain. Large variations were probably caused by varying classifications of programs and because sometimes participants may have been counted more than once. For example, a woman may have participated in a physical efficiency group, in women's gymnastics, and if she was employed in workers' gymnastics. Despite statistical irregularities, all the figures indicated considerable increases in participants. Table 16 shows an increase in participants from 6,500 in 1972 to 137,449 in 1975, broken down by various areas. One Cuban source claimed an almost threefold increase from 160,000 in 1977 to 450,000 in 1982.[43]

Statistics suggest that there was considerable success in the women's gymnastics program. Numbers increased from 4,000 in 1972 to 5,446 in 1975 to 90,777 in 1977.[44]While women entered basic gymnastics in considerable numbers, ongoing *machista* attitudes were reflected more strongly in organized sports, where Cuban women made far more limited advances (this will be discussed further below).

TABLE 16.
Participation in Physical Culture Programs, 1972 to October 1975

Program	1972	1973	1974	1975
Basic Women's Gymnastics				
Groups	81	875	1,484	2,166
Activities	81	875	1,484	2,043
Participants	4,000	16,417	31,295	50,446
Public Physical Efficiency				
Groups	107	1,872	1,622	2,428
Activities	107	1,872	1,622	2,393
Participants	2,500	56,213	59,570	80,225
Gymnastics at Work				
Centers	0	7	68	132
Groups	0	7	92	184
Activities	0	7	107	186
Participants	0	140	2,948	6,778

Source: Pickering, "Cuba," p. 163.

Women's gymnastics classes were specifically for women and included a number of different activities. One program lasted a year, with three forty-five-minute sessions each week. Thirty of these sessions were devoted to motor capacity; fifteen to physical development; six to sports; fifty-two to exercises of organization and control; and general physical development activities using some equipment. In addition, there were fifty-two classes on games and two on the LPV physical efficiency plans. The entire plan involved 209 classes under the supervision of the FMC with either a sports activist or a gymnastics instructor.[45]

An activist, an instructor, a mass organization, or a group could request pamphlets from INDER, along with a group instructor, if required, to establish a gymnastics group. These pamphlets described the details of the plan and listed the benefits, such as better health, better physical development, and improved fitness for defense and labor productivity.[46]

Most interesting for a socialist society, these pamphlets, as well as articles in the Cuban media, consistently refer to the role of gymnastics in improving women's figures.[47] Ironically, one article that described basic gymnastics as advantageous for women's figures also criticized "bourgeois" attitudes to women, which viewed women as objects of reproduction, pleasure, and decoration for men. The gulf between some of the ideals of the revolution and its reality were captured in such expressions:

Nature has given to women the highest responsibility of the essence of humanity: reproduction. It is she who from time immemorial was prepared for the interests of the dominant elements of society, especially within the bourgeoisie to be the objects of reproduction and pleasure; such as a decorative figure for masculine satisfaction.[48]

On the other hand, of course, a woman might wish to take care of her figure for health reasons alone, rather than to appeal to men. Such activities often contribute to the development of self-confidence, to a feeling of solidarity with other women, and to awareness about such machismo, as well as a greater sense of women's shared needs, desires, and rights, thus fulfilling (in part, at least) the revolutionary attempt to change general attitudes toward women. Unfortunately, there is no such attitude adjustment that routinely occurs in all-male sports activities (in fact, quite the opposite).

Cuba's physical culture administrators stressed that all age groups should exercise. In 1988 in Havana, Círculos de Abuelos (grandparents' groups) were opened to twenty thousand members over the age of sixty. In 1990, there were a hundred thousand participants in these grandparent *círculos*. Such centers and Therapeutic Areas were aimed primarily at improving health and, therefore, worked in cooperation with MINSAP and local health officials. These programs were begun on a trial basis in the city of Havana as a form of preventative health care, using exercises aimed at reducing obesity and related diseases. The plan was to provide one gymnasium per 45,000 people. In 1988 there were 54 of these centers with 15,000 members. Microgymnasiums were also planned in all municipalities with one gym for every 3,500 people. These centers and groups organize exercise programs and recreational activities such as short walks.[49]

These numerous plans were also seen as a way to encourage participation in physical activities, including organized sports. While many Cubans have contact with PE programs and recreation, participation in sports tends to be more restricted, with young male Cubans taking part in the greatest numbers.

MASS SPORT

Workers' Sports Games

The Workers' Games, like other sports competitions in Cuba, were organized with a broad base of participants, which was gradually reduced at regional competitions before the final national-level games. These games were first held in 1972, with subsequent games in 1975 and 1977, and at varying intervals thereafter. The first games included only four sports, the second eight, and the 1989 games included fourteen events, among them PE activities, chess, and basic gymnastics for women. In 1972, 82,000 workers competed in base-level competitions; in 1975, in the second games, 179,000 workers competed at this level, and by 1977, the number had risen to 620,000 workers.[50]

These games are organized by the CTC and INDER. Up to the provincial level, the seventeen syndicates that make up the CTC were responsible for organizing competitions. CTC executives and representatives from the syndicates organize provincial and national competitions. Equipment and sports officials are provided by INDER and the sports section of Poder Popular.[51] At the base level, teams represent individual work centers or a combination of several small centers. Larger centers hold intrafacility competitions. Municipal competitions come after this initial stage, followed by intraprovincial and then interprovincial competitions. In team sports, teams representing each of the seventeen syndicates compete with those from other provinces to determine the national representatives for each syndicate.

These various elimination rounds require considerable time. The competitions for the 1989 games began at the work-center level in 1986, with municipal competitions being held in the first half of 1987 and team interprovincial meets held later in the year. The final interprovincial meets were held throughout 1988. These extensive base-level competitions allowed workers to take part without time pressure and to participate in large numbers on a systematic basis. This approach was also thought to result in higher quality and to eliminate any rigging of events. At the municipal level, everyone competes against everyone else in team events (round robin), and there must be at least three base-level meets before anyone progresses to the national level.[52]

Syndicate and local officials are required to ensure as broad a participation as possible. They also have to submit the names of workers selected for higher-level competitions. Provincial authorities are required to present the names of representatives at the national level or risk the disqualification of their province. There are also various rules governing who can participate. Workers who were working when the base-level competitions began (that is, in December 1986 for the 1989 games) were able to compete at higher levels. Athletes on the Cuban national team who were workers when the base-level competitions were held could compete, as could top-level athletes, even if they had ceased working after the intercenter competitions. Small farmers and pensioners who had worked or given services to a work center were eligible as well. Those who did not compete in base-level competitions for a work center could not compete at higher levels. Authorities could request presentation of a competitor's identification card to ensure that these conditions were met. Thus, all competitors, including top-level athletes, had to compete at all levels in order to proceed to the national games. In addition to prohibiting any worker from automatic entry to a municipal, provincial, or national competition, there are awards for unions and provincial CTC branches with the highest participation numbers in various age groups at the base-level. All centers are urged to seek the participation, at some level, of 60 percent of their workers.[53]

The Workers' Games incorporate many workers at the base-level, but there are considerable numbers of Cubans (students, soldiers, or housewives, for example) who are not employed full-time. With the recent cutbacks, the number of unemployed Cubans, not otherwise gainfully occupied, will surely increase.[54] Students and soldiers have their own sports games, and meets are even organized for merchant sailors and their families![55]

Some housewives may have participated in physical education programs such as basic gymnastics, but women are less represented in sports. A woman who is not employed or who does not attend an educational institution may well find it difficult to enter sports competitions, unless she is capable enough to be accepted in a special area and also has enough free time to dedicate to her sport. For many Cuban women, this is not the case. Women may enter military service, which provides an opportunity to compete in sports, but it is not compulsory for them as it is for men.

Military Games and Military Sports

Like the Workers' Games, the Games of the Armed Forces (FAR) began at base level in 1972 (in military units) and advanced to a national level with teams from the Eastern, Central, and Western Armed Forces. The establishment of these games may, in part, have been due to increased contact with the armies of other socialist countries; Cuba joined the Sports Committee of Friendly Armies in 1969. Originally only small numbers competed in these military games (one thousand in 1973),[56] which included military skills, such as parachuting, grenade-throwing, and shooting activities that soldiers would be involved in during their training.

Civilians participated in these activities in SEPMI clubs, which were established in 1980. These clubs were intended to promote military-oriented sports, particularly among young Cubans. In 1986, there were 2,869 of these clubs with over 100,000 members. While they provided sports activities, it was likely that the main motive for SEPMI was to raise national defense capability at a time of heightened security concerns. As in the workers' sports, there were fewer women represented in the Military Games, with women comprising the smaller percentage of both the armed forces and the work force. (In 1986, only 37 percent of the Cuban work force were women.)[57]

Given these factors, it is not difficult to explain why fewer women than men participated in organized sports. The likelihood of this changing is closely related to changing attitudes to women's participation in competitive sports and in the work force (and to expansion of the work force itself).[58] It is in the school system that such changes in attitude might begin. Women's participation is greatest (proportional to that of men) in school sports.

PHYSICAL EDUCATION: "FROM THE MASSES, SPRINGS THE QUALITY!"

The diversification of mass sport—through the introduction of the people to the new disciplines of swimming, volleyball, weightlifting, judo, and others, along with the expansion of sports throughout the country—constitutes one of the fundamental premises of INDER for extending the possibility of the participation of the people in these physical activities and thus assuring that there are high-caliber athletes capable of representing Cuba in international competitions.[59]

One criticism of the Cuban sports system is that it has opened sports up to the masses only as insurance against passing over a potential champion at the lower levels. Surely this argument is not completely valid, since there is no hope that a champion will emerge from an FMC gymnastics class or from a class at a psychiatric hospital. On the other hand, the Cubans do go over all possible recruits with the fine-tooth comb that is their PE and sports system.

In the new constitution, under the section "Education and Culture," Article 38 states:

The state orients, foments, and promotes education, culture and science in all their manifestations. Its educational and cultural policy is based on the following principles: . . . c) the state must promote communist education of the new generations and the training of children, young people and adults of social life. In order to make this principle a reality, general education and specialized scientific, technical, or artistic education are combined with work, development research, physical education, sports, participation in political and social activities and military training. . . . h) the state promotes, foments, and develops all forms of physical education and sports as a means of education of contribution to the integral development of the citizens.[60]

That physical education and sport are mentioned so prominently in the constitution certainly underlines their important role in the development of Cuban citizens. Indeed, Fidel himself has said that the "physical education of the people is the basis of sport."[61] It is clearly an integral part of Cuban education.

Sports and physical culture activities are viewed as important for health and well-being, as well as for physical development. School programs are also regarded as important in developing the communist attitudes of the "new man" who would be a well-rounded, selfless person.

In keeping with the characteristics of its Revolution and the country's particular conditions, Cuba is developing a new type of man that the revolutionary process requires. This process is based on specific morality and an ideology determined chiefly by active participation of the people in the tasks set by the Revolution. . . .

From the beginning, our education is aimed at the complete formation of man and joins in a harmonious whole, study, work, defense, sports, art, and recreation.[62]

Physical education in all forms enables the Cuban government to have control over an important part of the developmental process of forming the new Cuban man:

The physical development of the child is the basis of his general development. Without physical culture and sport, it is impossible to form a generation with the capacity to work if it is not physically developed. . . . Physical education contributes in a special way to the achievement of this great goal in the formation of the communist personality.[63]

Physical Fitness for Babies and Toddlers

The physical side of Cuban education, and the subsequent government involvement, begins very early, long before the child is exposed to formal education. In fact, from the time the children are forty-five days old, their mothers are encouraged to begin exercising them. INDER produces a number of pamphlets for this purpose, such as "The Home Is the Gymnasium," *Matrogimnasia,* and *Mamá, Papá, Hágan Ejercícios Conmigo* by Jana Berdychova.[64]

Another pamphlet, *Para Ejercitar al Pequeño,* attacks traditional attitudes toward babies, such as the belief that fat babies are healthy. It also includes indoor and outdoor exercises similar to those in child-care centers. A major objective of these programs is to provide physical activities for children who do not attend child-care centers. *Matrogimnasia,* for example, is held twice weekly in fifty-minute sessions. Almost a million children aged from three to four took part in this program in the late 1970s. The attempt to educate parents and involve children in physical activities has led to the production of a weekly television program on these exercises. In addition, children are put into the water at the age of eight months to show them the first movements of swimming. This is an attempt to overcome what has been traditional Cuban weakness in water sports (the ultimate irony for a country surrounded by water).[65]

According to a Cuban saying, "the child lives when he plays and learns to live while playing." The Cubans believe that a child's instinctive capacity for movement reflects his personality and his psyche. The goal is to identify the optimum means with which to develop the capability and physical potential of children. So instinctive forms of play are channeled toward serious evaluative tests to ensure the child's progressive development.[66]

The children are the inexhaustible source of socialist society: the unmolded clay through which various programmed activities and morning gymnastics achieve the psychic-organic development that they need for skeletal and muscular growth and strengthening.

> All infants possess an amazing energy that constitutes their natural wealth. The constant desire for movement and the dynamism are their principle characteristics and this plays a very important role in the physical education.[67]

One of the earliest steps taken toward introducing physical education in all schools was the INDER-MINED Plan of 1961. In addition to trying to raise awareness of both the value of PE and the practicalities involved in its development, education officials and INDER officials began planning PE programs and interschool competitions. These programs were to include all schools, even the special ones, such as the Abel Santamaría School for the Blind or the Ana Betancourt School. Physical education was also introduced to rural areas through the Mountain Plan, during the 1961 literacy campaign, and through schools for rural women. By the 1970s, where it was available, physical education was compulsory in all schools, extending from the elementary level to the first few years of university and other tertiary studies.[68]

In 1974, there was a major revision of all education. The review of physical education stressed the need to link school activities with extracurricular activities, and the need to provide opportunities for children who were unable to participate in mainstream PE programs. The 1974 Report on the Analysis and Orientation of INDER called for greater promotion of physical education and for more stress on developing communist attitudes, especially in Basic Secondary Schools in the Countryside (ESBECs).[69]

Despite calls for developing physical education, the percentage of the primary school curriculum devoted to physical education was actually reduced (slightly) to 9 percent in 1975. Prior to this, physical education made up an average of 11.5 percent of urban primary school courses and 11 percent of rural primary school courses. One foreign source stated that one hour a day was dedicated to physical education in the primary schools. This was contradicted by Cuban figures which said physical education and sports activities were held twice a week (fifty-minute sessions) in primary schools, high schools, and in technical institutions. By the 1980s, physical education and sports activities were held two or three times a week in most schools and daily in kindergartens and child-care centers.[70]

Yet problems remained. In the primary schools in 1977, for example, 40 percent of urban students did not receive PE instruction. In rural areas, this number rose to 90 percent. The sheer size of this population contributed to this poor showing. The 1974 INDER report also suggested that not all rural secondary schools were offering PE instruction. Another concern in school (and social) physical culture is the underuse of sports facilities both in schools and in public areas. Despite these problems, almost two million primary school children were receiving PE instruction in 1977.[71]

Physical Education: The Primary Levels

Compulsory physical education begins in the *círculos infantíles* (kindergartens and nursery schools). Like *matrogimnasia,* kindergartens are viewed as an important part of forming habits of participation in physical activities. In the 1960s, these centers also taught children the history of Cuba and about Cuban sports champions. The stress was on group activities, which was said to contribute to the development of a collective outlook. Preschools also emphasized group activities and respect for others; in fact, separation from a group was used as a punishment.[72] Initially, the approach was spontaneous with little formal organization. By the late 1960s and early 1970s, however, Cuba's educational leaders felt that it was more appropriate for youngsters to have some organized activities rather than only undirected activities. There was also a move toward employing trained teachers throughout the education system. These changes may have expanded the government's control over education.

At the level practiced in the *círculos,* physical education consists of programmed activities, morning gymnastics, games of movement, sporting exercises, outings, and independent motor activity. The programmed activity is conducted year round, preferably twice a week on the same days, for fifteen to twenty minutes a day. These activities develop general health and movement, such as dexterity, flexibility, strength, speed, and endurance in conjunction with sports-related motor activities such as marching, running, jumping, climbing, throwing, catching, and rolling. Morning gymnastics is conducted every day between 8:00 and 8:30 A.M. This consists of basic movements and development in general, such as alignment, posture, creative dance, and other modified activities necessary for the multilateral muscle development.[73] If children do not attend a day-care center of some sort, they will still receive the benefits of physical education through such programs as the street plans (mentioned above).

This increased emphasis on organized and competitive games was perhaps influenced by the organization of sports competitions and games at increasingly earlier levels of schooling. The School Games were first introduced among older children and teenagers and later extended to include games at juvenile levels and between pioneer-aged children.

School Sports Competitions

In the realm of formal physical education, as well as in the less structured areas of athletic emphasis within the society, the Cubans never lose sight of their overriding goal, namely, mass participation in sport. More than two million school children participating in sports constitute the base or foundation of the pyramid of the Cuban sports organization. At the tip of the pyramid are the top Cuban athletes who compete in the international arena. But the road that leads from mass participation at the bottom to international competition at the top is too important for the Cubans to leave it to chance. All Cubans are supposed to have the right to participate in athletics, and those with talent have the right to demonstrate and develop their talents.

In order to find these athletic diamonds in the rough, who might one day represent Cuba, all school children are tested frequently, either individually or through a well-organized system of competition. In 1991, school sport was described as the "columna vertebral" of Cuban sport.[74] The program of individual testing is made up of LPV physical efficiency tests, given at the end of each semester; the group testing is the School Games. Fidel Castro has said that, to the Cubans, the important thing in sport is not to win, but rather to compete.[75] Competition is actually called *emulación,* a socialist form of competition and self-improvement. There are no material prizes. The reward comes from having succeeded.

And compete they do, because through competition, athletes with the greatest talent and potential become more visible. Many of Cuba's top athletes began their successes in the School Games. According to Gilberto Herrera, coach of the Cuban men's volleyball team that won third place in Montreal, 90 percent of the national team had come from the School Games. Silvia Chivas (sprinter) and Roberto Urrutia (weightlifting) both began competing in these games. In 1975, Pablo Vélez, then an official of INDER and manager of the Cuban delegation to the Central American and the Caribbean Games, considered the school sports system the basis for national-level sport, with 95 percent of the top athletes beginning at the school level. In 1980, Huberto Gil of the programming department of INDER said that 60 percent of the Cuban athletes at the Olympic Games in Moscow came from the School Games. He speculated that, in the future, it would most certainly be 100 percent.[76]

The School Games began in 1963, with 39,843 students taking part in preliminary competitions in eight sports. By 1982, almost five million students participated at the various base levels in twenty-two sports.[77] Schools first compete with other schools in their region. The winners then compete against winners from other regions, progressing from municipal- to provincial- and then to national-level meets.

The School Games (1963), along with the Juvenile Games (1971) and the Pioneer Games (1977), provide an opportunity for large numbers of youngsters to take part in sports competition. They serve also as a source of outstanding young athletes for sports schools and, eventually, national teams. The Games are the culmination of the PE program. They encourage students to want to participate and to strive to excel. If a student does not meet certain athletic and academic (and as he matures, political) standards, he is not allowed to compete.[78]

The Cuban sports system has been compared to a fishing net "of very fine mesh to ensure that not even the smallest fish get through." In the Cuban system of competition, every person with talent is given the chance to be discovered, and the opportunity to develop that talent. At every level, beginning with the individual schools, a championship team emerges. At the same time another team, called *selección*, is chosen from the best players from all the losing teams at that level. For example, if ten teams competed for the municipal title, a *selección* would be chosen from the remaining nine teams. In this manner, two teams actually move on to the championship, representing their particular unit. This process is repeated at every level up to the national, and there have been times when the *selección* has beaten the original champions.[79]

There are two significant aspects of this system. First, the Cubans ensure that not one potential athlete will be lost along the path of competition. Second, there is the ideological factor. Before the revolution, there existed irreconcilable class differences. With the *selección*, sports help to achieve a greater degree of integration. When the individual athletes are appointed to the selección, they must no longer identify with the old unit of school, military unit, or factory. So they begin to identify with a geographical area:

> The love of the local area becomes translated into the love of
> the province. . . . He begins to realize that the entire country is

his territory, that its traditions, ideology, and principles are his. Therefore, when the athlete goes abroad to compete, he competes for powerful reasons. People don't understand this. The force of ideology is much more powerful than any steroid or artificial drug that is given to an athlete.[80]

The School Games and other activities provided for Cuban students demonstrate the considerable effort expended on encouraging student participation in athletics. Cuban leaders hoped these young people would take this habit of participation in sports with them when they left school. In order to achieve this objective, trainers, instructors, installations, sports equipment, and open access had to be provided. Consequently, much effort was put into these areas, which were high priorities for Cuba's new leaders.

MASS PARTICIPATION: THE RECORD

Participation and Access

Participation numbers for sports, physical education, and physical culture in Cuba since 1959 are impressive, but figures have been irregularly published and variable. Methods of collection and changes in classifications sometimes have caused wide variations in numbers, even in the same activity.[81] An excellent example of these statistical problems was the sports participation figure used in the 1987 INDER report. Participation was set at 10,810,904, a figure roughly equal to (or even greater than) the entire population of the island![82] Records were of "participations" rather than of the number of different individuals practicing an activity. Table 17 lists some of the various statistics on participation in sports and recreation, from 1959 to 1990. Even if the lowest numbers are taken to be the most accurate, it can be seen that participation has increased substantially.

Women's Participation

The information in table 17 also demonstrates that, although growing, the level of women's participation in sports has always been much less than men's participation. This could be partially explained by the popularity of sports that rarely include women. Many of these sports have a strong tradition in Cuba and are sports in which Cuba has performed well internationally. Foremost among these is the national sport of baseball. "While a few Cuban women

TABLE 17.
Participation in Organized School Sports and Organized Social
Sports: 1962–1985

	Number of Participations		
Year	School Sports	Social Sports	Social Women's Sports
1959	849[e]	129,291[e]	not available
1962	not available	104,231[a]	not available
1963	39,843[b]	129,304[a]	5,444[a,b]
1964	89,590[c]	309,951[c]	28,338[a]
1965[f]	145,708[f]	586,940	55,375
1966[d]	479,575	778,226	81,056
1967[d]	829,950	1,281,224	162,527
1968[d]	962,498	1,371,606	185,303
1969[d]	1,062,712	1,177,375	156,959
1970[d]	1,233,268	1,094,317	125,735
1971[d]	1,086,153	1,214,278	156,227
1972	466,821[d]	821,017[d]/819,219[f]	52,774[d]
1973	1,314,589[d]	1,060,210[f]/1,063,813[d]	93,666[d]
1974[d]	1,673,574	1,303,734	125,941
1975[d]	2,136,468	1,673,046	191,446
1976[g]	2,671,963	2,121,754	279,683
1977[g]	3,119,728	2,206,143	286,797
1978[g]	3,806,855	2,294,209	334,251
1979[g]	3,757,755	2,354,343	340,629
1980	4,260,040[g]	2,622,169[g]	448,927[g]/427,850[b]
1981[h]	4,787,800	3,021,500	521,700
1982	4,994,500[h]/4,998,361[b,d]	3,210,600[h]	637,000[h]/541,341[b]
1983[h]	5,330,800	3,268,800	545,500
1984[h]	5,603,200	3,590,700	613,700
1985[h]	6,016,800	3,816,300	699,600
1990	5,169,306[e]	883,385[e]	not available

Sources: Statistics are compiled from the following: (a) *Compendio estadístico*
(1965), p. 16; (b) *Mapa INDER*; (c) Pickering, pp. 151, 161; (d) *Anuario estadístico* (1975), p. 244; (e) González González et al., *Razones*, p. 68; (f) *Anuario
estadístico* (1973), p. 271; (g) *Anuario estadístico* (1980), p. 241; (h) *Anuario estadístico* (1985), p. 556.

do play baseball, particularly in schools, baseball is still predominantly a male sport."[83]

In 1962, there were reportedly 60,887 baseball players. By 1969,
the figure was reported at 222,738, with an estimated 493,000 in
organized baseball in 1977.[84] Baseball is also played informally, of
course, for which there are no statistics. Approximately 5 percent of
the population, or 9–10 percent of all men, played organized baseball at some stage in their lives.[85]

Other popular sports limited to men were wrestling, weightlifting, and boxing. Nonwhite Cubans feature strongly among Cuba's top boxers and baseball players, both sports in which they have a long tradition of participation. Certainly the practice of some exclusionary sports came with the decision to compete internationally. In addition, the continuation of traditional "men only" sports provided a sense of cultural continuity in a process involving rapid and disruptive change in most areas of Cuban life.

The problems in attempting to change deeply ingrained attitudes were especially apparent in women's participation in competitive sports. While women were well represented in exercise programs, especially in basic gymnastics, they were less active in organized competitive sports. Even by 1980, of 2,622,169 participants in organized sports, only 17 percent were women. They were conspicuously absent from sixteen sports. Women were most strongly represented in activities such as horseshoe throwing, gymnastics, fencing, volleyball, table tennis, and athletics. Cuban coaches and officials frequently called for increased women's participation in competitive sports.[86]

This slower growth rate in the number of women in competitive sports is reflected in Cuba's national teams. While this was partly because many international sports are for men only, there are still problems that limit women's participation in Cuban sports. At the Moscow Olympics in 1980, only 36 women were included in Cuba's delegation of 237 athletes. At the Central American and Pan-American Games, women have been present in greater numbers. At the 1962 Central American and Caribbean Games, there were 32 women, and there were 15 at the Pan-American Games the following year. By 1982, the number of women increased to 127 in the Caribbean Games, and to 100 at the 1983 Pan-American Games. In the 1964 Olympics, two women represented Cuba. By 1976, there were 26 on the national teams.[87]

While only 5,444 women participated in sports in 1963, by 1976 there were approximately a million women involved in organized sports. Of these, however, only 200,000 (a fifth) participated outside the school system. Despite the liberation that came with the revolution, Cuban women, like those in other societies, found limited time for sports, after working, caring for husbands and children, doing housework, and waiting in lines for rationed goods.[88] The lower level of male participation outside of the school system also reflected that the desire to practice sports is weakened outside the compulsory PE structure in the school system. The higher num bers of women in physical culture programs might mean that these activities are more attractive to women than organized competitive sports. This, however, also might reflect traditional values about the activities suited to and suitable for each gender.

Non-Hispanic Participation

There is no official information on the participation of non-Hispanic Cubans in physical culture and sports. It is possible, however, to draw reasonable conclusions from other information. Bans on the entry of non-Hispanics to beaches and clubs were removed very early in the revolutionary process. Schools and other educational institutions were also opened to all, thus providing young African Cubans and mulattoes with the opportunity to practice sports within the school system. Cuba's national teams were no longer dominated by Caucasians as had been the case before 1959. In baseball and boxing, non-Hispanic (males) continued to be well represented. The smaller numbers of non-Hispanics in some sports, such as water polo and swimming (an obvious trend in the United States and Australia as well), might reflect their relatively recent exposure to these previously exclusive sports.

Racist attitudes persisted among some individuals and non-Hispanics remained poorly represented at the top levels of power, but there are a number of non-Hispanic Cubans involved in sports administration. Many vice-presidents in INDER are non-Hispanics, particularly in sports such as boxing and baseball. This trend probably reflects several factors. First, there was a long tradition of nonwhite participation in some sports before 1959. This not only increased the likelihood that nonwhites with skills in these sports would enter administration, but also might signify that white Cubans accept the participation of African Cubans and mulattoes more in these sports. It may be that, as before 1959, young African Cubans and mulattoes view sport as an avenue for social advancement (again, not unlike the situation in the United States and Australia), especially as talented athletes receive not just material benefits, prestige, and the opportunity to travel (as they may have done prior to 1959), but also access to education.

Problems in Popular Sport

Despite the Cubans' admirable successes in popular sport, certain problems remain. Participation in sports in Cuba is no longer formally limited by race, class, gender, or race; however, there are problems in the participation of women, older Cubans, and to a lesser extent non-Hispanic Cubans. Such problems are due to lingering attitudes rather than formal sanctions. Hence, while the under-representation of women and non-Hispanics in positions of power demonstrates an extension of attitudes to state structures, this is less of a problem in the upper echelons of sports administration, especially as regards nonwhites. Men, however, are predominant among sports officials, especially among sports journalists. Only one woman, Irene Forbes, is a long-term and regular sports writer.[89]

Some students do not have proper PE classes. Problems with the maintenance and the underuse of facilities placed limitations on both the quality and quantity of physical culture participation. Further, some trainers in schools and public centers pay more attention to locating champions and winning medals than to expanding participation.[90]

Officials claim that this situation does not reflect the development of Cuba's sports system and physical culture. This champion-oriented interest is characterized as a recent phenomenon; but it may have existed earlier, given the political benefits of winning both national and international sports medals. In 1978, the Director of Aquatic Sports emphasized that there were many medals to be won in these sports (such as swimming and rowing), even though they were expensive and required special diets, which made the creation of a mass base impossible. "It must be shown that swimming and rowing offer many respectable medals."[91]

Another concern has been the superior sports situation in urban areas over rural areas. In the cities, sport is more organized and receives more staff, more attention, more facilities, and more equipment. Of the thirty-two social sports available in 1986, only some were available at competition level in all provinces.[92] However, since most Cubans live in urban centers, this differentiation must not be overrated as a problem.

Also indicative of problems was the drop in participation in several activities in the late 1970s and early 1980s, when there was a fall in the number of sports councils, sports activists, and sports school students, as in the production of sports equipment too. This was partly due to the provincial boundary changes and to the alterations in school PE courses.[93]

From 1984 through 1988, the Cubans recognized that there were other problems demanding rectification, and reforms were made in the sports industry. An investigation was launched into the sports schools. A study of the most popular sports aimed to discover which sports were most popular in each region, and which

sports were most suited to mass participation and to high performance. This emphasis may lead to increasing regional specializa-
tions throughout the country. The difficulty in linking the related
yet disparate goals of popular participation and high performance
was recognized in the 1987 review of INDER. Significantly, one response from the National Assembly was an expansion of less formalized recreational activities.[94]

CONCLUSION

Despite the success, the Cuban goal of true mass participation and
universal interest in sports has not been achieved. In 1977, *LPV*
sports magazine ran a contest. The prizes were signed photographs
of Cuba's best athletes. There were only 268 responses, which indicates either a limited readership or (more likely) a limited interest in
entering. One question asked for the name of the first Cuban to win
a gold medal in the Pan-American Games (Rafael Fortún). He was
identified correctly by only 28 entrants, which suggests either a
general lack of sports knowledge or, perhaps, a knowledge limited
to postrevolutionary successes.

Further, statistics show a lower rate of participation than desired. In 1977, approximately 1.5 million individuals (15 percent)
were active in sports. Of these, over half were students. More significant, less than 6 percent of Cubans who were not students were
practicing sports (this was equivalent to or higher than in many developed countries). Also indicative of the lack of regular physical activity was the level of obesity in 1988, although this was also a
dietary problem. Half of all Cubans, and one-fifth of infants, were
classified as overweight. Among adults, 25–30 percent were termed
obese.[95] With bread rationing throughout the island, announced by
the government in May 1991, it is unlikely that the reverse trend of
thinner Cubans would necessarily indicate a fitter, more athletic
population.

The growth of participation in all programs, however, is impressive, especially in comparison with pre–1959 levels and with the
level of participation in other lesser-developed countries. Critics
claim that the mass base was developed solely to produce champions to further the glory of the socialist fatherland. While Cuba does
provide specialized training for top performers (as will be discussed
in more detail in chapter 5), it is unlikely that these champions will
emerge from an FMC basic gymnastics class or a grandparents' círculo para abuelos.

5

Cuba's Success:
Top Performance Sports

A close look at the Cuban system of popular participation in sports makes it clear that quality does indeed spring from the masses. The Cubans have dual goals for their system of sports and physical culture: for sport to become a daily part of the life of every Cuban, young and old; and for international champions to emerge from this wellspring of mass sport. At first, perhaps, these two objectives appear mutually exclusive. Yet as long as the aim of sport for the masses is never abandoned once top-level talent is found, the two are highly compatible, and surely, the Cubans have achieved this compatibility.

The Cubans claim that "the first objective is to promote the development of sports, and the second objective is to seek champions."[1] Yet when one sees the resources, both financial and otherwise, that go into the search for and polishing of these "diamonds," the process of recruitment and training hardly seems to have been accorded second-place status. In the Cuban system, as soon as a child shows a particular talent, he is given every opportunity to develop it. "The more people practicing [sport], the more people from which to choose."[2]

Yet Cuba's status as a world sports power could not be solely attributed to an increase in numbers. A nation could, theoretically, increase popular participation in noncompetitive physical activities and decide either not to take part in or not to seek high standards in international sports while still maintaining competitive sports on a mass scale. However, Cuba chose neither of these options. Instead, success in international competition is highly regarded, although not to the exclusion of popular participation. Medals are viewed as evidence of Cuba's progress, and they bring prestige to this small nation.

A Cuban athlete with talent has access to special training, special facilities, and possibly a sports school, which may not be available to a less talented athlete. A high-performance athlete gains not only prestige, but also the concrete benefits of a more balanced diet, special medical attention, and the resources of specialized sports science.

The decision to develop champions created a potential contradiction between mass participation and the privileged "superathletes." Cuba has had to deal with issues including the use of drugs by top athletes, and the fixing of results.[3] The domestic notoriety gained by some athletes has won them election to the National Assembly and high positions within the Cuban Communist party (PCC).[4] There is, however, no reason for athletes to be excluded from these positions; they may, in fact, have useful knowledge to contribute, not just regarding physical culture but in other areas too, especially as they have the broadening experience of international travel.

THE SPORTS SCHOOLS

Cuba has developed an elaborate system for locating and selecting talented youngsters. By the 1980s, young athletes could enter a special sports school at the early primary level and continue right through to tertiary level, with full access to specialized training and facilities. This attention plays an important part in the improved performances of Cuban athletes in world competition. According to Cuban sports official Raudol Ruíz:

> The advocates of capitalism allege that the socialist countries triumph because they give their athletes intensive training and special living quarters. It is true that in Cuba, for example, a national pre-selection is held in each sport, according to a de-

termined cycle, but no special training can bear fruit if there has not first been wide participation in sports. From the millions of boys and girls who play sports in Cuba come the Juantorenas, the Stevensons, the Rodriguezes.[5]

The sports schools serve the important purpose of intensively training talented young athletes. Yet, at the same time, they are not inconsistent with the other major objective of Cuban sports, mass participation. To the Cubans, they encourage it. According to Fidel:

Now it is important that the selection of students for this type of school be perfected. It must not be as a result of testing in 400 or 500 schools or between 40,000 or 50,000 students in a province. The test must be given in all the schools and to all students in a province. It is not the same thing to make selections from 40,000 students and to make them from 320,000. It is necessary to organize the testing of all students so that we do not lose a single one with ability, so that we do not lose a single champion.[6]

In fact, to the Cubans, the very existence of champions encourages mass participation in sports, by virtue of its inspirational quality. As Castro has said:

These two objectives complement each other because the existence of these schools encourages the practice of sports. At the same time, these schools, with their selection of and the quality of their students, develop champions and we need champions because champions become symbols for the youth and children. Champions represent the extent of the social, educational, and cultural development of our revolution and our people. Champions become a measure of the character, will, and dignity of our people. And champions generate joy, honor, glory, and prestige for the country. We do not deny this. Therefore, this movement can perfectly help us attain both objectives. It is very important that we do not be mistaken, that in the search for champions we do not neglect the practice of sports.[7]

Scholarships for sports schools began with the establishment of the Escuelas de Iniciación Deportíva Escolares (Schools for the initiation of scholastic sports), the EIDEs. By the 1980s, there were no less than nine types of sports schools, as well as a large number of academies specializing in individual sports or in groups of a few related sports. The sports school system started in the pre-EIDEs at lower primary level and existed at all levels up to the tertiary level, at the Institúto Superior de Cultura Física (Institute for physical culture), or ISCF. A student could enter at any level, not necessarily having to pass through all levels. The possible progression of students through this network of sports institutions is shown in figure 1.

Athletes could be chosen for the national selection and the national team at any stage in the sports school system. The idea of providing specialized sports training (and of insisting that athletes obtain an all-round education) began early in the revolutionary process, before Cuba became allies with the Soviet Union. In the first month of the revolution, sports academies were encouraged as a way to provide specialized training for athletes. All athletes in these academies and all those involved in competitions were obliged to attend evening classes to complete at least primary-level schooling.[8]

By the 1963–1964 school year, there were at least 609 students receiving special sports training, as well as undertaking their gen-

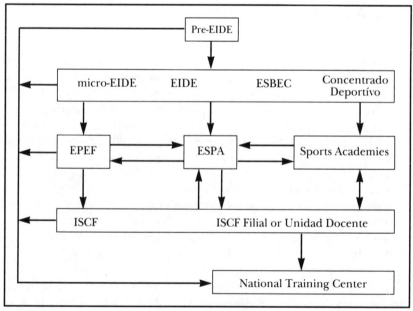

FIGURE 1.   Possible Progression Through Cuban Sports Institutions

eral education. By the following school year, there were 1,049 students in the recently established EIDEs. In 1978, sports school students numbered at least 5,610 and were distributed among eight sports schools.[9] By 1979, there were 9,743 students in Escuelas Provinciales de Educación Física (EPEFs) and in ISCF and its affiliates. By 1986, 2,372 students were enrolled for the bachelor's degree of physical culture at the ISCF. In 1988, students in sports institutions numbered 9,609. By 1986, these institutions included 9 EPEFs, 6 Escuelas Superior de Perfeccionamiento Atlético (ESPAs), 12 EIDEs, about 140 pre-EIDEs, 1 ISCF, 6 ISCF Filiales, 5 ISCF Unidades Docentes, 1 Concentrado Deportívo, 1 Escuela para Gigántes, plus a number of sports-oriented ESBECs, as well as a large number of academies specializing in one sport or several related sports. In 1987, the total number of specialized sports schools and sports areas (excluding EPEF and ISCF) was 1,439, with a total enrollment of 128,246.[10]

In 1984, however, Castro announced that the construction of sports schools was not going to be as high on the list of priorities in the foreseeable future. With so many already in existence, one might wonder if any more were necessary. Castro also indicated concerns about the functioning of sports schools and referred to an investigation being carried out by Alberto Juantorena (vice-president for high-performance sport in INDER) on the state of existing sports schools. Among these concerns were the condition of the facilities and the need to balance academic studies with sports training, perhaps indicative of an overemphasis on sports. Castro, however, indicated no doubt as to the continuing importance of top-level sports.[11] Even if the second half of the 1980s saw a slowing in the construction of sports schools and an emphasis on quality rather than quantity, Cuba already had an elaborate and extensive sports school network, which began in the pre-EIDEs.

Selection Procedures

Young athletes are recommended for a special sports area by a teacher or are chosen on the basis of their competitive results. The third possibility, developed in the late 1970s, is through a test of biotype, which determines stamina, coordination, speed, sports skills, and general health.[12] Via one of these three avenues, a talented youngster can enter a special sports area or even a sports school. A child's parents can also apply for a place for their child in some of these schools. Presumably, applications are assessed on the basis of sports results, biotype, academic performance, and trials in their sport.

Athletes can also be selected from any of several national games we described in chapter 4. The School Games and the Workers' Games, among others, begin in local-level meets and progress to regional levels, in a system intended to promote allegiance to a region rather than to a center, a school, or a team. These various national games incorporate many of the Cubans who participate in sports. The structure of these meets and the policy of selecting for higher levels the best players from the losing teams (the selección), not just from the best teams, means that greater numbers of Cubans are considered for specialized training. The School Games, in particular, have provided an avenue for many youngsters to gain entry to a specialized center or school. Many of Cuba's top athletes began in the School Games (see tables 18 and 19).

Sports Participation Areas

Once athletes with outstanding talent are selected, they are slated for more intensive training in their particular sport. The first level consists of the sports participation areas. These areas are, perhaps, similar to the playground or park district circuits in the United States, parks with equipment and with coaches or trainers, possibly volunteers, made available to developing athletes.

In 1977, there were 1,624 special areas in operation, with 65,500 students practicing 27 sports. In 1978, the numbers fell to 1,080 areas and 50,166 students. The reason for this reduction is un-

TABLE 18.
Cuban Medal Winners in Central American and Caribbean Games and Pan-American Games Who Competed in the School Games

	Caribbean Games				Pan-Am Games			
	1970	1974	1978	1982	1971	1975	1979	1983
Athletes from School Games	126	166	235	317	108	159	231	269
Percentage of team	40	60	73	68	39	51	75	72
Medals won	125	182	266	353	92	123	230	256
Percentage of medals won by ex-school games athletes	34	57	77	66	43	45	71	82

Source: *Mapa*, 1983, Dirección de Propaganda, INDER.

TABLE 19.
Cuban Medal Winners in Olympic Games Who
Competed in the School Games

| | Olympic Games | | |
	1972	1976	1980
Athletes from School Games	69	90	146
Percentage of team	49	54	7
Medals won	12	15	11
Percentage of medals won by ex School Games athletes	56	63	55

Source: Mapa, 1983, Dirección de Propaganda, INDER.

known, yet the Cubans still set a target of 3,000 areas with 109,476 students for 1980. Whether or not this goal was met when intended is unknown, but in 1985, numbers fell some 29,000 short of the 1980 objective. By 1988, there were 1,439 special centers for sports training, including 128,246 students in special areas.[13]

The decline from 1977 to 1978 could have been because of changing methods of collecting statistics or the closure of some special areas. The failure to reach the 1985 goal for sports areas by 1988 and the failure to reach the 1980 target for student numbers by 1985, however, might indicate economic constraints, a limit to the number of talented youngsters meeting the qualifying standards, or simply an overly ambitious planning official (the latter possibility was evident in target setting for economic and social plans, as well as in sports planning).[14]

Although goals are not always reached on time for special sports areas, there are still large numbers of young athletes using them. The 1987 INDER review, however, complained of the tendency to look only for champions, and of a lack of programs for teaching by categories and sports.[15] Many of the youngsters who, despite these problems, received places in special areas could aspire to attend one of the many sports schools.

Athletic Scholarships

Cuba's sports schools, since the late 1970s, have catered to special students from early primary level through the university level, most of whom are provided with tuition and full room and board. In the 1960s, scholarships for university and technical school students included board and 50 pesos per month for single students or from 90 to 150 pesos for married students or those with dependents. Students were not permitted to have paid employment or other sources of income.[16]

In the 1963–1964 school year, sports scholarships numbered just 609. By 1966, there were 3,736 scholarships granted by the state at a cost of 981.7 thousand pesos (see tables 20 and 21).[17] Thus, each student was allocated an average of 263 pesos per year. These figures almost certainly excluded the cost of board for these students, most of whom received it in full.

DIFFERENT TYPES OF SPORTS SCHOOLS

The Pre-EIDEs

In 1984, there were 140 pre-EIDEs (Schools Before the Initiation of Scholastic Sports), with 22,000 students. The goal was to build a pre-EIDE in each of the 169 municipalities. In the 1987 INDER report, however, there were criticisms of the failure to fulfill plans and of the poor growth in the number of pre-EIDEs.[18]

The first pre-EIDEs were established in the 1976–1977 school year. Students generally attended pre-EIDEs from the ages of eight through twelve. The pre-EIDE Camilo Cienfuegos in Havana takes students as young as six years old. Enrollment ranged from 100 to as many as 800 in each school. Pre-EIDE Rubén Bravo in

TABLE 20.
Sports Scholarships and Total Number of Scholarships Granted in Cuba: 1962–1963 to 1967–1968

	Number of Scholarships	
Year	*For athletics*	*For all of Cuba*
1962–1963	none	75,023
1963–1964	609	88,567
1964–1965	1,049	86,247
1965–1966	2,061	110,990
1966–1967	3,736	136,352
1967–1968	est. 6,347	est. 143,101

Source: Roberts and Hamour, *Cuba,* p. 107.

TABLE 21.
Value of Scholarships Granted in Cuba
and for Sports Schools (in thousands
of pesos)

Year	Value of Scholarships	
	Sports Schools	All Scholarships
1961	no scholarships granted	
1962	no information available	
1963	no scholarships granted	
1964	no scholarships granted	
1965	588.2	213,822.6
1966	981.7	225,060.8

Source: Roberts and Hamour, p. 91.
Note: There were no sports schools before 1965.

Marianao (Ciudad Habana) began in 1978–1979 with 727 students
and 37 teachers, offering 12 sports. The pre-EIDE in Camaguey
had 16 sports and a student-teacher ratio of 10–25 students to one
teacher. By 1987, there were 31,267 pre-EIDE athletes.[19] Graduates
could then pursue their sports specialization in an EIDE or at a
sports ESBEC.

Escuelas de Iniciación Deportíva Escolares, or EIDEs

The next level of intensive training for those showing talent are the
EIDEs, directly modeled after the sports schools of East Germany
and the former Soviet Union. The EIDEs combine a specialization
in sports with the regular academic curriculum. Students attend on
a daily or boarding basis, from the third or fourth grade of elementary school through the last year of preuniversity or high school.[20]

The first EIDE was founded in 1964, with an initial enrollment
of 1,049. By 1984, there were eleven of these schools and 13,000
students. Two years later, another EIDE had been added. By 1987,
there were still eleven EIDEs in existence (one had been destroyed
by a cyclone), with 11,742 students. Cuba, then, was well on its way
toward its goal of having at least one EIDE in each of the fourteen
provinces.[21]

The EIDEs have clearly evolved with time. Baseball player Rodolfo Puente Zamora spoke of his student life in the early 1960s,
"converging with athletic practice in the EIDE in Arroyo Naranjo,

Ciro Frías." Puente's account paints a picture of this particular EIDE at this particular time as, perhaps, a school he attended after finishing his regular day at a regular school. Curiously, a report made by the Cuban Ministry of Education in 1967 to the UNESCO Conference on Public Instruction does not include any schools that are identified as EIDEs or sports schools.[22] It is possible that they were simply not listed separately.

In any case, the EIDEs of the early 1960s were far less elaborate and much smaller than those that exist today. In November 1976, the EIDE in Holguín was opened with much fanfare, touted as the "first in the country for its characteristics" (see table 22 for the number of students attending the EIDE in Holguín in 1976):

> Independently of receiving their general preparation and of accomplishing their sports training in order to achieve a better performance, the students successfully combine the principles of communist education by mixing cultural activities, recreational activities, productive work, and formal education as the right way to instill in our youth and children the communist morality. . . .
>
> We will not hold back efforts so that each day our students will be better students, outstanding athletes, and exemplary revolutionaries.[23]

The Capitán Manuel Orestes School in Santiago de Cuba is similar to the one in Holguín. Over 1,500 students are taught by a staff of 69 teachers for academic subjects and 139 coaches and other sports specialists. The various facilities of the school include a massive gymnasium, three swimming pools (including one of Olympic size), a diving tank, two baseball diamonds, track and field facilities, a handball court, and four tennis courts, and there is a velodrome planned for the future.[24]

Over two thousand students enjoy similar facilities at the Mártires de Barbados in Havana Province:

> The school, built with the Girón system of prefabricated sections, consists of two blocks of classrooms; a building housing the kitchen and dining room; four blocks of dormitories; and a great number of sports facilities, among them two Olympic-size pools; one training pool; one diving tank; and a large gym for basketball, fencing, gymnastics, table tennis, judo, box-

TABLE 22.
Numbers of Students Practicing Different Sports in
the EIDE in Holguín, Levels, and Professors in 1976

Sport	Females	Males	Total
Chess	13	29	42
Track and Field	65	48	113
Basketball	66	54	120
Soccer	—	—	—
Boxing	—	—	—
Baseball	—	87	87
Cycling	—	42	42
Diving	24	10	34
Fencing	27	25	52
Gymnastics	21	31	52
Modern Gymnastics	44	—	44
Judo	—	25	25
Wrestling	—	66	66
Swimming	26	34	60
Water Polo	—	41	41
Weightlifting	—	60	60
Tennis	16	33	49
Sport Shooting	15	24	39
Table Tennis	21	33	54
Volleyball	46	46	92
Levels			
Primary	539		
Secondary	618		
Preuniversity	15		
Professors			
Graduates of ESEF, EPEF	42		
Total	73		

Source: Lissette Ricardo Torres, "EIDE: Dónde se gesta el futuro de
deporte cubano," ¡Ahora!, Holguín City (12 November 1976), p. 4.
Note: Facilities being developed to include synchronized swimming,
rowing, kayak, and handball.

ing, and wrestling. There are also baseball and soccer fields;
track and field areas; and outdoor basketball, volleyball, and
tennis courts.[25]

The number of staff at this school is impressive: 169 coaches and
trainers, and 70 academic teachers. Although students do get a taste
of general physical education, the basic formula is "one child, one
sport, year round."[26]

The Cubans claim to know the one sport in which the child excels by the time he is nine years old. Joel Despaigne, star of the Cuban men's volleyball team at the 1991 Pan-American Games and the 1992 Barcelona Olympics, entered an EIDE in Santiago when he was twelve years old. Two years later, he was moved to Havana to play on the junior national team and was already attracting international attention.[27]

A student can be selected for an EIDE from a special sports area, from the School Games, or from a pre-EIDE. But students in EIDEs are not allowed to be more than one year behind in school; the previous year of studies must be successfully completed. (There is no information on how "flexible" these rules are.) In addition, medical certification of age and health must be presented.[28] Involvement in a mass organization (almost all Cubans belong to a mass organization), as a voluntary sports activist, or as a sports monitor in a regular school, works in favor of a student who is applying for entry into an EIDE.

In addition to outstanding talent and promising biotypes, students may also be chosen because they have unusually advantageous characteristics for a particular sport, such as height for basketball. This is similar in logic to the recruitment, direct from Africa, of 7'7" Manute Bol to play basketball in the United States, when he had no background in the sport. The attempt is made to decide on a child's potential in a particular sport, in order to begin intensive training as early as possible.

However, the Cubans are not so rigid as to ignore a good reason to change from one sport to another, if developing talent justifies it. Boxer Teófilo Stevenson used to play baseball; middle-distance runner Alberto Juantorena was originally slated for basketball.[29] When it became clear how fast Juantorena could run in bulky basketball shoes, his prescient coaches began to speculate on what he could do on a track with the proper training and equipment.

Once accepted, students must pass each year of regular schoolwork in order to hold their place. Students are expected to combine sports training, academic studies, and sometimes productive work. Theoretically, at least, failure in any of these areas could cost the student his place in a sports school. However, there is no information on whether any outstanding athletes have been expelled for failing to meet these other requirements. Three hours of the school day and after-hours training are devoted to sports, with the remainder of the school day left for academic studies.[30]

From fifteen to twenty-five sports are practiced in the EIDEs, all Olympic sports, including baseball. The EIDE Mártires de Barbados in Havana has twenty-five sports, and Pedro Díaz Coello in Holguín has eighteen. These schools boast some of the best coaching and athletic facilities in the country. In 1978, the EIDE in Santiago de Cuba had 139 sports teachers for 1,500 students, as well as three pools, two baseball diamonds, an athletics track, a handball court, four tennis courts, a large gymnasium, and a cycling track was planned. The approximately one thousand students attending the EIDE in Matanzas in 1978 had access to a gymnasium, two baseball fields, tennis courts, volleyball and basketball courts, an athletics track, a cycling track, a shooting range, and three pools.[31] A similar list of facilities is available in other EIDEs.

Apparently, it is not enough. In 1984 and 1988, there was criticism of the poor maintenance and the underutilization of EIDE facilities. This in part might have motivated the 1984 investigation conducted by Alberto Juantorena and other sports officials. By 1988 there were complaints that the potential of EIDE students was growing more slowly than expected, given the level of development in Cuban sport.[32]

In some cases, the Cubans have found it necessary to emphasize a particular sport, usually the ones that have been traditionally weak on the island. Cuba has developed one of the best water-polo teams in the world, yet swimming remains its weakest sport. There is an EIDE on the Isla de la Juventud (Isle of Youth, formerly the Isle of Pines), where the emphasis is on the water sports: swimming, diving, canoeing, sailing, and water polo.[33] In 1977, Castro spoke of strength in some events and weakness in others. "We do not go anywhere with the discus. We do not go anywhere with the javelin. It is a good thing that we do not have to live off hunting like primitive man because we would certainly starve to death."[34] The strategy worked. In the 1980 Olympics, Cuban María Caridad Colón (who attended an EIDE) placed first in the javelin, the first Latin American woman ever to win Olympic gold; Luís Delís placed third in the discus.[35]

Despite the perquisites of life in the EIDEs—individual attention from talented coaches, access to high-quality facilities, and more and better food than is rationed for the general population (and this is more true in the 1990s than ever)—entrance to one of these schools does not spell a life of leisure. Standards for these modern EIDEs are well defined. Students' progress is recorded meticulously, and they are continually evaluated not only for their athletic performance but also for the academic level they maintain and their degree of political commitment. Castro cautioned the athletes:

> You are not going to be professional athletes; you are not going to make a living at sports. . . . You will make it from your *work.* You will be able to go as far as you wish in sports, but you will also be able to go as far as you wish as citizens and as professionals and technicians.[36]

The outcome is a system very unlike the athletic scholarships given in the United States.[37] Three young basketball players (two were former EIDE students, all three were current ESPA students) emphasized how important it was that they keep up in their academic studies. All three made cutting motions under their chins to show what would happen if they did not obtain the required grades.[38] Castro described the system during his dedication at the school Mártires de Barbados:

> Of course, it is known that students come to these schools based on their merits, capability, and aptitude. However, a point where we can never fail, and we cannot condone failure in this area even to the champion of champions, is the fulfillment of obligations as students. We cannot permit that an athlete be a poor student. Before violating this principle we would prefer to lose a champion. Therefore, as a golden rule, an athlete must be a good student and must pass his course. Secondly, an athlete must develop his sports and physical capabilities to the maximum. He must not neglect this. The third rule: selection must be continuous in these schools. The fact that someone has entered in a specific grade . . . does not mean that he has to remain in the school until he finishes. There must be a renewal of students because if . . . better prospects emerge, those who have been in the school and have not shown the same abilities must yield their place to the new ones. . . . Renewal of students is a principle that must be applied. There must never be a place occupied here when there is a student with better capabilities unable to join the school.[39]

After seeing the talent that was beginning to amass in these schools, in 1979 INDER officials found it necessary to change the system of competition for the School Games. Prior to that time, all schools competed among themselves, including the EIDEs with the non-EIDE schools. As the talent became concentrated in the EIDEs, the non-EIDEs were invariably eliminated by the special sports schools. After 1979, the system was changed into two parallel structures, in which the regular schools compete among themselves and the EIDEs compete among themselves. With this change, the EIDEs and the regular schools never meet in competition.[40] This gives more incentive to the students in the non-EIDE schools and, in turn, gives the talent scouts more new talent to observe (especially given the system of selección that we discussed in chapter 4).

Escuelas Secundarias Básicas en el Campo, or ESBECs

The EIDEs were the first of Cuba's sports schools and had some of the best facilities available. They were, however, in or near cities, usually provincial capitals. Although students who were not local were provided with their board, the decision to establish Escuelas Secundarias Básicas en el Campo or ESBECs (Basic secondary schools in the countryside) might have been motivated by a desire to offer specialized sports training to more students in rural or sparsely populated areas. These sports schools in rural areas were established so that students could also take part in agricultural labor, thereby receiving a more comprehensive education and developing a respect for manual as well as mental labor. A sports center, the Concentrado Deportívo, was even established to meet the needs of students on the Isle of Youth.

The ESBECs with sports emphasis operate parallel with the EIDEs. Students range in age from twelve to fifteen years old. In each ESBEC, there are usually about 500 students, although there were 1,082 students in 1979 in Las Tunas. In ESBECs, as in other sports schools, the physical condition and biotype of students is assessed, and only selected students are accepted.[41] Like the mostly urban-based pre-EIDEs, the ESBECs are intended to provide facilities at a local level, but in rural, not urban areas.

One ESBEC in Santiago de Cuba was made into a micro-EIDE. This school took from seventh- to ninth-grade students and gave preference to those from rural areas.[42] Why this change was made, or whether other ESBECs were or will be converted to micro-EIDEs is unknown.

Another school similar to the EIDEs, the micro-EIDEs, and the ESBECs, was the *concentrado deportívo* on the Isle of Youth. Originally an ESBEC, this school became the Mijail Frunze Concentrado

Deportívo. In 1977, there were 396 students aged from twelve to fifteen. Their days were long—fourteen hours of classes and work, including agricultural labor. There were forty-four teachers, twenty-four sports trainers, and fifteen apprentice sports trainers. Sixteen sports were practiced. There are at least twenty-eight specialized schools on the Isle of Youth, many with sports facilities especially for rowing, kayaking, canoeing, and water sports.[43]

Graduates from Mijail Frunze as well as the micro-EIDEs, EIDEs, and ESBECs could then attend one of several higher-level sports schools.

Escuela Superior de Perfeccionamiento Atlético, or ESPA

The Escuela Superior de Perfeccionamiento Atlético (Higher school of athletic perfection), or ESPA, was established in the early 1960s in Havana.[44] It underwent a major reconstruction for use in the World Youth Festival that was held in Cuba in 1978. According to Hector Rodríguez Cordoso, who defected to the United States, ESPA is based in the old Cubanacán Country Club and provides athletes with special treatment such as extra food, clothing, and high-quality housing.[45]

In a sense, the EIDEs and the other sports schools serve as a sort of "farm system" for this next level of training. From ESPA come all the teams that represent Cuba in international competition. It is the culmination of the movement from mass participation toward expertise in a sport. This scientific process of development or training cycle never takes less than six years or more than ten. And, as at all levels of development, there are more athletes than necessary chosen for this elite school. This prevents an attitude of complacency. A student is never allowed to take for granted a team position that he may hold at one time. He must continue to work for it.[46]

Three students from ESPA (en route to a basketball tournament in Poland) described a typical day. After breakfast (of better food than that served in the regular schools), they studied academic subjects from 8:00 A.M. until 1:00 P.M. The afternoon and early evening were reserved for practice and training in each individual sport.[47]

In 1975, 126 students graduated from ESPA, including the sprinter Silvio Leonard. The content of the courses and the training provided have not been released. In 1985, a law was passed requiring trainers at ESPA and the National Training Center Cerro Pelado to hold a bachelor's degree in physical culture. Later that year, more legislation required trainers at ESPA to be high-level graduates from a special sports area.[48]

By 1979, the first of several provincial ESPAs was established in Pinar del Rio. There were 62 teachers and 40 sports trainers who taught 389 students specializing in a choice of 19 sports. In the 1980s, four more provincial ESPAs were opened to cater to more top athletes. Yet, the ESPAs, like the EIDEs, were criticized for failing to develop their full potential.[49]

THE TRAINING OF SPORTS PERSONNEL

Institúto Superior de Cultura Física, or ISCF

With a countrywide emphasis upon sports participation for the masses, it is essential that INDER have enough qualified instructors, trainers, and other personnel to meet the need. In 1959, the new revolutionary government had faced a dearth of physical education teachers, and in 1963, Manuel Fajardo was created to fill this need. At first, this school for training PE teachers was designed to train as many people as quickly as possible, and the first class numbered seven hundred students.[50]

By 1970, Cuba had begun to construct similar institutions in the provinces. With the growth of these, Manuel Fajardo was upgraded to the Escuela Superior de Educación Física Comandante Manuel Fajardo (Higher school for physical education), or ESEF. Between 1963 and 1973, there were sixteen hundred graduates from ESEF. After the initial short courses, regular courses of three and a half years' duration were organized and included studies in the theory and practice of sports and recreation. Entry requirements in 1966 included completion of basic secondary school, proof of age (between fifteen and twenty-five), and a health certificate, as well as evidence of having been a sports monitor in a regular school. Further prerequisites included, of course, proof of athletic experience and ability and evidence of participation in a revolutionary organization, such as a CDR.[51]

In 1973, the ESEF was upgraded to university level and changed its name to the Institúto Superior de Cultura Física, or ISCF. Within the next two years it began to offer correspondence courses (1975) and evening classes (1974). In 1977, ISCF affiliates were opened in six provinces to provide similar studies outside Havana. In 1982, there were seven Filiales. In the 1980s, postgraduate courses were also offered. The course at ISCF was extended to five years in 1982 and, by 1985, 4,452 students had graduated from the tertiary level.[52]

Entry to ISCF is apparently not easy. Students need a 90 percent grade average and superior athletic ability. The domination of the ISCF team in national tertiary-level competitions suggests that the conditions on athletic ability are strictly enforced.[53] ISCF graduates are also well placed to gain the best employment positions in physical culture. Presumably, trainers in ESPAs and in the National Training Center Cerro Pelado (who are required to have physical culture degrees) are ISCF graduates. It is likely that, increasingly, INDER officials will be ISCF graduates.

Most new ISCF students have already spent four years in an EPEF, and therefore receive as many as nine years of specialized training in either sports, physical education, or recreation, and a sound general training in all three. Students also receive a tertiary education in general studies. In 1986, the ISCF included a Faculty for Workers (practicing teachers and trainers). Other facilities were the Armed Forces (FAR) Faculty; the Faculty of Postgraduate Studies; and the Faculty for High-Performance Athletes, which offered a special seven-year course for top athletes.[54]

All students must take academic and physical culture courses (or cycles) as well as basic military training, and they have to present an investigative thesis. Students can specialize as a sports trainer (438 hours of classes) or in recreation and physical education (300 hours of classes and practical teaching in the countryside). The details of the 4,638-hour course for 1986–1987 included over two thousand hours of physical culture courses. The ISCF, like other sports institutions, has many sports facilities as well as access to those in the nearby Ciudad Deportíva.[55]

ISCF produces highly trained physical culture specialists. It also provides vocational training for many of Cuba's top athletes, who may have already attended a sports school or other specialized training center for their particular sport.

National Training Centers

Cuba also established numerous sports academies to provide training for talented athletes. Before 1959, such academies had existed only for boxing and baseball, but similar academies for soccer, jai alai, swimming, volleyball, athletics, judo, basketball, fencing, wrestling, waterskiing, and kayaking were soon founded in 1959. By the end of 1959, there were 2,035 students in these various institutions. The number of academies grew throughout the island, and by the mid–1970s, each province had its own baseball academy. By 1987, there were 11,858 students in eleven provincial academies; 1,202 students in three juvenile national centers; and 885 students in four national centers.[56]

The end of the 1970s saw the emergence of national schools for other sports as well, such as fencing, equestrian sports, aquatic sports, gymnastics, and sprinting. Other special centers were established also, such as the "School for Giants" and the CEDA Manuel Permuy center (Experimental school for athletic development), in the city of Havana. The School for Giants began in April 1979 and had 123 students aged between 11 and 18; it offered training for very tall youngsters. The CEDA Manuel Permuy, in La Lisa Municipality, had 508 students aged between 11 and 13 in 1978, one year after it opened. This center assessed the physical qualities of its students and analyzed diet, metabolism, and related functions. The course involved 850 hours of classes, taught by 12 teachers, including 100 hours of physical activities in a program that also included work, social work, and military training.[57] These two centers are indicative of Cuba's growing emphasis on scientific approaches toward the detection of sports ability.

Besides sports schools and academies, some of Cuba's vocational schools have excellent sports facilities. Included among these was the Máximo Gómez Vocational School, with two gymnasia, an athletic track, and a baseball field, as well as basketball and volleyball courts. High priority was also placed on providing swimming pools in vocational schools. The most famous vocational school in Cuba, however, had perhaps the best sports facilities outside of the specialized sports schools. The Lenin School, established at the suggestion of Fidel Castro, is in an area of 300,000 square meters near the Lenin Park in Havana and had about 4,500 students in 1974. Facilities include saunas, two Olympic pools, a diving tank, ten basketball courts, ten volleyball courts, three baseball diamonds, two tennis courts, a fencing center, and a gymnastics hall.[58] The Lenin School is also mysteriously absent from public tours of Cuba's other showcase facilities, such as the Havana Psychiatric Hospital and Ciudad Deportíva.

In addition to these centers and sports institutions, special training and medical supervision is also available through the sports unit of the Revolutionary Armed Forces.[59]

EPEFs

At all levels, the Cubans take the training of a PE teacher very seriously. According to Cuban journalist María Elena Gil:

> It is not the only objective of the EPEFs to create teachers who impart sports knowledge to their students. The professor of physical education that INDER proposes to forge, in conjunction with MINED, should be one who forms the youth of tomorrow, a complete guide who knows to include in his method of teaching the practice of sport, the assimilation of the habits of discipline, of conscience, will and perseverance that ought to unite all athletes and all revolutionary youth in general.[60]

Today, ISCF trains the PE professors at the highest levels, while the EPEFs concentrate on producing middle-level technicians.[61] Graduates from ISCF, all of whom have mastered the three areas of sports, physical education, and recreation, number over a thousand per year.

Those EPEFs located in the provinces are called Escuelas Provincial de Educación Física or EPEFs. By 1983, there were eight EPEFs. In the 1977–1978 course, there were 6,664 students in the EPEFs, including 2,051 undertaking practical teaching experience. The students usually ranged in age from 13 to 18 years, but older, practicing PE teachers could also study at EPEF, while also receiving their full salary.[62]

ESBEC graduates were given preference in these teacher-training schools, presumably with the intention that they would return to their rural districts to teach after graduating. In 1975, entrance to primary-level teacher-training courses was opened to males who were from 13 to 14 years old and to females who were from 13 to 16 years old. Students must have completed the seventh grade, without any failures. For secondary school teacher training, students must be between 13 and 14 for males and between 13 and 18 for females. They are required to have completed ninth grade, without any failures. In 1979, prospective students also needed to have passed LPV tests and be good at sports. By 1981, students also needed to pass a medical test and a personal interview, in addition to obtaining a 160 point grade average (presumably out of a maximum 200) in seventh and eighth grades. The usual maximum age was also lowered to 16, although 17-year-olds from rural areas were still considered.[63]

The four- or five-year course at EPEF includes practical teaching experience for half of each academic year from the second year onwards. This experience is typically undertaken in an isolated school, thus providing PE teachers (albeit inexperienced) in regions where they might not choose to work permanently. Courses at the EPEFs include general academic subjects and pedagogy, as well as training in sports, popular physical culture, or recreation. The EPEF in Holguín, for example, teaches topics such as Spanish, English, mathematics, physics, chemistry, history of physical education, Marxism, morphology, physiology, psychology, theory and methods, pedagogy, and sports medicine, in addition to practical classes in at least seventeen different sports. Upon graduating from such a program, students are full-fledged PE teachers, prepared to enter, if desired, studies at ISCF. Beginning in 1980–1981, EPEF graduates emerged with a specialization in two sports. In addition, work toward the diploma includes a work notebook, in which the student records his completion of up to ten different projects, six of which are obligatory. Students must also complete an investigative work, addressing solutions to some fundamental problems that Cuba faces in physical education and sports.[64]

Even though students training to be PE teachers do not have to be world-class athletes, they are organized to continuously hone their own skills. Inter-EPEF games, held nationally, also underscore the emphasis on competition:

> The end result of this meeting is that the future professors can practically apply, for themselves, the theoretical-tactical knowledge that was given to them in the halls of [EPEF]. One cannot conceive, for example, of a swimming trainer who is not an acceptable swimmer. . . . Further, they constitute a valuable stimulus for the students to practice sport daily.[65]

EPEFs also served as centers for the provincial sports medicine institutes and for Unidades Docentes or Filiales of the ISCF. These provincial centers offered some of the services available in the main institutions in Havana.

In terms of facilities, ISCF (ESEF), EPEFs and ESPA have the most advanced facilities and equipment, which are usually not available for public use. In Santiago de Cuba, the EPEF (with a 1,000–1,500 student capacity) has a twenty-five-meter pool, diving tank, water-polo pool, plus the use of the INDER-Santiago facilities, located adjacent to the school in the Guillermón Moncada Stadium. This includes one of the two tracks on the entire island with a Rekortán surface, imported from East Germany.[66]

International Exchange

The ISCF and the EPEFs now train PE instructors at the university and postgraduate level. But this is a relatively recent development. Prior to 1972, these facilities served to provide the country with as many middle-level technicians as possible, just to ameliorate the tremendous lack of qualified teachers that existed in the cities and throughout the countryside.

According to Juan Kindelán, an official with INDER-Santiago, when he was in school it was necessary to go abroad. He obtained his master's degree in East Germany. This problem is slowly being addressed. (With the closing of opportunities to study in Eastern Europe and the Soviet Union, due to the massive changes in these nations, the necessity to develop an independent training capacity within Cuba has become paramount.) By August 1980, there were twenty-three doctoral candidates enrolled at ISCF. By 1990, there were fifty doctoral students.[67]

If instructors for the primary levels did not exist, then there would be no specialists in particular sports capable of training the best athletes. And the Cubans were unwilling to wait the twenty years required to develop their own expertise in the various athletic fields. Help came in the form of coaches and trainers from other countries, especially from the Soviet Union and Eastern Europe. "There are many cases of proletarian internationalism in sport."[68]

According to Jorge García Bango, former director of INDER, "We pay whatever is necessary to bring them," to arrange for foreign coaches. The Soviet Union, East Germany, Czechoslovakia, and Hungary have all provided Cuba with the greatest technical assistance. Andrei Chervonenko of the Soviet Union has trained, in the past, Teófilo Stevenson, Orlando Martínez, and other Cuban boxers. The Hungarian Karoly Laky worked with the Cuban waterpolo team, which is now one of the best in the world. Alberto Juantorena received the able coaching of the late Zigmunt Zabierzowski, who returned to Poland after seeing his charge through two gold medals in Montreal. In 1967, Soviet gymnastics coach Zinaida Podolskaya went to Cuba to help with the women's gymnastics movement there. She was soon followed by Diana Sivokava and Maria Vinogradova (Zaitseva). Evgenii Vov and Alberto Aznavurian also worked on the gymnastics program. Leonid Shcherbakov, Soviet Olympic triple jumper, coached Pedro Pérez Dueñas and other Cubans until 1976. Evgenii Cheroposki worked with Eduardo John on the fencing foil. Nikolai Durnev went with the Cuban marksmen to the twentieth Olympics in Munich. Leonid Gusevski also worked with the marksmen. Yuri Zamiatin helped develop wrestling, and Stephen Boutatas coached the basketball team that won third place in Munich. Other names include Valentin Samkhvolov, for track and field; Vasilii Romanov, for boxing; Evgenii Boechin, for cycling; Yuri Melnikov, for diving; Chitov Viatcheslav, for physical culture; Oleg Pozanov and Igor Isakov, for fencing; Evgenii Matseev, Vladimir Medvediev, and Vasilii Muraviov in ISCF; Anotolii Nikonov and Oleg Stokin, for gymnastics; Evgenii Rysin, for weightlifting; Yuri Ribalko, for wrestling; Yuri Stoida, Elena Matveva, and Nina Borozina on language translation. Florian Stoenescu of Romania worked with the handball team. In 1976, Yutsaka Matsudaira, coach of the Japanese volleyball team, gave a course at INDER for Cuban volleyball coaches and trainers.[69] (Table 23 shows the foreign technical assistance Cuba received in sports from 1961 through 1975.)

Cubans have also been sent abroad, at times, to sharpen their coaching or athletic skills. Gymnastics coaches Juana Bravet Quesis and Verania Pinera both studied in the Soviet Union. Until recently, the only sports official in Cuba with a doctorate in the field, Hernández Corbo, obtained his degree in Bulgaria.[70] Often, the simple contact with other athletes serves as a training experience.

As the Cubans advanced, the network of foreign assistance began to flow in the other direction. In 1972, Cuban sprinter Enrique Figuerola coached Soviet athletes in Odessa and Minsk. Cuban coaches and trainers have been sent to Angola, Panama, Mexico, Jamaica, Guyana, and Chile. They were reportedly imprisoned by the junta after Allende's assassination in Chile in 1973. In 1976, Yugoslavia announced it was going to follow the "Cuban recipe" in training its boxers. In addition, Cuba encourages students from other countries to study at Manuel Fajardo (ISCF) on an exchange program. As of 1978, there were students from a number of other countries in Latin America and at least one student from the United States.[71]

It is more important, perhaps, that Cuban coaches abroad are now earning valuable hard currency, which is pumped back into the state. In the 1970s, there were forty-two foreign coaches in Cuba. In 1992, there was only one for the Olympics, in archery. There are

TABLE 23.
Foreign Technical Assistance by Country of Origin

	Country of Origin										
Year	*USSR*	*Bulg.*	*Pol.*	*Cze.*	*Hun.*	*GDR*	*N.Kor.*	*Rom.*	*PRC*	*Other*	*Total*
1961	—	—	—	2	—	—	—	—	—	—	2
1962	14	1	—	3	—	1	—	—	—	—	20
1963	4	1	1	3	—	1	—	2	—	—	12
1964	13	1	—	1	2	1	—	—	2	—	20
1965	2	1	—	1	—	3	—	—	1	—	8
1966	17	3	1	3	3	5	1	—	—	—	33
1967	18	2	2	2	4	3	1	—	—	—	32
1968	14	4	6	3	8	4	1	—	—	—	40
1969	14	6	6	4	6	3	4	—	—	1	44
1970	22	9	6	6	6	3	6	—	—	2	60
1971	28	9	5	6	8	2	2	—	—	1	61
1972	26	18	4	3	10	2	1	—	—	1	65
1973	17	15	3	3	7	—	1	—	—	—	46
1974	21	14	2	2	7	6	—	—	—	—	52
1975	28	10	1	1	7	7	—	—	—	—	54

Source: Pickering, "Cuba," p. 155.
Note: Many of these visiting coaches and specialists came on contract usually for a three-year period; some renewed those contracts to stay for six. One Cuban who has taken US citizenship and coaches the Los Angeles Dodgers visits Cuba each year to run coaching clinics on baseball.

150 Cuban coaches working throughout the world. Nine countries at Barcelona had Cuban boxing coaches, while others have hired Cubans in volleyball, weightlifting, track and field, and other sports.[72]

Cuba established sports exchange programs with countries outside of Eastern Europe. These included Mexico, Canada, Algeria, Portugal, Nicaragua, Angola, Cape Verde, Jamaica, and Grenada, among others. Cuban sports specialists worked in thirty-three foreign countries, and foreign students were given places in the ISCF and in the EPEFs.[73]

THE SCIENTIFIC SYSTEM

Recruitment and Selection

There has been no attempt to keep the dual goal of the Cuban sports program a secret. Above all, for purposes of mental and physical health, recreation, and general well-being, sports should play a part in the life of every Cuban. The most effective way to instill this desire for physical activity is through the PE program. Castro described how the more talented athletes will emerge from the resulting mass movement in sports:

> One day we shall have thousands of young people studying physical education, excellent sports facilities in all schools, and interschool competitions as a means of selection. However, there is more to it than selection, for sport should be pursued not just to win competitions. Competitions are important; but there is something more important—sport as a cultural and recreational activity for the people. Of course, if everybody practices a sport, if all children pursue a sport, we shall have champions.[74]

In fact, each goal merely serves to feed the other. The more people who participate in sports, the greater the chance for true talent to develop and be discovered. The subsequent success that such talent achieves serves as a strong stimulus to encourage even more people to become actively involved in sports. This point was made clearly by José Ramón Fernández Alvarez, former vice-president of the Council of Ministers, minister of Culture, Sports, and Education, and member of the Politburo until the 1991 congress, when he greeted the Cuban athletes returning from Moscow:

> These successes [in the 1980 Olympics] should be a stimulus for people so that in the future the base of the pyramid is broadened, with each Cuban being able to demonstrate his or her true abilities, and among all the people—among those hundreds of thousands of young people, students and workers from the cities and the countryside—we can choose those with the best qualifications to go to the Olympics.[75]

With a national population smaller than that of New York, London, or Tokyo, Cuba can hardly afford not to consider all possibilities for development, in its search for talent. The Cubans claim to know a child's best sport by the time that child is nine years old. Yet, it is in their best interests to be open-minded about the selection process. The well-organized system of evaluation they have—in both the physical efficiency tests and the different levels of competition—serves as a fine-mesh net, ready to catch any late developers who exhibit their talent later in life, and in some cases, athletes who may have been funneled into the wrong sport.

The recent change in the organization of the School Games to keep the regular schools and the EIDEs separate was certainly a calculated move. More time and attention are thus given to young athletes who are not students at an EIDE. Experience has already taught the Cubans that there is a wealth of talent hidden in these students. Among those who have been "discovered" at the School Games are names such as Urrutia, Duenas, Leonard, Puente, Casanas, Romero, Chivas, Caridad Colón, Delis, and Despaigne. "[The School Games] are considered a furnace from which are forged the future members of the national teams."[76]

The emphasis on competition extends past the educational system. In 1976, 6,000 people participated in the Family Games, which are handicapped according to age. There were almost 600,000 participants in the 1976 Workers' Games, 105,000 of which were women. By the mid–1970s, more than one-quarter of the population engaged in INDER-sponsored competition in more than twenty sports.[77] These contests provide a tremendous source of recreation, both passive and active, for the Cuban people.

Selection and Training

It is instructive to look more closely at the selection process by which national athletes are chosen and the methods by which they are trained. The process by which the more talented athletes are selected out for more intensive training has evolved, with time and experience, into a scientific procedure. All children are evaluated when they are quite young, and at frequent intervals as they grow and develop. In addition, the network of competition, within school and outside of it, helps INDER officials to catch potential talent that they may have missed in the individual evaluations. These officials are trained for several purposes. One group serves as talent scouts out in the field, while the other group works on the more scientific, research side of selection. These research people report to the talent scouts out in the field which scientific measures they should be looking for; if biotype A or biotype B correlates higher with this or that sport, for example; or which type of muscle fiber makes a better sprinter or a better distance athlete, and which athlete has which type. If, after a number of years and frequent evaluations, the athlete still exhibits potential talent, he will be sent to ESPA for training, in order to represent his country in international competition. The older competitors remain students at ESEF while they continue their training.

When asked about his specific training regimen, Alberto Juantorena has said more than once that it is a "state secret." And one begins to believe it, from the amount of information available on the subject. In direct imitation of the former East German and Soviet systems, the Cubans are attempting to give athletic training a scientific base. There is also a strong effort to draw on as many scientific fields that could have any bearing on athletic activity as possible. For each sport, there is a scientific team, headed by a physician who is responsible for the care of the athletes in the sport, for the development of the sport, and presumably for breakthroughs in the selection process. The physician in charge of this group is one of the "technical members" of the "governing body" of the particular sport. Then each national team has a Coaching Committee, described by Ron Pickering:

> Every national coach has direct contact with the Institute [of Sports Medicine] and the Coaching Committees which arrange the annual training program of each athlete or event group. The Coaching Committee consists of the national coach, a sports physician, a sports psychologist and a member of the technical committee of the governing body who knows the dates and venues of all fixtures.[78]

The psychologist spends more time working with the coaches than with the athletes. According to officials at INDER-Santiago, he helps overcome the competition anxiety of both coaches and athletes. In addition, he serves to motivate and inspire, as well as to give relaxing exercises and the like.

The increasingly scientific bent of INDER can be seen in the development of several of its newer departments. Within INDER is the Centro de Investigaciones e Información de Deporte (Center of investigation and information in sport) or CINID. There are two separate departments within CINID: one is the Centro de Computación Estadística y Matemática Aplicada (Center for statistical computation and applied mathematics), or CEMA. The function of the center has been described only very superficially in the Cuban press. CEMA keeps cards on all the athletes who make up the different levels of national teams. Records are kept of their various performances, and projections are made as to their progress in their different events. CEMA also keeps complete records of the performances of all the athletes who participate in the control.[79] A control is a regularly scheduled contest of the upper level athletes, conducted under "meet" conditions. It serves as an evaluative measure for team and individual progress. It can also be useful in the selection of athletes for an international event, based on their performance in the control. This is especially true for sports in which progress is measured by time.

The other section of CINID is the Centro de Documentación e Información Científico-Técnica (Center for documentation and scientific and technical information), or CEDOC. CEDOC is concerned with information of a broader nature. Its purpose is to provide trainers and coaches with up-to-date information about progress in the various sports and, in particular, the achievements recorded by other countries in athletic endeavors and in training methods.[80]

According to Huberto Gil, former head of CINID, CEDOC serves as an invaluable information center. The statistics compiled and stored in CEMA enable sports officials to study the necessary data needed to train athletes more efficiently. By calling up on the computer the information stored on an athlete, a trainer can see the progression in the athlete's performance and training methods in relation to a specific block of time in order to predict the athlete's level of achievement by a certain date. In the case of a runner, for example, a trainer can consider how he should conduct his training for the next four years if he wants to peak for the 1996 Olympics and perform well at the various international contests between now and then. This is already done (albeit at an unknown level of sophistication and with an unknown degree of success) at INDER-Havana.[81]

INDER has decided to expand this program to Santiago de Cuba. The Centro de Informática del Deporte (Sports information center) there supplies the same type of information to the coaches and trainers at the EIDE Capitán Orestes Acosta in Santiago. The plan is that each EIDE in the country will have this capability in the future.[82] But one wonders how far this scientific method can filter down. However, this concerted effort to make the sports program as scientific as possible clearly mimics the system the East Germans have used for years, and with tremendous international success.

Juan Kindelán of INDER-Santiago said that, after all, the Cubans would rather amass champions than statistics. For purposes of evaluating the Cuban system, there is never enough specific information given to assess the methods used, the success rate achieved, or even the level of sophistication reached. A somewhat reliable indicator, at least of the level of sophistication, might be to evaluate the hardware used. In 1975, it was reported that INDER had two computers, a CID-201-A and a CID-201-B. Five years later, only the latter was mentioned in the press.[83] This level of computer is very small, very slow, and very unsophisticated. In 1992, the INDER central office was using a Cuban C300 as well as IBM and IBM-compatible microcomputers, purchased from transnational corporations. Software is made in Cuba. The collapse of socialism in Europe has not had a major negative impact on this aspect of Cuban sports. However, all the INDER computers are now stored in the one room that still has air-conditioning.[84]

A clear and frequently used test measures the maximum oxygen-consumption capacity. Yet this experiment is difficult to conduct without expensive laboratory equipment. The Cubans discovered a close correlation between the rate of oxygen utilization and physical-work capacity. Both are standard measures of physical efficiency as applied to athletes. The pulse rate of 170 beats per minute approaches the maximum physical-work capacity. "Training" involves pushing the pulse rate to a certain level, such as 170, and sustaining it over a period of time. However, to monitor an athlete's pulse at such a high rate over any period of time would also require relatively sophisticated equipment. But the Cubans found a way to circumvent this problem: they found a nearly linear relationship between work rate and pulse rate. This means that they could measure pulse rates for two fixed submaximal work rates, plot the linear relationship between the two points on a graph, and then extrapolate to determine the work rate needed to achieve a pulse of 170 (see figure 2).

For example, a runner's pulse could be taken after he has run a mile in eight minutes. Next, his pulse would be taken after a six-minute mile. After plotting these two points, the line between them could be extended to find at which speed his pulse would reach 170, in this case, perhaps at the four- or five-minute mile. For a nonrunner, a twelve-minute mile and a ten-minute mile might show that an eight-minute mile for this person gives the required 170. Using the step test, the Cubans have devised a chart, for both athletes and nonathletes according to age, showing how many steps per minute are required to produce 170 beats per minute (see table 24).

In the 1980s, four provincial information centers were formed, extending this specialized information service to areas outside Havana. They provided limited services to the majority of Cubans. In

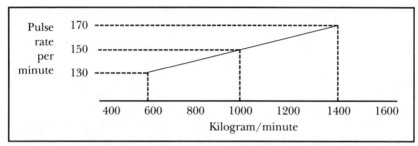

FIGURE 2.   Determination of Physical Work Capacity (PWC) for Optimum Pulse Rate

Source: José A. Yañez, Sergei A. Barantsev, "PWC170: Test para determinar la capacidad de trabajo físico," *LPV*, 647 (12 November 1974), pp. 30–33.

a similar manner, the Sports Medicine Institute was primarily concerned with top athletes, and like sports science, was extended to include provincial centers.[85]

Sports Medicine

One of the most advanced areas of the Cuban sports system is that of sports medicine. Its growth is proof of the scientific bent of present-day Cuban sports and of the revolutionary government's dedication to the sports system.

TABLE 24.
Recommended Workload for Determining the Physical Work Capacity at 170 Pulse Rate (PWC170)

	Age							
	10	*11*	*12*	*13*	*14*	*15*	*16*	*18*
Nonathletes								
First Workload	200	300	350	400	500	550	600	600
Second Workload	360	400	450	550	600	700	750	800
Athletes								
First Workload	350	350	400	450	500	500	600	600
Second Workload	400	450	500	600	800	900	1000	1000

Source: José A. Yañez and Sergei A. Barantsev, "PWC 170: Test para determinar la capacídad de trabajo físico," *LPV* 647, 12 November 1974, pp. 30–33.

René Iglesias y Rodríguez Mena has been a witness to the field both before and after 1959. He graduated from medical school in 1940. In 1944, in his spare time, he began to specialize in sports medicine. This specialization was academically sound but suffered from lack of government support. In those days, specialists were able to offer little more than medical assistance; because there was no budget, they could attend only to boxers and baseball players. Even then, a clinical exam consisted of nothing more than a test to determine whether an athlete was in condition to compete, or to help them when they were sick, and even in these cases, the doctors were dependent on specialists in other areas. Their equipment consisted of a simple X-ray machine and basic laboratory equipment.

In 1962, the Institute of Sports Medicine was established. It began with the international exchange of specialists in different fields: other socialist countries gave technical aid, and many Cubans went abroad for further training. This is the point at which sports medicine ceased to be merely medical assistance and became a scientific and technical area.[86]

The Institute is located in the same complex as INDER and Ciudad Deportíva in Havana. In 1982, it was headed by Dr. Arnaldo Pallares, a former national champion in the javelin, and the staff consisted of at least 142 workers and technicians, 42 physicians, 17 psychologists, 6 dentists, 3 biologists, 17 physiotherapists, 2 dieticians, and 4 statisticians. In 1990, there were 80 sports medicine specialists. The Cubans have found it helpful if most of the staff are themselves athletes. The physicians and the psychologists have had two years of study in their specialty beyond the normal degree. In addition, the Institute includes other departments: Management and Administration, Research, Teaching, Medical Assistance (working in combination with a local hospital and with the Department of Traumatology for surgery and other more complex cases), and Physical Development.[87]

Every athlete of national caliber has a current medical dossier. Twice a year, this folder is updated with a thorough medical exam and a comprehensive program of tests encompassing recordings of agility, coordination, concentration, reaction time, equilibrium, IQ, memory, and motivation, which brings in the psychological state of the athlete. At the research institute, the staff also study the possibilities and the reserves of the athlete through anthropomorphic and neuromuscular studies. They experiment with a controlled diet containing the necessary amount of calories and protein. Dentists advise on possible therapeutic and preventative measures.[88]

Armed with this information, the doctors work as part of the Coaching Committees. The goal is to make world-class athletes by eliminating their deficits, shortcomings, and hangups and by enhancing their natural skills and talents.

The Institute also functions as an instructional facility, teaching courses in conjunction with ESEF.[89] Future plans apparently include Provincial Centers of Sports Medicine connected to the existing and planned EPEFs. There are two other centers besides the main institute in Havana. In Pinar del Río, a Centro Provincial de Medicina Deportíva (Provincial center for sports medicine), or CPOMEDE, was inaugurated in 1977. Initial departments included cardiology, a respiratory and laboratory clinic, as well as nursing and stomatology. In 1977, Dr. Aramis Mazorra headed a staff of three doctors who were specialists in sports medicine, a stomatologist, midlevel technicians, and other qualified personnel.[90]

The major goal of the Center is to improve the quality of sport in the province. The staff aims for "strict control of the sport in terms of the amount of training to apply to each athlete, which requires medical supervision on the fields and in the laboratories." Medical assistance is developed from the general point of view, and from the point of view of injury suffered with the athletes in training and in competition, through a counseling program.[91] Medical counseling is developed from the general point of view, and from the specific point of view of injury suffered by the athletes in training or in competition.

Another provincial center for sports medicine was opened in Matanzas in 1980, with Armando Pancorbo serving as director, and Marcos Acebo and Oscar Ramírez as his assistants. This center included departments of physical development, physiotherapy, cardiovascular study, respiration, nursing, and stomatology. Rowing, baseball, boxing, weightlifting, and kayaking received special attention, although the center attends to all sports. The staff also worked closely with the EPEF to train future physical education instructors.[92]

This emphasis upon highly scientific sports medicine is in direct imitation of the training methods used in East Germany and the Soviet Union, which in the more developed socialist countries have resulted in the marriage of an early and meticulous selection process to an individual training system based on intensive medical and physiological research. Nothing is left to chance. Muscles are monitored to show precisely which ones are to be warmed up prior to training and how this is to be done. Athletes strive for the "perfect style" in their sport, which has been determined through scientific analysis of the body's musculature and its movement through air or water. During training, blood tests are taken to determine the amount of lactic acid buildup that allows a trainer to know the athlete's precise level of exertion. Armed with this information, trainers know exactly how hard an athlete can push before he enters the gray area of overtraining, which leaves him susceptible to injury. This is the technological level to which the Cubans aspire, but the available evidence suggests that this goal has not yet been reached.

Evaluation

Once the Cubans achieve a high level of proficiency in a sport, they will work hard to maintain it. Athletes are evaluated constantly, through means such as the control referred to earlier. No one is ever allowed to think that he or she is irreplaceable, since there is always someone else further down the line being primed for the same position. At the EIDE Mártires de Barbados, according to Thomas Boswell of the *Washington Post,* "each child is also measured, graphed, studied, coached against arbitrary performance standards that he is expected to meet."[93]

These evaluations are not just limited to the area of sports. Athletes are expected to maintain high academic and political standards also. In Cuba, if one does not work or study, one cannot be an athlete. Some 95 percent of national athletes are students, and the simple rule is that they have to study. Pablo Vélez gives the example of Richard Spencer, a national champion in the high jump and a medalist in the Central American Games who was prohibited from leaving Cuba to compete because he had not achieved the required grades. On the other hand, officials have said that to prevent an athlete such as Juantorena from competing because of grades would be counterproductive. Instead, upon returning from the contest, he would have to work harder to catch up.[94]

Motivation and Incentives

There are also more practical motivating factors. Although it is true that Cuban athletes do not receive disproportionate wages that set them apart from the rest of society, they are given special consideration in many ways. A worker who is an athlete will be given time off from his job to train and to compete. His coworkers will take up the slack caused by his absence.

The case of Armando Capiro, former "outstanding athlete and one of our National Team's home run hitters," was described at length in the Cuban press. When the baseball season started, he was granted a "sports leave of absence" (an accepted procedure in Cuba) from his job as a technician at the Havana Psychiatric Hospital. He continued to receive his full salary. According to Silvio Borges:

> This demands, however, that Capiro be a good worker because if not, there are problems. If he does not enjoy the respect and admiration of his co-workers and have a good work attitude, each time he asks for a sports leave the hospital director can say to us, "It seems that Capiro has not earned the privilege of participating in the national competition because his work attitude is very bad and his co-workers do not approve of his participation." The decision about his work attitude is made through the trade union organization by the workers who are there on the job with him. Any worker can object to an athlete's sports leave, "because we aren't willing to do what he isn't here to do." When an athlete is on leave his post must be covered by his co-workers because no extra personnel are assigned. . . . The opinion of the workers has enormous influence on an athlete, and this is positive because it helps shape an athlete in a well-rounded way and avoids sports professionalism. We want athletes to be involved in their jobs and improve their skills.[95]

Extensive research, however, has not revealed any examples of fellow workers successfully vetoing the sports leave of absence of a major Cuban athlete. With the current closure or winding down of Cuban work centers now occurring, sports licenses may be even less likely to be revoked.

A student athlete, working toward a future profession, is paid during training and competition the salary that he will make when he begins a job in his chosen field. He is given the extra time necessary to complete his degree, such as six years instead of the usual four because of the required time off. In addition, whereas food is rationed throughout Cuban society (and ration lists are growing rapidly today), athletes from the EIDEs on up receive more and better quality food to adequately sustain them.[96]

Medal winners from the major international contests are routinely flown home on special flights to be met personally at José Martí Airport by Fidel Castro, in much the same way that U.S. sports personalities are congratulated on their return by the president at the White House.[97] The Cuban athletes, however, do not instantaneously earn $100,000 for saying, "I'm going to Disney World!" as have Mark Rypien, Michael Jordan, Doug Williams, Joe Montana, and other famous professional North American athletes. In addition, there are certain perquisites that come with international travel, such as the opportunity to buy goods that are unavailable to the rest of Cuban society. At the school level, the athlete's every need is cared for, free, from toothbrushes to clothing.

To hear the Cubans tell it, however, the greatest motivation is political. According to Zulema Bregado Gutiérrez, a Cuban gymnast who defected, "at least 30 minutes of political indoctrination is mandatory before every training session." Perhaps this is true. It is certainly true that political courses are required study in the schools, whether the school is a regular one, an EIDE or perhaps one for musicians or dancers. Judging from the comments made in public by athletes like Juantorena or Stevenson, it is clear they have been well coached; they respond to questions with apparently stock, revolutionary slogans. But it is also true that life in Cuba is, in every way, much more political than life in the United States, Peru, or Australia, for example. Their critics state that Cuban athletes express no thoughts of their own. Such a charge, however, is hard to prove. Perhaps Stevenson really does believe his now-famous statement, "What is one million dollars compared to the love of eight million Cubans?"[98] Surely Stevenson has had ample opportunity to defect and collect in the lucrative world of professional boxing, as have other athletes in other sports.[99]

Essentially, all of Cuba's national athletes are products of the revolution, as they were quite young or not even born when it occurred. Several top-ranked athletes described their feelings:

Alberto Juantorena: Without the Revolution, I wouldn't have been able to be what I am. My victory in Montreal would never have been imagined; nor would there have been so numerous a Cuban delegation there. The people make it possible for athletes to go to the Olympics with their own work, with their dedication. And, we, in turn, dedicate the medals to the people. One thing is the result of the other. The Revolution is the same for both.

Aldo Allen Montalvo, specialist in the five and ten thousand meter events and the marathon (upon winning a 30K race in Managua, Nicaragua): I am aware of [the degree of training involved in the longer distances], and because of that, every day I practice with a passion, not only to please myself, but also to do my duty for Fidel, for the Party, for the Revolutionary Government, for my comrades and for my people. . . . I dedicate this victory to the people of Nicaragua and Cuba and to all of the countries of Latin America. I am proud for having participated in this marathon, for its significance celebrating the first anniversary of the triumph of the Sandinista Revolution.

Nancy Aldama Rulloba, gymnast: Everything I obtained in my sports career I owe to the Revolution which gave me all that was necessary to prove myself.

Joaquín Carlos Díaz, chess grand master: All that I am, I owe to the Revolution; I belong to the people and in another time I would have had to devote myself to searching for the means to guarantee subsistence for my family.[100]

Third baseman Omar Linares, a member of the Poder Popular, has said that "we are not going to be overrun by the United States. We prefer to die in our country before we submit it. It doesn't matter if we eat eggs alone, we will be able to resist."[101]

SUCCESS OF THE SYSTEM

The Modern Athlete

In order to judge the success or failure of the Cuban sports system, it is necessary to look at a number of indicators. One of these is the type of athlete INDER officials seek to develop; another is the kind of athlete that has actually emerged. According to Raudol Ruíz:

We do not aspire to have athletes like robots, or athletes who represent our country at the cost of their own alienation. We want men and women who represent this nation who can relate to other people educated in the revolutionary process, who are capable of feeling the Revolution as a natural feeling, not as something imposed and who are capable of defining the Revolution as a result of their own feelings. Moreover, they must acquire a cultural level which allows them to understand and evaluate what goes on in the world and be able to identify clearly its ideological framework. Further, they must have sufficient sophistication to recognize their own efforts and to value them. They should be able to converse with the trainers, doctors, psychologists, and not be just on the receiving end of orders. Only in this manner can we really obtain the kind of athlete who is revolutionary.[102]

On top of this order, the Cubans absolutely insist that there are no stars or heroes. An individual athlete is singled out only when his performance has been extraordinary. In addition, the publishing of the technical aspects, such as rules and tips for playing, helps to demystify sports. This prevents sport from being the sole preserve of naturally talented individuals. Such a philosophy serves to greatly reinforce the Cuban government's commitment to mass participation. Ostensibly, this closes the gap between ordinary people playing for fun and health and Olympic gold medal winners.[103]

There are seven principles that might comprise the Cuban philosophy of sport. According to Ron Pickering, they are also important indicators of the type of person the system produces:

1. The best have to work with the less able at all times.
2. The territory should be more important than the institution or the individual. No prima-donnas!
3. The system works against the concentration of athletic power and in favor of mass participation, albeit in competition.
4. Since everyone participates and sporting progress is linked to educational or work progress, it obviates excessive elitism since the best workers become the best athletes—not the worst workers becoming the best athletes. If you do not advance in studies and in work, you cannot participate in sport.
5. No good athletes or teams are lost in the system. Constant motivation and search are encouraged.
6. As soon as teams are selected (on merit rather than whim) there is immediate integration of factory, university, military unit, etc., which is politically and socially desirable.
7. The system avoids recruitment by any one team or unit since no athlete is allowed to move from his home or job without priority being given to his vocational needs.[104]

So how do the Cubans rate on the type of individual they have developed? Enormously successful. As evidenced by some of the athletes quoted above, Cuba has produced an amazing blend of athlete and revolutionary. Indeed, a chance meeting with Alberto Juantorena in 1980 (four years after his successes in Montreal) provided a glimpse of this famous Cuban sports hero out of the lime-light. He and his family were staying at the same hotel as one of the authors in his hometown of Santiago de Cuba. Repeated, random meetings consistently showed a self-assured but modest young man, who appeared to have a healthy perspective on his accomplishments. At no point was he ever mobbed by adoring fans, as certainly Michael Jordan would have been, in the United States. Rather, he was greeted occasionally by other Cubans as a friend whom one has not seen in some time.[105]

In the early stages of international competition, the Cuban representatives took themselves and their politics too seriously. Press articles and comments from U.S. opponents depicted Cuban sportsmen and women as being "out for blood." The 1971 Pan-American Games were fraught with rumors about defections and the physical beating of a top sprinter who supposedly tried to defect. Domingo Gómez, a trainer for the Cubans, reportedly cried "Down with Fidel" as he leapt to his death from the top of the Cuban building in Cali, Colombia. Another committed suicide in the village hospital. In addition, what began as a group of Canadians and North Americans stealing flags developed into a grand melee when the Cubans saw them take their flag and went after them. North American gymnast James Culhane supposedly had to be rescued from the Cubans by the U.S. water-polo team.[106]

In another little-known incident, during the First Northern and Central American and Caribbean Cup Games, the procedure before each volleyball match was for the two teams about to compete to exchange gifts, usually pins representative of that country. The North American women discovered later in discussion that each of them had been stuck by the Cuban as she gave her the pin! Rumor had it that, to the Cubans, it was bad luck not to prick the receiver when giving a pin! But at these games, the Cuban women were reportedly extremely hostile. During the final match against Mexico, one Cuban in particular had to be physically restrained by her teammates to prevent her from attacking the referee for a call that favored the Mexicans.[107]

Over the years, however, the Cubans seem to have grown in maturity and sophistication (although they are still susceptible to poor behavior when provoked, as at the Pan-American Games in Indianapolis, see chapter 6). The Cuban athlete of today is exemplified by the following incidents.

Upon returning from the seventh Pan-American Games, and representing the seventy women who participated, Carmen

Romero spoke: "Comrade Fidel, we dedicate our medals with all our hearts to the First Party Congress, to the Cuban people and especially to you, who have always inspired us with your example. Fatherland or Death! We will win!" At the same meeting, Teófilo Stevenson spoke for all of the athletes:

> As a demonstration of our admiration for you, of our respect, of our affection, of our recognition of your constant concern for sports and the happiness of the people; in the name of the Cuban sports movement, in the name of the Delegation that had the honor of representing the first socialist country in America in the VII Pan-American Games, I ask that you accept this medal, the final one, medal 119, with which we more than fulfilled the contracted agreement with you, with the Party, and with our people.[108]

Alberto Juantorena

There are several athletes who epitomize the Cuban athlete. Considered by their countrymen as "pearls of the Antilles," it is instructive to look at them more closely. Alberto Juantorena and Teofilo Stevenson are probably the most famous. Beatriz Castillo, a sprinter, provides a second look at the world of Cuban track and field.

Among many other titles, Alberto Juantorena holds the distinction of being the only person to have won Olympic gold medals in both the 400- and the 800-meter races. Because of this accomplishment, he was voted Athlete of the Year in 1976. His name has become synonymous with Cuban sport. He is consistently described as modest, simple, affable, unaffected, open, and trusting.[109] Born in 1951, he is married to a former gymnast and is the father of two children. Behind Fidel himself, he is one of the best spokesmen for the revolution. Upon returning from Montreal in 1976, on behalf of the Cuban delegation, he presented Castro with a plaque reading, "Fidel: We are a product of Moncada and Granma, so our successes are inspired by them and the determination of our people to win." To a crowd gathered in his honor, he gave a statement quite typical of others he has made as a representative of his country:

> I want to thank the working people who have made it possible for Cuban sport to have been present in Montreal. My victory is not an isolated one. It is a victory of socialism, a system that has demonstrated itself to be superior. This reception is worth

as much as an Olympic victory, but for an athlete of the Revolution, nothing is more valuable than the affection and the recognition of his people.[110]

Juantorena's career presents a good example of the athlete-student. During his active athletic career, he studied postgraduate economics at the University of Havana, on a schedule that was designed to allow for his necessary absences for training and competition. Instead of the usual three years to complete the program, he had at least six. While studying, he received a grant equivalent to the money he expected to make as an economist, approximately 320 pesos a month in the late 1970s and early 1980s. This was also based in part on his domestic situation, with three dependents. There were no time constraints, either academic or athletic. In a typical day, Juantorena was at the University from 8 A.M. until about 1 P.M. The rest of the afternoon was spent on training. He was allowed to finish his degree at his leisure, although he did commiserate with one of the authors about the tedium that comes with spreading a degree out over a number of years.[111]

He began his active athletic career playing basketball. In 1971, two of his trainers, Eneas Muñoz and José Salazár, convinced him that if he could run the 400 in 51 seconds in basketball shoes, he had better try his hand at track. Zigmunt Zabierzowski convinced him to train for both the 400- and the 800-meter races simultaneously.[112]

Zabierzowski returned to Poland after seeing his efforts come to fruition in Montreal. Jorge Cumberbatch then took over as Juantorena's coach. The most detailed answer he gave to questions about his training was that he ran the 150-, 200-, and 350-meter distances for speedwork and that, for endurance, he ran from 22 to 25 kilometers a day.[113]

Whatever his regimen, it was abruptly interrupted by an operation on his Achilles tendon in March of 1980. This setback clearly affected his performance in Moscow only four months later, where he scratched from the 800-meter heats and placed fourth in the final of the 400. Sportswriters began to say that he was "washed up" and a "fading star." At the end of 1974 and the beginning of 1975, Juantorena underwent two operations on one of his feet, which kept him off the track for eight months. Gold medals in the 400 and 800 were still ahead of him.[114]

Despite the natural end to his active athletic career, Juantorena as vice-president of INDER continues to be a highly visible and supportive spokesman for his beloved island. He (along with Stevenson) has been an elected delegate to the assemblies of the Poder Popular. At the 1991 congress of the PCC, he was elected to the PCC Central Committee.[115] It takes a certain type of person to dedicate his first gold medal to the heroes of Moncada, and to actually give the second one to Fidel to "share" with the people of Cuba. Although many of his answers may appear predictable revolutionary boilerplate, Juantorena at least gives a very clear impression of believing what he says. With these victories, he was "fulfilling his duty to the revolution."[116]

Teófilo Stevenson

The other "pearl of the Antilles" is Teófilo Stevenson. He is the most consistently successful Cuban athlete in international competition, winning gold medals in boxing in three successive Olympics. He too began his athletic career in a different sport—baseball. In addition, he too combined sports and studies, taking a degree in engineering. Like Juantorena, Stevenson is also an official at INDER. An official from INDER-Santiago (Juantorena's hometown) described Stevenson as "even more noble" than Juantorena.

Yet where Juantorena has been described as "expansive, informal, poetic, trusting, easily amused and absorbed by politics and history," Stevenson has been termed "withdrawn, suspicious, imperial, and often sullen." He appears to be as self-protective outside of the ring as he is in it.

Stevenson's training regimen begins early, "in the Cuban boxing team barracks on a farm 20 miles outside Havana near El Cano." Sprints are run in heavy boots on paths through a mango grove amidst the guinea hens, pigs, and cows. Yet the rural setting belies the scientific training environment: "A battery of trainers, psychologists, and scientists infests the camp, testing strength and reflexes, the results of the latest hush-hush boxing techniques that Cuba is adamant about developing."

The elusive Stevenson, in stark contrast to his U.S. counterparts, is a man of very few words who studiously avoids photographers. A long-time bachelor, Stevenson's smiles appear reserved for pretty women, not mere foreign admirers or journalists. He allegedly does not enjoy the rigorous training that makes him the world's best heavyweight fighter. Many of his bouts in international competition are won by forfeit—no one wants to face him. "When I am training and sweating, I do not like to think about the forfeits. I must be prepared to fight every bout because if I am not ready, they will see it and suddenly everyone will be anxious to fight." For that reason, his critics think that he is seldom challenged. "Either my opponents are very bad, or perhaps I am not so bad." According to Cuban sports photographer Jesús Rocamora, "He is just a big, docile boy. He enjoys a good game. He is just as glad to have someone else tell him what to do. He is a good, simple boy with natural dignity. Like Joe Louis."[117]

Beatriz Castillo

In another case of a less famous athlete, sprinter Beatriz Castillo, former national champion in the 400 meters, was a student at an EIDE in the late 1960s until she switched to ESPA in 1970. From there she went to ESEF to become a professor of physical education. Although she finished her postgraduate Licenciatura (or masters) work in 1975, she continued to study so that she had the time to train, all the while collecting the salary of her chosen profession.[118]

Beatriz claimed to have had the same coach as Juantorena, Jorge Cumberbatch. According to Castillo, what made his training methods so successful was that they were so different. The typical distance and speed work can make the athlete's regimen, and therefore condition, suffer out of sheer boredom. Of course, some regimented speed and distance work are necessary. But, according to Castillo, often a training session consists of a series of games, played with the other athletes. Sometimes it would be soccer, a game that combines continuous running (distance work) with frequent sprints (speed work), thus completing training requirements. The important part was not the game but rather that the athletes continued to run during it. The philosophy behind this method is presumably that, if the running is more enjoyable within the context of the game, the athletes will do more of it, and therefore derive more benefit from it than if it were sprint intervals. Swimmers (in a sport with a very high burnout rate) could possibly play different versions of water polo. In the United States, for example, some swimming coaches intentionally break up the year-round training with a few months of water polo. At the university level, the two seasons complement each other, rather than overlap.

The Athlete's Privileges

Given their athletic abilities, athletes are a "natural elite." Materially, however, they also receive benefits, which constitutes a form of "unnatural elitism." Gymnast Zulema Bregado Gutiérrez told the

CIA when she defected that athletes in Cuba were really professionals, because sport was their main employment. Their combined
benefits gave them definite advantages over most other Cubans.
Bregado claimed that athletes trained for four hours a day, six days
a week (a schedule comparable to that of top athletes in other countries). She also claimed that training included a half hour of political indoctrination, including instructions on how to respond to
foreigners. Another defector, Hector Rodríguez Cordosa, claimed
that sports victories are used to divert attention from failures in
other areas.[119] This may well be the case. However, sport is a far
better diversion from hardship and austerity than the consumption
of alcohol and drugs, which is also found frequently in both communist and capitalist countries. The more important question is
whether the sports program diverts funds that would be best used
in more practical and deserving areas of Cuban society.

The validity of the claim of political indoctrination cannot be
easily ascertained. The issue is also a relative one. Athletes in most
countries claim to be inspired by patriotic symbols, the national an-
them, for example, and the flag. Clearly, Cuban athletes are expected to be Cuban patriots who, in this case, see themselves as
revolutionaries. Their very entrance to sports schools and participation as representatives of their country could be denied if they
are not. Cuba also uses sports victories for prestige and nationalist
sentiments, but these would not necessarily distract a Cuban from
severe economic hardship for very long. The disjunct between
riding to sports practice in a Russian car, while one's countrymen
pedal bicycles is hard to ignore. However, Bregado's claims of material benefits are close to reality:

> This select group of athletes . . . achieve a new status and are
> cared for by the state. But . . . Cuba's athletes are not isolated
> and pampered with extra care, services, and pay. Often they
> are given physical education teaching jobs and sometimes work
> in regular factories. But their pay is within the confines of
> other Cuban workers' salaries, 150–400 pesos monthly, de-
> pending on responsibilities. They do receive free travel ex-
> penses, food, . . . sports instruction, and time off from their
> work [or studies] for practice and training.[120]

Outstanding sports performance might provide a lever for dealing with the bureaucracy. "Most Cuban ballplayers deny that baseball . . . has provided them with anything more than a few shortcuts

through the sometimes unfathomable bureaucratic maze."[121] Any assistance in dealing with the cumbersome Cuban bureaucracy would be useful, but Cuba's athletically talented will not get rich through sports. As sport provides better access and efficiency in dealing with the bureaucracy, however, it could be argued that this was an antidemocratic tendency. Yet it does not give Cuban athletes (unlike Soviet ones) the right to disregard the laws of Cuban society, and if they do, they are likely to be punished.[122]

There are, however, numerous examples of Cuba's high-profile athletes receiving benefits not available to the average Cuban. In 1982, the team and the officials for the Central American and Caribbean Games and their immediate families were given a one-week holiday at the Varadero beach resort, for example. This reward, and similar ones, were granted for other outstanding efforts also, such as very productive "vanguard" workers.[123] One could argue that the athletes, like the workers, were giving a service to the state. In addition to the time-consuming training, athletes play a major role in socialization and in bringing prestige to the island.

There are many other examples. Miguel Cuevas, a baseball hero in Cuba, said that baseball had given him everything—an education, a home, furnishings, a television, and a Russian car. More recently, according to José Fuentes, manager of the Cuban national baseball team, "Our government has a general assistance [policy] for all people who are outstanding. I think the people who do the greatest effort should be the prized ones." The government provides third baseman Omar Linares with a car. Second baseman Antonio Pacheco has "a driver at my disposal . . . and when I need a [free] airplane flight [within Cuba], I just make a call."[124]

Alberto Juantorena was driven to training, was given a home, and received an allowance of 320 pesos a month while he was still a student. Along with Teófilo Stevenson, Juantorena is now a high official of INDER. Another athlete who received a house was the wrestler Alcides Salazár. The sprinter Beatriz Castillo, like Juantorena, received a study allowance, which continued even after she had completed her degree. Stevenson was offered a second house (which he allegedly designed himself), with four bedrooms, luxurious by Cuban standards.[125] The election of Juantorena and Stevenson, and possibly others, to the National Assembly surely was based in large part on the status (and name recognition) they had gained as athletes. (The elections of U.S. politicians Bill Bradley and Tom McMillen and the Australian Darryl Baldock were also not hurt by their earlier professional sports careers.)

Cuban Victories

One of the clearest and most "measurable" indicators of success or failure in sports can be seen in the number of medals won in international competition. In the first decade after the ouster of Batista, Cuban athletes began to show a promise that would later be fulfilled. Cuba continued to do well in the sports in which it was traditionally strong. In 1960, the professional boxer Benny "Kid" Paret won the world welterweight title, and headed a strong contingent of professional Cuban boxers. At the 1962 Central American and Caribbean Games, Cuban amateur boxers followed up their fifth place at the 1954 Games (two medals) with a first place, a position they have held in all subsequent Central American Games. Cuba's first place in 1962 was based on four gold, two silver, and two bronze medals. By the 1982 Games, Cuba's boxers were dominant, capturing all the gold medals (see table 25).[126]

In the Pan-American Games, where competition was stronger, Cuban boxers also performed well, particularly from the late 1960s onward (see table 26). The high international standard of Cuba's boxers was also evident in the Olympic arena. In 1968, Cuba won two silver medals. In the 1980 Moscow Olympics, Cuban boxers swept the field, winning ten medals, six of them gold. At the 1992

TABLE 25.
Boxing Medals Won by Cuba in Central American and Caribbean Games, 1935–1982

Year	Gold	Silver	Bronze
1935	2	3	3
1938	0	0	0
1950	3	2	3
1954	0	1	1
1962	4	2	2
1966	5	1	3
1970	5	2	1
1974	6	1	1
1978	5	3	1
1982	11	0	0
Cuban Total	41 (40.2%)	15 (13.8%)	16 (11.1%)
Medal Total	112	109	144

Source: Jesús Domínguez, Boxeo cubano en Juegos deportivos centroamericanos y del Caribe (Havana: Editorial Científico Técnica), pp. 67–76.

Table 26.
Boxing Medals Won by Cuba in Pan-
American Games, 1951–1983

Year	Gold	Silver	Bronze
1951	0	1	0
1955	no boxing competition		
1959	0	0	0
1963	1	1	0
1967	3	3	1
1971	4	0	3
1975	7	2	2
1979	5	0	2
1983	8	2	0
Cuban Total	28	8	8
Medal Total			
(to 1979)	71	71	99

Source: Salmerón and Castillo, pp. 12–15. R. Alonso
Fornaris, "Medallas por País," *LPV*, no. 887, p. 24.
W. Kramer-Mandeau, *Sport und Korpererziehung* (Koln:
Pahl-Rugenstein, 1988), pp. 176–181.
Note: The number of possible medals increased in the
1970s with the introduction of more divisions.

Summer Olympics in Barcelona, the Cubans bested themselves,
with seven gold and two silver.[127]

Cuba continued to perform well in its other traditional sport—
baseball. The Cuban team finished fourth at the 1959 Pan-
American Games, but Cuba's best players might have belonged to
the U.S.–based professional team, the Havana Sugar Kings. After
the abolition of professional sports in 1961–1962, Cuban amateur
baseball teams dominated international competition, as they had
prior to 1959. Cuba won the Amateur World Series in 1961, 1969,
1970, 1971, 1972, 1973, 1978, 1979, 1980, and again in 1987. In the
Central American and Caribbean Games and the Pan-American
Games, Cuba captured most of the titles (see table 27).[128]

These two traditional sports and athletics were the sources of
most of Cuba's international medals, particularly in Olympic and
Pan-American arenas. In Pan-American Games since 1951 (up to
and including 1983), boxing and athletics made up 26 percent of
Cuba's medals (respectively 7 percent and 19 percent). In these regional games, Cuba also performed well in weightlifting and wrestling (respectively 17 percent and 9 percent of their medals). These
four sports made up 52 percent of Pan-American medals won by

Table 27.
Cuban Standings in Baseball Competitions Since 1959

Year	C.Am.	P.Am.	World Series	Intercont. Cup	Olymp
1959		4th			
1961			1st		
1962	4th				
1963		1st			
1966	1st				
1967		2nd			
1969			1st		
1970	1st		1st		
1971		1st	1st		
1972			1st		
1973			1st		
1974	1st				
1975		1st			
1978	1st		1st		
1979		1st	1st	1st	
1980			1st		
1981				2nd	
1982	2nd				
1983		1st		1st	
1987			1st		
1991		1st			
1992					1st

Source: Compiled from various sources.

Cuba from 1951 to 1983 (and 56 percent of medals won from 1959 to 1983). In the Olympic Games from 1960 to 1980, boxing and athletics were the sources of 80 percent of Cuba's medals (see table 28).

Although Cuba traditionally did well in professional boxing, it did not win an Olympic medal in boxing before 1959. Cuba also became a power in several other sports that it had not been prominent in before the revolution. Most noticeable of these were shooting, weightlifting, wrestling, volleyball, and water polo. The rise of the women's volleyball team—from a virtual unknown to equal number one with China in 1987—was a particularly notable example of Cuba's rise in sports. Another is the water-polo team's entry into the top six. Ruíz had commented on the team at the Central American and Caribbean Games in 1962, saying "We were lucky half of them didn't drown, they were so bad."[129]

By the second decade of the revolution, Cuba dominated the Central American and Caribbean Games; was ranked second only to the United States in the Pan-American Games; and finished

Table 28.
Medals Won by Cuba in the
Olympic Games Since 1968

Year	Gold	Silver	Bronze
1968	0	2	0
1972	3	1	1
1976	3	3	2
1980	6	2	2
1992	14	6	11
Total	26	14	16

Source: E. Martin, pp. 99–101.
Washington Post, 10 August 1992,
p. C8.

eighth in the 1976 Olympics and fourth in the partially representative Moscow Olympics in 1980. Cuba boycotted the Olympic
Games in 1984 and 1988, but indicated its continued strength at the
1987 Pan-American Games, winning all the gold medals in weightlifting. The young Cuban Javier Sotomayor held the world high-
jump record and Ana Fidelia Quirot, a female Cuban runner,
finished fourth in the 1989 World Cup athletics meet in Rome.[130]
Certainly, the Cubans performed even better in the 1992 Olympics
in Barcelona, placing fifth overall in the gold medal tally.

Perhaps even greater proof of Cuba's success is that there exists
depth behind the gold medal winners. Cuba has not taken just one
or two especially talented individuals and molded them into world
champions. Behind each individual success, there are dozens of others: the second- or third-place winners or those who simply make a
good showing. With every international contest (and Cuba enters
most of them), the Cubans are growing in experience and ability,
moving toward winning gold. This depth is a clear result of Cuba's
dedication to the goal of mass participation. Without a solid emphasis on sport at all levels, immature talent would never have the
opportunity to develop. In boxing, for example, perhaps the world
only knows of Teófilo Stevenson, but behind him have been Cubans
in other weight classes who also won, such as Savón, Garbey, Hernández, Rodríguez, Correa, Pedroso, Herrera, Gómez, Martínez,
Aldama, Horta, Ramos, Aguilar, and Rojas, sixteen thousand boxers
on the island in total.[131] This is one reason why Cuban athletes are
never allowed to think they are indispensable. Behind everyone is a
host of promising talent, waiting to be given the chance to compete

on a national team. In a country the size of Cuba, such depth could only come from a system dedicated to mass participation.

In baseball, Cuba seems to have a never-ending supply of first class talent. Jerry Kindall, coach of the U.S. baseball team at the Pan-American Games in 1979 and a major league player for ten years, could not praise the Cubans highly enough:

> They're better than several clubs in the major league. . . . At least five of their regulars could step into a big-league lineup tomorrow. . . . this is just the next generation after Tony Pérez, Luís Tiant, and Mike Cuellar—same quality. Before that, Cubans were half the Washington Senator team—the better half. . . . Right now, Cuba is the best of its breed.[132]

That year, the Cubans continued a winning streak that began in 1967 and lasted for over thirteen years. Even more interesting, perhaps, is that the Cuban teams play to burn out early, but for some reason they do not. Some of the members have been playing in international contests for decades.

The likelihood that Cuba would continue to be a sports power in the future seemingly had been guaranteed by two factors—the widened base of mass participation and the availability of specialized training for talented athletes. The fall of socialism in Europe, however, reduces Cuba's current and future capacity to maintain both these factors.

THE PROBLEMS

So far, this chapter has focused on the phenomenal success of the Cuban sports program and how this has been achieved. However, the system is not without problems.

The obvious existence of privileges for outstanding performance in sports is, in one sense, a form of elitism that is incompatible with the communist society envisioned by Marx and Engels, to which the Cubans ostensibly aspire. Rewards for athletes are comparable to other material incentives, which were (and are) often frowned upon in Cuba, especially by Che Guevara and other revolutionary leaders.

The discrepancy between theory and practice became difficult to avoid once the decision to compete internationally was made. International sports successes offered prestige and the "ultimate test" for aspiring athletes. Yet athletes can no longer perform successfully at the international level without specialized training and an adequate diet. The untrained, "amateur" athlete is rare in contemporary international competition, and even rarer on the winner's podium.

Material rewards such as special housing and payment for practice and competition is, however, a potentially dangerous policy. Athletes might develop elitist attitudes, and other Cubans without these privileges might feel (justifiably) deprived. There is the danger that the status of star athletes might result in political privileges as well, such as election to the National Assembly or membership in the Communist party. Cuban exiles claim that antirevolutionary sentiments can lead to exclusion from top sports, for example, and if this charge is accurate, then this could ensure that athletes are revolutionaries with political merits (from the Cuban viewpoint).

The appeal of success in international sports competitions could result in problems such as the taking of drugs, or the corruption of athletes and officials. There is the danger that officials could become more concerned with high-performance sports and could ignore the goal of popular participation. It is clear that producing top athletes is beneficial to both coaches and officials. High results give personal satisfaction and prestige to an official who is also a good worker. In the 1987 review of INDER, concern was raised about these possibilities, particularly in the selection of people for special sports areas. There is evidence that all these problems have emerged to some extent in Cuba, but certainly not to the degree that they have in the Soviet Union.[133]

Gambling and Corruption

In Cuba, where there is a long tradition of gambling, it is perhaps not surprising that gambling continued after 1961, when it was officially outlawed. In 1964, two baseball players were paid by gamblers to fix a game, and they were subsequently suspended. Gambling continued into the 1970s and 1980s. In the late 1970s, several baseball players were banned for accepting bribes. Among them was Barbaro Garbey, a member of the national team, who now resides in the United States. In 1982, seventeen players and coaches were banned for involvement in fixing games. Their names were removed from the records, and they became liable to prosecution.[134] Cuban officials were clearly concerned about this problem and instituted significant, if not judicial penalties.

They responded in a similar manner to athletes caught using drugs. The weightlifters Daniel Nuñez and Alberto Blanco were expelled from the ninth Pan-American Games in 1983 for using anabolic steroids. In this instance, however, it was their trainer, Manuel Gul Sing, who accepted the blame, and he was fired from the national training staff. There is limited evidence of drug use by Cuban athletes, but this does not mean that drugs are not used. It is also possible that Gul Sing's expulsion was a response to the embarrassment the Cubans felt at being caught for drug use. Cuban officials are publicly opposed to drug usage, which had been one of the symptoms of the corruption of Cuban society in the 1940s and 1950s. The charging and execution of General Arnaldo Ochoa, commander of Cuba's armed forces in Angola in 1989, for alleged drug trading was indicative of this official antagonism.[135]

Distribution of Resources

There also existed problems in seeking a balance between the distribution of resources between popular participation and elite sports. The Cubans appear to straddle the fence, unable to decide which sports to emphasize. On the one hand, they often develop major sports to a good international level before introducing new ones. On the other hand, they emphasize and encourage many new sports. Castro complained of Cubans being weak in some areas, such as swimming and long-distance running. It was important, therefore, that some provinces or schools did not overemphasize the most popular sports. "There are some sports which are more popular than others, but we can't let sports be decided by popularity alone."[136]

Despite an obvious interest in diversifying sports in Cuba, a survey begun by INDER officials in 1985 sought to assess which sports were popular in which regions, perhaps indicating concern about the level of mass participation.[137] Varying positions as to which sports to encourage and practice might exist in different parts of Cuba. While central INDER officials may have a generalized concern for mass participation in any physical activity, some officials within the provinces may have an interest in one group of sports or even a particular sport. Castro may prefer a diversification in sports, yet if Cubans preferred some sports over others, providing resources for new sports was misdirected, given the commitment to mass participation. On the other hand, more people could be attracted to new sports, rather than the traditionally popular ones, a reasonable expectation especially for women. However, the continuation of traditional gender stereotypes, as well as the existence of people uninterested in sports, means that physical culture can be extended only to a given point, unless Cuba is able to transform such attitudes.

BASEBALL, THE NATIONAL PASTIME

In 1961, an intelligence analyst in the United States was studying aerial photographs taken over Cuba. He noticed a military camp. The usual soccer field had been marked off and some of the men were playing a game. Upon second thought, the analyst remembered that Cuban military installations always set up baseball diamonds, not soccer fields. With closer examination, the camp turned out to be Russian, set up to help install missiles in Cuba.

Contrary to popular belief, the tradition of baseball in Cuba precedes the American presence on the island. Both the Tainos Indians and the Siboney had games that were played with a bat and ball. The Siboney Indians called their game *batos*. But with the arrival of the Americans came their form of the game, which became the most popular sport on the island and remained so even after the abolition of professionalism. Basketball comes second, and soccer is back in fifth place.[138] In South America, kids travel the streets with a soccer ball at their feet, while in Cuba it is a bat and ball (or something equivalent) in their possession at all times, just in case there is a pick-up game.

Baseball in Cuba is more than a pastime, it is an obsession. According to Sigfredo Barros, a sportswriter for the newspaper *Granma*, "Baseball is not our national sport. It's our national passion. It's our love." There are baseball diamonds everywhere. Play is year round, although top-level play is tied closely to the other important season on the island, sugar. Fidel has said that "Baseball helps the harvest; it is tied to the heart of our economy." Over half a million Cubans play organized baseball in one form or another. The rest participate as "active" spectators. According to Wilfredo Sánchez, the right fielder for the Matanzas team, "After every game, I have nine and a half million people waiting outside the stadium who want to explain to me, for the good of Cuba, what I did wrong."[139]

In 1874, the first baseball stadium in Cuba, Palmar de Junco, was inaugurated in Matanzas. Today, this stadium is a museum to the sport. The first game was played there on 27 December 1874, and Havana defeated the home team 51–9. Havana's left fielder was Emilio Sabourín, who helped to organize the country's first professional league in 1878. He died in 1897 in the Spanish prison, Castillo del Hacha, during the Cuban War for Independence.[140]

Cuban baseball has traveled a long road since 1874. Along the way, the sport has seen some legendary players develop, most of whom migrated to the professional leagues in North America. There were people such as Estéban Enrique Bellán (the first Latin American to play in the United States), Adolfo Luque, Martín Dihigo, Camilo Pascual, Minnie Minoso, Conrado "Connie" Marrero, Dagoberto "Bert" Campaneris, Rigoberto "Tito" Fuentes, Tony Olíva, Mike Gonzáles, Tony Pérez, Mike Cuellar, Luís Tiant, Tony Taylor, José Cardenal, Pedro Ramos, and Cookie Rojas. Many of these players are worth special mention. Those who came before the revolution such as Martín Dihigo, Adolfo Luque, and Minnie Minoso have been highlighted elsewhere (see chapter 2).

Mike Cuellar

There have been many others who came later, and Mike Cuellar was one of these. As was the case with so many other Cubans, Cuellar first pitched in a sugar-mill amateur league and during a stint in the Cuban army. He was spotted by Bobby Maduro and signed with the Havana Sugar Kings. He started with a bang in 1957, then followed the Sugar Kings to New Jersey in 1961. Again, as with so many Cuban players, he hit a bad slump, but Maduro remained confident: "Cuellar's going to be just like [Orlando] Peña and like a lot of other Cuban players. They all do well at the start of their careers, then slump for three or four years, then come back stronger than ever."[141]

Cuellar moved around from team to team for several years with a mixed record. In 1968, he was traded to Baltimore. In 1969 he went 23–11 and won the Cy Young Award. That same year, he opened the 1969 World Series for the Orioles, pitching a six-hitter to beat the Mets 4–1. Even though the Mets beat the Orioles in five games, Cuellar was the most effective pitcher of the Series, with 13 strikeouts and a 1.13 ERA. Cuellar bested himself the next year, leading the American League in wins (24–8), starts (40), complete games (21), and winning percentage (.750). In the last game of the 1970 World Series, Cuellar held Cincinnati scoreless for eight innings. "As Cuban Dolf Luque had done 37 years before for the New

York Giants, Cuellar was on the mound for the final out to gain the world championship for his team."[142] All told, between 1969 and 1976, Cuellar won 143 games for Baltimore:

> Cuellar was the major leagues' best Latin left-handed pitcher. He had a career .587 winning percentage, with 185 wins and 130 losses, a 3.14 ERA, and 36 shutouts. For six years he teamed with Dave McNally and Jim Palmer to make up the best pitching staff in baseball.[143]

Dagoberto Blanco Campaneris

Another Cuban star from the same era was Dagoberto Blanco Campaneris. His father worked in a rope factory and had been a catcher in his youth. Campaneris was playing in a tournament in Costa Rica with a semipro team when the Bay of Pigs invasion took place in 1961. Then and there, he and teammate Tito Fuentes were signed by Felix Delgado for the Kansas City A's. They were able to leave Cuba just before Castro closed the borders in 1962. That same year, "the ambidextrous Campaneris pitched two innings, left-handed to the lefty batters and right-handed to the right-handed hitters. He struck out four and gave up only one run. Campaneris also played the outfield, all infield positions, and catcher in 1962."[144]

Campaneris debuted in the majors in 1964 against Minnesota and homered off the first pitch, only the second player in history to do so. In his fourth at bat, he homered again. In 1965, reminiscent of Martín Dihigo, he became the first major-league player to play all nine positions in the same game. When the A's moved to Oakland in 1967, their record (and Campaneris's career) took off. He led the league in stolen bases six times, was named to the All-Star team five times, and was with the A's for three straight World Series victories. He finished with a .259 average.

Tony Pérez

Like so many other Cuban ball players of the time, Atanasio Rigal "Tony" Pérez also played on a sugar-factory team and went professional just before the borders closed in 1962. He signed with the Cincinnati Reds in 1960 when he was just seventeen years old. He experienced the same slow start as so many other Cubans and began to shine in 1967, when he helped the National League All-Star Team to victory. That year, he was voted the Reds' Most Valuable Player and finished with a .290 average, 26 home runs, and 102 runs batted in.

Pedro Olíva

Pedro Olíva was one of ten children from a family in Pinar del Río, Cuba. When Joe Cambria heard about him, he gave him the airfare to come and try out in the United States. When he could not find his passport, he borrowed his brother Antonio's passport and thus became Tony Olíva. Six days after he left, the Bay of Pigs invasion started, and Tony Olíva became the last Cuban to be signed by Joe Cambria. Minnesota called him up from the minors after he started to hit in 1963. "In 1964 he established a rookie hit record with 217 and is the only American League rookie to win a batting title (.323). He also led in doubles and runs scored."[145] He led Minnesota to the pennant in 1965 and the American League in hits five times through 1970. After several injuries, Olíva began managing in the winter leagues in Mexico and Colombia. He coached in the minors and has been instrumental in developing young players, most notably Kirby Puckett.

Luís Tiant, Jr.

Against both his mother's wishes and the advice of his father, Luís Tiant, Jr., was determined to follow in his father's cleats. Luís "Lefty" Tiant, Sr., had been "one of the finest spitball pitchers in the Negro leagues."[146] The talent of Luís Jr. was first spotted by Cleveland Indians scout Bobby Avila in 1959. In his major league debut against the Yankees in 1964, Tiant allowed only three hits and struck out eleven. His big year was 1968, when he threw four consecutive shutouts and in three other games struck out forty-one batters, a new record.

In 1972, with the Boston Red Sox, Luís Jr. led the American League with a 1.91 ERA and a 15–6 record. In August 1975, Fidel Castro allowed Tiant's parents to leave Cuba. Lefty Tiant threw out the first ball during a game, as the Boston fans roared their approval. Boston went on to win the pennant, with Tiant shutting out Cincinnati 6–0 in the first game of the Series. But Cincinnati won the Series 4–3. The elder Tiants died after the 1976 season.

Luís played several more years and finished his career in 1982 with a 229–172 record, 49 shutouts, 2,416 strikeouts, and four 20-win seasons.

American Baseball in Cuba

With the revolution came the abolition of professional baseball in 1962. If anything, the change strengthened the Cuban game. The better players stopped migrating north, and from 1963 to 1991, Cuba has won every gold medal for baseball in the Pan-American Games—except one, in 1987, when they were beaten by the U.S. team led by Jim Abbott, who went on to pitch in the major leagues for the California Angels and the New York Yankees.

The Castro government has clearly been supportive of the expansion of baseball. In 1971, Gran Stadium was upgraded to Estadio Latinoamericano, with a 55,000–seat capacity, which was 20,000 more than before. In Matanzas, a new 30,000–seat stadium was built near the original Palmar de Junco, one of nine stadiums in Cuba with a capacity over 20,000. It was named Estadio Victoria de Girón, to commemorate the Cuban victory over the United States at the Bay of Pigs.

It is ironic that the game remains the common denominator between Cuba and the United States (baseball is not something that Cubans could share with the socialist brotherhood). As Don Miguel Cuevas—perhaps the greatest living baseball hero in Cuba—said, "The Russians have yet to come up with a good left-handed hitter."[147] Unfortunately, the political situation allows Cuba and the United States to share only the memories of baseball in days gone by. Even today, the most influential American players in Cuba are probably Ted Williams and Mickey Mantle, who were featured in the last training films that were shipped to Cuba before relations were severed. It is the era of Williams and Mantle that is remembered by the older Cubans now coaching the younger players, and about which they reminisce.

It has been said that "Cuba has two distinct baseball generations: that which remembers and that which does not."[148] Those who have grown up with the revolution can say with conviction that they have no interest in the U.S. major leagues. Nothing of American baseball is reported on Cuban television, on the radio, or in the press. But for those over forty years old, sometimes it seems they remember too much. The life he led as a pitcher for the Washington Senators brings back fond memories for Connie Marrero. And the memories are recalled in infinite detail, made more vivid by the decades of being rehashed, with others who also remember.

Cuban baseball fans are a blend of all ages and colors, but predominantly of only one gender. The most interesting group of *aficionados* is the older men who, during the entire game, talk of nothing but old-time baseball. Some of these discussions become rather high-spirited (to put it mildly), as the men discuss vintage American baseball, including the Negro leagues and obscure players from the 1930s. Although it is almost a point of honor to display a complete lack of interest in North American baseball, there is still an enormous amount of information that is circulated, especially when it is almost all by word of mouth. A South Dakotan traveling through Cuba on a basketball tour was shocked to meet a Cuban who knew that Ken Griffey of the Cincinnati Reds once played minor-league ball for Sioux Falls, for example.[149] The attitude toward the major leagues is clearly ambivalent.

It is a love-hate relationship, and its symbol is perhaps a "nervous, wizened gentlemen" named Edel Casas. Casas keeps himself and everyone else in Cuba abreast of the "Great Leagues" by daily visiting the Agence France Presse and through an information column he used to write for *Listos Para Vencer:*

> No American trivia expert could surpass Casas on the genuinely trivial. He knows the date of every well-known American baseball happening from Johnny Vander Meer's nohitters to how many thirds of an inning Walter Johnson pitched in the World Series of 1924 and 1925. . . .
>
> "McNeely's bad-hop hit struck a famous pebble," Casas is told. . . . "Was that pebble in front of first, second, or third base?"
>
> Casas seems justifiably hurt by such a sneaky, such a trivial question. "Second base," he says tentatively. And, of course, incorrectly.
>
> "Marvelous," he is told. "That's right."
>
> The little middle-aged man relaxes. His performance cannot trip him up in front of his superiors.
>
> "I want very much for the United States and Cuba to have an exchange of games," he says. "You see, I have never seen an American Great League game with my own eyes."[150]

This "tangled fascination and antipathy for the Great Leagues" often takes the form of a strong desire for the chance at one game against the "Yanquis" (not necessarily the New York variety). Láz-aro Pérez, now in his early fifties, reached his peak in the early 1960s. He caught for the Cuban national team for decades, the same team that has won all the gold medals but one at the Pan-American Games since 1967. "I never want to sell myself for money, but I have waited for years to play against the professionals." Al-though the Cuban players insist they are uncomfortable discuss-ing their market value, they still brag about it. Manuel Zayas of INDER claimed that "the Japanese have offered millions for [Omar] Linares." At a tournament in Edmonton in 1985, when Linares was only seventeen, the Toronto Blue Jays offered him a contract that would have allowed him to play only home games, thereby not having to travel to the United States. He turned them down.[151]

In 1977, Fidel Castro invited an all-star team from the United States to come and play against the Cubans. The deal fell through. Castro then invited the Yankees to play in Havana. The trip was canceled by the U.S. State Department because of "Cuba's involve-ment in Angola." Bill Veeck, owner of the Chicago White Sox, went to Cuba to scout talent and to attempt some "ping-pong diplomacy." Even an exhibition match in Mexico between the Seattle Mariners and a Cuban team was aborted.[152]

If the best of the United States and the best of Cuba were to play against each other, it certainly would be an interesting match. Isolated by the revolution, baseball in Cuba has developed differ-ently from the game in the United States. The most obvious weak-ness is the pitching. Most Cuban pitchers lack variety. They are junk-ball specialists, throwing mainly fastballs and sidearm curves. Certainly, contact with the technically superior North American leagues could improve the quality of the game. That the Cubans want no part of it is hard for those involved with U.S. baseball, such as Preston Gómez (a Dodger coach and a Cuban), to understand:

> Baseball is the only sport there is where the players don't have the opportunity to compete with those better than they are. . . . Those players reach a certain age, and then they stand still. They don't make progress. They have several players there that, if they had had the opportunity five or six years ago to come to the States would be playing in the big leagues now. Ir-relevant, say the Cubans. "We have our game," says Las Villas First Baseman Antonio Muñoz, "and you have yours."[153]

Cuban Baseball

On the plus side, Cuban baseball is characterized by tremendous talent: "speed, recklessness, superb defense, and fascination with rules and strategy."[154] And this fascination with rules and strategy is as true of the fans as of the players and managers. "After all, this nation worships subtlety in its baseball. Marrero was once given a standing ovation for his windup. The crowd was on it feet cheering Marrero's head-bobbing gyrations before he ever released the pitch."[155] But subtlety is not enough by itself. All the wonderful windups in the world will not satisfy Cuban fans in a 1–0 pitchers' duel. They leave. Cuban fans will take nothing less than pure excitement with scoring, stealing, and strategy.[156]

In postrevolutionary Cuba, it is easier to leave early than it was before the revolution. The fans are not sacrificing their entrance fee, because there is none. Admission to all games is free, on a first-come-first-served basis. And in Cuba, all foul balls are returned; there is even an extra official to collect the returned balls. This is one example of what appears to be a truly cooperative effort (unknown in the United States since perhaps World War II). And there are other differences, especially in contrast with the USSR. Crowd behavior is impeccable. Although they are ready at the drop of a bat to show disapproval for a bonehead play, the crowd, players, and officials treat each other with the utmost respect. On all sides, anger is as subdued as is humanly possible, and all this without a policeman in sight. The umpire is in total control of the game. The violence in the stands that was so common in the 1950s is now gone:

> Cuba's top hitter, Wilfredo Sánchez, was once called out by a "blind" umpire in Matanzas when he was safe by a yard, leaped high in the air, spun around and made the psychic transformation from complete disbelief and fury to resigned composure before he returned to the earth. He walked off the field without any show of displeasure except that four-foot vertical catapult when he first saw the umpire's thumb. . . .
>
> Cuban ballparks may be the only ones in the hemisphere that combine rabid partisanship, ferocious noise and umpire baiting with a sense of total personal security.
>
> The crowd has its right to yell, "We are being robbed" and "We are playing nine against thirteen." But when the ump has

heard enough, he calmly raises a hand like a school principal and the sound turns off like a faucet. It is an impressive and somewhat unnerving sight.[157]

The continual arguments in the stands are confined to a level out of earshot of those on the field. The freest speech in Cuba can be heard at the corner of Paséo de Martí and San Rafael in Havana where dozens of men hotly discuss every aspect of the game and its players. Often, the arguments seem to be about a game that was played two or three decades earlier, rather than the one in progress at the time. In addition, in order to help people "think collectively," Cuban sportswriters are not supposed to use personal nicknames, a practice that supposedly emphasized the importance of the individual over the team. In the stands, however, it is hard to discover the real names of the players for the number of nicknames used.[158]

Although in many ways, baseball seems to be the least political of Cuba's sports, the revolution is never far from view. The stadiums themselves are a testimony to it:

The Estadio [*Latinoamericano* in Havana] itself is really two ball parks, pre- and post-revolution. The 46-year-old covered grandstand has been gussied up with fresh paint and new seats. The outfield sections were completed in 1971 by volunteer labor, the product of revolutionary sporting fervor. The whole— 25,000 old seats, 30,000 new—looks as if it is one part Comiskey Park and one part Riverfront Stadium. The hybrid is Cuba's largest stadium, an impressive structure for all the commingling. The outfield fences are somewhat closer to the plate than in most major league parks—325 feet at the foul lines, 345 in the power alleys and 400 to dead center—but the air is heavy and balls do not seem to carry well. The fences are painted a subdued green, unblemished, of course, by advertising signs, there being none in Cuba. However, the foul poles are lighted for night games, an innovation the big leagues would do well to consider. The electric scoreboard does not transmit quizzes and cartoons, nor does it welcome the Kiawanis from Matanzas, but it does list the batting orders and advise the fans of each hitter's average.[159]

Fans go to see the game and to talk to each other rather than to partake of the hoopla that characterizes American baseball. And they do so sober. "Baseball is thought to be sufficient inebriation for any Cuban." Base paths are swept by "middle-aged groundskeepers in coveralls" rather than by "nubile teenagers in hot pants." In fact, the game itself tends to be much shorter, seldom over two hours. "The single-deck stadium offers no advertising [besides a few pro-revolution billboards], no ushers, no concessionaires, no hawkers, no panty-hose night, no exploding scoreboards, no inessential public address announcements."[160]

The players on the field are conspicuously shorthaired and clean shaven. And they all are amateurs who show a marked disdain for professionalism. They must arrange for time off from their jobs or their studies to train and to play. The workplace or university must approve their leave of absence. The players continue to draw their regular pay or stipends. Their schedule more closely resembles the barnstorming teams of the 1930s, more so than the major or minor leagues of today. They play more than a hundred games a season on regional teams, sleeping in stadium dormitories as they travel. Conditions are worse than those in the lowest minor leagues in the United States. For the play itself, they say they do it for "pride, patriotism, incalculable public adoration, and government fringe benefits."[161]

But there are apparently some attractive perquisites. According to one recent source, players are free from food-rationing and from harvest-season drafts. They also have access to the very best coaches, doctors, and psychologists outside the U.S. major leagues.[162] Don Miguel Cuevas says that it is because of baseball that he has a home, furnishings, a TV, a Russian car, and most important to him, a diploma. Until 1964, he had only a seventh-grade education. In 1977, he became a PE instructor. His diploma is rivaled only by a scroll, personally signed by Fidel, that commemorates his retirement from baseball in 1974, after twenty years of distinguished play, the only such scroll ever awarded a Cuban baseball player.[163]

Although in some ways the Dominicans have replaced the Cubans on the Caribbean baseball circuit, the island remains the source of the highest caliber of play. A professional team in Mexico, the Sultanes, recently hired several Cuban instructors and a sports physician, including pitching coach Julio Romero. The Sultanes went on to break a twenty-nine-year losing streak by winning the national championship. These support staff (unlike the players) are free to work outside Cuba, but their earnings go to the state. "More than 100 Cuban coaches and sports doctors are working in Spain, Italy, Venezuela, Mexico, and Nigeria, mostly with amateur organizations." Indeed, when the Sultanes went into a recent slump, they brought back a Cuban sports psychologist.[164]

Despite its very recent elevation to Olympic status, baseball has always enjoyed an equal place in the EIDEs.[165] In 1977, Augusto Fonseca, senior baseball coach at the Havana Province EIDE, said that the twenty-five students were chosen from over two thousand boys from throughout the province. These athletes, aged between eleven and thirteen, had daily three-hour afternoon training sessions. Held at the former Havana Yacht Club, the practices included slalom runs around the palm trees, which supposedly simulate weaving around opponents while running bases. Like all other student athletes, if they do not keep up their academic grades, they are ineligible for competition.[166]

Cuban Political Refugees

There is, of course, another side to the baseball story: the counter-revolutionaries. In 1980, Johnny Carson made the comment that "Bowie Kuhn [then Baseball Commissioner] isn't worried about the baseball players going on strike. He's got 65,000 replacements who just got to Miami ready to step in."[167] He was referring to the wave of Cuban refugees who had just arrived in Florida during the "Mariel boatlift." It was a joke, of course, but one that was lost on many of the people in question, such as Julio Soto, Eduardo Cajuso, and Julio Rojo. These men were members of the "Free Cuban Baseball Team," which was formed from the more than ten thousand refugees at Eglin Air Force Base in Florida. They had left their families and their pasts in a quest for their lifelong dream: a shot at the Major Leagues. According to Cajuso, "I would give my left arm to play in the major leagues. All I've ever dreamed of is playing in the big circus. I would only ask for my right arm and my legs so I could play well."[168]

These men lived and breathed baseball. Soto says, "Every year at Christmas, I got the same present from my parents: a new baseball uniform. It was all I ever wanted." Rojo inherits his love for the game from his father, who played in the old Negro leagues for a team called the New York Cubans.

Their story smacks of politics, however. They were all prohibited from playing ball in Cuba because they were anti-Castro. This is certainly consistent with INDER's demands on Cuban athletes in the realms of sports, academics, work, and politics. The refugees claim that baseball players are second-rate compared to the other athletes, because the game cannot be exported for political purposes as can the Olympic sports. However, in 1992, baseball became an official Olympic sport. Contrary to what INDER and most of the Cuban players say, the refugees think that Cuban boys consider the Cuban leagues only a stopping point on their way to the Great Leagues. Although the first goal of these men is to make the majors, the second goal is political. "Someday, I want to go back to Cuba and play on the exhibition tour. I want to show people what a free Cuban can do, given the chance. I want to go back and prove what they wouldn't let me prove before."[169] They admit that the only reason they came to the United States was to play baseball. And at first it seemed as if they would get their chance. Within seventy-two hours of the refugees' arrival, the Cincinnati Reds had two scouts there. They were there until Commissioner Kuhn said the Cubans could not be recruited until their status was established.

One "Marielito" who came closest to the Major Leagues is Barbaro Garbey, the designated hitter on the 1976 Cuban national team, and the first Cuban in over twenty years to break into major-league baseball. In 1982, *Granma* reported that a group of top players and coaches were banned from the game and the record books for accepting bribes to fix games in Cuba. One of these was Barbaro Garbey. Despite this, Garbey was signed by the Detroit Tigers within days of arriving in this country. He batted .364 in his first season and starred on Detroit's AAA farm club in 1982. He was placed on probation after the *Miami Herald* reported Garbey's acknowledgment of game fixing in Cuba. "I know I did right, because I had to do it [to feed my family]. A lot of people say it was wrong. I still say it was right." Although he continued to play well with a .321 average, he was suspended after allegedly striking a rival fan with a bat.[170] He continues to play professional ball in Mexico.

Miami Cubans

A Cuban may try to forget many things about his country to protect himself from the pain of his own memories, but he will not forget baseball. It is in his blood, and he wants to pass it on to his sons. American coaches in the Miami area have had to adjust to the intense involvement of the entire Cuban American family in the game played by the sons and beloved by the fathers.

> If you've got ten native Americans on a team maybe three of them will have fathers who played baseball seriously. But if you

have ten Cuban-Americans on a team, probably nine of them have fathers who have played. They're very involved. They never miss a game.

Sometimes you'll work with a kid on something for hours, trying to get him to do it a certain way. You'll get it down, then send him home. The next day they come back doing it differently. You ask them why. They tell you they've been working with their fathers.[171]

Cuban parents tend to be overprotective and overinvolved. And the Cuban kids are less likely to defy their parents than are their American counterparts. The parents do not want the boys involved in any other sport but baseball, not even the weightlifting required to gain hitting power (the lack of which is a well-known Cuban weakness).

And it is not just the fathers. Although Danny Tartabull's father, José, played nine seasons in the majors (he is now a hitting instructor in the minors), Danny's mother is the one he calls Little General:

Tartabull's mother cooked him steak for lunch almost every day because, she told him, if he was going to be a ballplayer he had to eat right. She saw to it that Danny made it to high school safely by driving him to the front door in the morning, and she was there to pick him up again at the end of the day, even though the school was only three blocks from the Tartabull's home. Danny never walked, not once.[172]

In one way, the overemphasis on the game has worked. The large Cuban American population has produced several major-league players, such as José Canseco, Danny Tartabull, Rafael Palmeíro, and Nelson Santovenia, three of whom played on the same Little League team in Miami.[173] Phil Philbin—a Philadelphia Phillies scout—coached an American Legion team that, for over twelve years, was all Cuban; Ralph Davis—baseball coach at Miami High School for more than twenty-eight years—has not coached a non-Cuban player in over ten years. No one else was good enough to survive the last cut to eighteen players.

In another way, the overemphasis has not worked. There are not nearly the number of Cuban Americans in the big leagues as many people have expected, and the reasons are many. First, before the revolution and the great exodus to the United States, there were eight million Cubans to choose from, and now there are only about eighty thousand refugees living in the United States. Second, Cubans are said to peak very early, at fifteen or sixteen, because they play no other sports, and they just never improve after that. Third, it could be prejudice. The stereotypical Cuban player is quick, small, not a power hitter, and according to Ralph Davis, black. Fourth, the motivation is certainly different here than it ever was in Cuba. On the island, there is nothing but baseball. Here, there are many other distractions, from further education, to other sports, to cars and easily available entertainment.

In an attempt to overcome what many Cuban Americans consider "sub-Cuban" baseball, there has developed in the Miami area a system of baseball schools. All 15 of these are Cuban-run. Almost all of the students are Cuban Americans, from the ages of five to fifteen. One is the Academia Pascual, run by Carlos (Camilo Pascual's brother) and his son Juan. Carlos is in his early sixties. This man's life is, literally, baseball. When he is not at the school with the 250 athletes, which is held 50 Saturdays a year, he is a scout for the Baltimore Orioles. In the winter, he manages a Venezuelan team.[174]

Talent Scouts in Cuba

More recently, it seems, the Major Leagues are not waiting until Cuban refugees arrive on U.S. shores. Scouts are already visiting Cuba regularly, in an attempt to get to know the best players, for when and if they are allowed to leave. The defection to the United States before the Pan-American Games in July 1991 of René Arocha, a pitcher from the Cuban national team, raised the hopes for such a prospect even higher. Yet many Cubans doubt that others will follow. According to Pablo Gutiérrez Véliz, the team psychologist, "Few would take that step. No one travels as a prisoner in bondage." It is what they travel without that makes the difference. Arocha left behind his twenty-year-old wife and an eight-year-old daughter from a previous relationship.[175]

According to Arocha, "Everybody [the Cuban athletes] wants to play here because they think they are wasting their time in Cuba." After pitching for the Louisville Redbirds, the AAA team for the St. Louis Cardinals, for two seasons, Arocha recently made his debut with the Cardinals. Yet, despite Arocha's treachery, even Cuban Baseball Commissioner Domingo Zabala is ambivalent about him. In one breath he declares him a "traitor to Cuban baseball" and says "it is as if he died at birth." The next moment he asks how he is doing.[176]

The lack of friendly relations between the United States and Cuba forces scouts to be creative about making Cuban contacts. They took advantage of the 1991 Pan-American Games to make further contacts. Frank Wren, formerly the Montreal Expo's Latin American scouting supervisor and now with the Miami Marlins, visited Cuba under the sponsorship of the Cuban Baseball Federation. Because U.S. Treasury Department regulations prohibit spending money in Cuba, Wren was asked if the Federation was paying his expenses. "Well, they make it easy for me, let's put it that way. . . . I'd really not like to get into the specifics of it." On the other hand, Los Angeles Dodger scout Mike Brito has traveled to Cuba three times in the last six years as a guest of Mexico's national baseball team, not technically as a Dodger scout. "It's very tough because we American citizens have to get a special permit from Washington. But because I go with the Mexican team, it's easy for me." He already has four hot prospects: Omar Linares, Antonio Pacheco, Germán Mesa, and Lazaro Valle.[177]

The U.S. teams are counting on the economic situation in Cuba to force Castro's hand until he allows Cuban players to leave. (Stranger things have happened. Former Soviet athletes are now playing in the National Hockey League, for example.) According to Brian Sabean, the New York Yankees' vice-president for scouting, "Castro needs dollars and he needs favorable publicity to deflect his problems. And Castro knows that athletes are one of his resources." The Cuban team has won nine world amateur championships since 1969. If the doors were opened, some say that "Cuba would one day surpass the Dominican Republic as the leading producer of major league talent from Latin America." According to Mike Brito, who discovered Fernando Valenzuela in Mexico, "If they ever come over to the U.S., there's going to be a Cuban player on every team."[178]

Indeed, the René Arocha case is an interesting one. His defection on 10 July 1991 was apparently facilitated by Manuel Hurtado, a former Cuban pitching coach who had defected some years earlier. "[Defecting] was easy. All I had to do was find an exit sign." Hurtado had a car waiting for him.

Hurtado had arranged tryouts for Arocha. Eight teams were interested in him so a special lottery was held; St. Louis was the name pulled out of the hat. In his first season in the Triple A league,

Arocha went 12–7 with a 2.7 ERA in 25 starts. He came to the United States with the reputation of being the fourth best pitcher in Cuba. Major league scouts are anxious to see the other three.[179]

Like most other Cuban athletes, baseball players claim they play solely for the love of the game and of the revolution. Yet if given the opportunity to leave, most Cuban athletes would abandon socialist slogans and go, according to René Arocha:

> Of course they say they're not playing for money because that's true. You can't be playing for money when you're hardly making any. I earned 230 pesos a month [about $300 at the official rate of exchange], and nobody on the team has a car, not even the older players. And, yes, the players complain about these things—privately, of course.

In the 1970s and early 1980s, members of the national team were allowed to buy a car, at a discount, upon retirement. But now, even that option has been removed. In 1990, coaches and directors were given a Soviet Lada car, but not the players.[180]

Preston Gómez, the California Angels' executive and a former major-league manager and Washington Senator, is a long-time acquaintance of Castro's, a well-known figure from prerevolutionary Cuba, and one of the four hundred Cubans signed by Joe Cambria. To Gómez, the defection of Arocha may be the long-awaited "foot in the door." "When someone defects, the whole country knows about it. Outside of Fidel Castro and a few *comandantes*, baseball players are the best-known people on the island."[181]

> My feeling is Castro will allow his baseball players to turn pro next year after they try to win a gold medal at the Olympics in Barcelona . . . because the economic situation in Cuba is so bad. You know what breaks my heart? When I go to Cuba and these former Cuban players come up to me and they want a pair of socks. Or they have a daughter and she needs a dress. The heat is on. Fidel Castro is struggling. So, before long, I believe he will be forced to open up everything, including baseball.[182]

If the gates were opened, scouts would be eyeing prospects such as third baseman Omar Linares, left fielder Orestes Kindelán, second baseman Antonio Pacheco, and shortstop Germán Mesa.

SPORTS AND POLITICS

Cuba has been accused of making sport an instrument of politics. Castro does not deny that sport is political; it is almost as if he were accused of being Latin American. Why deny it? Instead, he merely tries to clarify the Cuban position.

> Really, it is just the other way around. Politics is an instrument of sports. That is, sport is not a means, but rather an end, like every other human activity, every other activity that has to do with man's well-being, just as education, health, material living conditions, human dignity, feeling, and man's spiritual values are all the objectives of politics.[183]

To the Cubans, politics or the revolution exist to serve the ends of the people, that is, to serve all human activity. Sport is merely one of those activities.

Scientists say that it is healthy to exercise. Desirous of a more fit population, the developed countries like the United States, Australia, and Great Britain have for several decades tried to encourage people to get out and practice some sport, to exercise. The results have been less than overwhelmingly successful. Cuba, on the other hand, seems to have succeeded where these countries have failed. "State monopoly works wonders in sports, whatever its shortcomings in other fields."[184]

> Cuba's successes in the development of sport have to be located in the political and social context in which they occur. It is impossible to understand one without looking at the other. Sport is an important part of the Cuban culture available to all and, at the same time, a means of asserting Cuba's independence and evidence of the tangible successes that have been made in other spheres.[185]

With the revolution came the task of restructuring Cuban society. For at least the first decade, until the new system was well on its way, policy was directed toward implementing change, rather than maintaining the status quo. After the early 1970s, the aim of the revolutionary government became to secure the new radical status quo. Just how far did Cuban society have to travel to get from the old system to the new one imposed from above by the revolutionary government? Jorge Domínguez, a professor at Harvard University and a long-time observer of Cuba, provides an intriguing view of Cuban political culture, both old and new, and of the relationship between the two. The topic is beyond the scope of this book, although it does have pertinent policy implications:

> Socialism found fertile soil in Cuba. Participation, cooperation, approval of government intervention, and political awareness are none of them new to Cuba. While not all socialist values are equally consistent with prerevolutionary attitudes and while opposition and resistance to change did occur, many socialist goals found their echo in Cuban traditions. Much of the prerevolutionary political culture continues into the revolutionary era, quite in harmony with the aims of the new government.
>
> The persistence of the past and the changes that occurred independent of any policy decisions made by the ruling elite suggest that individuals retained a more substantial degree of autonomy in belief and behavior than would have been allowed in a genuinely totalitarian state. The Cuban revolutionary government has extraordinary powers; it curtails the freedom of action of organizations and of individuals to a far greater extent than any of its predecessors had ever attempted. Yet, in part through the resilience of its citizens, not everything has changed that the government wanted changed, and some things have changed in spite of opposition from the government. The processes that account for change in Cuba are primarily related to modernization but have also resulted quite generally from the experience of the revolution itself, at times changing structures unexpectedly; these processes often begin outside government policy and are likely to remain independent of it.
>
> Although the past has not faded entirely and has helped to shape the present, the extent of the change is substantial, most of it in the direction of modern socialist values. There is more variation within the political culture than had existed before the revolution; Cuban citizens may now hold rather sharply differentiated political values. This cultural heterogeneity may become a new source of tension between government and society in the decades ahead.

If the coming of a socialist revolution to Cuba was not inevitable, the spread of socialist values, though also not inevitable, is less surprising. Government intervention was already extensive before the revolution and prepared the way for the state that burgeoned after it. Political participation, an essential part of Cuban revolutionary politics, is not new to Cuba either, although it has taken novel revolutionary forms.[186]

Sport is one of these "novel revolutionary forms," and such novelty, especially in the form of baseball, may be the salve to smooth and soothe the scars left by years of hostility between the United States and Cuba.

6

Cuban Sport in the 1980s and 1990s

The last decade in Cuba has been one of major political and economic changes. These changes were reflected in changing sports policies. New security concerns—arising from the anti-Cuban foreign policy of the Reagan and Bush administrations and the more recent withdrawal of much of the Soviet support for Cuba—contributed to an increased emphasis on defense, which was reflected in the formation of military sports clubs in the 1980s. Economic decline—as a result of problems within Cuba's socialist system, world recession, and more recently, the withdrawal of many Soviet supplies and subsidies—probably prompted cutbacks in sports spending (except for the 1991 Pan-American Games) and a refocusing on popular sports participation in the mid–1980s. In the 1990s, Cuban leaders may try to use sports to break the political isolation they now face, but the economic crisis could force the leadership to cut back on sports aid programs, teams sent to competitions, top athletic training, and programs for mass participation in sports.

THE POLITICAL AND ECONOMIC CONTEXT

In order to understand the direction of Cuban sports policy in the 1980s and 1990s, it is necessary to explore briefly the broader economic and political situation. A full explanation of Cuban econom-

197

ics and politics since the beginning of the 1980s would be a complex and lengthy task and would also be inappropriate to a study of sports. The broader social situation has been addressed elsewhere.[1] Yet, this economic and political setting is relevant to recent (and future) developments in Cuban sports. Consequently, in this section, we shall provide a brief summary of the conditions faced by Cuba in the late 1980s and early 1990s, as well as Cuban reactions to this situation. Only the years 1990 and 1991 will be considered in detail as these years are broadly indicative of Cuban policy since 1986.[2] These two years also incorporate the impact on Cuba of the process of change in Eastern Europe and the former USSR.[3]

The sweeping changes that occurred in the former USSR and in Eastern Europe disrupted the Cuban economy and created political pressures for major reforms in Cuba. The rapid pace of change in the old socialist bloc, in combination with previously existing economic problems, made it hard to establish a clear direction in Cuban policy.[4] This was made more difficult because Cuban rhetoric does not always correspond to actual practice. Cuba's leaders appeared uncertain as to how to respond to the crisis faced by their country. The Cuban response, in reality, was to attempt to reform the economic and political structures of Cuba within a socialist framework.[5] This standpoint was reaffirmed in 1990 and 1991, as well as at the Fourth Congress of the Cuban Communist party in October 1991.[6]

Even before the rapid transformations in Eastern Europe and the USSR, Cuba was facing several economic difficulties. Principle among these was a severe shortage of hard currency. Perestroika and the subsequent abandonment of socialism in East Europe and the Soviet Union intensified the existing economic crisis in Cuba. Indeed, according to Jorge Domínguez, "From 1989 to 1992 the Cuban economy contracted sharply with imports shrinking from $8.1 billion to $2.2 billion."[7]

The Cuban Economy in the 1980s

In May 1986, Cuba temporarily suspended interest payments on its $3.5 billion debt to the West. In that year Cuba suffered a $520 million trade deficit. By the end of 1989, the debt to the West and to Japan was $6606.5 million. This suspension added to Cuba's considerable difficulty in conducting trade outside the then socialist bloc. Shortly afterward, Cuba's major socialist trading partners turned toward expanding their ties with the West and were less inclined to trade with Cuba, especially if Cuba could not purchase goods with exchangeable currency. This tide may be turning. Spain recently announced a $40 million loan to alleviate the food shortage in Cuba. Madrid had suspended credits in 1986 because of "Cuba's failure to make payments on its $1 billion debt."[8]

Falls in sugar and oil prices in the late 1980s contributed to a 25 percent cut in Cuba's hard currency earnings.[9] These developments, along with reductions in Cuban production of tobacco and coffee, added to the burden created by other international events, such as the devaluation of the U.S. dollar (the main foreign currency held in Cuba), increased protectionism in the West, and the tightening of the U.S. economic embargo.[10] Further, the Cuban debt is not held in U.S. dollars, so the devaluation against other currencies hurts the value of the debt.[11]

Thus, in the late 1980s, Cuba was forced to reduce imports (adding to the existing shortage of consumer goods) and to increase efficiency in an attempt to increase its export revenue. Nevertheless, in June 1989, Cuba's hard currency reserves had plummeted to a meager total of $87 million ($69 million in cash), which was less than six weeks' worth of imports from the West.[12]

In the late 1980s and the early 1990s, Cuba sought new sources of hard currency: through tourism and through new trading partners in Asia (especially China) and in Latin America (especially Brazil).[13] Between 1986 and 1992, Cuban tourism services improved substantially, although services are still slow and some prices have increased.[14] At the 1991 Congress, Carlos Lage stated that tourism had earned over $400,000,000 for Cuba.[15]

Joint ventures, sanctioned since 1982, have also received renewed attention, especially in recent years. The changing situation in the socialist bloc has placed additional pressure for Cuba to seek such potential sources of convertible currency, together with an increased emphasis on import substitution and self-sufficiency, especially in foodstuffs. These policies were stressed more under the "Special Period in Peace Time" adopted at the end of 1990 and were restated at the Fourth Congress of the Cuban Communist party in October 1991.[16] Despite these efforts, however, in 1991 Cuba's hard currency reserves were estimated at a paltry $50 million.[17]

The Collapse of Socialism in Europe and its Effects on Cuba

Existing economic problems, the ousting of the communist parties in Eastern Europe, and disruptions in Soviet trade led to a 5 per-

200 Sport in Cuba

cent decline in Cuba's economy in 1990 and food shortages in 1990 and 1991. Deliveries from the Soviet Union to Cuba were severely disrupted. At the beginning of 1990, rural strikes in the Soviet Union resulted in delayed shipments of wheat and chicken feed, which led to a scarcity of bread and eggs in Cuba.[18] In 1990, Soviet deliveries of oil, which Cuba had reexported for hard currency, were also curtailed substantially, and this cost Cuba a loss of $620 million in hard currency earnings.[19] In 1991, only 7.3 million tons of oil were delivered, one-third of what was expected and thus, no surplus could be reexported. Domestic use has also been severely curtailed. By mid–1992, there had been a 50 percent cut in oil since 1987.[20] Vital Eastern European supply lines have also been disrupted, and Cuba could not afford the hard currency demanded by newly established private East European firms.[21]

In 1992 Cuba faced even greater difficulties. Under the Soviet-Cuba Trade Agreement of 29 December 1990 all exchanges from March 1991 (including oil purchases) were to be made in U.S. dollars. Although this condition was subsequently postponed until 1 January 1992, world market prices for Cuban commodities were established. The agreement also stated that as of 1995 Cuba's debt to the USSR (estimated at between 10 and 15 billion dollars) would become payable in hard currency.[22] The recent demise of the Soviet Union may lead to an advancement of this aspect of the agreement, especially as the 1990 agreement was for only one year, not for five as in past agreements. The demand that Cuba pay 10 percent of freight costs for oil placed additional strain on Cuba as this cost was equal to about half of Cuba's foreign currency reserves.[23]

The collapse of the Gorbachev-controlled central Soviet government makes Cuba's position in the future even more uncertain. Should Yeltsin remain as the most prominent and powerful leader in whatever is left of the USSR, prospects for Cuba are likely to deteriorate further. Yeltsin supported bringing an end to Soviet subsidies to Cuba and may seek cheaper alternative sources for goods now purchased from Cuba. On 27 December 1991, Yeltsin announced that the 1991 Trade Pact with Cuba had ended and that no new agreement had been made. He stated that Russia would no longer subsidize Cuba, that any future ties would be of a commercial nature, and that trade would be conducted in hard currency. This was to include any future oil purchases, which were possible but which would not be sufficient to meet all of Cuba's needs. Russian officials also declared their support for "freedom and democracy" in Cuba and stated that Russian troops in Cuba would not defend the Castro regime should it be threatened. Interestingly, the

Russian announcement coincided with the opening of a Moscow office of the anti-Castro Cuban American National Foundation (CANF). The office was opened "to get the point of view of free Cubans into spheres of influence of democratic Russia."[24]

Cuba has talked to several republics and made one barter agreement with Belarus in September 1991. In December, Cuba's foreign trade minister visited several former Soviet republics, including the Baltic states.[25] On 26 December 1991, Cuba recognized the new Commonwealth of Independent States and also Georgia. A desire to retain the "ties of friendship and collaboration created over the past three decades" was also expressed in the news dispatch from Havana. A more significant development, the Cubans announced that "most-favored-nation" trade agreements had been established with the oil-rich republic of Kazakhstan and with the food-producing Republic of Ukraine. The trade agreement would include supplies of oil and wood to Cuba in exchange for sugar, medicines, and fruit at market prices. These agreements with three republics indicate that Cuba may be able to retain trade with some republics in the USSR, but the fact that 80 percent of goods shipped to Cuba pass through the Russian republic places Yeltsin in a position to severely disrupt any trade with Cuba. However, in May 1993 Russia's first deputy prime minister, Vladimir Shumeiko, went to Cuba to review bilateral trade accords that were not being completed satisfactorily. It was the first high-ranking Russian government official to visit Cuba in more than two years.[26]

Cuban Policy in the 1990s

At the end of 1990, austerity measures already adopted in the late 1980s were expanded in Cuba under the rubric of "The Special Period in Peacetime." This special period will temporarily (for from two to five years) end the construction of schools, daycare centers, polyclinics, and houses. The measures also included cuts in the availability of gasoline, reductions in the number of publications, and an expansion of the list of rationed goods (including foodstuffs and clothing). The legal parallel markets that sold goods at higher prices than rationed goods were finally closed in November 1990 after previously being restricted to luxury items. Use of fuels was cut—oxen replaced tractors and bicycles replaced cars. In a ridiculous twist of fate, with old technology now leading the new, the Cuban military has adapted horse-drawn carts and tricycles to transport supplies and heavy weapons, such as anti-aircraft guns. In late 1991, taxi service was virtually halted, television broadcasting was restricted to five hours daily, and bus services were limited. Even nighttime baseball games were halted. On top of all other hardship, "a mysterious epidemic has afflicted thousands of Cubans in the past 18 months," causing vision problems and limb numbness. The illness shows no signs of being contagious and the poor Cuban diet is under suspicion.[27]

In early 1992, bus routes outside Havana were cut by one-third, cinemas were open only a few hours daily and some only one day a week, taxi service was further curtailed, and air-conditioning and street lighting were reduced significantly. These cuts are indicative of the severe economic (and possibly social) crisis faced by Cuba as the 1990s decade opens. According to Russian sources, in 1989 Cuba's GNP fell by 10 percent and by a further 20 percent in the first half of 1991. The source also claimed that in 1992 Cuba's GNP would decline by a staggering further 80 percent. With virtually no hard currency reserves and only 70 percent of expected imports arriving in 1991, Cuba faced growing external and internal pressures for far-reaching economic and political reforms.[28]

The Cuban response during the Special Period—of increasing voluntary labor in order to grow more food and of declarations that socialism would be maintained even if horse power had to be used—could have several different results. There could be increased repression, likely to prompt U.S. and/or Cuban exile intervention. At the end of 1991, three Cuban exiles were caught trying to infiltrate the northeastern coast of the island, armed with forty-one explosive devices. After a trial in Cuba, one was executed, the others jailed. In May 1993, nine armed exiles, members of the militant, anti-Castro Alpha 66 group, were arrested in the Florida Keys, equipped with hand grenades, pipe bombs, AK-47 semiautomatic weapons, and a grenade launcher.[29]

It could result in the further undermining of the legitimacy of socialism within Cuba, which was already evident in the emergence of human rights activists and in the burgeoning number of legal and illegal Cuban exiles.[30] Yet the trend appeared short-lived. Several weeks after the arrest of the three armed exiles in 1991, five Cubans were arrested after allegedly killing three policemen in a foiled attempt to escape the island. Following these events, several human rights activists were arrested and one dissident (with bruises on his body) claimed he had been beaten. A crackdown had begun.[31]

The Rapid Action Brigades, begun in concern with the Mariel boatlift in 1980, began to step up their activities, such as staging progovernment demonstrations at the homes of dissidents. Within the last two years, dissident activity has clearly subsided. Like everyone else in this "Special Period of Peace," human rights activists must spend the better part of the day and night standing in line, walking or biking to work, and scrambling just to survive. Such a hand-to-mouth existence leaves little time for the luxury of dissent. According to Jorge Domínguez, "Although many abroad expected that economic hardship would increase support for opposition groups, the short-term effects of this hardship have weakened and disorganized them, making it easier for the regime to endure. . . . Cuba's would-be Boris Yeltsins have thus far been cowed. Its would-be Violeta Chamorros and Václav Havels are in prison or in Miami."[32]

Like the invasion at Playa Girón thirty years earlier, the U.S. embargo has served to strengthen the resolve of the Cuban people as well as of Fidel Castro. The one fact that all Cubans—those in Miami and those in Havana—can agree on is that they are a very proud people. According to Alberto Juantorena, "Americans *live* in a country; we Cubans are *building* a country. We are small and still rather poor, but very big with sentiments of liberty." Current U.S. policy gives ordinary Cubans a reason to support the call for austerity and reaffirms Castro's greatest psychological asset: the United States as the enemy. Cuban Americans anxious to recapture their homeland violate Cuban sovereignty, frightening Cuban listeners of Miami radio "with the prospect of the return of exiles who will demand property restitution."[33]

The Cuban Democracy Act (also known as the Torricelli Amendment) was passed in 1992, signed by President Bush, and endorsed by President-elect Clinton. Besides deepening the bite of the embargo, this law seeks to apply U.S. law to other countries. Foreign subsidiaries of U.S. companies may now be prosecuted for trading with Cuba. "Ships carrying cargo to or from Cuba are barred from U.S. ports for six months." It has been "denounced worldwide as an infringement on international trade law." The most stinging indictment of U.S. policy came with the vote of the U.N. General Assembly on the resolution entitled "Necessity of ending the economic, commercial and financial embargo imposed by the United States of America against Cuba." The vote was 59–3, with 71 abstentions, with only Israel and Romania aligning with the United States. Before the Cuban Democracy Act, it was Castro's Cuba that was isolated internationally. U.S. policy toward Cuba has swung the pendulum, with the United States and Cuba trading places in international public opinion. Continued pursuit of such a policy will likely preclude U.S. influence on post-Castro Cuba, which has been the entire point of U.S. policy since 1960.[34]

Castro has stated several times that Soviet reforms would not be replicated in Cuba. Yet, this is at least as much a rhetorical expression of Cuban independence as it is an outright rejection of Soviet-style reforms. This is not to say that the Cuban leadership is unaware of the problems it faces, rather it is a rejection of any external attempt to force Cuba's hand. Cuba's leadership has sought its own solutions, but several reforms point toward liberalization in the economy as well as an attempt to improve political accountability and responsiveness.[35] On the other hand, the Fourth Congress of the PCC appeared to sanction ideas and policies previously enacted or raised by either Fidel or his brother Raúl, in his speech to the congress, and this indicated both that control still rested largely with Cuba's political elites (especially the PCC) and that many leaders feared the effects of political decentralization and expanded empowerment of the Cuban populace.[36] The particularly severe economic situation also requires rapid decision making, which is not easy to combine with the goal of expanding participatory democracy.[37]

Conversely, decisions to allow material incentives, especially in agriculture, despite recent official criticism—together with allowing greater foreign investment, encouraging enterprise self-financing, and allowing privatization in some areas of the economy—indicate that some reform occurred in Cuba, and that reform may well continue as the decade of the 1990s unfolds.[38] As in the economy, the international context Cuba found itself enmeshed in during the late 1980s and early 1990s also prompted attempts to reform political structures on the island.

The Fourth Congress sanctioned direct elections to the Cuban Provincial and National Assemblies, attempted to democratize the PCC and, as at the 1986 Third Congress, sought to renovate the top levels of power in the PCC. Carlos Aldana Escalante, Carlos Lage, and Roberto Robaína, all members of a faction in the PCC said to favor perestroika-type reforms, were promoted to the Politburo.[39]

The Cuban leadership appeared to adopt a position between that of these reformers and that of the old guard, who feared the consequences of reforming too much. The apparent ambiguity of Cuban policy in recent years reflected the divergent views within the PCC, the effects of the economic crisis in Cuba, as well as attempts to contain discontent. The Cuban elite attempted to reform socialism and thereby to retain the legitimacy of the elite among Cubans, in an increasingly difficult context.[40] The deteriorating economic situation and growing political isolation, however, makes this task—and the survival of socialism in Cuba—increasingly difficult. Should all or most previous ties with the republics of the former Soviet Union be removed, the future of Cuba's revolutionary experiment with socialism looks bleak.

In an attempt to rejuvenate the political leadership, Castro dismissed several high-ranking officials. "Carlos Aldana, former party secretary for ideology and international relations and among the most pragmatic and open-minded of the senior leadership, was dismissed in 1991 for corruption and negligence of duty." Aldana had greatly expanded his duties within the party and the government as recently as 1989. Humberto Pérez, alleged architect of the economic recovery twenty years ago, had been sacked in 1985 for "excessive reliance on market mechanism." General Arnaldo Ochoa, hero of Angola, was executed in 1989 for drug-trafficking and corruption. This move appears designed to teach many lessons, not the least of which is to keep the army loyal.[41]

Roberto Robaina González appears to be profiting from the recent shake-ups. The thirty-seven-year-old leader of the Communist Youth organization was named—apparently to his own surprise— as Cuba's foreign minister, replacing Ricardo Alarcon de Quesada, fifty-five, who was reassigned as president of the National Assembly of People's Power. Analysts reason that the choice of Robaina is more important domestically than internationally. "With more than 50 percent of the Cuban population under 35 and nearly 40 percent between 14 and 30, the revolution definitely needs to be responsive to the younger generation."[42]

Whether the political and economic reforms will be contained within a socialist framework remains to be seen, but it seems increasingly less likely without major change, perhaps including direct (and perhaps more representative) elections.[43] The 1980s also witnessed numerous changes in the sports policies in this Caribbean island. With changes in Soviet sport and the revelations of corruption in sports in the GDR, it will be useful to follow the direction of Cuban sports policies in the 1990s. In the current decade, Cuba's leaders will be hard pressed just to survive. Unless Cuba can turn sports into a moneymaker through the cash awards of the athletes and the salaries of sports professionals overseas, sport seems to be a likely and logical area in which to make cuts.

CUBAN SPORTS POLICIES

The desire for mass participation in physical culture and the desire for outstanding athletes have been constant commitments in Cuban sports theory, despite shifts in emphasis between the two desires over the course of the revolution. Cuban leaders constantly refer to the links between physical culture, health, discipline, and defense. Cuban praxis is complex and contains many different elements, often operating simultaneously. Although it seems that either mass participation or high performance dominated in some periods, both goals have continued to be important. New approaches to one aspect or the construction of facilities for a particular activity did not mean that other aspects or activities were suddenly ignored or excluded. This was true both before and after 1961 when Castro declared that the revolution was socialist. The changes in physical culture were in the methods adopted to achieve the various goals of Cuban theory, and in the shifting placement of emphasis among these goals.

The promotion of communist ideology through physical culture was also consistently stated as a goal, particularly after 1960, but the method for achieving this objective varied, especially before and since 1970. The emphasis placed upon pursuing physical culture for health and defense purposes has similarly varied since January 1959. Many of these variations in Cuban policy can be linked to shifts in general Cuban theory and practice of revolution and socialism. This is evident in the different approaches used to encourage both mass participation and world-class performances. In general, emphasis was placed upon trying to achieve egalitarianism in physical culture via revolutionary consciousness during the 1960s, especially between 1966 and 1970. In the 1970s and early 1980s, increasing standards and developing specialized sports training centers appeared to dominate physical culture policies. After 1970, economic growth and quality improvements were viewed increasingly as ways to make egalitarianism possible. This was in line with the change in Cuba's general theory of socialist transition at that time. Beginning in 1984 and intensifying in 1986, there was a reconsideration of the best ways to advance both egalitarianism and economic growth. An attempt was made to balance the ideas developed in the 1960s and 1970s.

Massive changes in Eastern Europe and the USSR and the economic effects of these on Cuba mean that sport will be less of a priority, even though the encouragement of international cooperation through sports may be desirable to help reduce Cuba's political isolation. The near collapse of Cuba's economy, however, means that priority will be elsewhere; if indeed, the regime survives.

Cuban Sports Policy up to 1980

During the first two years after the revolution, the roles given to physical culture were within a liberal-democratic tradition, and there was little indication of the part that physical culture would later play in political socialization. At this early stage, Cuba's physical culture administrators concentrated on extending access. Physical culture programs in these two years emphasized the value of physical culture for health and recreation, especially for children. Physical culture was also used as part of military training.

These uses continued following the declaration of socialism in 1961. Physical culture was viewed as an agent of social change, a means to promote the development of communist attitudes, a part of well-rounded development; athletes were seen to be at the vanguard of this ideal and were expected to provide examples of revolutionary consciousness. Both these aspects remained crucial to Cuban theory, but the methods to fulfill these objectives have varied over the years since 1961. In the 1960s, athletes, like other prominent public figures, were expected to be revolutionaries, students, and workers (not just athletes) who were disciplined and modest. This expectation continued into the next decade. Athletic success and competition were, however, stressed increasingly in the 1970s. Yet, mass programs—and notably exercise groups—continued to be important and were expanded. Success stemmed from the technological advances in Cuban physical culture and was portrayed as important.[44] As in most areas, there was a reorientation of policy toward qualitative advances following the quantitative development emphasized in the 1960s.

In the late 1960s, developing revolutionary consciousness and using moral incentives were the most important vehicles for achieving both egalitarianism and economic growth. In the 1970s, however, material incentives were used increasingly as a means to develop Cuba's productive base. In production, this meant that both collective and individual material incentives replaced some of the moral incentives that had been emphasized between 1966 and 1970. In politics, education, and employment, merit would be the prime basis for selection rather than just revolutionary commitment: "merit will be what distinguishes one citizen from another."[45]

Cuban Sports Policy in the 1980s and 1990s

This change in the methods intended to achieve economic growth, quality, and egalitarianism during the socialist transition was stressed after 1976 and was maintained into the early 1980s. Material incentives continued, as did the policy of distribution according to ability and productivity. The role of physical culture in the economic development of Cuba was given new emphasis. Economic growth was viewed as a prerequisite for making the future achievement of egalitarianism possible in all areas including physical culture. Health, fitness, discipline, and increased productivity were reemphasized as values linked with participation in physical culture.

From the mid–1970s on, there may also have been a greater willingness to provide top athletes with some material rewards in return for their achievements that, as well as creating prestige for the revolution, provided other Cubans with role models. The prestige for both Cuba and socialism gained from success is a source of pride for many Cubans, not just for political leaders. Greater emphasis was laid on competition in sports and also on some exercise programs. In the late 1970s, raising standards became more important in Cuban policy, possibly at the expense of relaxation and recreation.[46] As the 1980s progressed, the stress on organized sports and specialized training for athletes was reexamined.

Between 1980 and 1984, there were limited changes to physical culture policy, although spending on sociocultural activities was reduced. In 1981 and 1982, the production and export of sports equipment fell as well. New programs in all aspects of physical culture were limited in these years, except for the formation of military sports clubs or SEPMI, which aimed at teaching Cubans basic military skills and educating them in the importance of defense capabilities. Besides this one new policy in physical culture, the ideas of the 1970s emphasizing the importance of economic growth and technology along with revolutionary consciousness were maintained. The Cubans were still building new sports schools until the mid–1980s. Recreation facilities were provided as part of collective material incentives in the workplace. There was, however, one program that pointed to concern about raising participation levels: in 1982 a renewed emphasis was placed on providing facilities in rural areas of Cuba.[47]

In 1984, Cuba's leaders turned away from constructing specialized sports schools. Cubans were urged to make better use of existing facilities, and Castro stated that no new sports schools or swimming pools would be constructed in the immediate future. In the following year, workers in the sports industry were urged to be more efficient so as to meet domestic demand for equipment. Programs using locally made equipment or makeshift equipment that was readily available in the home were also encouraged.[48] This was in line with various measures adopted in many areas in response to economic difficulties and reforms in the late 1970s and early 1980s. In 1986, INDER began surveys to determine which forms of popular physical culture could be easily and cheaply provided with facilities across the island.

As in several government and party organizations, new personnel were appointed in INDER, including a new president, Martínez Corona, and a new vice-president for high-performance sports, Alberto Juantorena. These changes appeared to culminate in the 1987 review of INDER that criticized the tendency of some physical-culture trainers and bureaucrats to concentrate on producing champions at the expense of mass participation. Since 1985, new programs for extending mass participation in physical culture, especially recreation, have also been introduced, including an anti-sedentary campaign to combat obesity and smoking, and clubs (círculos de abuelos) that are intended to promote recreation among older Cubans. These programs were probably introduced because many Cubans did not participate in physical culture, and perhaps also because the process of rectification then occurring in Cuba resulted in the reassessment of a number of economic and political policies adopted in the mid–1970s.[49]

The revision of physical culture since the middle of the 1980s indicated the ongoing attempt to balance the policy goals of mass participation and top-level athletes, which has existed since the beginning of the revolution. The stress on making more efficient use of existing facilities probably came from problems in economic growth, which limited the resources available for investment in areas such as physical culture. State control of prices and currency rates meant there was little or no price inflation for most goods until 1981, when wages and retail prices were increased by an average of 10 percent.[50]

This meant that the apparent increase in budgetary spending in all areas was actually a reflection of price reforms. Spending on physical culture, however, continued to increase until 1983, when all expenditures were cut. In 1984, Castro stressed the importance of making better use of existing facilities, because Cuba could not afford new ones. "In the immediate future, we are not going to be able to set up more sports schools."[51] Cuba's sports school program suffered a setback in 1984 when the EIDE in Ciego de Avila was destroyed by Cyclone Kate. Another example of the drop in government spending was the inclusion of physical culture facilities as part of incentive funds for workers. Two-thirds of these funds were for bonus pay, while one-third went to sociocultural activities including recreational clubs and gymnasiums as well as vacations and housing.[52]

Despite some cutbacks in physical culture funding in the 1980s, spending on basic military training and on military sports clubs was expanded. Military sports clubs were established in January 1980 and expanded rapidly in 1981 and 1982, which runs counter to the policy of cutting back on spending in physical culture, particularly as equipment for these clubs is generally expensive and must be imported. This commitment was related to security concerns arising not only from the aggressive foreign policy of the Reagan administration in the United States, but also from a number of internal security concerns, such as the Mariel exodus and the occupation of foreign embassies by Cubans wishing to leave the island.[53]

Foreign trade and sports aid, both financial and technical, was an important part of Cuba's physical culture economy. Cooperation with the socialist bloc was particularly important in military-related sports and in high-performance sports, which also received considerable funding. Nevertheless, spending on mass physical-culture programs is considerable, and the economic pressures of the early 1980s necessitated limits on elite facilities as well as on new facilities for the general populace. There was also an attempt to encourage mass activities that were not expensive, such as physical-culture plans that used articles found in the home.[54]

Despite these cutbacks, Cuba's leaders did not renege on their commitment to host the 1991 Pan-American Games, at considerable cost. In fact, these Games were probably the major contributor to the 1991 sports budget of $150 million (a 50 percent increase on the 1988 budget and a 12 percent increase on the 1990 budget of $117 million).[55] This commitment was made more remarkable given the recent radical changes in the European socialist countries.

Changes in the Socialist Bloc and Cuban Sports

The general economic situation and the radical changes in Eastern Europe and the Soviet Union make it likely that Cuban spending on sports will be reduced. As President Castro has acknowledged, sport is considered important but not the first priority. As the island realizes the loss of Eastern European trade and the cutoff of subsidized trade with the USSR, Cuba will be forced to focus on meeting the most basic needs of its population. This will probably lead to cuts in sports funding even though there are reasons for continuing the commitment to sport. Changes in Eastern Europe and the Soviet Union also reduce the possibility that Cuba will continue to receive the technical and sports training facilities previously available to it, or that, at the very least, such assistance will be charged for in hard currency. This, together with the reduction of the sports equipment trade, has serious implications for Cuba's future capacity to maintain mass participation and top-level sports. Since 1988, imports of sports equipment from COMECON countries have fallen substantially.[56] It will also make it difficult for Cuba to continue supporting sports development in other less developed countries, which may serve to increase the island's already substantial isolation.

In addition to these economic effects on the Cuban sports system, revelation of corruption in the former East German and Soviet sports systems (like exposures of party and state corruption in the old socialist bloc) will put increased pressure on the ideological underpinnings of political, economic, and sports structures in Cuba. The Soviet sports system, on which much of Cuba's sports system is modeled, has been subjected to considerable criticism during the process of perestroika and glasnost in the USSR.

Vladimir Sysoyev, a member of the Soviet Olympic Committee, criticized sports officials for ignoring sport as a source of health and fun and accused the State Sports Committee of stressing Olympic sports. He criticized the sports body for issuing padded reports with inflated statistics. The president of the State Sports Committee, Marat Gramov, was voted out by the People's Deputies. During six hours of discussions held over two days, he was bombarded with questions, which he failed to answer adequately and which included several about previous spending on mass sports and on the upkeep of officials. Valeri Lobanovski, a soccer coach, was critical of sports policies that paid no attention to mass sports and that concentrated on Olympic sports. In 1991, only 6–8 percent of Soviet citizens practiced sports. Lobanovski also accused the Sports Committee of taking hard currency winnings from Soviet athletes (80 percent of top athletes' earnings or about $100 million dollars) and spending the money on the committee's bureaucracy, on foreign trips, and on bonuses for the officials that traveled overseas with the Soviet sports teams.[57]

Top athletes have sought to end this practice of their hard currency winnings going into the state coffers. Some tennis players have apparently ignored the rules in recent years. According to Lobanovski, sports bureaucrats have resisted the perestroika process. Chess player Gary Kasparov stated that the Sports Committee should only handle sports that could not be put on a cost-accounting and self-improvement basis. Tennis player Andrei Chesnokov wanted to see the Sports Committee closed down.[58]

It is difficult to know whether similar complaints or problems are common in Cuba. It seems likely that some athletes would like to receive the money earned from their sporting efforts. René Arocha, a Cuban baseball pitcher who recently defected to the United States, claimed that all Cuban baseball players want to play in the United States and believe they are wasting their time in Cuba. Arocha claimed he received 230 pesos a month. Players, unlike coaches and trainers, could not buy cars, and the right (in the 1970s) to purchase a car at a discount when a player retired has been recently removed. Probably some Cuban athletes would like to earn money from their sports in the West, and allowing athletes to do so could provide a source of valuable hard currency for the beleaguered Cuban regime. In 1991, there were frequent rumors that this practice would soon be permitted by Cuban officials, but so far there have been no agreements. In 1977, the United States outlawed the importation of Cuban baseball players and prevented baseball scouts from attending the 1991 Pan-American Games held in Cuba.[59]

While Cuba has appeared to be more committed to mass sport than the Soviet Union, there still exists the potential for a contradiction between mass and elite sport. It is probable that there are corrupt officials in Cuba, although the small contingent of officials sent with the Cuban team to the 1987 Pan-American Games is in stark contrast to past Soviet sports delegations. Revelations of abuse in the USSR may prompt further reviews of Cuba's sports system and may perhaps add to the political isolation of the island.[60] Cuban athletes may also be moved to follow their Soviet compatriots in pushing for reforms in the payment of athletes. Cuba's substantial investment in top athletics may stimulate criticisms within Cuba, especially with the intensifying economic pressures that threaten to destabilize the entire political system. Spending on elite sports is not likely to be applauded by Cubans who face increased rationing and a reduction in the availability of already-limited consumer goods. Even if Cuba can survive the current economic turmoil, this may require not only massive cuts in the sports budget (including the diversion of athletes' earnings to other areas) but also longer working hours for less return.[61] Neither of these contingencies will encourage an expansion of mass participation in sports among the island nation's population.

The Fall of Soviet Sports

Some of the most rapid and radical changes to take place since the failed August 1991 coup attempt in the USSR have been in sports. The once great Soviet sporting nation has begun to collapse. It is conceivable that the Commonwealth of Independent States will not host the 1994 Goodwill Games, even though the Russian Olympic Committee has signed a contract with Ted Turner. It is an extreme example of the radical reversal of Soviet views that, by the 1988 Seoul Olympics, sports were seen not as a source of prestige for the USSR and for socialism, but rather as a means to open new trading markets. At the 1992 summer Olympics in Barcelona, the Baltic states fielded their own independent teams. The remaining republics competed on the Unified Team, as they had at the winter Olympics. If nothing else, the athletes shared a desire to see the old Soviet sports dynasty "make an honorable exit from the arena of Olympic sports competition" before the final breakup; and that is what they most certainly did, winning the most gold (thirty-two) and the most total medals (seventy-eight) of the summer games.[62]

Probably more threatening to the sports strength of the USSR was the decline of resources for sports (exacerbated by the falling value of the ruble) and the exodus of athletes and coaches for the riches of professional sports in the West. Soccer players, a gymnastics coach, and water-polo players are among the athletes who have left the Soviet Union. The world-record holder in the pole vault, Sergi Bubka, has also stated his intention to move to France, although he competed on the Unified Team at Barcelona. In the meantime, he represents Nike clothing and Nike shoes and runs his own athletic school in Berlin.[63]

Once-famous and well-funded sports clubs and schools are faced with shortages of money, equipment, and even food. One club in Liebsk was forced to grow flowers and vegetables for sale in order to raise money to pay for a recreational park. Access to several important training sites was blocked because of ethnic wars in the former republics of Moldova, Georgia, Armenia, and Azerbaijan. The gymnastics team, which shone in Barcelona, claimed to owe its success to the hospitality of the Italian Olympic federation. The Italians hosted the Soviet team for weeks at an athletic complex in the resort town of Porto San Giorgio. According to Vitali Scherbo from Minsk, Belarus, who won a record six gold medals, "Training facilities were excellent, the best we'd ever seen. It was an island of stability that helped us relax and concentrate on the games."[64]

The athletics and soccer federations have sought sponsorship, breaking away from the centralized Soviet Sports Ministry (Gosport), although 7 percent of their earnings are still sent to Gosport. In athletics, competitors give 10 percent of their earnings to the Athletics Federation. A gymnastics training center has resorted to offering training camps for children from the United States for $100 per day.[65]

Should funding for sport be further reduced, athletes already expressing a desire for monetary gains may leave the Soviet Union in even greater numbers. Those in weaker sports with limited professional opportunities will find it increasingly difficult to pursue their sports. Although poor by Western standards, Soviet athletes were, and remain to some extent, a privileged group. Soviet citizens are unlikely to tolerate large state subsidies for athletes, especially as the wider economy is further privatized. Yet, athletes may be reluctant to forego the perks to which they have become accustomed.[66]

Will Sport in Cuba Self-Destruct?

At this stage Cuban sport is not experiencing the same degree of turmoil. These developments in the USSR, however, may well be repeated in Cuba should socialism begin to unravel there. Cuban athletes may also exert pressures for reform in regard to their sports earnings at a time when the general populace of Cuba is being subjected to increased hardships. Thus far, however, there is limited evidence of a breakdown in traditional patterns within the Cuban sports system.

In the 1980s, Cuba pursued its general commitment to using physical culture as part of socialization but did not return to the radical 1966–1970 methods of trying to (rapidly) develop a communist society through the use of moral incentives. The idea of using physical culture as an agent for social change (by promoting communist attitudes) has been maintained, just as the promotion of physical culture for integral development, health, and defense purposes has been present since the early years of the revolution, despite the shifting in emphasis.

Although Cuba successfully hosted the 1991 Pan-American Games, the costs involved served to intensify the economic problems emerging as a result of the collapse of socialism in Eastern Europe and the USSR. This expenditure, in combination with the end of the Soviet subsidies to Cuba, will make it extraordinarily difficult, if not impossible, for Cuba to maintain its past sports policies. Sport is an area quite likely to be reduced, as pressure for more basic requirements intensifies and increases the possibility of the collapse of Cuba's socialist system.

THE GAMES

Cuban Performance in the 1980s and 1990s

Cuba first emerged as a world sports power in the 1970s. This success continued into the 1980s and 1990s. Although Cuba boycotted both the 1984 and 1988 Olympic Games, it began the decade credibly, finishing fourth at the 1980 Moscow Olympics. While only eighty-one countries attended these games (the United States led a boycott over the Soviet invasion of Afghanistan), Cuba demonstrated its continuing strength in world sports by winning eight gold medals, seven silver medals, and five bronze medals.[67]

During the 1980s, Cuba also continued its domination of the Central American and Caribbean Games, finishing first (with 271 medals) at the 1982 games, which were held in Cuba and which cost 12 million pesos to host. Cuba was again victorious in 1986 and 1990, winning 271 medals in Santiago de los Caballeros, Guatemala, in 1986 and 322 medals in Mexico City in 1990. Similarly, Cuba continued to be a world power in a number of sports, notably baseball, boxing, women's volleyball, women's weightlifting, athletics, and to a lesser extent wrestling. Cuba was a prominent performer at the 1991 World Athletic Championships in Tokyo, finishing twelfth.[68]

This continuing sports strength has been underscored by recent Cuban successes. At the 1983 and 1987 Pan-American Games, Cuba finished ahead of Canada and second only to the United States, capturing 163 medals in 1983 and 175 medals in 1987. As host nation for the 1991 Pan-American Games, Cuba won 265 medals, including ten more gold medals than the United States. Throughout the 1950s, the island never won more than thirty medals in the Pan-American Games, yet since 1971, Cuba has never won less than a hundred medals. Through the 1980s, only the United States won more medals than Cuba in the games.[69]

The Cuban success story continued at Barcelona for the 1992 Summer Olympic Games, although not on quite so grand a scale as at the Pan-American and Caribbean Games. Cuban athletes won fourteen gold, six silver, and eleven bronze medals. Out of the record number of 172 nations competing, they placed fifth in gold and sixth in total medals. Cubans were bested only by the Unified Team (112 medals, 45 gold); the United States (108, 37); [unified] Germany (82, 33); China (54, 16); and Hungary for total medals (37, 11).[70] Cuban gold medals were won in boxing (a record seven gold), two in wrestling, women's volleyball, women's discus, men's high jump, women's judo, and (most important) baseball.

On a medals-won-per-capita basis, Cuba has long been the best performer in the Western hemisphere, and in amateur baseball, Cuba remains king. Cuba has dominated Pan-American baseball, losing its first game since 1967 at the 1987 games. Despite losing six medals at the 1983 games due to drug use, Cuba proved to be a weightlifting stronghold by winning all the weightlifting medals at the 1987 Pan-American Games. Cuban boxers also dominated these games, winning a record ten medals in 1987. By 1991, with the demise of the GDR as an independent country, Cuba became the world's best sports performer on a per-capita basis.[71]

The Politics at the Games, in America

These successes at the games and world championships brought prestige to Cuba; but there were other political implications, both positive and negative, that resulted from its international sports participation. Sport has been used by Cuba for various political purposes. Games involving Cuba have often prompted political activity, and sometimes involved violence. This has been the case particularly in sporting contacts that involve both Cuba and the United States.

Even before the 1987 Pan-American Games in Indianapolis began, there was considerable controversy over Cuba's participation. This was to be the first time Cuba had competed in a multisport event within the United States since 1959, the year of the revolution. Games officials received criticism for trying to encourage the Cubans to participate in the games, following a Cuban threat to boycott the games if charter flights from Cuba to Indianapolis were not permitted. In general, all (the rare) flights from Cuba are required to pass customs in Miami and U.S. State Department officials, in a rigid adherence to policy, saw no reason to change the regulations to accommodate Cuba. Cuban officials argued that the government could not afford commercial flights, and Castro claimed that it was illogical not to allow charter flights direct to Indianapolis. Given the large, vehemently anti-Castro Cuban exile community in Miami, it is quite possible that Cuban officials were concerned about security. Moreover, the opening ceremony, originally intended to be in a downtown mall, had to be shifted because the local branch of the American Legion objected to flying the Cuban flag in what was a Legion memorial mall, claiming that one of their members had been killed in the early years of the Cuban revolution. In addition to these early controversies, a number of anti-Castro organizations had come to Indianapolis to push their viewpoint. Three groups were involved in various protests at the games. These included the Washington-based Cuban American National Foundation, which had set up a temporary office in Indianapolis during the games; the group Cuba Independiente y Democrática (CID), and the Freedom Now Committee (linked to the *Soldier of Fortune* magazine).[72]

Anti-Cuban activities began at the opening ceremony. A large banner displaying a telephone number for Cubans wishing to defect flew over the ceremony. The Cuban delegation was showered with leaflets encouraging Cubans to defect. Similar leaflets appeared on the first day of the games and were tossed at the Cuban baseball team during their first game (CID claimed responsibility). Some of Cuba's team members tore the leaflets up and threw them back. The Indianapolis police chief described the leaflet throwing by CID members as provocative, and security was increased around the Cubans and at their events. The Cuban American Foundation admitted that it had printed ten thousand cards, saying "Brother Cubans, Welcome to the Land of Liberty" and listing three telephone numbers: the Foundation, emergency, and immigration. They subsequently agreed not to distribute the cards. The Freedom Now Committee admitted to printing about the same number of leaflets offering $25,000 in gold to the first Cuban or Nicaraguan security or intelligence officer to defect. In a thinly veiled explanation, John Coleman, editor of *Soldier of Fortune* magazine, later claimed that this was not an attempt to encourage defections but was intended to assist any defector in making the transition to a new society.[73]

Various other minor events occurred, which resulted in several letters of protest from the Cuban delegation: verbal abuse of González Guerra, president of the Cuban Olympic Committee; the Cuban condemnation of Roberto Urrutia, a weightlifter who defected, as a traitor whose defeat by Cuban weightlifters showed the power of dedication and principles over imperialist money; and the Cuban claim of a right to respond to provocations. Other incidents included the replacement of a Puerto Rican gymnastics judge for allegedly favoring Cuba over the United States; the claim that a Cuban player attempted to provoke a fight at the end of the United States–Cuba handball match; a verbal exchange between the Cuban and U.S. boxing teams; and a bomb threat at the swimming venue.[74]

By far the most serious incident at the games was a brawl between Cuban boxers and officials on one hand and a group of anti-Castro CID members on the other. The exact nature of the incident remains unclear. From five to twelve Cubans were accused of being involved. As they had warned, before the games, "This country is promising us protection, but we are ready to protect ourselves."[75] With good reason. One Cuban boxer claimed he was slapped by a spectator; CID claimed the Cuban boxers tried to take an anti-Castro banner from them. Whatever the truth, other Cuban boxers and officials appear to have come to the aid of the boxers in the crowd, and a scuffle ensued: one CID member was arrested, the boxers were said to be uninjured, and security around the boxers was increased. Three spectators (CID members) claimed they were injured and subsequently filed three lawsuits requesting that criminal charges be laid against Cuban boxers and officials, accusing them of a conspiracy to commit battery. CID also filed a suit against Alberto Juantorena for alleged defamation of CID members. The chances of any such action being accepted by the Cubans was remote, and nothing appears to have happened after the games. The political nature of the incidents also made any sanctions by sporting authorities against Cuba unlikely, according to the director of the U.S. Boxing Federation.[76]

Controversy also arose over the closing ceremony, which the Cubans threatened to boycott. The Miami dance band chosen to play at the closing ceremony irked the Cubans because lead singer Gloria Estefan's father was apparently a bodyguard of the ousted dictator, Fulgencio Batista. In the end, the Cubans did attend, and even their Minister for Education and Sport, José Ramón Fernández Alvarez, was present for the hoisting of the Cuban flag as the next Pan-American Games host country. Fidel Castro described the games as "un Girón deportívo," a sports Bay of Pigs. Although concerns were expressed about security—especially as the minister had commanded forces at the Bay of Pigs invasion—no political incidents occurred at the ceremony.[77]

Despite controversy over Cuban boycotts of the 1984 and 1988 Olympics, such intensely political activities involving Cuban sports as those surrounding the 1987 Pan-American Games did not occur again. The rest of the decade was mild, by comparison, although controversy did emerge again at events involving both the United States and Cuba.

Minor controversy occurred over the 1984 and 1988 Olympic Games, both of which Cuba boycotted for political reasons: "even in the Olympics, when sports was the only link between Cuba and the United States and we didn't go to Los Angeles or Seoul, the latter out of loyalty to the Democratic People's Republic of Korea, because we don't sell out principles."[78] In the 1984 Los Angeles Games, Cuba was among the last countries to join the Soviet-led boycott, which was largely a retaliation for the U.S.–led boycott of the previous Moscow games. Cuba also claimed it was concerned about security in the United States.[79]

In Seoul

The 1988 Olympic Games in Seoul were far more controversial for Cuba. Cuba again raised security concerns, but its major complaint was that North Korea was not joint host with South Korea of the 1988 games. Cuba maintained this position even though, of the other socialist countries, only Albania and North Korea decided to boycott the games. The decision not to go unless the games were cohosted by North and South Korea was apparently made as early as 1985.[80] The main political repercussion of this decision was the claim that Cuba might lose the right to host the 1991 Pan-American Games. Allegations appeared in U.S. papers that Cuba's hosting of the Pan-American Games was contingent upon Cuba attending the 1987 Pan-American Games and the 1988 Olympics. Cuba responded by saying that the Pan-American Games had nothing to do with the Olympics and asking why Cuba should lose the Pan-American Games for Olympic boycotts when no such policy was instituted against the United States for its boycott of the 1980 Olympics. As it turned out, no such condition was imposed.[81]

In New York and Seattle

Controversy involving Cuba and the United States emerged again in 1988 when a Cuban chess player, Guillermo García, finished second in the New York Open event, winning $10,000 in prize money. Under the Trading With the Enemy Act of 1911, he was not permitted to take the money back to Cuba, having access to it only through a blocked account that could not be used unless he left Cuba permanently. Garcia claimed sport should not be included under the act. Organizers of the competition were shocked by this law, but did not plan to challenge it.[82]

Whereas sporting exchanges occurred between the two countries in the mid–1980s, by the end of the decade relations had become rather strained. Events at the 1990 Goodwill Games in Seattle were indicative of this antagonism between Cuba and the United States. José Ramón Fernández Alvarez, who had been present at the closing ceremony for the 1987 Pan-American Games in the United States, was denied a visa to attend the Goodwill Games. Government officials claimed that granting Fernández a visa would be inconsistent with U.S. foreign policy. Yet, Fernández had been allowed into the United States for the 1987 Pan-American Games and this made U.S. policy appear rather inconsistent, especially considering the very concept of the Goodwill Games. The refusal of a visa was an expression of President Bush's antagonism toward Cuba and an expression of the U.S. dissatisfaction with Cuba's refusal to follow the path of Eastern European socialism.[83] This increased antagonism between Cuba and its northern neighbor was also evident in the lead-up to the 1991 Pan-American Games.

In Cuba

Besides speculation in U.S. newspapers that Cuba could lose the Pan-American Games because of its decision to boycott the 1988 Olympics, relations were further strained as a result of wrangling over the U.S. television coverage of the games and the refusal of the U.S. government to allow a U.S. company to construct bowling lanes in Cuba for the games. As early as 1987, Cuban officials had held discussions with Brunswick Bowling and Billiards Corporation about the construction of a bowling center for the 1991 games. In the end, Cuba had to contract a Japanese firm to build the lanes, because the Trading With the Enemy Act, enforced under the economic embargo of Cuba by the United States, prevented the Brunswick Corporation from building anything in Cuba. This added four million pesos to the cost of hosting the games. Such policies also prevent U.S. firms from taking advantage of business opportunities in Cuba.[84]

Twenty-one new installations—including a stadium, gymnasiums, and a velodrome—were constructed for the games. A further forty-six sites were renovated and fifty-five buildings were constructed to house the athletes. This effort cost Cuba $24 million in hard currency and 100 million pesos (over $124 million, at the January 1992 Cuban exchange rate), which placed considerable strain on Cuba's limited foreign reserves at a time of major economic difficulties.[85] President Castro admitted that Cuba could not really afford the games and that, if the decision had not been made five years earlier, the island would not have been the host. The number of sports was reduced from the planned thirty to twenty-five.[86]

As well as denying Brunswick Corporation permission to construct the bowling center for the games, the Bush administration displayed reluctance to allow ABC television to pay for television rights to cover the games. ABC Sports had made an agreement with Cuban officials to pay about $9 million for the TV rights to the 1991 games, but this required a special license because of the economic blockade of Cuba by the United States. The ABC request to the Federal court to allow a payment of $8.7 million to the Pan-American Games Organizing Committee (75 percent of which would go to Cuba to help pay for the games) was denied by the U.S. Treasury Department. An appeal was launched for an exception for gathering and disseminating news; it was pointed out that refusal to allow the television coverage payment was inconsistent with the decision to send a team to the games. The U.S. government wanted the money to be placed in a blocked account whereby the United States would decide when relations with Cuba were sufficiently satisfactory to merit the release of the money. Cuban officials objected, claiming that the money was to help cover the cost of the games and that, if the money was not released, TV coverage by the United States would be impossible. The U.S. government continued to press for the appeal to be refused. ABC pursued its request, claiming the government was denying free speech. ABC won its case, but was only able to broadcast the games by signing an agreement waiving the fee.[87]

Despite the economic burden, the 1991 Pan-American Games were largely successful for Cuba. Cuba won more gold medals than the United States, which sent a team of 750 athletes; and Cuba won

its first-ever Pan-American gold medal in the swimming pool. A total of thirty-eight countries attended the games which were, on the
whole, of a high standard. Some U.S. athletes praised the standard
of most facilities, and U.S. journalists were generally favorable on
the presentation of the games, if not on the facilities for journalists
and on services in general.[88] Although a Cuban-made kayak was
overweight and there were problems with basketball backboards,
the games were hosted successfully.[89]

The major complaints were voiced by the U.S. men's basketball
team, which made an unusual decision to shuttle its players from
Miami to Cuba, rather than staying in the athletes' village. Whether
intended or not, this decision was an insult to both Cuba and the
spirit of the athletes' village. Cuba made no statement, but some
other U.S. athletes criticized basketball officials for their actions. In
an ironic twist of fate, several members of the U.S. men's basketball
team contracted diarrhea in Miami. U.S. boxers also complained
about the quality of food and accommodations (the athletes' village
apparently had no toilet seats). The U.S. Olympic Committee
stated, however, that the facilities in Cuba were as good as any outside the United States, and no other complaints from the other
thirty-six competing teams were reported.[90] This, together with
Cuba's excellent performance, no doubt brought some prestige to
the island as had been hoped among Cuban officials. "The leadership hopes that the [Pan-American] Games will bring Cuba a good
deal of hard currency, an improvement in its image beyond the Caribbean and Latin American region, and a dash of optimism to raise
the spirits of the islanders."[91]

While Cuba probably did win some prestige from the games, no
profit was made (Cuba broke even), despite the decision to charge
entry fees for some seventeen thousand visitors, including photographers who were charged $150 for access to the Pan-American
events.[92] Further, the games probably did little to raise the spirits of
the Cuban population, which was beset by declining food supplies
and consumer goods. "Please don't ask me about the games," said a
middle-aged woman outside a market last week. "Ask me about
eggs, meat, chicken—these are the things that we need."[93]

While some Cubans may have felt a sense of pride over the
games, some like this woman probably felt resentful about the
money spent on the games in a time of economic hardship in
Cuba.[94] Some dissidents also used the games to express their dissatisfaction: Roberto Luque Escalona, for example, who allegedly

went on a hunger strike and was jailed as a result. This seems to have been the only protest during the games. U.S. papers claimed that special "Rapid Action Brigades" had been formed to repress any protests during the games.[95] Overall the games appeared to be successful, but they did not (nor could they) cause the economic problems on the island to disappear. Despite the controversies leading up to the games, relations between U.S. and Cuban athletes during the games proved to be friendly.

Cuba's desire to use sports to promote friendship and cooperation with the United States has, however, proved to be largely unsuccessful, particularly in the late 1980s and early 1990s when U.S. antagonism toward Cuba has actually increased. More success in encouraging links between Cuba and other countries has occurred through Cuban ties with the Soviet Union and the Third World. The Soviets provided aid, including for the 1991 Pan-American Games.[96] Cuba extended aid to a number of Latin American, Caribbean, and African nations. The subsidized relationship between Cuba and the former USSR is a thing of the past. Cuba will be less able, and perhaps less willing, to provide sports aid and promote exchanges with other countries, despite the role that this aid and sports competitions may play in breaking the island's political isolation.[97] Indeed, expertise in sports is, for Cuba, a salable commodity that earns valuable hard currency for the Castro government.[98]

Changes in Soviet Sport Evident at Barcelona

The fallout in sports from the breakup of the former Soviet Union was watched with great interest at the 1992 Barcelona Olympics. As for the Unified Team, "to the average Soviet athlete, [it] was little more than a forced marriage engineered by IOC president Juan Antonio Samaranch to alleviate a housing shortage in the Olympic Village." Unless other arrangements are made, which is unlikely, this is the last time the former Soviet republics will compete as one team. The Baltics have already gone their own way. Defections of the nonpolitical kind are already legion. Leonid Arkaev, coach of the Unified Team men's gymnastics team, is leaving after the Olympics. "I will leave because one has to earn some money to live." The man responsible for making the USSR a volleyball powerhouse, Vladislav Platonov, will move to Finland to coach there. The same is probably true for the men's soccer coach, Anatoly Bishovitz. The only way the team can compete at all is because the American vodka manufacturer, Smirnoff, sponsored the Unified Team for Barcelona in 1992.[99]

In fact, the Unified Team closed out an illustrious Olympic career with a bang. They won in both medal totals with 112 (United States had 108) and the most gold medals with 45 (United States had 37). This time, Soviet athletes had an even more powerful incentive: money. The medal winners from the Unified Team were "compensated through a special fund set up by the Olympic federations: $3,000 will be awarded for each gold medal, $2,000 for silver, and $1,000 for bronze." Their biggest problem will be earning a steady income. Where once they were revered as heroes of the state, the athletes are now seen as targets of envy.[100]

The access to facilities once enjoyed by athletes and coaches is gone. The winter training camps for swimmers in the tropical climate of Georgia and Armenia have been closed because of civil war and conflict. At least four hundred of the once-famous network of sports schools have been shut down. In June 1992, Boris Yeltsin established the Russian Olympic Committee (ROC), an organization that is supposed to be independent of the state and self-financing. Modeled after the U.S. Olympic Committee, the ROC has begun to cultivate marketing opportunities. Head of the ROC, Vitaly Smirnov, and his deputy, Alexander Kozlovski, both have ties with corporations such as Coca-Cola and Adidas. Adidas has pledged $15 million to the ROC; a Yugoslav company, Goma, is making the uniforms; and there is a deal in the works with Collegiate Licensing Company of Atlanta for the burgeoning T-shirt industry. The ROC has already signed a contract with Ted Turner and CNN for the coverage of the Goodwill Games in St. Petersburg in 1994.

So far, the money has not trickled down to the athletes. Sports schools are shutting down throughout the republic and, although it is still open, Moscow's Olympic Club for Water Sports is feeling the pinch. Vladimir Sichov, deputy director of the club, describes problems faced by many other countries which are now new to Russia:

> Our mission here was to make sure the children swam and studied at the same time, and for this the trade unions gave us money. Now the trade unions have no money, and we must raise the money ourselves. We have to earn 2.4 million rubles, so now we have to charge the kids 10 rubles a month to swim. Before, we took swimmers according to ability and potential. Now our main goal is to make money, so we take only those who can pay. We were forced to fire 14 coaches in May and

turn 2,500 kids onto the street. This is happening in all sports, all over the union. Those 2,500 kids aren't going to be busy. Who knows, they might organize into gangs and thieves.

There may be a bright spot amid the gloom, something the Cubans recognized thirty years ago. The reorganization plan signed by Yeltsin established a state-financed Committee for Physical Fitness. The mandate of this body is to provide athletic facilities for the average Russian citizen. According to Boris Fyodorov, the author of the plan and deputy on Yeltsin's Advisory Body on Sports and Physical Culture, "Before, all the money went to elite or higher-level sports." The Russians have come full circle in sports. Now they are beginning to sound like the Cubans did when they first established their revolutionary sports system.

CONCLUSION

Sports may be a source of pleasure, serving as a temporary diversion from day-to-day life, or it may bring political prestige (all qualities that could inspire governmental support), but it is not likely to be at the top of the nation's list of priorities. Whether Cuba's leadership responds to the current crisis by returning to some form of capitalist economics, lesser reforms, or repression, economic survival will take precedence over other areas, including sport. This is all the more likely if efforts are made to retain such social benefits as cheap education and free health services. The collapse of Castro's regime would mean a probable return to limited sports for many Cubans. An attempt to institute reforms (such as self-financing sports) would probably result in a reduction of access to sports activities for the less-well-off Cubans. Hence, given the survival of the regime and of the desire to maintain mass sports, Cuba's leadership could be forced to cut its investment in elite sports, even though this may reduce its ability to use sport as a vehicle for political prestige and for developing ties with potential new trading partners. On the other hand, money earned through athletics, currently used to fund sports, may be used for more essential purposes, such as buying food.[101] The choice (if indeed there is a choice in the face of economic crisis and possible political upheavals) remains a double-edged sword for Cuba. Either elite sport suffers, which brings a loss of the prestige resulting from sports victories, or mass programs are reduced, which adds to growing dissatisfaction prompted by near economic collapse.[102] The recent policy appears to be cuts in both areas, with the exception of spending on facilities for the 1991 Pan-American Games. Entry to games events was free for Cubans and these facilities were to be opened to the public following the games. However, such spending may provoke complaints among Cubans whose food rations have recently been reduced. In summary, it seems unlikely that Cuba can continue to expand its sports program or, perhaps, even to maintain its current commitment to sports at either the elite or the mass level, despite believing it will continue because it is a fundamental part of a well-rounded education.[103]

7

Cuba Today and Tomorrow:
A Home Run for Sports,
a Strikeout for the Economy?

Within fifteen years of revolution, Cuba changed from a country that was very undistinguished in the sports arena to being one of the top ten sports nations in the world. What accounts for the tremendous success of the Cuban sports system? The answer is a combination of factors, but undoubtedly one of the most important is the Cuban determination to invest resources both in the expansion of mass participation in physical culture and in specialized training for those with talent. The unity of purpose, which is perhaps relatively easy to achieve in a small country with a strong sense of nationalism, is another factor; and the improvements in living standards that result from sports participation, especially in food intake and health, are also important factors.[1]

In sum then, it is Cuba's transformation to socialism that explains the island's sporting success. However, the stability that has come from the rise in per capita gross domestic product and the financial and technical support of the Soviet Union (both important to Cuba's success) is now threatened. Assistance from the former Soviet Union has been withdrawn almost completely, which damages Cuba's sports system considerably, through reductions in the import of sports equipment.[2]

ACHIEVEMENTS AND PROBLEMS IN CUBAN SPORT

Mass Participation

Theoretically, the Cuban revolution is dedicated to the creation of egalitarianism in all areas of society. In physical culture there is an attempt to balance equality with encouraging high standards, just as there is an attempt to balance egalitarianism in standards of living with economic expansion. The twofold objective in physical culture—high performance and mass participation—is based not only on Marxist-Leninist theory, but also on Cuban views about the nature of their society before 1959.

Cuban leaders claim that physical culture did not exist for most Cubans before 1959, because the clubs were exclusive and denied entry to most Cubans on economic and racial grounds. Cuba's leaders also criticize the dominance of U.S. interests in many sports, as well as the corruption and limited government interest in physical culture. This critique is in large part justified, despite the tendency of Cuban leaders to overstate the lack of facilities and to ignore the breakdown of racial restrictions in a few sports, such as the ubiquitous baseball. Equality of opportunity to participate, however, did not exist. Physical culture also tended to reflect the racial, gender, and class divisions that characterized Cuban society prior to 1959. Access was, in most instances, restricted to Cubans who were rich, white, and male.

Since 1959, Cuban leaders have criticized the inequality and underdeveloped state of Cuban physical culture and have dedicated themselves to changing these conditions. They have tried various methods for achieving these objectives, with considerable success. At the beginning of the revolutionary transformation, Cuban leaders concentrated on the removal of legal barriers (and some socioeconomic barriers) to participation in physical culture. With the transition to a socialist and then to a Marxist-Leninist philosophy, the island's leadership pursued a policy of extending access through direct state control. They also sought to alter the social structure of the nation, and to break down gender, race, and especially class barriers to participation.

Important factors for promoting egalitarianism in physical culture were the provision of new facilities and the production and distribution of sports equipment. The establishment of the Cuban sports industry in 1965, which grew rapidly, extended the amount of sports equipment available. The number of facilities also increased substantially. By 1988 there were over 9,500 installations on the island. By 1990, there were 11,122 sports facilities. Although there were certainly problems with work standards and quality control in the sports industry, the expansion of facilities and equipment made it possible for growing numbers of Cubans to practice physical culture.[3]

Cuba's leadership also introduced a wide variety of programs that were aimed at encouraging participation. In the 1960s, considerable emphasis was placed upon developing programs for young Cubans. Attention was directed at providing physical culture activities in regions outside the major population centers. These concerns continued into the 1970s and 1980s. In these decades, attention was also given to competitive sports as well as activities, often of a recreational nature, for older Cubans. Cuba extended its participation programs to include a diverse group of activities for Cubans of various ages. Programs for sports, exercises, and recreation were steadily developed, improved, and expanded. Attitudes also began to change, especially negative attitudes to women's participation. Change, however, is a slow process (especially in a Latin American country), inhibited by the slowness of raising the educational and cultural awareness of both parents and teachers.

Cuba has, on the whole, achieved its target of mass participation in physical culture. Indeed, Cuba has probably progressed further in *massovost* than the former Soviet Union had, where the dual goals of massovost (mass participation) and *masterstvo* (high quality) were developed. In a sense, Cubans are duty bound to participate in physical culture as a sign of their commitment to the revolution, and most Cubans participate in physical culture activities at some stage in their lifetime, especially at school. At least 15 percent of the population participates in some sport.[4]

The goal of mass participation has encountered several problems and obstacles, and primary among them is the prioritization of basic needs and economic expansion over other objectives. The limited availability of resources, intensified today by reductions in Soviet subsidies and the collapse of socialism in Eastern Europe, means that physical culture will likely suffer severe cuts in the near future. Even though athletes' earnings (appearance money and prize money) are used to support sports, resources for construction of facilities and for mass programs will probably be reduced; the money from athletes will probably be needed for basic expenditures.[5] The reduced availability of hard currency will probably result in a reduction of imported sports equipment and perhaps a focus on producing sports items for export rather than for internal use. These economic problems may well lead to cuts in both mass participation programs and the training of top athletes, which will make it even more difficult to overcome existing limits to mass participation, such as dropping out after leaving educational institutions, sexism, racism, and bureaucratic inefficiencies.[6]

While the extent of some of these defects is difficult to assess (especially racism), sexism is clearly evident. *Machismo* (and probably *marianismo*) is still evident despite the efforts of the revolution to combat it.[7] Women are excluded from some sports (such as boxing and baseball), and the number of women on Cuban teams is still quite small, especially compared to those of the former USSR and the former GDR. Nevertheless, the growth of women's participation in Cuban physical culture cannot be dismissed, nor can the fact that Cubans now have the opportunity to participate in many activities from which they were excluded prior to the revolution.

Another likely result of Cuba's development of physical culture is the benefits of such activities for the health standards of the island's population. This has certainly been a major objective in Cuban policy, but it has been hindered by the nature of the Cuban diet and the difficulty in getting adults to exercise. In fact many Cubans are overweight, so it appears that only a proportion of the Cuban people have participated in sporting activities for health reasons.[8]

Elite Sports

Another achievement in Cuba's sports system has been the development of opportunities for those with talent, evident in the success of Cuban teams in international sports. Almost all Cubans with ability may aspire to athletic careers through access to specialized training and facilities in sports centers or schools.[9]

This fact, however, creates its own problems, notably the difficulty in balancing bureaucratic and funding emphases between mass programs and elite sports. Tensions have arisen and were recently raised publically.[10] There is also the problem that athletes receive certain privileges, such as access to a wider variety and a greater amount of food, and this may become increasingly irritating to ordinary Cubans as the effects of the dissolution of the socialist bloc bite more deeply into the economy of the island. Similarly, corruption and advantages for athletes in dealing with the burdensome Cuban bureaucracy could incur the ire of growing numbers of the population in a period of increasing political and economic isolation and hardship. The ability and willingness of the Cuban system and its people to support elite athletes will probably decline. The reduction of Soviet financial and technical assistance in sports, on which Cuba has been partially dependent, will add to the pressures and will no doubt be detrimental to both *massovost* and *masterstvo* in Cuba.

Athletes may well be asked to accept fewer privileges and to dedicate themselves even more to the revolutionary cause than they do now. This could lead to pressures from athletes who might want to retain their winnings, as was recently the case in the former Soviet Union.[11] Economic and political pressures may weaken the impressive Cuban sports system, together with the varied domestic and foreign policy roles it has traditionally played. Yet, at the same time, these pressures could make the use of sport for political purposes more attractive to Cuba's embattled and isolated leadership.

DOMESTIC POLICY

Cuba's economic problems together with the antagonism of the Reagan and Bush administrations led to an increased use of physical culture to promote fitness and military preparedness. The role of athletes as a vanguard for the revolution and the use of sports successes to create national pride and international prestige may be expanded. On the domestic front, the use of physical culture for socialization and perhaps for social control could intensify. These aspects of physical culture, however, are unlikely to have much impact if discontent continues to grow in the face of economic hardship and political isolation.

Military Preparedness

The use of physical culture within military training is common to all countries. In the socialist countries, sport was encouraged to promote fitness for defense among the population as a whole in the face of often hostile environments. This has certainly been the case in Cuba. It is not surprising that, in times of perceived or actual security threats, vigilance—including the use of physical culture for fitness and readiness purposes—has increased. The antagonism of the Reagan administration led to the formation of military sports clubs, which taught civilians basic military skills in combination with recreational activities. Should Cuba be threatened again (not an altogether unrealistic fear given the recent capture of armed Cuban Americans on Cuban shores), it seems probable that the use of physical culture for military preparedness will be maintained, if not increased.[12]

Political Roles

Athletes may also be called upon to intensify their role as revolutionary role models and as sources of national pride. Cuba's sports stars have already played a significant role in the revolutionary process, as has physical culture as a whole. Sport has affected three very important political factors: nation building, socialization, and political integration.

As Alberto Juantorena said, "Americans live in a country; we Cubans are *building* a country."[13] Through sports, Cubans are able to feel personally involved in the process. This creates strong feelings of national pride. People who feel they have helped to create something identify more closely with it. The goals of mass participation were to break down class differences and to promote cohesiveness. The result, it was hoped, would be a system or network between government and people and among the people as a whole that was mutually supportive. Certainly, the people's participation in numerous activities and their administration (including physical culture) may serve this purpose. On the other hand, the fact that decision making in physical culture (as in other areas) is highly centralized in the upper levels of the state and party structures—and, in the case of physical culture, at the top levels of INDER—may have undermined, to some extent, the goal of political integration and national unity.[14]

Socialization through physical culture and the use of athletes as role models may be more effective for unity and cohesion, especially in the long term. Outstanding sportsmen and sportswomen become role models for society as a whole. Cuban athletes usually acknowledge the role of the revolution and the Cuban people in their victories: for example, Stevenson refused a million dollars to retain the love of the Cuban people; Juantorena dedicated a gold medal to his compatriots and gave another gold medal to Fidel to share with them. Athletes are expected to display such revolutionary commitment as the vanguard for all Cubans.[15] With the growing economic problems, the Cuban "masses" may find inspiration in athletic victories, but may be less content to support privileges for athletes. Nevertheless, there is no denying the national pride inspired by Cuba's world-class sportsmen and women.

The probable decline in Cuba's capacity to support superstars will weaken part of the political socialization process that occurs through physical culture. The current economic problems in Cuba may undermine the socialization that comes from promoting the revolutionary ideology in physical culture at the mass level. Nevertheless, there has been considerable social pressure to conform to the revolution's ideology. Physical culture was regarded as a means to combat old values and to promote communist attitudes. While this leads to overt allegiance to the revolution, separate from coercion, socialization cannot guarantee social control. The evidence for this is obvious in the rapid dismantling of socialism in Eastern Europe and the Soviet Union. It is also important not to underestimate feelings of allegiance that arise from improved living conditions and the spirit of nation building. However, the fact that socialization does occur may become more evident in the former socialist bloc as people, accustomed to notions of guaranteed incomes, food, and shelter, face the prospects of rising inflation and growing unemployment. It seems improbable that socialization in Cuba will prove any stronger than it has in the exsocialist bloc or for that matter in the United States and in Australia during the Vietnam war. Socialization will certainly not lead Cubans to ignore, dismiss, or accept the difficulties they are facing today. Hence, the role of sport in domestic politics seems likely to be retained, if limited in its capacity to overcome the problems the island population is facing. Physical culture may well have a greater role to play in Cuban foreign policy in future years.

FOREIGN POLICY

Physical culture has traditionally been significant in Cuban foreign policy in the postrevolution period. With the prospect of growing political isolation, this role is quite likely to grow in importance, although funding problems may well undermine this avenue of foreign policy.

Sport can serve as a powerful international political tool, a fact that is not lost on many countries today:

> For this land, whose boundaries are set by the sea, sports has
> become a kind of Cuban equivalent of 19th century American

[U.S.] Manifest Destiny. The Olympics are their Oregon Trail, their Northwest Territory, their visible evidence of national accomplishment and a rallying point for morale.[16]

Surely the value of a victory in the Olympics, the Pan-American Games, or any international sporting contest goes beyond the gold medal. It is but a short distance from an individual athlete in his or her national uniform to the strong symbol of the country being represented.[17]

There are many uses for sport, some of which are closely interrelated.[18] Five of these are described below.

Diplomatic Recognition

One of the most concrete uses of sport is as a means of diplomatic recognition or nonrecognition. Sport is a clear but indirect way to communicate government policy. The most obvious examples have been relationships between East and West Germany, the People's Republic of China and Taiwan, South Africa and New Zealand, and South Africa and the British Commonwealth. At the 1966 Central American Games, for example, Puerto Rico denied Cuban athletes visas to attend the games and would not guarantee safe participation. The Cuban team was sent by sea on the *Cerro Pelado,* and despite a hostile reception and harassment, was allowed to compete. Cuban athletes dominated the games. Cuba's impressive victory in those games further enhanced the Cubans' political point. The U.S.–Cuban tensions at the 1987 and 1991 Pan-American Games are further examples. The Cubans made political statements by boycotting the 1984 and 1988 Olympic Games. The 1991 Pan-American Games may also have played a part in Cuba's current attempt to further break its isolation in Latin America.[19]

Propaganda

Sport provides a convenient stage for displaying the physical prowess (and superiority) of a country's athletes. The implication is clear: only a superior social system could produce such dazzling champions (the inferiority of the loser is implicit). So important was this function to the socialist countries that meetings were held regularly among the leaders of the propaganda sections of the sports associations of the entire bloc. The 1977 meeting was held in Cuba.

The revolutionary government has not lost the opportunity to capitalize on its sporting successes. After all, probably most people throughout the world identify Cuba first with the 1962 missile crisis, and second with Alberto Juantorena or Teófilo Stevenson, rather than Moncada, Granma, or even the Bay of Pigs. To the Cubans, sports success as propaganda is important throughout the world, but nowhere more so than in the rest of Latin America. Castro said, "I can assure you that one of the things most admired by our Latin American neighbors is our sporting successes. We can say that our athletes are the children of our Revolution and, at the same time, the standard-bearers of that same Revolution."[20]

What gives Cuba more credibility with the less developed countries is that Cuba is still "one of their own," a neighborhood kid made good. This position was strengthened as Cuba moved into a leadership role and gained the ability to provide technical assistance to other countries. "Cuba thus provides a powerful example of the potential of a small country whose resources are rationally deployed under what the Cuban leadership described as a 'superior social system.' "[21]

The collapse of most of Cuba's socialist allies means that this propaganda effort may be substantially weakened. The economic chaos in the former USSR and in Eastern Europe makes it harder for people and nations to believe Cuban claims to a superior social system. This also applies to Cuba's own domestic audience. The reduction of technical and economic aid will probably mean it will be harder for Cuba to maintain its current status as a world-class performer. Nevertheless, there will continue to be prestige in victories such as the ones at the 1991 Pan-American Games and the 1992 Olympics.

Prestige

Closely tied to propaganda is the function of sports in the search for national prestige. Athletes are sources of pride; victories are a bonus. Since the mid–1970s, Cuba has been a respected member of the international sporting community. This can be accredited not just to the nation's athletes, but also to the government officials and trainers who support the actual contestants. In 1976, Raudol Ruíz, a former prominent sports official in Cuba, became the first Latin American to be awarded the Philip Noel Baker prize for scientific investigation by the International Council for Sport and Physical Education. In Cuba this was considered a high honor.

Ruíz began his career as an athletic trainer. After the revolution, he moved in to direct Manuel Fajardo (ISCF). With further study, he received his Ph.D. from the GDR. In 1982, he was vice-president for Latin America for CIEPS and a professor at INDER. Ruíz's response upon receiving the award was in typical Cuban fashion:

> I think that in the first place although my name is on the award, this distinction corresponds to those who in the last fifteen years have given their cooperation to the development of national sport. Implicit here is the tremendous privilege of learning what the Revolution has given to us, and for this recognition, we are obliged to improve our work every day.[22]

Whether Cuba is able to maintain its sporting strength and the resulting prestige in the future remains uncertain, just as Cuba's important role in sports cooperation appears threatened by economic crisis. Both sporting strength with prestige and a role in sports cooperation however, have been, and will remain, valuable tools of foreign policy.

Cooperation

Perhaps the function of sport that carries with it the most hope is that it encourages cooperation among nations. The assumption is that any contact fosters understanding, perhaps even improved relations. Cooperation, which was especially valuable to Cuba, certainly occurred within the former socialist bloc, but since 1970 Cuba has also extended sports cooperation to less developed countries—notably Jamaica, where the Cubans have built sports facilities (including one for free).[23] Jamaicans and many other people from poor countries in Africa and Latin America have also received sports training in Cuba.

Since 1977, Cuba's overseas sports program has been greatly expanded: in Africa, Algeria, Angola, Benin, Congo (since 1984), Guinea (until the end of 1986), Guinea-Bissau, Malagasy Republic (up to early 1987), Mali, Mozambique, Nigeria, and Tanzania have all received Cuban sports aid. Iraq, South Yemen, Vietnam, Nicaragua, Panama, Peru, Brazil, and Venezuela have also been included in Cuba's sports program. In 1983, ninety Cuban sports specialists were working in a total of fifteen countries. By 1987, eighteen countries were assisted by forty-eight specialists. In 1990, there were four hundred foreign students from thirty-three countries on scholarships. Also in that year, there were a thousand technicians working overseas, and thirty-nine countries received technical aid. Hence, despite U.S. pressures to reduce Cuba's international influence in the 1980s, Cuba was assisting numerous countries in sports as well as in health and education.[24]

Cuba's commitment to socialist internationalism is promoted through such sports links. With the current concerns with internal problems and, indeed, the very survival of Cuba's socialist system, it will be harder for Cuba to sustain this sports aid to less developed countries. On the other hand, such programs could be used to raise revenue through the extension of commercial ties in sports, such as was believed to be the case with Kuwait. In October 1992, the sports institutes of Cuba and Venezuela tripled the extent of their previous sports cooperation agreement, increasing the number of Cuban specialists and trainers with the Venezuela national teams from 106 to 240. The two countries agreed to hold 62 practice and training contests, 33 in Cuba and the rest in Venezuela. The Fourth Congress sanctioned the sale of sports services.[25] Yet the upheavals in European socialism may also lead not only to increased antagonism between Cuba and other nations, but also to reluctance to accept Cuban sports aid or commercial sports contracts with Cuba.

Conflict

The role of sport as a signal of hostility may increase. Sport has often been a vehicle for the United States to express its hostility toward Cuba, and vice versa. Cuba's defeat of the U.S. volleyball team in Los Angeles in 1976 was hailed by Castro as a "sporting, psychological, patriotic and revolutionary victory."[26] Similar political hostilities surfaced in abundance at the 1966 Central American Games (over Cuba's boycott of the 1984 and 1988 Olympic Games), at the 1987 Indianapolis Pan-American Games, and at the 1991 Havana Pan-American Games. It has also been recently revealed that the access given a high-ranking Cuban sports official made him attractive to the Central Intelligence Agency. Alberto Puig de la Barca, now INDER's national director for education and physical culture, allegedly worked as a double agent, for both Cuban intelligence and the CIA.[27]

Most recently, however, Cuban athletes (if not their political leaders) exhibited warmer feelings toward athletes from the United States. According to Raúl Villanueva, a vice-president of INDER, "We have a great relationship in sports with the United States.

Politics has been a barrier in other areas between us, but never in sports."[28]

In the first game of the Basketball Tournament of the Americas, in which a team from North or South America qualifies to play in the Olympics, the United States routed Cuba 136–57. The U.S. team had been dubbed the Dream Team, with the finest professional players from the National Basketball Association, such as Michael Jordan, Magic Johnson, Larry Bird, and Charles Barkley.[29] The Cubans seemed resigned to an honorable defeat from the very beginning. Three minutes before the game began, in broken English they begged the U.S. team to come to center court for a group photo. The attitude of Cuban coach Miguel Calderón Gómez was best expressed in a Cuban saying, "You can't cover the sun with your finger." Rather than the rhetorical harangue about the Dream Team's professional status that may have happened in another year, Calderón's only comment was, "It was the first game between the NBA and an amateur team. It was an achievement for us just to play against them." As for the players, Cuban center Félix Morales expressed an attitude that would have been unheard of several years earlier: "I have followed the NBA players for years. To see them right there in front of you is definitely an awesome thing. For me, it was an honor. We saw the scoreboard, and it was a logical result."[30]

Even in baseball, which both countries claim as their "national pastime," sportswriter Tom Boswell spoke of a "delicious undercurrent of respect between the teams." After a summer of exhibition games in both countries, the two teams had at least gotten to know each other a bit. Players complimented each other. Star pitcher Omar Ajete said, "We play well against them [the United States] because they are mean competitors," despite the Cuban record of seven out of nine games. Phil Nevin claimed, "We've played them so much this summer that some of us have gotten to be pretty good friends." Indeed, Cuban first baseman Lourdes Gurriel told Nevin, "Good luck in the major leagues with the Astros. I hope I'll be able to see you there someday."[31]

Fidel did have harsher words for the Dream Team. At the ceremony welcoming the Cuban Olympic athletes home from Barcelona, Castro claimed that the U.S. team was an example of professionalism in sports. "This has nothing to do with the Olympic spirit. They did it to show off their supremacy and arrogance."[32]

The intensification of anti-Cuban feelings in the United States and Cuba's growing isolation may lead to further expressions of hostility between Cuba and the United States. On the other hand, Cuba may seek to use sport, as it has done before, as a means to expand ties with the United States, particularly with its desire to see the lifting of the U.S. economic blockade of the island.[33] A deepening of hostility, however, seems more likely.

CONCLUSION

The purpose served by sport in the international arena is invaluable. "International sport is one of the strongest, most direct, cheapest and least dangerous foreign policy weapons a nation can use to set the tone of relations."[34] And Cuba appears to have made astute use of this weapon. Indeed, Fidel—unlike his colleagues in Venezuela, Peru, and Colombia—made a rare personal appearance in Barcelona. His extended trip, coinciding significantly with the anniversary of his 1953 attack on the Moncada barracks (which sparked the Cuban revolution), was clearly a show of power.[35] Unfortunately for Castro, however, the propaganda value of his effort was diluted when, to the astonishment of his Spanish hosts, he rushed back to Cuba amid talk of violence and troop movements at home. The rumors were apparently the work of anti-Castro Cuban exiles.

Today, the tendency may be growing to use sport for prestige, to imply that "things are alright" in Cuba, and as a means to break political and economic isolation. The capacity for these uses to be effective, however, is limited, and probably more so before the Cuban leadership's domestic audience, where the effects of socialization may be weakened by very basic food shortages.[36] The probable decline in the ability of Cuba's economy to maintain current standards in both elite sports and mass physical culture will make this political task of physical culture all the more difficult to realize. Neither physical culture nor sport can solve the more pressing economic and political problems that threaten to bring down socialism in Cuba.

Sports will almost certainly suffer as a result of the current conditions. Expenditure on sports seems a likely and logical way to wisely invest scarce pesos and earn valuable hard currency in a time of economic hardship, and sports appearance money and prize money could be diverted to essential goods. If socialism disappears in Cuba, it may be hard for any successive government to wind back the clock on physical culture in Cuba, as it has become an important part of many Cubans' lives and is increasingly seen as a right of all people. As is evident in Eastern Europe and the Soviet Union, it is very easy to "throw the baby out with the bathwater." Much has been achieved in Cuban physical culture. While there are problems, the good features in the Cuban sports system would become unfortunate losses if the socialist system in Cuba collapses.

Notes
___
Index

Notes

CHAPTER 1. THE POLITICS OF SPORT IN CUBA

1. Bill Brubaker, "Cuba's Renewed Mission: Olympic Glory," *Washington Post*, 12 July 1992, pp. D1, D6.

2. Peter Katel, "The Best Team Money Can't Buy," *Newsweek*, 8 June 1992, pp. 62–63; see also Thomas Boswell, "Sí, Cubans' Ajete Is Ace of These Games," *Washington Post*, 5 August 1992, pp. F1, F9. The Dream Team is a reference to the U.S. men's basketball team, comprised of the very best players from the National Basketball Association, who easily won the gold medal (see chapter 7).

3. *USA Today*, 19 August 1991, p. C1; *Washington Times*, 19 August 1991, p. D5; Tom Knott, "Life Got You Down? Try Cuba's Wonders," *Washington Times*, 20 August 1991, pp. D1, D2; Lee Hockstader, "60,000 Cubans Cheer Baseball Team's 3–2 Victory Over U.S.," *Washington Post*, 12 August 1991, pp. C1, C7.

4. In December 1993, as many as 50 Cuban athletes (out of a delegation of 450), defected at the Central American and Carribbean games in Puerto Rico; see Christine Brennan, "Lower Return of Castro's Athletic Exports, *Washington Post*, 5 Dec. 1993, p. D3; William Booth, "For Cubans, Finish Line Is the U.S.," *Washington Post*, 2 Dec. 1993, pp. A1, A4. Warren Strobel, "Pan Am Games Could Invite Cuban Unrest," *Washington Times*, 2 August 1991, p. A7; George Vecsey, "Bay of Pigs Explains the Games," *New York Times*, 12 August 1991, p. C7; Spencer Reiss, "The Only Dream Left Is to Get Out," *Newsweek*, 12 August 1991, pp. 38–39.

5. Brubaker, "Cuba's Renewed Mission"; Knott, "Life Got You Down?" p. D2.

6. Brubaker, "Cuba's Renewed Mission."

7. Ibid.

8. Ibid. High jumper Javier Sotomayor was recently allowed to sign with a professional track and field club in Spain. The Cuban government will keep

his earnings. Christine Brennan, "Lower Return of Castro's Athletic Exports," *Washington Post* 5 Dec. 93, p. D3.

9. Jorge Domínguez, "Cuban Foreign Policy," *Foreign Affairs* 57 (Fall 1978): p. 83. See also Manfred Komorowski, "Cuba's Way to a Country With Strong Influence in Sport Politics: The Development of Sport in Cuba Since 1959," *International Journal of Physical Education* 14 (1977), pp. 26–32.

10. The concept of unconventional diplomacy in Cuba was first published in Paula J. Pettavino, "Novel Revolutionary Forms," in Georges Fauriol and Eva Loser, *Cuba: The International Dimension* (New Brunswick, N.J.: Transaction Publishers, 1990), pp. 373–403.

11. Geralyn Pye, observations, January 1992.

12. Basílio Gutiérrez, Institúto Cubano de Amistad de los Pueblos (ICAP), conversation with Geralyn Pye, 20 January 1992, Havana; see also Brubaker, "Cuba's Renewed Mission."

13. NBC Nightly News, 21 December 1991; C. Hughes, "Castro: Conditions to Worsen," *Times-Picayune*, 19 December 1991, p. A26; (AP), "Cuba Cuts Electricity, Job Hours," *Times-Picayune*, 21 December 1991.

14. Brubaker, "Cuba's Renewed Mission"; Orestes Vega, head of the section for sports automation, INDER, conversation with Geralyn Pye, 24 January 1992, Havana; "Cuban Bicycle Race Runs Out of Gasoline," *Washington Times*, 6 January 1992, p. A2.

15. John Otis, "Cubans Make Do Despite Shortages, *Washington Times*, 9 September 1993, p. A7. Giséla Labnada, Institúto Cubano de Amistad de los Pueblos (ICAP), conversation with Geralyn Pye, 24 January 1992, Havana.

16. Dr. Gusta Singer, "Health, Physical Education, and Recreation," in Lynn Vendien and John Nixon, *The World Today in Health, Physical Education and Recreation* (Englewood Cliffs, N.J.: Prentice Hall, 1968), p. 354; J. A. Bedia, ed., *José Martí: Reflexiones sobre el deporte* (La Habana: Centro de Estudios Martianos, 1991).

17. James Riordan, "Sport as an Agent of Social Change" (unpublished paper adapted from one given to the IOC Olympic Solidarity Course for Sports Coaches and Administrators, University of Sussex, August 1976), p. 2.

18. Karl Marx, *Capital* (Moscow: Foreign Languages Publishing House, 1961), pp. 483–84. Lenin practiced what he preached, exercising regularly, even when imprisoned. Marx, however, did not, preferring more sedentary activities like chess. See Paula J. Pettavino, *The Politics of Sport Under Communism: A Comparative Study of Competitive Athletics in the Soviet Union and Cuba* (Ann Arbor, Mich.: University Microfilm, 1982).

19. *Izvestiia tsentral'nogo komiteta RKP(b)* (July 1925), cited in John N. Washburn, "Sport as a Soviet Tool," *Foreign Affairs* 34, no. 3 (April 1956), p. 490.

20. Andrzej Wohl, cited in Gerald S. Kenyon and John W. Loy, *Sports, Culture and Society: A Reader on the Sociology of Sport* (New York: Macmillan, 1969), p. 10.

21. *Pravda*, 19 July 1954, p. 1, translated by the *Current Digest of the Soviet Press* 1, no. 29, 1 September 1954, p. 26 (hereafter referred to as *CDSP*).

22. G. I. Kukushkin, *Sovetskii sport,* 25 March 1951, p. 1, cited in Henry Morton, "Soviet Sports: A School for Communism" (Ph.D. diss., Columbia University, 1959), pp. 8, 9.

23. A description of the GTO program is beyond the scope of this effort; for further information, see Pettavino, *The Politics of Sport.* The Cuban LPV program is described at length in this volume, chapter 4.

24. For purposes of simplification, the authors will use "he," "him," and "his" for generic references that are both male and female.

25. "Glorious Jubilee," *SKDA, Sportivnoe obozrenie,* 20 April 1977, p. 1.

26. Andrzej Wohl, "Prognostic Models of Sport in Socialist Countries on the Background of Changes in Sports in People's Poland," *International Review of Sport Sociology* 6 (Warsaw: Polish Scientific Publishers, 1971), p. 43.

27. Raudol Ruíz, interview, "Sport—Why Cubans Win," *Cuba Review* 7, no. 2 (June 1977), p. 14. Ruíz is also a professor at INDER. Before the revolution, he was a trainer for the Cleveland Indians for part of the year and for the Havana Sugar Kings for the remainder of the year.

28. Irene Forbes, "Cultura física popular: Fruto de la masividad," *Semanario Deportivo Listos para Vencer* 14, 17 February 1976, p. 43; journal hereafter referred to as *LPV.*

29. *Massovost, masterstvo,* and *masividad* are used frequently in discussions of Soviet and Cuban sports. The Spanish word for mastery, *maestría,* is not. The Cubans speak of training champions, without using one specific term for the phenomenon as is done in Russian.

30. See B. Brubaker, "Baseball Scouts Ready to Slide Into Cuba," *Washington Post,* 4 August 1991, p. D10; and also this volume, chapter 6, for more details.

31. Manuel González quoted in Thomas Boswell, "1970s First Step Into the Bassinet," *Washington Post,* 12 January 1980, pp. E1, E7. Fidel Castro Ruz, speech at the dedication of the Havana City sports school the Mártires de Barbados, 6 October 1977. (The school is named after the members of the Cuban fencing team, killed in the explosion of a Cuban airliner off Barbados. An anti-Castro terrorist group claimed responsibility.)

32. Most Cubans belong to at least one mass organization, usually a Comité de la Defensa de la Revolución (CDR).

33. James Riordan, "Soviet Sport and Soviet Foreign Policy," *Soviet Studies* 27, no. 3 (July 1974), p. 322.

34. Henry Morton, "The Emergence of Soviet Sports," *New Leader,* 5 December 1961, p. 20.

35. Fidel Castro Ruz, *Discurso a la primera plenaria provincial de los Consejos Voluntarios Oriente, 1 de octubre de 1961* (Havana: INDER, 1961), p. 6.

36. Ruíz, "Sport—Why Cubans Win," p. 12.

37. Fidel Castro Ruz, *Discurso a la primera plenaria nacional de los Consejos Voluntarios, 19 de noviembre de 1961* (Havana: INDER, 1961), pp. 21, 25 (hereafter referred to as *Discurso*).

38. Rafael P. Cambo Arcos, *Organización deportiva* (Havana: INDER, 1963), p. 5.

39. There is much discussion as to the validity of Castro's now-mythical tryout for the Senators. See M. Siegel, "Senators Never Lacked in Supply of Cuban Imports," *Washington Times,* 24 August 1991, p. D6. In an ABC interview on 28 July 1991, Castro would neither confirm nor deny the allegation.

40. Officials from INDER-Santiago, interviews with Paula Pettavino, August 1980, Santiago, Cuba; Alfredo López Suárez, *Historia de la educación física* (1950), p. 59; F. Cuervo et al., *Educación física* 1 (Siboney Publishing), p. 26.

41. Victor Joaquín Ortega, "En el deporte," *La Juventud* (Havana: Editorial Gente Nueva, 1978), p. 15.

42. Ibid., p. 14. Carvajál was thirty-eight in 1904. *Andarín* comes from the Spanish verb *andar* meaning to walk, go, move, travel. *Andarín* means the tireless walker or traveler. See also Jesus Gregario, *Cómo, cuándo y dónde halló la fortuna el Andarín Carvajál* (Havana: Ediciones Union, 1978), a highly stylized play about Carvajál. On the cover is juxtaposed a photo of Alberto Juantorena (winner of the 400– and 800–meter races in Montreal in 1976) with a drawing of *Andarín.*

43. This was true of baseball to a far lesser extent. The Cuban winter baseball leagues had a life of their own (see this volume, chapters 2 and 5).

44. Pettavino, *Politics of Sport,* p. 138.

45. This fall in participation after people leave school is not unique to Cuba. It has been reported in Australia as well. See *Youth Sport* (Canberra: Australian Sports Commission, 1989), p. 13.

46. Some exiled Cubans claim they were excluded from baseball for political reasons. Pettavino, *Politics of Sport,* pp. 203–4.

47. Fidel cited in Anna Husarska, "Soft Cell," *New Republic,* 27 January 1992, p. 15. From 1982 to 1987, average annual value of sports equipment imports from COMECON equalled 3.5 million pesos; since 1988, this figure has fallen substantially. See G. R. González González, L. Robalcaba Ordáz, and G. Díaz Cabrera, *El deporte cubano: Razones de sus exitos* (La Habana: Ediciones ENPES, 1991), p. 52 (hereafter referred to as *Razones*).

48. Gutiérrez, conversation with Geralyn Pye; see also Brubaker, "Cuba's Renewed Mission."

CHAPTER 2. CUBAN SPORT BEFORE 1959

1. Jorge Domínguez, *Cuba: Order and Revolution* (Cambridge, Mass.: Belknap Press, 1978), pp. 184–85.

2. The information in this paragraph is taken from a variety of sources: Milo A. Borges, *Compilación ordenada y completa de la legislación cubana 1988–1950, indice alfabético* 3 (Havana: Editorial Lex, 1952), p. 286; González González et al., *Razones,* p. 1; Arnaldo Ribero Fuxa and Pedro Rodríguez, director and subdirector of teaching at INDER-Havana, interviews with Paula Pettavino, 18 August 1980, Havana.

3. Eugénio George Lafita, interviewed in M. C. Valle, "Trece años, trece testimonios," *LPV* 13, no. 609, 19 February 1974, p. 19 (hereafter this journal is referred to as *LPV*).

4. Angel Leíba Cabrera, cited in T. Canon, *Revolutionary Cuba* (Havana: José Martí, 1983), p. 21. Brooklyn was the black area; the white area was called Washington. Only U.S. citizens were allowed on Washington Street.

5. M. Llaneras Rodríguez et al., "Cuba: 25 años de deporte revolucionario," *Mensaje Deportívo*, special issue (May 1986), p. 157.

6. R. J. Pickering, "Cuba," in J. Riordan, ed., *Sport Under Communism* (Canberra: ANU Press, 1978), p. 159.

7. J. González Barros, "Baseball," *Granma Weekly Review*, 4 December 1966, p. 8 (hereafter referred to as *GWR*); Pickering, "Cuba," p. 159; J. Llanusa, "Speaks From the Canefields About Sports," *GWR*, 17 April 1966, p. 10.

8. Fidel Castro Ruz, "Sobre el deporte" (1974), cited in Pickering, "Cuba," p. 152.

9. See A. Arredondo, *Batista un año de gobierno* (La Habana: Editorial Ucacia, 1942), pp. 190–92; *Cuba en la mano enciclopedia popular ilustrada* (Miami: Mnemosyne, 1940, reprinted 1969), pp. 1174–76; F. Batista, *The Growth and Decline of the Cuban Republic* (New York: Devin Adair, 1964), pp. 87–88.

10. Arredondo, *Batista*, p. 189.

11. Jackie Robinson officially broke the color line in 1947. See Jules Tygiel, "Black Ball," in John Thorn and Pete Palmer, eds., *Total Baseball* (New York: Warner Books, 1989), pp. 548–62.

12. Guillermo de la Cuesta, director of Industria Deportíva, interview with Paula Pettavino, August 1980 (see also chapter 3). By most accounts, the story of Abner Doubleday is a myth: see Donald Honig, *Baseball America: The Heroes of the Game and the Times of Their Glory* (New York: Macmillan, 1985), pp. 1–6. The Cuban Sports Industry carries the trade name *Batos*. It is interesting that other countries also claim some sort of "prehistoric" version of the game as their own. For the North American version, see John Bowman and Joel Zoss, *Diamonds in the Rough: The Untold History of Baseball* (New York: Macmillan, 1989), pp. 39–76. The Soviet Union has actually claimed that baseball is derived from an ancient version of a game called *lapta*, brought to America by Russian immigrants in the mid–nineteenth century: see Steve Wulf, "The Russians Are Humming," *Sports Illustrated* 69, 25 July 1988; "Mighty Ivan at the Bat," *Newsweek* 110, 27 July 1987; Bill Barich, "Going to the Moon," *New Yorker* 67, 22 July 1991; Carroll Bogert, "First Steppes in Baseball," *Newsweek* 113, 17 April 1989; and John Leo, "Evil Umpires? Not in Soviet Baseball," *Time* 130, 10 August 1987.

13. For Nemesio Guillot, see E. A. Wagner, "Baseball in Cuba," *Journal of Popular Culture* 18, no. 1 (Summer 1984), p. 115; also Joseph L. Arbena, ed., *Sport and Society in Latin America: Diffusion, Dependency, and the Rise of Mass Culture* (Westport, Conn.: Greenwood Press, 1988), p. 118, cited in Michael M. Oleksak and Mary Adams Oleksak, *Béisbol: Latin Americans and the Grand Old Game* (Grand Rapids, Mich.: Masters Press, 1991), p. 6. For the students, who

also introduced other ball games from the United States, see E. Casas, J. Alfonso, and A. Pestana, *Viva y en juego* (La Habana: Editorial Científico-Técnica, 1986), p. 7; and Rob Ruck, *The Tropic of Baseball: Baseball in the Dominican Republic* (Westport, Conn.: Meckler Publishing, 1991), p. 2.

14. Oleksak and Oleksak, *Béisbol*, p. 6; also Bruce Brown, "Cuban Baseball," *Atlantic* 253 (June 1984), pp. 109–14. Bellán played before the color line in North American baseball was firmly in place. See Ruck, *Tropic of Baseball*, p. 99. For more information about blacks in organized baseball before the color line, see Bowman and Zoss, *Diamonds in the Rough*, pp. 135–49.

15. E. Martín, *Por las rutas del olimpo* (La Habana: Editorial Científico-Técnica, 1985), p. 51. See also Oleksak and Oleksak, *Béisbol*, p. 6; Ruck, *Tropic of Baseball*, pp. 2, 6; and Angel Torres, *La historia del béisbol cubano, 1878–1976* (Los Angeles: Angel Torres, 1976), p. 11.

16. E. Casas, J. Alfonso, A. Pestana, *Viva y en juego*, (La Habana: Editorial Científico-Técnica, 1986), p. 11; Oleksak and Oleksak, *Béisbol*, p. 6; Llaneras Rodríguez et al., "Cuba," p. 159; L. Agneles, "Palmar de junco un siglo de historia," *El Deporte* 3 (1975), pp. 41, 42.

17. J. R. Crespo and E. Mata, "El necesario rifle del equipo," *LPV* 810, p. 30; Wagner, "Baseball in Cuba," p. 116; Torres, *Historia del béisbol cubano*, p. 122.

18. Luís Hernández, "Un siglo de béisbol en Cuba," *LPV* 2 December 1969, p. 4, cited in Wagner, "Baseball in Cuba," p. 115.

19. Oleksak and Oleksak, *Béisbol*, pp. 6, 7.

20. John Krich, *El Béisbol: Travels Through the Pan-American Pastime* (New York: Atlantic Monthly Press, 1989), pp. 190–91.

21. Brown, "Cuban Baseball," p. 110; Ruck, *Tropic of Baseball*, p. 3; Casas et al., *Viva y en juego*, p. 22; Oleksak and Oleksak, *Béisbol*, p. 20.

22. Bowman and Zoss, *Diamonds in the Rough*, p. 149.

23. Ibid., p. 148.

24. Negro league player Willie Wells described his experience playing baseball in Mexico in an emotional letter: "I've found freedom and democracy here, something I never found in the United States. I was branded a Negro in the United States and had to act accordingly. Everything I did, including playing ball, was regulated by color. Well, here . . . I am a man" (Oleksak and Oleksak, *Béisbol*, pp. 23–24).

25. Ruck, *Tropic of Baseball*, p. 100. Phony documents were required validating whiteness. In addition, Marsans apparently had gone along only as Almeída's interpreter, but he played so well he was also offered a contract. See Oleksak and Oleksak, *Béisbol*, pp. 25–26, and Brown, "Cuban Baseball," p. 111.

26. George Compton and Adolfo Solorzano Díaz, "Latins on the Diamond," *Americas* 3 (June 1951), p. 10, cited in Oleksak and Oleksak, *Béisbol*, p. 26.

27. Bowman and Zoss, *Diamonds in the Rough*, p. 148, and Oleksak and Oleksak, *Béisbol*, p. 26.

28. Apparently, there had been several interracial teams in the mid–nineteenth century. Racism in baseball had hardened by the 1880s, however, with

the 1887 incident of Cap Anson, manager and first baseman for the Chicago White Stockings, who shouted "Get that nigger off the field!" referring to George Stovey, black pitcher for the Newark Little Giants. See Edna Rust and Art Rust, Jr., *Art Rust's Illustrated History of the Black Athlete* (New York: Doubleday, 1985), pp. 6–8. See also Art Rust, Jr., *Get That Nigger Off the Field* (New York: Delacorte Press, 1976).

29. Oleksak and Oleksak, *Béisbol,* pp. 27–30.

30. Daniel C. Frío and Mark Onigman, "Good Field, No Hit: The Image of Latin American Baseball Players in the American Press, 1871–1946," *Revista/Review Interamericana* (Summer 1979), p. 204, cited in Oleksak and Oleksak, *Béisbol,* p. 30.

31. Ruck, *Tropic of Baseball,* p. 100; Oleksak and Oleksak, *Béisbol,* pp. 26–30.

32. Oleksak and Oleksak, *Béisbol,* pp. 26, 27.

33. John Holway, *Blackball Stars: Negro League Pioneers* (Westport, Conn.: Meckler Books, 1988), p. 59, cited in Oleksak and Oleksak, *Béisbol,* p. 30.

34. Brown, "Cuban Baseball," p. 110 (for more information on the extent of Cobb's racist violence, see Bowman and Zoss, *Diamonds in the Rough,* pp. 144–46); Oleksak and Oleksak, *Béisbol,* p. 21; Rust and Rust, *Art Rust's Illustrated History* (New York: Doubleday, 1985), p. 15. It is ironic that Babe Ruth himself was, at times, the victim of racist remarks. Many fellow players called him "nigger" because of his broad nose and full lips.

35. Oleksak and Oleksak, *Béisbol,* pp. 20–21. The quotation comes from Charles C. Alexander, *John McGraw* (New York: Viking Penguin, 1988), p. 159, cited in Oleksak and Oleksak, *Béisbol,* p. 22. John McGraw—who started playing with the Orioles in 1891 and went on to manage the New York Giants for thirty years—worked actively, both on and off the field, to break the color line in baseball. He was unsuccessful. He employed Ed Mackall, a black trainer with the Giants for thirty years, but when McGraw retired in 1932, Mackall was fired immediately. Rust and Rust, pp. 10–15.

36. Oleksak and Oleksak, *Béisbol,* pp. 32–33; Rust and Rust, p. 12.

37. Oleksak and Oleksak, *Béisbol,* p. 33.

38. Brown, "Cuban Baseball," p. 111.

39. Holway, *Blackball Stars,* p. 244, cited in Oleksak and Oleksak, *Béisbol,* p. 33.

40. Brown, "Cuban Baseball," p. 112; Oleksak and Oleksak, *Béisbol,* p. 34; Ruck, *Tropic of Baseball,* p. 15.

41. Oleksak and Oleksak, *Béisbol,* p. 35. For statistics on Luís Tiant, Jr., see Thorn and Palmer, *Total Baseball,* p. 1964. Because of the racism he had faced, Lefty Tiant advised his son, Luís Jr., not to play ball. See Neil J. Sullivan, *The Minors: The Struggle and the Triumph of Baseball's Poor Relation from 1876 to the Present* (New York: St. Martin's Press, 1990), p. 199.

42. Brown, "Cuban Baseball," p. 112; see also Oleksak and Oleksak, *Béisbol,* pp. 53–54. For more information on Rickey, see also Rust and Rust, pp. 47–52. There are innumerable accounts of how Jackie Robinson broke the color line in 1947 (ibid., pp. 135–95, for example) as well as personal accounts

such as Jackie Robinson and Al Duckett, *I Never Had It Made* (New York: G. P. Putnam, 1972).

43. Oleksak and Oleksak, *Béisbol,* pp. 55–56.

44. Ibid., p. 58. Despite that record, he was still passed over for Most Valuable Player (see Oleksak and Oleksak, *Béisbol,* for information on the poor treatment of Latin American athletes by sports writers).

45. Ibid., pp. 58–59.

46. Ibid., pp. 59–60. His late entry to the major leagues was because of the color line.

47. Siegel, "Senators," pp. D1, D6.

48. Oleksak and Oleksak, *Béisbol,* pp. 42–45.

49. Brooklyn Dodger left fielder Edmundo Isasi "Sandy" Amoros was one of the least famous players in the 1955 Dodgers lineup. Yet, in the 1955 World Series, he made a dramatic catch of a ball hit by Yogi Berra and turned it into a double play, which was instrumental in sparking Brooklyn to victory. He also led his team for the series, hitting .333. In twelve at-bats, he hit a home run, scored three runs, and drove in three more. From 1947 through 1956, the Dodgers won six pennants but lost all of the series except the 1955 series, to the hated Yankee rivals. During a seven-year career in the majors, Amoros batted .255, hitting 43 home runs, driving in 180, and scoring 215. Amoros died of pneumonia on 28 June 1992 at the age of sixty-two (Richard Pearson, "Sandy Amoros, 62, Dies; Star of '55 World Series," *Washington Post,* 28 June 1992, p. B4).

50. Ruck, *Tropic of Baseball,* pp. 100–101.

51. R. Marquez and D. A. McMurray, *Man-Making Words* (Amherst: University of Massachusetts Press, 1972), pp. 150–53, 168. Translation of the poem is by the authors, as are all translations from Spanish original texts, unless otherwise noted.

52. Oleksak and Oleksak, *Béisbol,* p. 71.

53. Ron Luciano and David Fisher, *Strike Two* (New York: Bantam Books, 1984), p. 78, cited in ibid., p. 72.

54. Oleksak and Oleksak, *Béisbol,* p. 72.

55. Ibid., p. 73.

56. Ron Fimrite, "In Cuba, It's Viva El Grand Old Game," *Sports Illustrated* 46, no. 24, 6 June 1977, pp. 77, 73.

57. H. Senzel, *Baseball and the Cold War* (New York: Harcourt Brace Jovanovich, 1977), pp. 119, 190; Brown, "Cuban Baseball," p. 112; Oleksak and Oleksak, *Béisbol,* p. 75.

58. Rob Ruck, "Baseball in the Caribbean," in Thorn and Palmer, *Total Baseball,* p. 605.

59. Casas et al., *Viva y en juego,* pp. 45–47.

60. Fimrite, "In Cuba," p. 72.

61. Casas et al., *Viva y en juego,* pp. 48–49.

62. Ruck, "Baseball in the Caribbean," pp. 607–8.

63. J. L. Salmeron, "25 Experiencias del béisbol," *El Deporte* 188 (1986), p. 49.

64. Fimrite, "In Cuba," p. 79; Wagner, "Baseball in Cuba," p. 115.

65. Oleksak and Oleksak, *Béisbol*, p. 76 (see also p. 199).

66. Casas et al., *Viva y en juego*, p. 11.

67. R. Hernández, cited in O. Lewis, M. Lewis, S. M. Rigdon, *Neighbors Living the Revolution: An Oral History of Contemporary Cuba*, vol. 3 (Urbana, Ill.: University of Illinois Press, 1978), pp. 376–77.

68. Alan M. Klein, *Sugarball: The American Game, the Dominican Dream* (New Haven, Conn.: Yale University Press, 1991), p. 42.

69. Ruck, *Tropic of Baseball*, pp. 1–2.

70. Ibid., p. 118.

71. Oleksak and Oleksak, *Béisbol*, p. 8.

72. Gilbert M. Joseph, "Forging the Regional Pastime: Baseball and Class in Yucatán," in Arbena, *Sport and Society*, pp. 33, 34; Carlos J. García, *Baseball para siempre* (Mexico: EISW, 1979), p. 50, cited in Oleksak and Oleksak, *Béisbol*, p. 10.

73. Oleksak and Oleksak, *Béisbol*, p. 9.

74. Ruck, *Tropic of Baseball*, p. 5.

75. Klein, *Sugarball*, pp. 25, 59.

76. Bill Deane, "Foreign-Born Players," in Thorn and Palmer, *Total Baseball*, pp. 414–15; Klein, *Sugarball*, p. 61.

77. ABC interview with Castro, 28 July 1991. J. David Truby, in "Castro's Curveball," *Harper's* 278 (May 1989), pp. 33–34, claims that Castro was very seriously considered by the Senators, but that he declined the offer, preferring to continue college. T. Slack, "Cuba's Political Involvement in Sport," *Journal of Sport and Social Issues* (1982), p. 35. Oleksak and Oleksak, *Béisbol*, p. 45, claim that Joe Cambria scouted Castro (see also this volume, chapter 5, on baseball). U.S. and Cuban baseball of the 1940s and 1950s is relived in the constant reminiscences of the older fans in the stands at baseball games held throughout Cuba today.

78. I. Ballart, "Encuentro en Matahambre," *LPV* 869 (1979), p. 28; J. Alfonso, *Puños dorados apuntes para la historia del boxeo en Cuba* (Santiago de Cuba: Editorial Oriente, 1988), pp. 19, 20, 31, 33.

79. Unión Deportíva Cuba Libre, *Sports Without Freedom Is No Sport at All: Communist Sports as a Political Instrument*, a Cuban exile publication; E. López Sánchez, "Golpes, necesidad, y explotación," *LPV* 829 (1978), pp. 30–31, and R. Crespo, "Kid Chocolate," *El Deporte* 187 (1986), p. 19. Sardínas was asked what boxing is, and he responded, "El boxeo soy yo." See E. Menéndez and V. Joaquín, *El boxeo soy yo* (La Habana: Editorial Pablo de Torriente, 1990).

80. Alfonso, *Puños dorados*, pp. 75, 76; López Sánchez, "Golpes," pp. 30–31.

81. Alfonso, *Puños dorados*, pp. 80, 81.

82. M. M. Ballou, *Due South* (New York: Negro Universities Press, 1885), p. 59.

83. Unión Deportíva Cuba Libre, *Sports Without Freedom*, p. 10; W. Hulbert, *Gan-Eden* (New York: John D. Jewett, 1854), pp. 59, 73, 383.

84. W. C. Bryant, *Letters of a Traveller* (New York: George P. Putnam, 1850), p. 358. It is difficult to comment on the recreation of Cuban women because little reference is made to them.

85. Hulbert, *Gan-Eden*, pp. 46, 47, 51; Bryant, *Letters*, p. 362.

86. Hulbert, *Gan-Eden*, pp. 198–99; Ballou, *Due South*, p. 239; E. Montejo, *Autobiography of a Runaway Slave* (New York: Random House, 1973), pp. 29–31.

87. Fiestas in Havana were often based on African traditions, although activities common in other parts of Latin America (such as the children's game with papier-maché piñatas) were also played. F. Ortíz, "Los viejos carnavales habaneros," *Revista Bimestre de Cuba* 70 (1955), p. 257.

88. Hulbert, *Gan-Eden*, pp. 198–99. The celebration of El Día de Los Reyes later included processions and masquerade balls, Llaneras Rodríguez et al., "Cuba," pp. 157–58.

89. Montejo, *Autobiography*, pp. 88–89. Two of these games—the jug game and the biscuit game—were tests of manliness designed to exhibit the length and strength of the participant's penis (ibid., pp. 25, 26, 28).

90. Ortíz, "Los viejos carnavales," p. 256; Montejo, *Autobiography*, pp. 78–79.

91. P. C. Emmer, ed., *Colonialism and Migration: Indentured Labor Before and After Slavery* (Hingham: Klawer Academic Publishers, 1986), p. 272; Montejo, *Autobiography*,, p. 95.

92. R. J. Scott, *Slave Emancipation in Cuba* (Princeton: Princeton University Press, 1985), pp. 265, 268.

93. Ibid., p. 269.

94. W. Frank, *Cuba: Prophetic Island* (New York: Marzani and Mansell, 1961), appendix 3.

95. J. A. Saco, *Colección de papeles* 1 (La Habana: Dirección General de Cultura, MINED, 1960), p. 177 (quotation is from p. 182). See also A. Nuñez Jiménez, *La abuela* (Lima: Campodanico Ediciones, S.A., 1973), p. 36.

96. Apparently Saco's work would not have been published if he had criticized *las gallerias* (the cockpits) or called for them to be banned. Saco, *Colección de papeles*, pp. 184, 187–88, 191–93.

97. Alcaldia Municipal de San José de las Lajas (June 1985), "Un documento para la historia del juego en Cuba," *Revista Bimestre Cubana* 71 (1956), p. 186; E. Roig de Leuchsenring, "Apuntes para un estudio sobre la evolución de nuestros costumbres públicas y privadas," *Revista Bimestre Cubana* 30 (1932), semestre segunda, p. 228.

98. Cuban Ministry of Foreign Affairs, *Cuba: A Giant School* (Havana: 1966), p. 6; J. Rosales, ed., *La educación en Cuba* (Buenos Aires: Editorial Convergencia, 1975), p. 9.

99. Llaneras Rodríguez et al., "Cuba," p. 157; I. Huberman and P. M. Sweezey, *Cuba: Anatomy of a Revolution* (New York: Monthly Review Press, 1960), p. 96.

100. Pickering, "Cuba," p. 149; H. González Alonso, "La formación de cuadros," *Cultura Física Revista* 1, no. 1 (October 1985), p. 5.

101. W. Giusta Almíra, "Más de un medio siglo en el deporte," *LPV* 877 (1979), p. 29; González González et al., *Razones*, p. 1.

102. Ballou, *Due South*, p. 222; Hulbert, *Gan-Eden*, p. 123; J. Conangla Fontanilles, "El turismo y las corridas de toros," *Revista Bimestre de Cuba* 34, segundo semestre (1934), pp. 145–46.

103. The term *jai alai* means "fiesta alegre" in Basque and became the name for *pelota vasca* in Cuba. It is a court game somewhat like handball played by two or four players with a ball and a long curved wicker basket strapped to the wrist. A. Mendez Muñiz, *La pelota vasca en Cuba: Su evolución hasta 1930* (La Habana: Editorial Científico-Técnica, 1990), p. 12; L. Judson and E. Judson, *Your Holiday in Cuba* (New York: Harper and Brothers, 1952), p. 106; H. Portell-Vila, *Nueva historia de la República de Cuba (1898–1979)* (Miami: La Moderna Poesia, 1986), p. 142. Both squash and handball were also played in Cuba before 1930, see Mendez Muñiz, *Pelota vasca*, pp. 17, 142, 157, 158.

104. A. G. Robinson, *Cuba and the Intervention* (New York: Longmans, Green, 1905), p. 337.

105. J. Rodríguez, "La cancha puede ser de todos," *LPV* 847 (1978), pp. 26–27.

106. Bryant, *Letters*, pp. 368, 367, 375.

107. Hulbert, *Gan-Eden*, pp. 118–19; Montejo, *Autobiography*, pp. 88–89; Bryant, *Letters*, p. 367. The quotation is from Ballou, *Due South*, p. 210.

108. R. McLean and G. P. Williams, *Old Spain in New America* (New York: Association Press, 1916), p. 88; L. Nelson, *Rural Cuba* (New York: Octagon Books, 1970), p. 214.

109. C. A. Palácio, "Patrimonio de la humanidad," *El Deporte* 15, no. 154, 30 May 1983, p. 30; *Cuba en la mano*, pp. 1177–78; J. Caminada, "El arma de un estadio cincuentenario," *El Deporte* 12, no. 3 (1980), pp. 6–7. Moises Rivera described how, in the 1930s, makeshift balls were used and youngsters were scolded for wearing out their shoes (see O. Lewis, R. M. Lewis, and S. M. Rigdon, *Four Women Living the Revolution: An Oral History of Contemporary Cuba*, vol. 2 (Urbana, Ill.: University of Illinois Press, 1977), p. 146).

110. M. Torres, "Gimnástica," *LPV* 806 (1977), p. 30; J. Alfonso, *Guía de los panamericanos* (Santiago de Cuba: Editorial Oriente, 1991), p. 27; Llaneras Rodríguez et al., "Cuba," p. 159. De Aguera also wrote *Gimnástica moderna y de consulta* (1882), which was the first official text used in Cuban schools and institutions.

111. Torres, "Gimnástica," pp. 29, 30.

112. Llaneras Rodríguez et al., "Cuba," p. 160.

113. J. Caminada, "Desde sus raíces," *LPV* 809 (1977), p. 10, and M. Robainas Ortega, "LXV aniversario del tenis de Cuba," *El Deporte* 188 (1986), p. 35.

114. Torres, "Gimnástica," p. 30.

115. M. Torres, "Al rítmico paso del pedalista," *El Deporte*, no. 6 (1979), p. 8.

116. McLean and Williams, *Old Spain*, p. 96. The university was also active in fencing, baseball, basketball, and rowing. See D. A. Alvárez Guerra, L. Ramírez de Armas, A. Carbonell del Busto; G. R. González, and J. Pedro Heredia, *El deporte universitario: Cuna del deporte cubano* (La Habana: Ediciones ENPES, 1991).

117. Caminada, "Desde sus raíces," p. 10, and Robainas Ortega, "LXV aniversario," p. 35.

118. M. Torres, "El baloncesto síntesis de su historia," *El Deporte* 12, no. 9 (1980), p. 20; A. Prado, "El tenis de campo en sancti spiritus," *LPV* 861 (1978), p. 28.

119. M. C. Valle, "Trece años, trece testimonios," *LPV* 609 (February 1974), p. 21; M. Torres, "Entre malla y balón," *El Deporte* 20, no. 203 (March 1988), p. 47; *Cuba en la mano*, pp. 1179–80.

120. J. Caminada, "Deporte milenario," *El Deporte* 12, no. 7 (1980), pp. 17–18.

121. Judson and Judson, *Your Holiday in Cuba*, pp. 105, 111, 112. Most Cubans earned less than 1,000 pesos per annum before 1959. Moreover, the cost of living rose steadily from 1937 (100) to 1942 (132.4) and then increased rapidly until 1952 (253.8). The buying power of the Cuban peso declined in a similar fashion: from 1937 (100) to 1942 (75.5) and then to 1952 (39.4). *Anuario estadístico, 1952*, p. 285.

122. Fidel Castro Ruz, cited in Pickering, "Cuba," p. 150.

123. N. McWhirter and S. Greenberg, eds., *Olympic Records* (Harmondsworth, 1980), pp. 48, 51, 55.

124. See Rafael Fortun Chacon, interview in M. C. Valle, "Trece años, trece testimonios," *LPV* 609 (February 1974), p. 24.

125. Pickering, "Cuba," p. 149.

126. Scott, *Slave Emancipation in Cuba*, p. 266.

127. Ibid., p. 267.

128. *La Propaganda*, 26 February 1882 and 17 May 1885, and "Las fiestas en los campos," *Revista de Agricultura* 8, 2 September 1888, p. 385, both cited in ibid., p. 236.

129. Scott, *Slave Emancipation in Cuba*, pp. 8, 266, 268–69.

130. Ibid., p. 273; Fia, *Guía descriptiva e histórica de Trinidad* (La Habana: Maza, Caso, 1939), p. 23; Scott, *Slave Emancipation in Cuba*, p. 269.

131. Scott, *Slave Emancipation in Cuba*, pp. 266, 268, 269, 273. The quotation is from p. 270.

132. McLean and Williams, *Old Spain*, p. 96.

133. J. Martí, cited in M. Torres, "Reseñas deportívas," *LPV* 883 (1979), p. 28, and in "Pensamientos de Martí," *LPV* 884 (1979), p. 2. See also C. Enríquez, *José Martí y los deportes* (Mexico: Machado y Cia, 1948), and Bedia, *José Martí*.

134. Casas et al., *Viva y en juego*, pp. 18, 20; see also Brown, "Cuban Baseball," p. 110. The quotation is from González Barros, "Baseball," p. 6.

135. Casas et al., *Viva y en juego*, pp. 18, 20; Brown, "Cuban Baseball," p. 110.

136. C. Hoyos, "Los boy-scoutts [sic] y la protección de la niñez," *Revista Bimestre Cubana* 24, no. 5 (September–October 1929), pp. 728, 734, 785–88.

137. Arredondo, *Batista*, p. 191.

138. *Problems of the New Cuba*, report of the Commission on Cuban Affairs (New York: Foreign Policy Association, 1936), p. 176.

139. Arredondo, *Batista*, p. 175.

140. Caminada, "Desde sus raíces," pp. 8–10; Historiadores Deportívos de La Habana, "Julio Antonio Mella," *LPV* 872 (1979), p. 31; I. Forbes, "Algo sobre el 'Juan Abrante,'" *LPV* 656 (1975), pp. 20–22. See also Alvarez et al., *El*

deporte universitario, pp. 3, 14, 23–34. The quotation is from Forbes, "Algo sobre el 'Juan Abrante,'" p. 23.

141. Torres, "Gimnástica," *LPV* 807, p. 31; M. C. Pacheco González et al., *Apuntes para la historia del movimento juvenil cubana* (La Habana: Editorial Abril, 1987), pp. 43, 44, 68, 79.

142. Cited in Canon, *Revolutionary Cuba*, p. 211.

143. González Barros, "Baseball," p. 6; Llanusa, "Speaks from the Canefields," p. 10; Pickering, "Cuba," p. 159.

144. Lourdes Casals and Andres R. Hernández, "Role of Cultural and Sports Events in Cuba's Foreign Policy," p. 6. Preliminary draft prepared for the conference "The Role of Cuba in World Affairs," Center for Latin American Studies, University of Pittsburgh, 15–17 November 1976. See also *LPV* 14, nos. 732–22, 6 July 1976, pp. 20–23.

145. Lafita, in Valle, "Trece años," p. 19.

146. *GWR* 15, no. 33, 17 August 1980, p. 9.

CHAPTER 3. STRUCTURE AND ADMINISTRATION UNDER FIDEL

1. This introductory discussion avoids mentioning the 1980 Olympics in Moscow, the 1984 Olympics in Los Angeles, and the 1988 Olympics in Seoul, where the absence of many strong contenders because of boycotts would provide an unrepresentative picture.

2. The phrase *un mal rato* means a bad time or period and comes from Ribero Fuxa, interview with Paula Pettavino.

3. "En quince años, esfuerzos y victorias," *LPV* 14, 17 February 1976, p. 34.

4. Ruíz, "Sport—Why Cubans Win," p. 11. At the time of this interview, Ruíz was a professor at INDER.

5. P. Arrieto, director of social sports, INDER, interview with Geralyn Pye, 8 October 1986, Havana; "Entrance Fee for Sporting Events Abolished in Cuba (Law 546)" *Cuba Economic News* 3, no. 22 (April 1967), p. 11; Fidel Castro Ruz, *Main Report to the First Congress of the Cuban Communist Party*, 17 December 1975, Havana; Res. no. 1030, INDER, 16 March 1967, *Fundamentales*, Dirección Jurídica (1984).

6. *Index to Latin American Legislation*, vol. 1 (Boston: G. K. Hall, 1971), p. 449, compiled at the Library of Congress; *New York Times*, 12 December 1964, 2:5.

7. Ruíz, "Sport—Why Cubans Win," p. 11.

8. *National Atlas of Cuba in Commemoration of the Tenth Anniversary of the Revolution*, translations on Latin America, 525, 19 May 1971 (Havana: Joint Publications Research Service [JPRS], 1979), prepared by the geography institutes of the Cuban and USSR academies of science, pp. 128–31. The original was published by the Main Administration of Geodesy and Cartography of the USSR Council of Ministers (hereafter referred to as *National Atlas*).

9. The information in this paragraph was gleaned from the authors' personal observations and through interviews. Some information is included in Pickering, "Cuba."

10. Domínguez, *Order and Revolution*, pp. 244–46.

11. Resolutions no. 2 and 3, 15 March 1961; Res. no. 38, 2 September 1961; Res. no. 67D, 4 January 1962; Res. no. 75, 15 February 1962; Res. no. 83A, 9 March 1962; in *Fundamentales*.

12. Gutiérrez, conversation with Geralyn Pye.

13. All the data in this paragraph are taken from the United Nations, *Economic Survey of Latin America and the Caribbean, 1982* 1 (1984), Santiago de Chile, pp. 244, 267, 268 (hereafter referred to as *ECLA*).

14. E. Boorstein, *The Economic Transformation of Cuba* (New York: Modern Reader Paperbacks, 1968), p. 79; see also the plan of the fourth congress of the Cuban Communist party to export sport services, "Resolución sobre el desarrollo económico del país," point 5, *Congreso del Partido Comunista de Cuba*, 10–14 October 1991, p. 10 (hereafter referred to as *Congreso del PCC*); Llaneras Rodríguez et al., "Cuba," pp. 122–30.

15. Gutiérrez, conversation with Geralyn Pye; Domínguez, *Order and Revolution*, p. 185; Geralyn Pye, observations, October 1986, Havana.

16. C. Mesa-Lago, "The Economy: Caution, Frugality, and Resilient Ideology," in Jorge I. Domínguez (ed.), *Cuba: Internal and International Affairs* (Beverly Hills, Calif.: Sage Publications, 1982), p. 155; Fidel Castro Ruz, *We Are Born to Overcome, Not to Be Overrun*, speech at close of Sixth Congress of the Federation of Students Intermediate Education (FEEM) (La Habana: Editorial Política, 1984), p. 15; Carlos Alvarez, section of international relations, INDER, interview with Geralyn Pye, 8 October 1986, Havana.

17. In 1980, over 125,000 Cubans left Cuba. Some had occupied the unguarded Peruvian embassy and insisted on being allowed to leave. See Domínguez, *Internal and International Affairs*, pp. 44–45 (quotation is from p. 54).

18. James Riordan, "Soviet Sport," in B. Lowe, D. B. Kanin, and A. Strenk, eds., *Sport and International Relations* (Champaign, Il.: Stipes, 1978), p. 300; Arrieto, interview with Geralyn Pye.

19. United Nations, *ECLA*, p. 266.

20. Boorstein, *Economic Transformation*, chap. 4.

21. The introduction of charges for sports events might have absorbed some of the surplus income of Cubans. It is not known whether this was considered when charges were reviewed. Mesa-Lago, "The Economy," p. 143.

22. J. Yglesias, *In the Fist of the Revolution* (London: Penguin, 1968), p. 39; J. García Bango, then president of INDER, "Los VII juegos panamericanos se convierten en un compromiso moral de nuestros atletas," *LPV* 663, 4 March 1975, p. 13; Paula Pettavino, observations, Havana, August 1980.

23. Domínguez, *Internal and International Affairs*, p. 42. The system of Poder Popular was introduced in the mid-1970s. Elections followed the system of democratic centralism first used in the former Soviet Union. Direct elections were held at the municipal level only. That body, the municipal assembly, then elected the provincial assembly, which elected the national assembly. The national assembly then elected the Council of Ministers; candidates at all levels needed party approval. The system was recently changed to allow for direct

popular election of the National Assembly. See chapter 6 for further information.

24. Calculated from data given in C. Contreras, "Everyone in . . . for the Benefit of Everyone," *Cuba Today* 3 (October 1985), and C. Mesa-Lago, *Revolutionary Change in Cuba* (Pittsburgh: University of Pittsburgh Press, 1971), p. 262.

25. CDR president, conversation with Geralyn Pye, 21 January 1992, Havana (Calle Consulado between Trocadero and Colon); Domínguez, *Order and Revolution*, p. 255; Geralyn Pye, observations, October 1986.

26. "Resolución sobre el perfeccionamiento de la organización y funcionamiento de los órganos del Poder Popular," *Congreso del PCC*, pp. 7–9.

27. Llaneras Rodríguez et al., "Cuba," pp. 160–61; Wagner, "Baseball in Cuba," p. 117; CTC, Departamento de Deportes, *Convocatoria de los VII juegos deportívos* (1986) (see this volume, chapter 4, for more details).

28. J. L. Salmerón, "Five Months to the World Series," *GWR*, 20 June 1971, p. 9; A. Rojas, "The Work of a Million Hands," *GWR*, 3 October 1971, p. 8.

29. T. Díaz Castro, "What Are the CDRs?" *GWR*, 22 January 1967, p. 6; J. Yglesias, *Fist of the Revolution*, p. 39.

30. Domínguez, *Order and Revolution*, p. 262. The quotation is from Díaz Castro, "What Are the CDRs?" p. 6.

31. D. W. Bray and T. F. Harding, "Cuba," in R. H. Chicote and J. C. Edelstein, eds., *Latin America* (Cambridge: Schenkman, 1974), p. 672. The Plan de la Calle was a program to block off streets and provide physical recreation for children, especially during the 1960s when many parents went to the countryside to help with the sugar harvest.

The LPV tests had two main objectives: to raise the health of Cubans and to provide information about physical fitness for government authorities. The test was divided into levels according to age and gender and involved achieving set standards in such activities as running, jumping, and shooting. These tests were based on the GTO tests in the Soviet Union (see this volume, chapter 4).

32. Domínguez, *Internal and International Affairs*, pp. 43–44; Geralyn Pye, observations, January 1992, Havana.

33. Llaneras Rodríguez et al., "Cuba," pp. 17, 18, 22; J. Griffiths, "Sport: The People's Right," in J. Griffiths and P. Griffiths, *Cuba: The Second Decade* (London: Writers and Readers Cooperative, 1979), p. 250; G. Whannel, *Blowing the Whistle* (London: Pluto Press, 1983), p. 112; Pickering, "Cuba," p. 160; J. Caminada, "Héroes anónimos del deporte," *LPV* 809, 20 December 1977, p. 14.

34. See Griffiths, "Sport: The People's Right," p. 250; *Cuba '67: Image of a Country* (Havana: Cuban Book Institute, 1967), p. 324.

35. Whannel, *Blowing the Whistle*, p. 112.

36. J. García Bango, "Los VII juegos," p. 10 (translated by the authors).

37. Domínguez, *Internal and International Affairs*, p. 54; Llaneras Rodríguez et al., "Cuba," p. 30–31.

38. Domínguez, *Order and Revolution*, p. 170, see also pp. 275–76.

39. See Comite Organizador Cuba 78, *XI festival Cuba 78* (published in Cuba, undated).

40. Yglesias, *Fist of the Revolution*, p. 18.

41. See the introduction to Domínguez, *Order and Revolution*. For a contrasting view of Cuban democratic centralism, see Contreras, "Everyone," pp. 4–6. The quotation is from Domínguez, *Order and Revolution*. p. 391.

42. "Más deportes y menos vicios," *Revolución*, special edition, 30 December 1959, p. 10; "Cuesta de $2 a $6 ser Socio del Biltmore," *Revolución*, 16 May 1960, pp. 1, 12. No figures are available on membership after these changes. Perhaps there was a reluctance to enter these previously exclusive clubs.

43. Chatazo (nom de plume), "Gratis hoy la serie," *Revolución*, 28 May 1959, p. 10; P. Montesinos, "Sobre la permanencia de los Sugar Kings en la Habana," *Revolución*, 22 May 1959, p. 9; "Entrance Fee Abolished," p. 11; Arrieto, interview with Geralyn Pye (based upon the authors' observations).

44. "Free Admission to all Sport Events," *GWR*, 19 March 1967, p. 3.

45. J. García Bango, "The Cuban Revolution," *GWR*, 10 September 1972, p. 9.

46. "Más deportes y menos vicios," p. 14.

47. García Bango, "Cuban Revolution," p. 9.

48. *Boletín estadístico de Cuba, 1964,* (JUCEPLAN, 1964), p. 124; Fidel Castro Ruz, *Educación y revolución* 7th edition (Mexico City: Editorial Nuestro Tiempo, S.A., 1983), p. 101; García Bango, "Cuban Revolution," p. 9; Fidel Castro Ruz, "Nuestras victorias son una medida de nuestros esfuerzos," *El Deporte* 4, no. 10 (1971), p. 40.

49. González González et al., *Razones*, pp. 39, 153; J. Caminada, "Recuento de un análisis," *El Deporte* 20, no. 203 (March 1988), pp. 4, 5, and "Palabras de Conrado Martínez Corona," same issue, pp. 8, 9 (hereafter referred to as "Palabras de Corona").

50. *LPV* 14, 17 February 1976, p. 39. *Batos* is the name of a game similar to baseball played by the indigenous peoples of Cuba. See chapter 2.

51. Luís Sexto, "Cómo se inventó aquella máquina," *LPV* 14, 17 February 1976, pp. 50, 51.

52. De la Cuesta, interview with Paula Pettavino.

53. Pickering, "Cuba," p. 164.

54. De la Cuesta, interview with Paula Pettavino.

55. Llaneras Rodríguez et al., "Cuba," pp. 132–34,

56. Ibid., pp. 117, 128–29; F. Mastrascusa, "Honrar honra," *LPV* 681, 8 July 1975, p. 25, and García Bango, "Los VII juegos," p. 13.

57. Pickering, "Cuba," p. 164; Arrieto, interview with Geralyn Pye.

58. Jean Stubbs, *Cuba: The Test of Time* (London: Latin America Bureau, 1989), p. 60.

59. Thomas Boswell, "Idle Play Not in Cuba's Game Plan," *Washington Post*, 9 April 1978.

60. De la Cuesta, interview with Paula Pettavino. It is interesting to see how Señor de la Cuesta, a man in his fifties, arrived at his position as director of the Sports Industry in 1980. Before the revolution, he was an agricultural worker. A supporter of Castro, he led a battalion of men at Playa Girón. He

returned to agriculture and supervised all cattle raising in Havana Province. In 1973, he returned to finally finish high school and went on to complete a degree in economics. Diploma in hand, he began work in a tire factory and moved to the Sports Industry in 1979.

61. B. Castillo, speech, "Término reunión nacional de análisis del INDER," *Granma*, 14 January 1974, p. 6.

62. Caminada, "Palabras de Corona," pp. 8, 9.

63. García Bango, "Los VII juegos," pp. 8, 9, 13; J. L. Salmerón, "Las industrias locales apoyo a la masividad," *El Deporte* 20, no. 204, 30 March 1988, pp. 33, 34.

64. Arrieto, interview with Geralyn Pye.

65. González Alonso, "La formación de cuadros," p. 6; *Cuba '67*, p. 326.

66. Pickering, "Cuba," p. 157; A. Pallares Vera, "La ciencia y la técnica al servicio del deporte, " *El Deporte* 18, no. 186, 30 March 1986, p. 13; M. Torres and M. C. Valles, "X congreso panamericano de educación física, fuente de energia creadora," *El Deporte* 19, no. 192, 30 March 1987, p. 14; Caminada, "Recuento," p. 5; González González et al., *Razones*, p. 155; *Mapa 1983* (Havana: INDER, Dirección de Propaganda); González González et al., *Razones*, p. 67.

67. *Anuario estadístico de Cuba, 1975*, JUCEPLAN, p. 52; *Compendio estadístico de Cuba, 1965*, JUCEPLAN, p. 16; *Boletín estadístico de Cuba, 1965*, p. 26; *Gaceta oficial de la República de Cuba* 72, no. 24, 9 September 1974, p. 1010.

68. Llaneras Rodríguez et al., "Cuba," pp. 137–38.

69. Caminada, "Recuento," pp. 3–6.

70. Griffiths, "Sport: The People's Right," pp. 257–58; Casals and Hernández, "The Role of Cultural and Sports Events," p. 10.

71. Rolando Betancourt, "Sports, Movies Unlimited," *GWR*, 29 February 1976, p. 9. See also Casals and Hernandez, pp. 12–15.

CHAPTER 4. POPULAR PARTICIPATION UNDER FIDEL

1. Fernando Sandoval, "Cuba Catches Up," *Atlas World Press Review* (May 1976), p. 53, excerpted from *Veja* of Rio de Janeiro.

2. All constitutional references are from the *Constitution of the Republic of Cuba* (New York: Center for Cuban Studies), pp. 5, 12, 13, 14, 16.

3. Castro, speech at the Mártires de Barbados.

4. Llaneras Rodríguez et al., "Cuba," p. 161. See also Pickering, "Cuba," p. 164. The quotation is from Luís Sexto, *LPV* 14, 17 February 1976, p. 4.

5. *La Juventud* (Havana: Editorial Gente Nueva, 1978). In an interview in 1988, Raudol Ruíz spoke of 4.7 million "participations." By this he meant not the number of individuals who participated, but rather how many times a sports service (such as a bat, ball, pool, gym, or track) was used. He also estimated only about 25,000 such "participations" before the revolution. This corresponds to 1.5 million people, Ruíz estimated, between the ages of ten and forty. (From Ruíz, "Sport—Why Cubans Win," p. 13.) The figures from *La Juventud* were probably calculated the same way, representing "participations" rather than different individuals.

6. Rafael Cambo Arcos, cited in J. González Barros, "On Sport," *GWR*, 26 January 1969, p. 8. See also the survey form for "Conrado Benítez" Brigada de Alfabetización, Comisión Nacional de Alfabetización, MINED, 1961.

7. *Cuba '67*, pp. 326–30.

8. Llaneras Rodríguez et al., "Cuba," p. 148.

9. Ibid., p. 162; *Cuba '67*, p. 235.

10. Llaneras Rodríguez et al., "Cuba," p. 162; I. Forbes, J. Alvárez, F. Mastrascusa, C. A. Palacios, and J. L. Salmeron, "Dos fructíferas décadas del deporte revolucionario," *El Deporte* 11, no. 1 (1979), p. 15; I. Estrada, "El deporte en las montañas," *LPV* 891, 17 July 1979, p. 28.

11. J. Caminada, "El deporte y la Guayabera," *El Deporte* 157, 30 August 1983, pp. 18–23.

12. Griffiths, "Sport: The People's Right," p. 251.

13. *Cuba '67*, p. 327; O. Tapia, "Fit to Win," *GWR*, 30 October 1966, p. 2.

14. The term *cederista* comes from the Spanish pronunciation of the letters CDR (for Comites de la Defensa de la Revolución) made into a word; J. Paz, "No importa la edad para el deporte," *El Deporte* 11, no. 2 (1979), p. 12.

15. This does not mean 4,000,000. individuals, as several tests were given to the same participants. The information in this paragraph came from J. L. Salmerón, "¡A pasar las pruebas de eficiencia física!" *LPV* 15, no. 805, 22 November 1977, pp. 10–11; and González González et al., *Razones*, p. 67.

16. Doctor's interview with Paula Pettavino, 22 August 1980, Sierra Maestra. See also Herman Bosch, "La salud fluye por las venas de las historias cordilleras," *Bohemia* 67, no. 45, 5 November 1976, pp. 26–27.

17. Manuel González, quoted in Boswell, "Idle Play," pp. D1, D7.

18. Dirección Nacional de Educación y Cultura Física (INDER), *Ponte en forma* (no date); J. Caminada, "Motivos de satisfacción," *El Deporte* 19, no. 192, 30 March 1987, p. 56.

19. S. Guerrero Gutiérrez and H. O. Cuevas O'Gaban, *Recreación turística* (Havana: Editorial Pueblo y Educación, 1981), p. ix; Geralyn Pye and Paula Pettavino, observations in Havana in 1980, 1986, 1988, and 1992, when attempts to exchange Cuban pesos for U.S. dollars were very common. The rate of exchange on the black market in January 1992 was $1 = 25 pesos. In 1988, it was 6–9 pesos per dollar. Prostitution is also evident in Havana. By early 1992, such activity was growing and more blatant. Also by early 1992, the rate of crime in Havana had risen significantly. In 1987, the Cuban publication *Somos Jovenes* reported that there were about a thousand prostitutes in Havana, and that some were earning as much as 6,000 pesos per month, more than the average annual income for all other Cubans (cited in M. Azicri, *Cuban Politics, Economics, and Society* [New York and London: Pinter Publishers, 1988], p. 161).

20. Dominoes (and also chess and baseball) are played in many public places. During August 1980 at Guardalavaca in Holguín Province and during July and August 1988 near Havana, the beaches and pools of nearby hotels were crowded with throngs of Cubans. Foreigners were an unusual sight. By early 1992, there were significantly more tourists (Geralyn Pye and Paula Pettavino, observations, Havana). More recent efforts to rapidly develop tourism

as a source of hard currency has created a new system of "tourist apartheid," where Cubans are barred from certain hotels and facilities—welcomed as employees, but not as guests. See sources listed in chapter 6, note 13.

21. "In 1975, a week-long tour in a luxury bus complete with bar and toilet conducted vacationers from Havana to Santiago de Cuba and back at a cost of 180 pesos. A four-day trip to the Isle of Pines cost 90 pesos" [Jan K. Black, Howard I. Blutstein, J. David Edwards, Kathryn T. Johnston, David S. McMorris, *Area Handbook for Cuba*, 2d edition (Washington, D.C.: Foreign Area Studies of the American University, 1976), p. 229]; Geralyn Pye, observations, Havana, January 1992.

22. Geralyn Pye, observations, Havana, January 1992; A. Isidron del Valle, "The Ismaelillo Pioneers' Camp," *GWR*, 29 August 1976, p. 6.

23. The OCIODE study was conducted in the Regla municipality in the city of Havana. Llaneras Rodríguez et al., "Cuba," pp. 168, 164–65.

24. Ibid., pp. 165–66.

25. R. Escobar, "Round Up," *Cuba International* 4, no. 986, pp. 57–58; Paula Pettavino, observations, August 1980.

26. M. Díaz, director of recreation at INDER, interview cited in M. C. Valle, "La recreación y su importante papel," *LPV* 17, no. 872, 6 March 1979, p. 21; see also the 1981 Plan de Campismo Popular (UJC), González González et al., *Razones*, p. 37.

27. These very precise figures are cited in "A Full Week of 'Street Playground' to Coincide with Spring Vacation Period," *GWR*, 3 April 1966, p. 6.

28. Lewis et al., *Four Women*, vol. 2, pp. 391–92; Llaneras Rodríguez et al., "Cuba," pp. 162–63; B. Salamanca, "Many Thousand Children Take Part in Second INDER and UPC Giant Street Playground Plan," *GWR*, 18 December 1966, p. 6.

29. R. Pérez Betancourt, "Street Playground Future Champions," *GWR*, 6 March 1966, p. 10.

30. T. Díaz Castro, "CDRs Work for the Revolution," *GWR*, special feature, 22 January 1967, p. 6; I. Forbes and J. Alvarez, "Simientes de porvenir," *LVP* 17, no. 884, 29 May 1979, p. 20.

31. R. Fleites, "Hablemos de . . . Plan de la Calle," *LPV* 13, no. 657, 21 January 1975, p. 29; Geralyn Pye and Paula Pettavino, observations, 1980, 1986, 1988, 1992; see also Wagner, "Baseball in Cuba," p. 113 (throughout South America, on the other hand, the dominant street game is soccer); J. Caminada, "Los Planes de la Calle, hacia una nueva etapa," *LPV* 16, no. 821, 14 March 1978, pp. 24–27.

32. J. P. Coto, "Acerca de la recreación," *LPV* 18, no. 912, 11 December 1979, p. 26; I. Forbes, "Son felices mediante el juego," *El Deporte* 12, no. 7 (1980), p. 32. Almost all Cubans have televisions. In 1980, 53 percent of households had a television; by 1982, 67 percent of households had one. United Nations, *ECLA*, p. 248.

33. M. Torres, "Un innovador dedicado a la recreación física," *El Deporte* 12, no. 6 (1980), p. 13.

34. Forbes, "Cultura física popular," pp. 43, 44.

35. Paula Pettavino, observations, August 1980.

36. Llaneras Rodríguez et al., "Cuba," p. 143.

37. Paula Pettavino, observations, 1980 in Cuba, 1977 in El Salvador, and 1980 in Peru. Throughout Latin America, *piropos* (courteous or flirtatious remarks expressed frequently by men to women in public) are quite common. As much as the revolutionary government might like to think that sexism has disappeared, Cuba *piropos* have simply become politicized. Interestingly, Cubans called blonde non-Cubans *tvarishch* (the Russian word for comrade), apparently assuming that light-skinned, blue-eyed foreigners were Russian. Domínguez gives other examples: "Take me along to voluntary work, beautiful"; "You put an end to underdevelopment"; "Give me a scholarship in your heart"; "Honey, how many ration cards do you have?"; "Gorgeous, you are overfulfilling the norm"; "You are like the history of Cuba, old but interesting" (Domínguez, *Order and Revolution*, pp. 465, 623n).

38. J. Caminada, "Correr es vivir," *El Deporte* 18, no. 189, 30 June 1986, p. 42; J. Velázquez, "Maratón LPV," *El Deporte* 185, 28 February 1986, p. 46; E. Montesinos, "¡Más vida en los años!" *El Deporte* 20, no. 202 (January–February 1988), p. 2; Caminada, "Motivos de satisfacción," p. 54, and J. Caminada, "II Aniversario," *El Deporte* 18, no. 190, 30 July 1986, p. 36.

39. INDER, *Ponte en forma*, p. 1.

40. Llaneras Rodríguez et al., "Cuba," pp. 147–48, and Resoluciones Aprobados por el Segundo Congreso, *II congreso del Partido Comunista de Cuba, documentos y discursos* (Havana: Editorial Político, 1981), pp. 448–49.

41. Llaneras Rodríguez et al., "Cuba," p. 149; the 1990 figures are from González González et al., *Razones*, p. 66; J. García Rodríguez, "Programas para los grupos de educación física de adultos utilizando el deporte como un medio," in *Programas para el desarrollo de las actividades de la cultura física con la población*, Departamento Nacional de Cultura Física, INDER, Havana, pp. 41–42.

42. J. García Rodríguez, methodological inspector of physical education for adults at INDER, interview with Geralyn Pye, 8 October 1986, Havana; G. Casamayor Maspons, "Programa de gimnasia laboral para la población," in *Programas para el desarrollo*, pp. 59–62.

43. Llaneras Rodríguez et al., "Cuba," pp. 150–51; Pickering, "Cuba," p. 162.

44. Pickering, "Cuba," p. 162, 163; M. C. Valle, "Las madres, presencia decisiva," *LPV* 16, no. 831, 27 May 1978, p. 25.

45. D. Navarro Eng and C. Cannet Baro, "Programa de gimnasia básica para la mujer," in *Programas para el desarrollo*, pp. 5, 6, 8.

46. García Rodríguez, interview with Geralyn Pye.

47. *Compañera: ¿Conoce usted lo qué el la gimnasia básica femenina y la matrogimnasia?* (FMC and INDER pamphlet); C. Martínez, "Ellas," *El Deporte* 8, no. 5 (1975), p. 20.

48. Martínez, "Ellas," p. 18.

49. M. Torres, "La salud, primero," *El Deporte* 20, no. 202 (January–February 1988), p. 47; González González et al., *Razones*, pp. 67, 46–47; "La voluntad vence el cansancio," *El Deporte* 20, no. 204, 30 March 1988, p. 24.

50. R. Quiza, "Fiesta deportíva proletaria," *El Deporte* 8, no. 7 (1975), p. 9; *Convocotoria de los VII juegos deportívos de los trabajadores,* Departamento de Deportes, CTC, 1986, p. 4; Quiza, "Fiesta deportíva proletaria," p. 7; J. Caminada, "De la fábrica a la cancha," *El Deporte* 10, no. 8 (1977), p. 9.

51. *Convocotoria,* 1986, p. 3.

52. Ibid., pp. 3, 6–8.

53. Ibid., pp. 5–6, 7, 8.

54. "Resolución sobre el desarrollo económico del país," point 11, *Congreso del PCC,* p. 11. In conversations with a "dissident," it was noted that many Cubans now work for twenty-four hours and then "rest" for the next seventy-two. Geralyn Pye, observations, January 1992, Havana.

55. J. Paz, "Los hombres del mar," *El Deporte* 202, pp. 32–33.

56. F. Burgos, "Atletismo de las FAR doce records," *El Deporte* 13, no. 680, 1 July 1975, p. 33; A. Pérez Hebra, "Juegos militares," *El Deporte* 6, special edition (1973), p. 22.

57. J. Paz, "El deporte y la SEPMI," *El Deporte* 18, no. 189, 30 June 1986, p. 3; Fidel Castro Ruz, *Main Report at the Third Congress of the PCC* (Havana: Editorial Político, 1986), p. 12.

58. The number of women in the work force relates closely to the general pattern of expansion or contraction in the whole Cuban work force. In the mid–1970s when the Cuban economy and work force grew, so did the number of women workers. Similarly, in the 1980s, when there were economic difficulties and a reduction in labor demand, the participation of women in the Cuban work force fell. With the economic problems of the late 1980s and early 1990s, even men are finding access to full-time work difficult.

59. Inside front cover, *LPV* 18, no. 947, 12 August 1980.

60. *The Constitution* (of 1976), p. 12.

61. Fidel Castro, *Discurso, 19 de noviembre de 1961,* p. 11.

62. *School and Society* 97, no. 2318 (Summer 1969), p. 293.

63. David López Escalante, "Para qué la semilla germine," *LPV* 18, no. 947, 12 August 1980, pp. 5, 7.

64. Pickering, "Cuba," pp. 166–74; Griffiths, "Sport: The People's Right," p. 252. See also *GWR,* 23 October 1977. Jana Berdychova provides an obvious example of influence from the USSR or Eastern Europe.

65. N. Junco Cortez, *Para ejercitar al pequeño* (Havana: Dirección Nacional de Educación y Cultura Física del INDER, 1983), pp. 3, 8; the television show is called *Compañera: ¿Conoce usted?;* Forbes and Alvarez, "Simientes de porvenir," p. 22; Manuel Gonzales in the *Washington Post,* 9 April 1978, pp. D1, D7.

66. Ruíz, "Sport—Why Cubans Win," p. 16; Caridad Martínez, "Ellos son felices," *El Deporte* 8, no. 9 (1979), p. 36.

67. Martínez, "Ellos son felices."

68. Llaneras Rodríguez et al., "Cuba," pp. 136–37; R. Pérez Betancourt, "In Search of the Sun," *GWR,* 6 June 1971, p. 5; L. Chadwick, *A Cuban Journey* (London: Dobson Books, 1975), p. 74, and "Educación física a todos los escolares," *Revolución,* 3 October 1964, p. 5; Pickering, "Cuba," p. 169.

69. Llaneras Rodríguez et al., "Cuba"; García Bango, "Cuban Revolution," p. 9; Castillo, "Término reunión nacional," p. 6.

70. MINED, *Documentos directivos para el perfeccionamiento del sistema nacional de educación* (Havana: 23 April 1975), p. 34; Pickering, "Cuba," p. 169, and Cuban Ministry of Foreign Affairs, *Cuba: A Giant School*, p. 21; Señor Lima, vice-director for sports schools, interview with Geralyn Pye, 8 October 1986, Havana.

71. Ruíz, "Sport—Why Cubans Win," p. 12; Castillo, "Término reunión nacional," p. 6; Fidel Castro Ruz, "Speech at the Inauguration of General Máximo Gómez Vocational School," *GWR*, 12 September 1976, p. 3; also Caminada, "Recuento" and "Palabras de Corona," pp. 3–9; Valle, "¿Cómo crear campeones?," *El Deporte* 10, no. 10, 1978, p. 8, and Pickering, "Cuba," p. 169.

72. M. Leiner, *Children Are the Revolution* (Harmondsworth: Penguin, 1974), pp. 2, 48. Such methods are not limited to revolutionary societies. The "time-out" method of punishment popular among parents and teachers in the United States relies on separation from the group and its activities as the means for its effectiveness.

73. Ibid.

74. González González et al., *Razones*, p. vi.

75. Fidel Castro, *Discurso, 19 de noviembre de 1961*, p. 21.

76. Herrera cited in *La Juventud;* Pablo Vélez, *Areito* 2, no. 2/3 (September–December 1975), p. 74; Huberto Gil, *LPV* 946, 5 August 1980, p. 29.

77. H. Gil García, *20 años de juegos deportivos escolares* (Havana: 1983), p. 56.

78. *LPV,* 17 February 1976, pp. 6, 7, 18, 19, 20.

79. Griffiths, "Sport: The People's Right," p. 253; Ruíz, "Sport—Why Cubans Win," p. 13. Vélez, *Areito*, p. 74.

80. Ruíz, "Sport—Why Cubans Win," pp. 13, 14.

81. For a summary of the reliability of Cuban statistics, see C. Mesa-Lago, "The Availability and Reliability of Statistics in Socialist Cuba," *Latin American Occasional Papers* 1 (January 1970). This problem is not unique to Cuba. Australian officials have struggled with the same problem. See *Youth Sport*, p. 13.

82. Caminada, "Recuento," p. 5. The 1990 figures were given as 10,100,000 participations. González González et al., *Razones*, p. 160.

83. Wagner, "Baseball in Cuba," p. 119.

84. Ibid., p. 118; Fimrite, "In Cuba," p. 75. In the only reference to softball found by the authors, it was played by men. References to softball appeared in *Revolucion* throughout 1959.

85. Wagner, "Baseball in Cuba," p. 119.

86. A. Padula and L. Smith, "Women in Socialist Cuba: 1959–1984," in S. Halebsky and J. M Kirk, *Cuba: Twenty-Five Years of Revolution, 1959–1984* (New York: Praeger Publishers, 1985), p. 87; I. Forbes, J. Alvárez, F. Mastrascusa, C. A. Palacios, J. L. Salmeron, "Un pensamiento hecho realidad," *El Deporte* 11, no. 1 (1979), p. 9.

87. Slack, "Cuba's Political Involvement in Sport," p. 37; and *Mapa 1983*.

88. J. L. Salmerón, "Después de quince años," *LPV*, 7 February 1976, p. 11; also *Compendio estadístico de Cuba (1965)*, p. 16); see E. Stone, ed., *Women and the Cuban Revolution* (New York: Pathfinder Press, 1981).

89. See *LPV* and *El Deporte,* 1972 onward.

90. Caminada, "Palabras de Corona," p. 8.

91. P. Véliz, cited in J. L. Salmerón, "Les deportes acuáticos frente a un despertar positivo," *LPV* 16, no. 823, 28 March 1978, pp. 20, 21.

92. Arrieto, interview with Geralyn Pye.

93. García Rodríguez, interview with Geralyn Pye.

94. Arrieto, interview with Geralyn Pye; see Caminada, "Recuento," pp. 3–6, and Caminada, "Palabras de Corona," pp. 8, 9.

95. See *La Juventud;* García Rodríguez, interview with Geralyn Pye; J. Paz, "¿Se puede bajar el peso?" *El Deporte* 20, no. 27 (July 1988), p. 29. The Cuban diet is high in fats and sugar. Combined with cigars and cigarettes, this diet contributes to high rates of lung cancer, heart disease, and other circulatory problems. *Salud pública* (Havana: MINSAP, Dirección de Estadísticos, 1983).

CHAPTER 5. CUBA'S SUCCESS

1. Castro, speech at the Mártires de Barbados.

2. Vélez, *Areíto,* p. 76.

3. "Sancionados peloteros del delito de traición," *Bohemia* 56, 2 October 1964, p. 51, cited in L. Salas, *Social Control and Deviance in Cuba* (New York: Praeger, 1979), p. 47; Brown, "Cuban Baseball," p. 114; M. A. Masjuan, "La pureza del deporte cubano," *Bohemia,* 16 September 1983, p. 40; Juan M. del Aguila, *Cuba: Dilemmas of a Revolution* (Boulder, Colo.: Westview Press, 1984), p. 172.

4. Alberto Juantorena was chosen as a member of the central committee at the fourth congress of the PCC. See *Congreso del PCC,* p. 16. One of Cuba's best baseball players, Omar Linares, has been elected to a seat on the Poder Popular (he also allegedly refused an offer to play for the Toronto Blue Jays). Brubaker, "Cuba's Renewed Mission," pp. D1, D6.

5. R. Ruíz, "Playing Field Politics," *Cuba Review* 7, 2 June 1977, p. 25.

6. Castro, speech at the Mártires de Barbados.

7. Ibid.

8. "Instrucción primaria a los atletas," *Revolución,* 19 January 1959, p. 11.

9. Cuban Ministry of Foreign Affairs, *Cuba: A Giant School,* p. 24; *La Juventud.* Other sources give larger numbers for sports school students: 7,000 in N. Suárez, *Nosotros los jovenes cubanos* (Havana: Editorial de Ciencias Sociales, 1978), p. 50; 12,805 (6,805 in EIDEs) in J. García Bango, "Estamos en la obligación de trabajar con mayor voluntad para vencer las dificultades," *LPV* 819, 28 February 1978, p. 5.

10. F. Mastrascusa, "Reunión nacional de análisis y orientación del trabajo en el INDER," *LPV* 867, 30 January 1979, p. 19; Caminada, "Recuento," p. 5; *Mapa 1983;* Fidel Castro Ruz, *We Are Born to Overcome, Not to Be Overrun,* speech at close of Sixth Congress of the Federation of Students Intermediate Education (FEEM) (La Habana: Editorial Política, 1984), p. 14; and interview with Raudol Ruíz by R. Agacino, "¿Por qué los triunfos de Cuba?," *El Deporte* 161, 30 December 1983, p. 9; González González et al., *Razones,* p. 154.

11. Castro, *We Are Born to Overcome*, pp. 13–14.

12. K. Shaw, "Cuban Sportswomen," *Cuba Times* 3, no. 3/4, (Spring–Summer 1983), p. 31.

13. García Bango, "Estamos en la obligación," p. 5; Suárez, *Nosotros los jovenes cubanos*, p. 50; *Mapa 1983;* Caminada, "Recuento," p. 5.

14. The target set for LPV tests in the mid–1960s was an example of inaccurate planning. See *Boletín estadístico de Cuba, 1965,* p. 148.

15. Caminada, "Palabras de Corona," p. 8.

16. Cuban Ministry of Foreign Affairs, *Cuba: A Giant School,* p. 22.

17. C. P. Roberts and M. Hamour, eds., *Cuba: 1968 Supplement to the Statistical Abstract of Latin America* (Los Angeles: University of California, 1970), pp. 91, 107.

18. Castro, *We Are Born to Overcome*, p. 14; Caminada, "Palabras de Corona," p. 8.

19. J. Alvarez, "¿Qué son las pre-EIDEs?," *LPV* 874, 20 March 1979, p. 14; M. C. Valle, "¿Han cumplido su papel las pre-EIDE?," *LPV* 886, 12 June 1979, p. 16; González González et al., *Razones*, p. 154.

20. Parental attitudes are similar to those in the Soviet Union. There was an initial reluctance to enroll a child in a boarding school. In Cuba, once parents saw there was an effort on the part of the government to conserve the parent-child relationship, fears began to dissipate, however. Parents were also encouraged to participate in school activities with their children, and they were relieved of financial responsibilities. From Jan K. Black and Howard Blutstein, *Area Handbook for Cuba*, pp. 141–42.

21. J. Caminada, "¿Cómo funcionan las EIDE?" *LPV* 848, 19 September 1978, p. 29; Castro, *We Are Born to Overcome*, p. 14; A. Pallares Vera, "La ciencia y la técnica," p. 13; González González et al., *Razones*, p. 154; M. C. Valle, "¿Qué son las EIDE?," *LPV* 16, no. 834, 13 June 1978; I. Forbes, "Un momento a la vida y al recuerdo impercedero," *LPV* 12 (1977), pp. 15, 19.

22. Rodolfo Puente Zamora, quoted in Jorge Alvarez, "Yo me desarrollé en la EIDE," *LPV* 18, no. 921, 12 February 1980, p. 22; Cuban Ministry of Education, *Report to the XXX International Conference on Public Instruction*, convoked by the OIE and UNESCO, Geneva, 6–15 July 1967 (Havana, 1967).

23. Alvaro Corella, quoted in Lissette Ricardo Torres, "EIDE: Donde se gesta el futuro del deporte cubano," *¡Ahora!*, Holguín City, 12 November 1976, p. 4.

24. Griffiths, "Sport: The People's Right," p. 254.

25. Marta Jiménez and F. G. Davalos, "Fidel Inaugurates School for Basic Training in Sports in City of Havana Province," *GWR*, 6 October 1977, pp. 1, 3.

26. Boswell, "Idle Play," p. D7.

27. "In Cuba, Sport Is a Mass Effort," *Chicago Tribune*, 20 March 1977, p. 5; William Nack, "Put-Down Artist," *Sports Illustrated* 77, no. 3, 22 July 1992, pp. 157, 159.

28. "¿Quiénes integran la matrícula de una EIDE?," *LPV* 878, 17 April 1979, p. 6.

29. Alberto Juantorena won the gold medals in the 1976 Montreal Olympics in the 400– and 800–meter runs. He has since become a vice-president of INDER. Teófilo Stevenson is a world class heavyweight boxer, probably the Cuban athlete most widely known throughout the world.

30. J. Caminada, "El deporte en las EIDE," *El Deporte* 158, 30 September 1983, p. 35; Valle, "¿Qué son las EIDE?" p. 15.

31. Griffiths, "Sport: The People's Right," p. 254; "Main Report on Work of the Party Since March Last Year, Presented," *GWR*, 23 November 1975, p. 5.

32. R. López Rodríguez, "Bastión de futuros atletas," *LPV* 811, 3 January 1978, p. 21; Castro, *We Are Born to Overcome*, p. 13; Caminada, "Recuento," p. 8.

33. Richard Taylor and Ron Pickering, *Cuba: Sport and Revolution*, BBC/TV (1977), cited in Griffiths, "Sport: The People's Right," p. 257.

34. Castro, speech at the Mártires de Barbados.

35. See F. Guiral, *María Caridad Colón: La Jabalina de oro* (La Habana: Editorial Científico-Técnica, 1986). Miguel A. Masjuan, "El valor de una medalla," *Bohemia* 72, no. 33, 15 August 1980, pp. 36–39, and Ken Denlinger, "Soviet Judges Said Cheating; Officials Protest," *Washington Post*, 31 July 1980, pp. F1, F6. The discus throw was measured by a Soviet official who placed his feet on the spot where the discus landed then stooped forward. He measured the toss from where his knees touched the ground, costing Delís about two feet. Delís came in third, 13 inches behind a Soviet athlete.

36. Fidel Castro Ruz, quoted in Griffiths, "Sport: The People's Right," p. 254.

37. Top-level college basketball and football in the United States is rife with examples of students who play for as long as their eligibility can be extended, yet who never graduate from college and are not of the caliber to move on to professional sports. It is the rare university that enjoys a reputation for the unique combination of a competitive basketball team along with a high rate of graduation for student-athletes, such as Duke University and the University of Notre Dame.

38. Cuban basketball team, interview with Paula Pettavino upon their return from international competition, Havana, August 1980.

39. Castro, speech at the Mártires de Barbados.

40. Officials from INDER–Santiago, interview with Paula Pettavino. Also mentioned in Huberto Gil, *LPV* 946, 5 August 1980.

41. E. López Segura, "Centro de tradición deportíva," *LPV* 17, no. 879, 24 April 1979, p. 27; E. Roldán Hernández, "Una visita y nuevas experiencias," *LPV* 807, 28 November 1977, p. 16.

42. F. Albizua, "La micro-EIDE en contramaestre," *LPV* 813, 17 January 1978, p. 23.

43. J. Caminada, "La Mijail Frunze cantera deportíva," *LPV* 808, 13 December 1977, pp. 22–23; M. Jiménez, "Where a Prison Once Stood," *GWR*, 22 April 1973, p. 4.

44. Alvarez, "Yo me desarrollé." Yet, so soon after the revolution, the ESPA referred to is probably a less sophisticated version. In his speech inau-

gurating the Mártires de Barbados in 1977, Fidel Castro spoke of "building ESPA," which probably meant modernizing and upgrading it for the World Youth Festival in Havana the following year.

45. R. Quiza, "Cómo y qué se hace," *LPV* 835, 20 June 1978, p. 2; Hector Rodríguez Cordosa, cited in Jack Anderson and Les Whitten, "Castro's 'Force-Trained' Athletes," *Washington Post*, 13 August 1976, p. D15.

46. Ruíz, *Cuba Review*, p. 18.

47. Students from ESPA, interview with Paula Pettavino, Havana, 16 August 1980.

48. Resolution 1, 10 January 1985, and Resolution 63, 17 July 1985, *Divulgación jurídica*, Dirección de Propaganda del INDER, no page numbers.

49. J. Herrera Calzada, "Inauguran una ESPA," *LPV* 912, 11 December 1979, p. 24; Pallares Vera, "La ciencia y la técnica," p. 13; Caminada, "Palabras de Corona," p. 8.

50. Vélez, *Areito*, p. 75.

51. Jaime Caminada, "Una necesidad del deporte," *LPV* 846, 5 September 1978, p. 29; E. Menéndez, "Fajardo: A Forge of Instructors," *GWR*, 8 May 1966, p. 10.

52. J. Paz, "Los primeros frutos," *El Deporte* 5 (1980), pp. 31–33; B. Castilla, "La aplicación de la ciencia y la técnica no es una aspiración, sino una necesidad para elevar los niveles de desarrollo alcanzado," *LPV* 819, 28 February 1978, p. 11; González González et al., *Razones*, p. 38; Llaneras Rodríguez et al., "Cuba," pp. 72, 73.

53. F. Ward, *Inside Cuba Today* (New York: Crown Publishers, 1978), p. 133; J. González Barros, "Un ingreso en ESEF 'Fajardo,'" *Mujeres* 6, no. 12 (December 1966), pp. 124, 125; Llaneras Rodríguez et al., "Cuba," p. 75.

54. Pickering, "Cuba," p. 173; assistant to the rector, Manuel Fajardo school, ISCF, interview with Geralyn Pye, 8 October 1986, Havana.

55. The ISCF is across the road from the Ciudad Deportíva in Havana. Students from the institute use the facilities in both. Authors' observations, August 1980 and October 1986. See also Pickering, "Cuba," p. 156.

56. "Funcionarán académias deportívas," *Revolución*, 19 January 1959, pp. 11, 12; F. Miranda, "Polvo de estrellas," *Revolución*, 20 January 1959, pp. 1, 2; "Más deportes y menos vicios," *Revolución*, special edition, 30 December 1959, p. 14; J. L Salmerón, "Acerca del próximo clásico de béisbol," *LPV* 804, 15 November 1977, p. 17; González González et al., *Razones*, p. 154.

57. This information was collected from articles in *LPV* and *El Deporte;* also Mastrascusa, "¡Ahora, a trabajar en firme!" *LPV* 888, 26 June 1979, p. 8; F. Mastrascusa, "Centro experimental de desarrollo atlético 'Manuel Permuy' una escuela que mira al futuro," *LPV* 825, 11 April 1978, pp. 16, 17. See also J. Velázquez, "La gacela oriental," *El Deporte* 24 (1982), p. 41.

58. Rosales, *Educación en Cuba*, pp. 57–58, p. 125; M. C. Valle, "La casa de todos," *El Deporte* 23 (1982), pp. 20, 21.

59. R. Quiza, "Después de la IV espartakiada," *El Deporte*, no number, p. 12.

60. María Elena Gil, "Hacia la tecnificación del deporte," *LPV* 14, no. 727, 25 March 1976, p. 5.

61. Officials from INDER-Santiago, interview with Paula Pettavino.

62. Griffiths, "Sport: The People's Right," p. 255; *Mapa 1983;* C. A. Palacio and A. Hernández, "Escuelas provinciales de educación física," *LPV* 823, 28 March 1978, p. 32; R. Fleites, "EPEF: Donde se garantiza la técnica deporte," *LPV* 672, 6 May 1975, p. 4.

63. Fleites, "EPEF: Donde se garantiza la técnica deporte," p. 4; M. Cabrera Sánchez, "¿Cómo ingresar a las EPEF?," *LPV* 869, 23 February 1979, p. 8; *Gaceta oficial de la Republica de Cuba* 79, no. 11, 9 December 1981, p. 1715.

64. *Gaceta oficial,* p. 1715; Arnaldo Ribero Fuxa, quoted in M. C. Valle, "De interes para todos," *LPV* 17, no. 943, 15 July 1980, pp. 26–27.

65. *LPV* 18, no. 932, 29 April 1980, p. 28.

66. Paula Pettavino, observations, August 1980. For information on other facilities at other EPEFs, see J. Herrera, "Pinar del Río—estudiantes Bulgaros," *LPV* 673, 13 May 1975, p. 26; Fleites, "EPEF," p. 6; and Cabrera Sánchez, "¿Cómo ingresar a las EPEF?," p. 11.

67. Ribero Fuxa, interview with Paula Pettavino; González González et al., *Razones,* p. 67.

68. *La Juventud.*

69. Jorge García Bango, quoted in Sandoval, "Cuba Catches Up," p. 53 (excerpted from *Veja* of Rio de Janiero); *La Juventud;* Pickering, "Cuba," p. 154; Griffiths, "Sport: The People's Right," p. 256; *Chicago Tribune,* 20 March 1977; *Cuba Review,* p. 9; *Sport in the USSR* 6, no. 172 (1977), p. 13; "Desarrollo del deporte y la cultura física," *LPV* 13, no. 609, 19 February 1974, pp. 5, 6; *Cuba Internacional* 9, no. 92, April 1977 (La Habana: Prensa Latina: Agencia Informativa Latinoamericana), pp. 53–54; *GWR,* 10 October 1976.

70. *Sport in the USSR;* Vélez, *Areito,* p. 75.

71. Griffiths, "Sport: The People's Right," p. 256; interview with Paula Pettavino, August 1980, INDER-Santiago; *Granma,* 12 August 1976, p. 4; Pickering, "Cuba," p. 173.

72. Brubaker, "Cuba's Renewed Mission"; William Rhoden, "You Need an Olympic Coach? Cuba May Have the Answer," *New York Times,* 5 August 1992, pp. A1, B10.

73. Llaneras Rodríguez et al., "Cuba," p. 5. See for example "Top Cuban and Angolan Sports Officials Sign Joint Communique," *GWR,* 27 June 1976, p. 2; M. Hernández and A. Nacianceno, "Bases for Cuba-Mexico Exchange in the Field of Sport Established," *GWR,* 16 February 1965, p. 7; and D. Roguera, "Canada Will Invite Cuba to Pre-Olympic Events," *GWR,* 5 January 1975, p. 9. See also T. Bedecki, "International Sports Relations," in M. Ilmarinen, ed., *Sports and International Understanding* (Berlin: Springer-Verlag, 1984), pp. 312–15.

74. Castro cited in Pickering, "Cuba," p. 173.

75. José Ramón Fernández Alvarez, *GWR,* 17 August 1980, p. 1.

76. Jorge García Bango, in J. L. Salmeron, "Despres de quince años," *LPV* 15, 17 February 1976, p. 14.

77. Black and Blutstein, *Area Handbook for Cuba,* p. 186.

78. Pickering, "Cuba," pp. 165–66.

79. Jaime Caminada, "Importancia de la información," *LPV* 17, no. 919, 29 January 1980, p. 5. At the suggestion of Alberto Juantorena, Paula Pettavino visited CEMA in August 1980, but she was told that not only was research not allowed, but there was no one there who could say what CEMA did!

80. Ibid., pp. 5, 6.

81. Ibid., pp. 6, 7.

82. Ibid.

83. Ibid.

84. Orestes Vega, head of section for sports automation (SAD), part of CEDOC, interview with Geralyn Pye, 24 January 1992, Havana.

85. INDER Resolution 72, 25 November 1982, cited in Llaneras Rodríguez et al., "Cuba," pp. 97–98.

86. René Iglesias y Rodríguez Mena, quoted in *LPV* 609, 19 February 1974, pp. 20–21.

87. González González et al., *Razones,* p. 67; Pickering, "Cuba," p. 165;Max Novich, "Why Cuban Athletes Succeed," *New York Times,* 2 November 1975, 2:1.

88. *LPV* 609, 19 February 1974, pp. 20–21.

89. Novich, "Why Cuban Athletes Succeed," 2:1

90. Ramón Briguela Roque, "Inauguran en Pinar del Río centro de medicina deportíva," *Juventud Rebelde,* 28 October 1977, p. 3.

91. Ibid.

92. *LPV* 951, 9 September 1980, p. 16.

93. Boswell, "Idle Play," p. D7.

94. Vélez, *Areito,* p. 76; Pickering, "Cuba," p. 168.

95. Servio Borges, "Play Ball," *Cuba Review,* p. 23.

96. Norman Diamond, "Thinking Politically About Sports," *Cuba Review,* pp. 8, 9; Fernando Sandoval, "Cuba Catches Up," *Atlas World Press Review,* May 1976, p. 53; Pickering, "Cuba," p. 168; INDER officials, interview with Paula Pettavino, Havana; Alberto Juantorena, interview with Paula Pettavino, Santiago, August 1980; Anderson and Whitten, "Castro's 'Force-Trained' Athletes," p. D15; *Chicago Tribune,* 20 March 1977; Griffiths, "Sport: The People's Right," p. 259; Novich, "Why Cuban Athletes Succeed" p. 1.

97. *Atlas World Press Review.*

98. Z. Bregado Gutiérrez cited in Anderson and Whitten, "Castro's 'Force-Trained' Athletes"; Stevenson quotation from Tex Maule, *Sports Illustrated* (March 1974), cited in Pickering, "Cuba," p. 152.

99. Several of the top baseball players from the Cuban national team have allegedly been offered lucrative contracts and have refused them. See Brubaker, "Cuba's Renewed Mission."

100. "Alberto Juantorena: Running for the Revolution," *Cuba Review* 7, no. 2 (June 1977), p. 28; Aldo Allen, quoted in Jaime Caminada, "Imágen de un esfuerzo," *LPV* 18, no. 947, 12 August 1980, p. 18; Nancy Aldama, quoted in Jaime Caminada, "Del ballet a la gimnástica," *LPV* 17, no. 944, 22 July 1980,

p. 21; Joaquín Carlos Díaz, quoted in José González Vera, "Pinar del Rio: Todo lo debo a la revolución," *LPV* 16, 17 February 1976, p. 64.

101. Brubaker, "Cuba's Renewed Mission."

102. Ruíz, "Humanizing Sports," p. 20.

103. Diamond, "Thinking Politically," p. 8. Griffiths, "Sport: The People's Right," pp. 257–58.

104. Pickering, "Cuba," p. 159.

105. Observations by Paula Pettavino, August 1980.

106. Neil Amdur, "Russians Coach Cubans at PA Games," *New York Times*, 8 August 1971, 1:2; Andrew Strenk, "The Thrill of Victory and the Agony of Defeat: Sport and International Politics," *Orbis*, Summer 1978.

107. Nancy Holm, member of the U.S. women's volleyball team, in correspondence with Paula Pettavino.

108. Romero and Stevenson quoted in *LPV* 699–700, 18 November 1975, p. 7.

109. Thomas Boswell, "Cuba's National Treasures," *Washington Post*, 8 April 1978, pp. D1, D5; *Cuba Internacional* (4/77), pp. 56–61; Griffiths, "Sport: The People's Right," p. 259.

110. *Granma*, 2 August 1976, p. 1; *GWR*, 15 August 1976, p. 1; *Granma*, 2 August 1976, p. 4.

111. Pickering, "Cuba," pp. 167–68; Griffiths, "Sport: The People's Right," p. 255. Alberto Juantorena, interview with Paula Pettavino, Santiago, August 1980.

112. "Alberto Juantorena: Running for the Revolution," *Cuba Review*, p. 26; *Cuba Internacional*, April 1977, p. 60; *Bohemia* 68, no. 53, 31 December 1976, pp. 38–39.

113. "Alberto Juantorena: Running for the Revolution," *Cuba Review*, p. 27; *Cuba Internacional*, April 1977, p. 60; J. L. Salmerón, "¿Cómo esta Juantorena?" *LPV* 921, 12 February 1980, pp. 6, 7.

114. Ken Denlinger and Kevin Klose, "Viren, Juantorena, Are They Fading Stars?," *Washington Post*, 25 July 1980, p. D4; *Cuba Internacional*, April 1977, p. 56; Salmerón, "¿Cómo esta Juantorena?," pp. 6, 7.

115. *Congreso del PCC*, 10–14 October 1992, p. 16.

116. *Granma*, 28 July 1976, p. 5; 30 July 1976, p. 4; *GWR*, 15 August 1976, p. 9; Griffiths, "Sport: The People's Right," pp. 255, 259.

117. *Washington Post*, 8 April 1978, pp. D1, D3; Griffiths, "Sport: The People's Right," pp. 255, 259; official from INDER-Santiago, interview with Paula Pettavino.

118. Beatriz Castillo, interview with Paula Pettavino, Santiago, August 1980.

119. Gutiérrez and H. Rodríguez Cordosa, cited in Anderson and Whitten, "Castro's 'Force-Trained' Athletes," p. D15.

120. Ward, *Inside Cuba Today*, p. 132.

121. Fimrite, "In Cuba," p. 72.

122. For more information on Soviet athletes, see Pettavino, *Politics of Sport*.

123. R. Quiza, "Premio al esfuerzo," *El Deporte* 150 (1982), pp. 22–29; Mesa-Lago, "The Economy," p. 155. Such workers are not unlike the "Stakhanovites" in the Soviet Union.

124. Cuevas cited in Fimrite, "In Cuba," p. 72; Fuentes and Pacheco cited in Brubaker, "Cuba's Renewed Mission," pp. D1, D6.

125. Pickering, "Cuba," pp. 167–68; R. Pickering, "The World About Us, Cuba: Sport and Revolution," BBC television script, screened on 9 October 1977; Yglesias, *Fist of the Revolution*, p. 110; S. Freeman and R. Boyes, *Behind the Scenes of Sport* (North Ryde, Australia: Cassell, 1980), p. 73. According to a U.S. report, Stevenson was given two houses and two cars. Corona, president of INDER, said that Stevenson's family needed to be comfortable while he was away, so he would not be worried, and that it was also in return for his commitment to Cuba when he refused an offer of a million dollars to turn professional. Bill Brubaker, "A Boxer to Whom Money Didn't Talk," *Washington Post*, 21 February 1989, p. A1.

126. "Campeon," *Revolución*, 28 May 1960, pp. 1, 17; Jesús Domínguez, *Boxeo cubano en juegos deportívos centroamericanos y del Caribe* (La Habana: Editorial Científico-Técnica, 1985), p. 63.

127. J. L. Salmerón and L. L. Castillo, "Nuestra trayectoria," *LPV* 17, no. 887, 19 June 1979, pp. 12–15; Martín, *Por las rutas del olimpo*, pp. 99–101; Steve Sneddon, "Experts: Cubans as Professionals Would Be Mixed Bag," *USA Today*, 18 August 1992, p. 8C.

128. J. L. Salmerón, "Campeones por decimoctava ocasión," *El Deporte*, 30 March 1987, p. 36; see also *Revolución* (October 1959).

129. F. Ruíz, cited in "In Cuba, Sport Is a Mass Effort," *Chicago Tribune*, 20 March 1977, 3:5.

130. "Cubans Take All the Pan Am Gold," *Sunday Times*, 14 August 1987; *Sport Report*, SBS Television, Australia, screened on 1 August 1989.

131. Tom Weir, "Cuban Dynasty Still Packs Punch," *USA Today*, 5 August 1992, p. 3E.

132. Thomas Boswell, "Cuba Nine in a Class by Itself," *Washington Post*, 11 July 1979, pp. D1, D5.

133. Caminada, "Palabras de Corona," p. 8; for more extensive information on the Soviet sports system and the abuses within, see Pettavino, *Sport Under Communism*.

134. "Sancionados peloteros," *Bohemia* 56, 2 October 1964, p. 51, cited in Salas, *Social Control and Deviance*, p. 47; Brown, "Cuban Baseball," pp. 110, 114.

135. Masjuan, "La pureza del deporte Cubano," p. 40 (see also del Aguila, *Cuba*, p. 172, and Andres Oppenheimer, *Castro's Final Hour* (New York: Simon & Schuster, 1992). There is also the contention that Ochoa was framed for drug charges, when his real crime was to be the popular leader of an influential faction within the Cuban leadership. See R. Orozco, "Droga y corrupción," *Cambio* 16, no. 919, 10 July 1989, pp. 98–100; J. Smolowe, "Reading the Coca Leaves," *Time*, 10 July 1989, pp. 18–19; and C. McGillion, "Cuban Squeeze," *Age Magazine*, 14 October 1989, pp. 116–20, 124–25.

136. Pickering, "Cuba," p. 152; Griffiths, "Sport: The People's Right," p. 257. Quotation is from Castro, *We Are Born to Overcome*, p. 15.

137. García Rodríguez, interview with Geralyn Pye.

138. Officials from INDER-Santiago, interview with Paula Pettavino; López Suárez, *Historia de la educación física*, p. 59; Cuervo et al., *Educación física*, p. 26; *Atlas World Press Review*.

139. Barros cited in Brubaker, "Cuba's Renewed Mission"; Castro cited in Thomas Boswell, "Baseball: The Passion of the Game," *Washington Post*, 5 April 1978, pp. F1, F4; Sanchez cited in Thomas Boswell, "Island Aches for Yankee Visit," *Washington Post*, 7 April 1978, pp. E1, E3.

140. Boswell, "Baseball: The Passion of the Game"; Fimrite, "In Cuba," pp. 68–80. (For more on the history of Cuban baseball, see this volume, chapter 2.)

141. Oleksak and Oleksak, *Béisbol*, pp. 114–15. All the information in the following paragraphs is taken from this work, (pp. 116–27, 141–49, 190), and only the quotations will be given direct references.

142. Ibid., p. 117.

143. Ibid., p. 118.

144. Ibid., p. 120.

145. Ibid., p. 143.

146. Ibid., p. 145.

147. *La Juventud;* Fimrite, "In Cuba."

148. Thomas Boswell, "Great Leagues Live for Some," *Washinton Post*, 6 April 1978, pp. D1.

149. William Greider, " 'New Man' in Cuba Is Just Plain Folks," *Washington Post*, 10 April 1977, pp. A1, A22.

150. Boswell, "Great Leagues Live for Some."

151. Pérez cited in ibid; see also Robert DiNardo, "Can Cuba Beat the Yankees?" *Mother Jones* 2, no. 7 (August 1981), pp. 15, 16; Zayas cited in Katel, "The Best Team Money Can't Buy," pp. 62–63; Linares story from Merrell Noden, "Happy Days in Havana," *Sports Illustrated* 75, no. Z9, 26 August 1991, pp. 26, 27.

152. "Fidel Castro invita á selección de beis de E.U.," *La Prensa Grafica* (San Salvador, El Salvador), 13 April 1977; Oleksak and Oleksak, *Béisbol*, pp. 190, 191. The term *ping-pong diplomacy* refers to the role that a U.S.–Chinese ping-pong competition played in the opening of more normal relations between those countries in 1972.

153. Fimrite, "In Cuba"; Boswell, "Island Aches for Yankee Visit."

154. Boswell, "Island."

155. Boswell, "Great Leagues Live for Some."

156. Boswell, "Baseball: The Passion of the Game."

157. Ibid.

158. Paula Pettavino and Geralyn Pye, observations, 1980 and 1988 (there are continual arguments among the fans as to whether the Cubans could beat the United States); Katel, "The Best Team Money Can't Buy," pp. 62–63; Fimrite, "In Cuba."

159. *Sport International*

160. Quotations in this paragraph come from Boswell, "Baseball: The Passion of the Game"; Fimrite, "In Cuba." In 1988, Geralyn Pye saw coffee being sold in the crowd at the stadium.

161. Katel, "The Best Team Money Can't Buy," p. 63.

162. Ibid.

163. Fimrite, "In Cuba"; *La Juventud;* Boswell, "Baseball: The Passion of the Game."

164. Katel, "The Best Team Money Can't Buy," p. 63.

165. Baseball was considered an Olympic exhibition sport. This practice began at the 1936 Olympics. The exhibition status was dropped when actual Olympic baseball competition began in Barcelona in 1992. Oleksak and Oleksak, *Béisbol*, p. 66.

166. "Through Baseball, U.S., Cuba Share Common Bond," *Times-Picayune*, 6 March 1977, 6:10.

167. Johnny Carson, quoted in John Feinstein, "Cuban Refugees Ache for Shot at 'American Great Leagues,' " *Washington Post*, 25 May 1980, p. F1.

168. Ibid., p. F14.

169. Ibid.

170. Brown, "Cuban Baseball," p. 114.

171. Lou Reilly, quoted in John Feinstein, "Father-Son Game," *Washington Post*, 26 May 1980, pp. B1, B6.

172. Bruce Newman, "Bright Lights, New City," *Sports Illustrated* 76, no. 11, 23 March 1992, pp. 56–59.

173. Ibid. Tartabull recently signed a $25.5 million, five-year contract with the New York Yankees.

174. John Feinstein, "Hopes High, the Changes Slow," *Washington Post*, 27 May 1980, pp. D1, D3.

175. Katel, "The Best Team that Money Can't Buy," p. 63. Arocha's wife apparently had no idea of his plans to defect. She went to meet him at the airport when the team returned. He has since married again, to a Cuban American. Steve Wulf, "Sports People," *Sports Illustrated* 78, no. 15, 19 April 1993, p. 60.

176. Arocha cited in Brubaker, "Baseball Scouts," pp. D1, D10; Zabala cited in Katel, "The Best Team Money Can't Buy," pp. 62–63.

177. Quotations from Brubaker, "Baseball Scouts"; news of the hot prospects from Noden, "Happy Days in Havana."

178. Sabean, quoted in Brubaker, "Baseball Scouts"; Brito, cited in Noden, "Happy Days in Havana."

179. Steve Wulf, "Sports People," p. 60.

180. Brubaker, "Baseball Scouts."

181. Oleksak and Oleksak, *Béisbol*, p. 43; Brubaker, "Baseball Scouts."

182. Brubaker, "Baseball Scouts," p. 298. See also Barry Hochberg, "Make Room on the Bench," *South Florida* (July 1993), pp. 51, 61, 62.

183. Fidel Castro Ruz, cited in "Peking and Havana: Sports as a Political Exercise," *New York Times*, 22 August 1971, 1:3. See *La Juventud*.

184. Katel, "The Best Team Money Can't Buy," p. 63.
185. Griffiths, "Sport: The People's Right," p. 258.
186. Domínguez, *Order and Revolution,* p. 465.

CHAPTER 6. CUBAN SPORT IN THE 1980s AND 1990s

1. See, for example, R. P. Rabkin, *Cuban Politics: The Revolutionary Experiment* (New York: Praeger, 1991); and S. Halebsky and J. M. Kirk, *Transformation and Struggle: Cuba Faces the 1990s* (New York: Praeger, 1990).

2. Although Cuban policy has varied in small ways since 1986—there was increased liberalization in 1987 and 1988 followed by the arrest of dissidents in 1989 and 1991–1992—Cuban policy since 1986 has been largely characterized by an attempt to reform within socialism. Reforms have focused on some liberalization in the economy as well as attempts to make Cuban officials more efficient and more responsive to public demands. At the same time, rhetoric has tended to reaffirm a commitment to Marxism-Leninism, which reflects Cuba's disapproval of changes enacted by its one-time socialist allies. In practice, however, Cuban policy represents pragmatic responses to the economic difficulties encountered since the mid–1980s.

3. The rapid pace of change in the country until recently known as the USSR makes it a difficult task to apply an appropriate term for that region. Unless otherwise stated, in this book we shall refer to the former USSR as the Soviet Union or the USSR, and to the present-day state as the former Soviet Union or Russia. There will also be separate references to the individual former Soviet republics.

4. Cuba's main economic problems in the 1980s were negative trade balances and the inability to meet debt payments. See Rabkin, *Cuban Politics,* p. 180. Other problems included shortages of goods and their poor distribution.

5. The Rectification of Errors Plan adopted in 1986 was characterized by declarations of adherence to socialism and the need for moral incentives and developing revolutionary commitment. Among the stated goals were efficiency, the abolishing of corruption, and the discouraging of laziness and absenteeism. It is important to consider practice rather than rhetoric when assessing Cuban policy, however (this has been the case since at least the late 1960s), and in practice, material incentives were not abandoned and, despite the official declarations, there was also liberalization and decentralization in the economy as well as liberalization in politics, at least in 1987 and 1988. On rectification see Rabkin, *Cuban Politics,* p. 180, and C. Bengelsdorf, "The Matter of Democracy in Cuba: Snapshots of Three Moments," in Halebsky and Kirk, *Transformation and Struggle,* pp. 35–52.

6. Nieves Alemany, secretary of the Cuban Women's Federation in Santiago de Cuba and a member of the Central Committee of the Cuban Communist party until 1991, and Eva Seone Domínguez, vice-president of ICAP, conversation with Geralyn Pye at Flinders University, South Australia, October 1991. See also G. Gunn, "Cuba in Crisis," *Current History* 90, no. 554 (March

276   Notes to Pages 198-99

1991), p. 104; Raúl Castro, "Llamamiento al IV congreso del partido," *Casa de las Americas* 30, no. 180 (May–June 1990), pp. 2–12; "Faintest Glimmers of Change," *Latin American Weekly Report*, 24 October 1991, p. 3, and *Congreso del PCC*.

7. G. Gunn, "Will Castro Fall?" *Foreign Policy* 79 (Summer 1990), p. 134; Jorge I. Domínguez, "The Secrets of Castro's Staying Power," *Foreign Affairs* (Spring 1993), p. 97.

8. Rabkin, *Cuban Politics*, p. 180; N. Leon Cotayo, *Beleagured Hope: The U.S. Economic Blockade of Cuba* (La Habana: Editorial Cultura Popular, 1991), p. 63; Gunn, "Will Castro Fall?" p. 133; J. Carranza Valdes, "The Current Situation in Cuba and the Process of Change," *Latin American Perspectives* 18, no. 2, issue 69, trans. by Clare Weber (Spring 1991), p. 14; "Spanish Loan for Cuba," *Washington Post* 12 Mar. 1993, p. A25.

9. M. Benjamin, "Things Fall Apart," *North American Congress on Latin America* 24, no. 2 (August 1990), p. 15. In 1979, the USSR paid 44 cents for a pound of Cuban sugar, which was five times the world price for sugar at that time. Also in 1979, the Soviets charged Cuba $12.80 for a barrel for oil, that is, one-third of the current OPEC price. R. Rabkin, "Implications of the Gorbachev Era for Cuban Socialism," in H. M. Erisman and J. M. Kirk, eds., *Cuban Foreign Policy Confronts a New International Order* (Boulder, Colo.: Lynne Reinner, 1991), p. 24. See also S. Jenkins, "Western Europe and Cuba's Development," in Erisman and Kirk.

10. Benjamin, "Things Fall Apart," p. 15; A. Zimbalist, "Introduction: Cuba's Socialist Economy Toward the 1990s," in A. Zimbalist, ed., *Cuba's Socialist Economy Toward the 1990s* (Boulder, Colo.: Lynne Reinner, 1987), p. 4; and A. Zimbalist, "Does the Economy Work?" *NACLA* 24, no. 2 (August 1990), p. 18.

11. Cotayo, *Beleagured Hope*, pp. 60–61.

12. See Gunn, "Will Castro Fall?" p. 134.

13. Ibid., pp. 137–38, and Gunn, "Cuba in Crisis," p. 103. Cuban trade with Latin America in 1988 was worth $1.33 billion (Rabkin, *Cuban Politics*, p. 202). Relations between Cuba and China were fully normalized in August 1991. See "China, Cuba to Close Ranks After 30 Years," *The Advertiser*, 5 August 1991, p. 6. See also Douglas Farah, "Catering to Foreigners Instead of Cubans Puts Castro on Defensive," *Washington Post*, 9 August 1992, p. A31; Tom Carter, "Cuba's 'Volunteers': Hookers, Tourism Go Hand in Hand," *Washington Times*, 22 October 1992, pp. A1, A8; Lee Hockstader, "Tourists Royally Entertained in Cuba, the Penurious Communist Holdout," *Washington Post*, 22 May 1992, p. A33.

14. Workers in the tourist industry are fairly well paid (maximum = 325 pesos a month) and also have access to dollars through tips and possibly to goods in tourist shops. Workers are supposed to have learned a second language by 1993 and are expected to be active revolutionaries who behave "correctly" with visitors. As jobs in tourism are now contracted for periods of a few years, workers behaving inappropriately may lose their employment. Workers in the tourist industry, discussions with Geralyn Pye, and the noticeboard in the Hotel Lido, Havana, January 1992.

15. "Introducción a la discusión del Proyecto de Resolución sobre el desarrollo económico, realizado por el compañero Carlos Lage Davila," *Congreso del PCC*, p. 9.

16. Gunn, "Will Castro Fall?" pp. 137–38; Gunn, "Cuba in Crisis," pp. 104, 133. See (AP), "Congress Grants Cubans New Direct Voting Rights," *Canberra Times*, 15 October 1991; L. Hockstader, "A Hint of Capitalism in Socialist Cuba," *The Age*, 16 October 1991; *Congreso de PCC;* and "Whatever It Looks Like, Cubans Say It Is Not a Form of 'Backdoor Perestroika,' " *Latin American Weekly Report*, 14 November 1991, p. 1.

17. C. Lane "Low Fidelity," *New Republic*, 7 and 14 January 1991, p. 28.

18. K. Hart, "Will Cuba Follow the Kremlin's Example?" *Swiss Review of World Affairs* 14, no. 1 (April 1991), p. 11. For an extensive list of failed deliveries in 1991, see Fidel Castro Ruz, "Discurso pronunciado en la inauguración del IV congreso del partido comunista de Cuba, 10 de octubre de 1991," in Fidel Castro Ruz, *Independientes hasta siempre IV congreso del partido comunista de Cuba* (La Habana: Editorial Político, 1991), pp. 17–29. The shortage of bread was particularly problematic as it is a staple part of the Cuban diet and the failed deliveries forced Cuba to spend vital hard currency on imports from elsewhere. Other goods were in short supply in 1990 and 1991 also: rubber, tires, ammonia, rice, peas, condensed milk, butter, construction materials, fertilizers, matches, sulphur, wood dust, wood pulp, metal plates, spare parts for consumer goods, antibiotics, caustic soda, penicillin, medicines, soap, powdered milk, fats, sodium carbonate, cooking oil, canned meat, vegetables, tobacco, chicken, grains, cereals, cheese, pasta, and oil. See L. Hockstader, "Communists Press Forth—By Oxcart," *Washington Post*, 12 September 1991, pp. A1, A31–32. See also Benjamin, "Things Fall Apart," p. 15.

19. Hockstader, "Communists Press Forth," p. A32. Cuba gets about 99 percent of its oil from the Soviet Union (C. D. Deere, "Cuba's Struggle For Self-Sufficiency," *Monthly Review* 43, no. 3, p. 56). See also Hart, "Will Cuba Follow Kremlin's Example?" p. 11; M. Benjamin, "Soul Searching," *NACLA* 24, no. 2 (August 1990), p. 2; and "Postscript-Economy," *Latin American Weekly Report*, 17 January 1991, p. 12.

20. J. Rice, "New Year Looking Grimmer to Cuba," *Times-Picayune*, 4 January 1992, p. A17. See also A. de Borchgrave, "Russians Seeking Castro's Downfall," *Washington Times*, 30 September 1991, p. A8; "Any Real Benefit for Cuba? Closer Look at the Trade Agreement With Moscow," *Latin American Weekly Report*, 13 June 1991, p. 8; "Postscript-Economy," p. 12. In December 1991 electricity was rationed, working hours and jobs were reduced, television transmission was cut to five hours a day, and air conditioning was cut off in public buildings. "Cuba Cuts Electricity, Job Hours," *Times-Picayune*, 21 December 1991.

21. Douglas Farah, "Wanted: Rm w/vu of Old Havana," *Washington Post*, 6 August 1992, p. A35; Benjamin, "Things Fall Apart," p. 15; and Carranza Valdes, "The Current Situation in Cuba," p. 14.

22. Hart, "Will Cuba Follow Kremlin's Example?" p. 11; Gunn, "Cuba in Crisis"; and "Any Real Benefit For Cuba?" pp. 6–7. See also de Borchgrave,

"Russians Seeking Castro's Downfall," p. A8. Rabkin (*Cuban Politics*, p. 180) claims that the Cuban debt to the Soviet Union is at least $10 billion, while Lane ("Low Fidelity," p. 28) claims the debt is $15 billion.

23. Hart, "Will Cuba Follow Kremlin's Example?" p. 11; Gunn, "Cuba in Crisis," p. 101; J. Bernstein, "Is It the End of a Beautiful Friendship?" *Insight*, 30 September 1991, p. 19.

24. (AP), "Cuba Cut Off by Russia, Exile Says," *Washington Post*, 28 December 1991 p. A16; "Russia Won't Prop Up Castro's Regime in Cuba," *Washington Times*, 28 December 1991, p. A2. Kasey Vannett, "Cuban Americans Set Up Office in Moscow," *Times of the Americas*, 25 December 1991, p. 14.

25. "Has Gorbachev Signalled Cut-Off?" *Latin American Weekly Report*, 26 September 1991, p. 4; "Moscow Serves Notice of Changes," *Latin American Weekly Report*, 12 September 1991, p. 9.

26. "Havana Recognizes Commonwealth," *Washington Times*, 27 December 1991, p. A9; Rice, "New Year Looking Grimmer," p. A17. In September 1991, Gorbachev stated that Cuban-Soviet trade would continue because "There are things that we want to continue to receive, such as sugar, citrus, fruit, and nickel. I think that should continue because it's good for both of us. Cuba also needs some things from us" ("Cuba Shocked by Plan for Soviet Pullout," *Washington Times*, 12 September 1991, p. A8). De Borchgrave, "Russians Seeking Castro's Downfall," p. A8; Reuters, "Russian Official in Cuba for Talks," *Boston Globe*, 21 May 1993, p. 61.

27. Fidel Castro Ruz, speech at the close of the fifth congress of the FMC, 7 March 1990, in Fidel Castro Ruz, *Faithful to the Ideals of Socialism* (La Habana: Editorial José Martí, 1990), p. 31; Deere, "Cuba's Struggle," p. 60; Gunn, "Cuba in Crisis," pp. 104, 133; *Cuba Internacional* (July 1992), cited in *Washington Times*, 7 July 1992, p. A2; NBC Nightly News, 21 December 1991; Hughes, "Castro: Conditions To Worsen," *Times-Picayune*, 19 December 1991, p. A26; (AP), "Cuba Cuts Electricity"; Sandy Rovner, "Baffling Blindness Afflicts Thousands in Cuba: Medical Researchers Believe Nutrition May Be Partly at Fault," *Washington Post*, 1 June 1993, Health News, p. 7.

28. Geralyn Pye, observations, Havana, January 1992; S. Francis, "Awaiting a New Ally?" *Washington Times*, 7 January 1992, p. F4; Nieves Alemany and Eva Seone Domínguez, discussions with Geralyn Pye, in Adelaide, Australia, October 1991.

29. Benjamin, "Things Fall Apart," p. 22. The fourth congress stressed the need to develop self-sufficiency in food, especially for Havana and in mountain regions. See "Plan de Alimentación" and "Plan Turquino," in *Congreso del PCC*, p. 10; George Gedda, "U.S. Warns Exiles Not to Attack Cuba," *Times Picayune*, 25 January 1992, p. A1; Louie Estrada, "Death Verdicts in Cuba Spur Outcry," *Times of the Americas*, 22 January 1992, p. 1; on Alpha 66 group, see *Washington Post*, 22 May 1993, p. A9.

30. There are a number of human rights groups in Cuba. Most are aligned in the Democratic Cuban Consortium (CDC), which was founded on 4 September 1991. See *Latin American Weekly Report*, 17 October 1991. In 1990 nearly 20,000 Cubans emigrated to the United States. In 1991 some 15,000 fol-

lowed this course of exile, until the Bush administration froze visa applications in early August. (AP), "U.S. Visa Policy Altered to Stem Flow of Cubans," *Times-Picayune*, 4 August 1991; G. Gedda, "Castro Defies Fall of Communism," *Times-Picayune*, 11 August 1991; S. Reiss and P. Katel, "The Only Dream Left Is to Get Out," *Newsweek*, 12 August 1991, p. 38. In December 1991, a bizarre attempt to escape on a homemade swing tied to the wheel cover of a jet to Miami was unsuccessful. "Addenda," *Washington Post*, 28 December 1991, p. A9.

31. Anna Husarska, "My Three Friends in Cuba," *Washington Post*, 24 January 1992, p. A23; Observations by a member of the Australian Cruz del Sur Work Brigade, conversations with Geralyn Pye, Havana, January 1992. See (AP), "Cuba Arrests 3 in Death of Agents," *Washington Times*, 11 January 1992, p. A7; R. Castillo, "Exiles Are Skeptical About Bungled Cuba Mission," *Washington Post*, 26 January 1992, p. A20; P. Fletcher, "Dissent Means Death, Cubans Warned," *Washington Times*, 22 January 1992, p. A1; and C. Hughes, "Cuba Tightens the Screws on Dissidents," *Washington Times*, 19 January 1992, p. A18.

On the crackdown, see Anne-Marie O'Connor, "Revolutionaries Joining Movement Against Castro," *Times-Picayune*, 20 September 1992, p. A32. Lee Hockstader, "Own Revolution Fought by Castro's Daughter," *Times-Picayune*, 15 April 1992, p. A15. Kevin Noblet, "Dissidents Pay Dearly to Oppose Castro's Regime," *Times-Picayune*, 15 November 1992, p. A25. Pascal Fletcher, "Dissent Means Death, Cubans Warned," *Washington Times*, 22 January 1992, pp. A1, A10. Douglas Farah, "Dissident Children of Cuba's Revolution," *Washington Post*, 2 August 1992, pp. A29, A31. America's Watch, "Cuba: Behind a Sporting Facade, Stepped-Up Repression," 11 August 1991, Washington, D.C., and New York.

32. O'Connor, "Revolutionaries Joining Movement," p. A32; Dominguez, "Secrets of Castro's Staying Power," pp. 100, 101.

33. For Juantorena's comments, see Thomas Boswell, "Cuba's National Treasures," *Washington Post*, 8 April 1978, p. D3. On U.S. as enemy, see Douglas Farah, "Castro Uses Stiffer U.S. Embargo to Justify Economic Straits," *Washington Post*, 17 December 1992, pp. A33, A44. On return of exiles, see Domínguez, "Secrets of Castro's Staying Power," p. 103.

34. See Peter James Spielmann, "U.N. Panel Condemns U.S. Embargo on Cuba," *Times-Picayune*, 24 November 1992, p. A10; Shawn Miller, "Castro's Cuba: Time to End the Embargo?," *Insight on the News* 9, no. 23 (23 May 1993), p. 8; Dominguez, "Secrets of Castro's Staying Power," pp. 103, 104; Marcus Mabry, "Putting the Squeeze on Fidel," *Newsweek*, 14 September 1992, p. 48.

35. See Benjamin, "Things Fall Apart," p. 22. Castro has rejected copying Soviet reforms several times since 1988. See Fidel Castro Ruz, *Fidel Castro Speeches 1988–9: In Defense of Socialism* (Sydney: Pathfinder, 1989); "Havana Recognizes Commonwealth," p. A9. See Gunn, "Cuba in Crisis," p. 134; Benjamin, "Soul Searching," p. 30; D. Evenson, "Channelling Dissent," *NACLA* 24, no. 2 (August 1990), pp. 27–28.

36. See Castro, "Llamamiento"; Gunn, "Cuba in Crisis," p. 133; *Congreso del PCC*; J. Petras and M. Morley, "The New Model of Accumulation and Cu-

ba's Foreign Policy," in R. H. Ireland and S. R. Niblo, eds., *Cuba: Thirty Years of Revolution* (Melbourne: ILAS La Trobe University, 1990), p. 71.

37. On this point, see Gail Reed, *Island in the Storm: The Cuban Communist Party's Fourth Congress* (New York: Center for Cuban Studies, 1992), p. 115.

38. Gunn, "Cuba in Crisis," p. 133; "Whatever It Looks Like," p. 1; "Resolución sobre el desarrollo económico del país," point 7, *Congreso del PCC*, p. 10; Hockstader, "A Hint of Capitalism."

39. "Party Gives Direct Voting to Cubans," *Australian*, 15 October 1991, p. 8; "Resolución sobre el perfeccionamiento de la organización y funcionamiento de los organos del Poder Popular," point 1, *Congreso del PCC*, p. 8; Philip Brenner, William M. LeoGrande, Donna Rich, and Daniel Siegel, *The Cuba Reader: The Making of A Revolutionary Society* (New York: Grove Press, 1989), pp. 145–48; "Faintest Glimmers of Change," p. 3.

40. "Faintest Glimmers of Change," p. 3. In addition to the growing number of exiles and the emergence of human rights activists, discontent has been manifested within Cuba through a protest rally by artists and painters in 1988 and by disturbances in food lines. See E. Cordova, *El trabajador cubano en el estado de obreros y campesinos* (Miami: Ediciones Universal, 1989), p. 210, and "The Cuban Time Bomb," *Parade Magazine*, 20 October 1991.

41. Domínguez, "Secrets of Castro's Staying Power," p. 100; "Third Most Powerful Leader in Cuba Booted from Office," *Times-Picayune*, 25 September 1992, p. A19; Geralyn Pye, "Cuba: Prospects for the 1990s," *Current Affairs Bulletin* 69, no. 8 (January 1993), pp. 18–26. According to Domínguez, the army's loyalty is also motivated by the promise of Cuban exiles, through the Voice of Miami radio, to hold "Nuremberg-style trials" (p. 100).

42. Mimi Whitefield, "New Foreign Minister Climbs Ladder in Cuba," *Times-Picayune*, 1 April 1993, p. A24. Hugh Davies, "Castro Protege Attempts to Save Collapsing Cuba," *Washington Times*, 13 April 1993, p. A9.

43. According to one Cuban intellectual (who wished to remain anonymous), Cuba's socialist system could survive at most between five and ten years. He claimed that a major change, such as allowing free circulation of U.S. dollars and floating the peso, was needed in the next few years. He felt that this would be hard and that the reformers in the PCC would have difficulty in challenging the military hardliners in the PCC who were very strong. Yet Castro surprised the world and did just that during a speech on 23 July 1993: he legalized the use of dollars by Cubans to take effect 14 August. Several weeks later, he legalized a broad free market in services, allowing those without employees to work on their own. "We have serious problems and we have to solve them to survive. There are two different sets of things: the things we have to do to perfect socialism and the things we have to do for the revolution" (Douglas Farah, "Making Change in Cuba," *Washington Post National Weekly Edition*, 23–30 August 1993, p. 19).

Such risky policies come with a social—and perhaps, ultimately, political—cost. The government is now allowing economic power outside of state control. These policies also create new privileged sectors of Cuban society; ironically, those with dollars are those with greater ties to Miami. According to Jorge Domínguez, "The result is a particularly pernicious kind of inequality. The more loyal you were the less advantage you have today." Carlos Lage, vice president of the Council of State and Cuba's leading economic planner, acknowledges the problem: "This will create differences among people, greater than what we have now and greater than we are used to having since the revolution. It is necessary for our people to understand we need the hard currency for the benefit of the entire population, and that the inequality or privilege than can be created are realities we must allow" (p. 19). See also Conversations with Geralyn Pye, Havana, January 1992; "Cuba Goes for New Free Market Trial to Boost Economy," *Times-Picayune*, 10 September 1993, p. C2.

44. I. Fonseca, interview with A. Nancianceno, in *GWR*, 5 October 1975, p. 10; Fidel Castro Ruz, in *Granma Weekly Review*, 12 September 1976, p. 3.

45. Fidel Castro Ruz, speech at the Fourth Congress of the UJC, 4 April 1982, in Fidel Castro Ruz, *Speeches at Three Congresses* (La Habana: Editorial Político, 1982), p. 70.

46. E. Wagner, "Sport After Revolution: A Comparative Study of Cuba and Nicaragua," *Studies in Latin American Popular Culture* 1 (1982), p. 70.

47. C. Mesa-Lago, "The Economy Caution, Frugality, and Resilient Ideology," in Domínguez, *Internal and International Affairs*, p. 155; Llaneras Rodríguez et al., "Cuba," pp. 126, 128; Domínguez, "Revolutionary Politics," p. 54. See Caminada, "El deporte y la Guayabera," pp. 18–23.

48. Castro, *We Are Born to Overcome*, p. 15; Salmerón, "Las industrias locales," pp. 32–33.

49. M. Janofsky, "In Cuba, the Call Goes Out for Less Smoke, More Action," *New York Times*, 4 May 1987; E. González, "U.S. Policy Objectives and Options," in Domínguez, *Internal and International Affairs*, pp. 208–9; C. Brennan, "Castro Takes Firm Steps Against Flab," *Washington Post*, 23 April 1987, p. B1. See A. Zimbalist, "Incentives and Planning in Cuba," *Latin American Research Review* 24, no. 1, 1989, pp. 65–94.

50. United Nations, *Economic Survey of Latin America and the Caribbean, 1982*, vol. 1 (Santiago de Chile: 1984), pp. 244, 267.

51. Castro, *We Are Born to Overcome*, p. 15.

52. Alvarez, interview with Geralyn Pye; Mesa-Lago, "The Economy Caution," p. 155.

53. Domínguez, "Revolutionary Politics," p. 155. In 1980, over 125,000 Cubans left their homeland. Some had occupied the unguarded Peruvian Embassy to insist on being allowed to leave. See ibid.

54. Arrieto, interview with Geralyn Pye. Between 1982 and 1987, the average annual value of sport imports from the socialist bloc was 3.5 million pesos (González González et al., *Razones*, p. 52).

55. T. Knott, "Medals Won't Help This Tarnished Land," *Washington Times*, 2 August 1991, p. D2; J. Powers, "On a Mission From Havana," *Boston Sunday Globe*, 16 August 1987, p. 46. The 1989 INDER budget was 116.2 million pesos. González González et al., *Razones*, p. 152.

56. González González et al., *Razones*, p. 52.

57. V. Sysoyev, "Push for Olympic Gold Brings Drop in Sports Participation," *Survey* 133, no. 5 (June 1990), pp. 14, 16; C. Brennan, "Mighty Red Star Is Dimming," *Washington Post*, 16 June 1991, p. A23.

58. Brennan, "Mighty Red Star Is Dimming"; "Champions Call for Sacking of Soviet State Sports Committee," *Survey* 12, no. 9 (October 1989), p. 16.

59. Brubaker, "Baseball Scouts," pp. D1, D10; (AP), "No Scouts, Please," *New York Times*, 13 August 1991.

60. M. Janofsky, "Cubans Concerned About Definitions," *New York Times*, 5 August 1987. Reviews of INDER have occurred several times, the highly self-critical 1987 report, for example (see Caminada, "Recuento," p. 8).

61. Work hours have been cut to save electricity, but there is pressure to do more voluntary work. This work is often labor intensive because of the lack of availability of gasoline and spare parts for agricultural machinery.

62. Christine Brennan, "Playing Catch-Up in a New Arena," *Washington Post*, 18 June 1991, p. A14; R. Demak, "Do Svidaniya Goodbye—Maybe—to the Great U.S.–USSR Sports Rivalry," *Sports Illustrated* 75, no. 11, 9 September 1991, p. 9; William Drozdiak, "A Team Unified by Individual Goals," *Washington Post*, 4 August 1992, pp. A1, A6. See also "Soviets Unite for Olympics," *Washington Post*, 13 September 1991, p. F1.

63. Brennan, "Mighty Red Star," p. 6; (AP), "Official Says Soviet Sports Not Bankrupt," *Washington Times*, 25 June 1991, pp. D6, 7nn; Brennan, "Mighty Red Star," p. A23; Drozdiak, "A Team Unified by Individual Goals."

64. Drozdiak, "A Team Unified by Individual Goals."

65. Christine Brennan, "Factory of Dreams Put in New Light," *Washington Post*, 17 June 1991, p. A15.

66. At a gymnastics competition in the United States, Soviet coach Leonid Arkaev and gold medalist Dmitri Bilozerchev had a heated verbal disagreement over monetary winnings. See Brennan, "Factory of Dreams," p. A15, and Christine Brennan, "For Soviet Athletes, to the Would-Be Victors Go the Sports," *Washington Post*, 17 June 1991, p. A5.

67. W. Kramer-Mandeau, *Sport und Korpererziehung auf Cuba von der Sportutopie eines Entwicklungslandes zum Sportmodell Lateinamerikas?* (Koln: Pahl-Rugenstein Verlag, 1988), p. 192.

68. See *El Deporte*, 1982; E. Montesinos and S. Barros, *Centroamericanos y del Caribe los más antiguos juegos deportívos regionales del mundo* (La Habana: Editorial Científico-Técnica, 1984), p. 442; Kramer-Mandeau, *Sport und Korpererziehung*, pp. 166, 167; González González et al., *Razones*, p. 171. See *El Deporte* and *LPV*, for Cuban sports performances in the 1980s; and also *The Australian*, 2 September 1991, p. 14.

69. Kramer-Mandeau, *Sport und Korpererziehung*, p. 181. See *The Australian*, 20 August 1991, p. 20. Jorge I. Domínguez, *To Make a World Safe for Revolution: Cuba's Foreign Policy* (Cambridge: Harvard University Press, 1989), p. 150.

70. *Washington Post*, 10 August 1992, p. C8.

71. F. C. Klein, "On Sports: Pan Am Games," *Wall Street Journal*, 8 November 1987; J. Powers, "U.S. Ends Cuba's Winning Streak, 6–4," *Boston Globe*, 16 August 1987, p. 67; "Cubans Take All the Pan Am Gold," *Times on Sunday*, 14 August 1987; M. Moran "Battered American Boxers Assess Effort," *New York Times*, 24 August 1987, p. C5; P. Fletcher, "Cuban Athletes Try to Outdo U.S. Rivals," *Washington Times*, 5 July 1991, p. D6.

72. I. Wilkerson, "Indianapolis Rouses for Joy and Headaches of Pan Am Games," *New York Times*, 12 January 1987; M. Janofsky, "Castro Tells Officials He Is Optimistic on Cuba's Participation," *New York Times*, 19 August 1987, section 5; "Sports World—Change in Ceremonies," *New York Times*, 27 July 1987; M. Janofsky, "Visa Granted to Cuban Official," *New York Times*, 22 August 1987, pp. 47–48; M. Janofsky, "Action and Distractions for Cubans at Games," *New York Times*, 11 August 1987, pp. A1, A21. See also Kenny Moore, "Indy Lights Up," *Sports Illustrated* 67, no. 8, 24 August 1987, pp. 18–24.

73. Moore, pp. 18–24; Powers, "On a Mission," p. 46; Janofsky, "Action and Distractions," p. 121; "Group Denies Involvement in Games Incident," letter from J. Coleman to the editor, *New York Times*, 5 September 1987.

74. "Group Denies Involvement in Games Incident"; Powers, "On a Mission," p. 67; G. Vecsey, "Cooling-Off Time," *New York Times*, 18 August 1987; S. Jenkins, "Cuban Tempest Buffets Indianapolis: Political Controversies Swirl Around Leaflets, Flags and Bands," *Washington Post*, 19 August 1987, p. B3; Janofsky, "Action and Distractions," p. A21.

75. Moore, "Indy Lights Up."

76. Jenkins, "Cuban Tempest," p. B1; (AP), "Charges Sought Against Cubans," *New York Times*, 20 August 1987, p. D24; "Suit Filed Over Fight," *New York Times*, 22 August 1987, p. 48; M. Wilson, "Cubans Go to Court at the Pan Am Games," *Washington Post*, 20 August 1987, p. E6; Moran, "Battered American Boxers," *New York Times*, p. C5.

77. Jenkins, "Cuban Tempest," p. B1; Fidel Castro, cited in E. Capetillo, *Un girón deportívo* (La Habana: Editorial Pablo de la Torriente, 1988), p. 92 (this book provides a Cuban view of the 1987 Pan-American Games); S. Jenkins, "Cuban Official Invited to Games Will Represent Host of 1991 Event in Closing Ceremonies," *Washington Post*, 22 August 1987.

78. Castro, *Faithful to the Ideals of Socialism*, p. 13.

79. Although Cuba was having some disagreements with the Soviet Union at this time, it eventually decided to join the boycott of the 1984 Games for "solidarity" (see Domínguez, *To Make a World Safe*, p. 105); J. Stubbs, *Cuba: The Test of Time* (London: Latin American Bureau [Research and Action], 1989), p. 110. Such harassment continues outside of sports as well. Cuban exile protesters recently marred an academic conference on the history of Tampa, Florida, on the campus of the University of South Florida. When invited speakers from Cuba attempted to speak, demonstrators forced the closing of the session. The Cubans had to be escorted from the auditorium under a hail of debris and verbal abuse. One speaker was hit with a picket sign. Louis A. Pérez, Jr., "Cuba, Cubans, and the Climate of Intolerance," *LASA Forum* 23, no. 4 (Winter 1993), pp. 1, 3–6.

80. Stubbs, *Cuba: The Test of Time;* M. Janofsky, "Cubans Turn Their Backs on the Seoul Olympics," *New York Times*, 16 January 1988, p. 47; M. Janofsky, "Cuba, North Korea Prepare to Be Hosts," *New York Times*, 19 January 1988, p. D27; M. Janofsky, "Cuba Discusses Decision on Seoul," *New York Times*, 11 February 1988, p. B14.

81. Janofsky, "Cubans Turn Their Backs," p. 49; Janofsky, "Cuba Discusses Decision," p. B14; (AP), "Cuba Still Pan Am Site," *New York Times*, 12 April 1988.

82. D. Hevesi, "Chess Grandmaster Barred From Taking Prize to Cuba," *New York Times Metropolitan News*, 10 April 1988, p. 34.

83. M. Janofsky, "U.S.–Cuba Gulf Is Still There," *New York Times*, 22 July 1990.

84. M. Janofsky, "All They Need Is a Bowling Lane," *New York Times*, 20 August 1987, p. D24; Janofsky, "U.S.–Cuba Gulf"; G. Vecsey, "Pins Are Toppling, even if Castro Isn't," *New York Times*, 11 August 1991. See also Spencer Reiss and Peter Katel, "After Fidel, a Deluge of Deals," *Newsweek*, 29 June 1992, p. 42.

85. (AP), "Castro Uses Games to Display a Happy Face," *The Age*, 15 August 1991. See also González González et al., *Razones*, pp. 63–64; Gutiérrez, conversation with Geralyn Pye; L. Hockstader, "Cuba Sports New Slogan: 'Let the Games Begin,' Castro Set to Open World Athletic Meet," *Washington Post*, 29 July 1991, p. A14.

86. Knott, "Medals Won't Help," p. D2; Fidel Castro, interview on ABC TV, 28 July 1991. Cuba broke even on the games. Gutiérrez, conversation with Geralyn Pye.

87. M. Janofsky, "Pan Am Games Eye Problems," *New York Times*, 25 August 1987, p. A17; M. Janofsky, "ABC Seeks Court Order to Show Cuban Games," *New York Times*, 6 December 1989; M. Janofsky, "Tentative Agreement for ABC on '91 Rights," *New York Times*, 17 May 1989; Janofsky, "ABC Seeks Court Order"; (Reuters) "Capital Cities Loses Ruling," *New York Times*, 4 December 1990; "ABC Works Out Its Pan Am Deal," *New York Times*, 4 December 1990. See also Reed, *Island in the Storm*, pp. 10–11.

88. J. Laber and J. S. Rubin, "Let Americans Go to Cuba," *New York Times*, 1 June 1991, p. 23. The gold medallist was sixteen-year-old Mario González who won the 200–meter breaststroke. (AP), "Roundup—Swimming," *Washington Post*, 17 August 1991, p. D3; Knott, "Medals Won't Help," p. D2; Christine Brennan, "U.S. Team Blends In as Castro Declares Pan Am Games Open," *Washington Post*, 3 August 1991, pp. D1–D2; G. Vecsey, "Where the Sickle Meets the Saddle," *New York Times*, 13 August 1991, p. 10; K. Allen, "Best, Worst of Games," *USA Today*, 20 August 1991, p. C7; L. Hockstader, "No Service, No Smile, Little Sauce," *Washington Post*, 5 August 1991, p. A12.

89. A backboard broke in the warm-up for a men's basketball match between Cuba and the United States, causing the game to be delayed for thirty minutes. The problem was not necessarily substandard equipment. Breakage of backboards during a game has become a somewhat common occurrence in NBA play, as players hone the gratuitous and costly practice of hanging from the rim after a shot. See Christine Brennan, "U.S. Men's Basketball Stumbles, Doesn't Fall," *Washington Post*, 4 August 1991, p. D7; also "Shattered" and "Can You Spare a Boat?" *Washington Times*, 5 August 1991, pp. C1, C9.

90. Christine Brennan, "U.S. Men Return, Dispatch Bahamas," *Washington Post*, 8 October 1991, p. D5; "How Suite It Is," *Washington Times*, 24 August

1991, p. D6; also Christine Brennan, "Spotlight of Americas on Cuba," *Washington Post*, 2 August 1991, p. F2, and "U.S. Is Criticized for Pan Am Shuttle," *Washington Post*, 8 August 1991, p. B1; M. Wilbon, "Amateurism, at Best and Worst," *Washington Post*, 17 August 1991, p. D1.

91. Hart, "Will Cuba Follow Kremlin's Example?" p. 11.

92. Gutiérrez, conversation with Geralyn Pye; S. Wulf, "Running on Empty," *Sports Illustrated* 75, no. 5, 29 July 1991, p. 65; Brennan "Spotlight of Americas," p. F1; Christine Brennan, "U.S. Swimmers Get Rolling, Win 5 of 5 at Pan Am Games," *Washington Post*, 13 August 1991, p. E1.

93. Hockstader, "Cuba Sports New Slogan," p. A14.

94. According to Alberto Juantorena, "The Cuban people see these Games as something of their own. Half a million people have participated in some way. It's a matter of national pride, national dignity. . . . The ultimate goal of the construction is to give a higher standard of living to the average citizen." Cited in Christine Brennan, "Juantorena Doesn't Fault U.S. Shuttle," *Washington Post*, 8 October 1991, p. D5.

95. Strobel, "Pan Am Games Could Invite Cuban Unrest," p. A5; "Cuban Sports New Slogan," p. A14; (AP), "Castro Uses Games."

96. Vecsey, "Where the Sickle Meets the Saddle," p. 10. Also see this volume, chapter 7, on Cuban and Soviet sports cooperation.

97. The Fourth Congress declared it would look at exporting sports services rather than sports aid, which, like all Cuban aid, is likely to be cut. See "Resolución sobre al desarrollo económico del país," *Congreso del PCC*, p. 10. Military aid has already been cut, and although Castro stated that civilian aid would continue, his declaration "We have problems at home, and internationalism begins at home" suggests that cuts are likely in all aid. Fidel Castro Ruz, cited in P. Fletcher, "Cuba to Halt Military Aid to Revolutions," *Washington Times*, 14 January 1992, p. A7. See also T. Harvey, "Cuba: New Foreign Policy," *Times-Picayune*, 16 January 1992.

98. Rhoden, "You Need An Olympic Coach?," pp. A1, B10.

99. All quotations in this paragraph are from E. M. Swift and Jeff Lilley, "Soviet Disunion," *Sports Illustrated* 77, no. 2, 13 July 1992, pp. 46–48.

100. Drozdiak, "A Team Unified by Individual Goals." All the information and quotations in the next four paragraphs come from this work. In an unprecedented move, the U.S. Olympic Committee recently announced a policy of grants that will entitle American athletes who excel at the Olympics to bonuses. The USOC will give an athlete $15,000 for a gold medal, $10,000 for a silver medal, $7,500 for a bronze, and $5,000 for a fourth-place finish. For world championships and other non-Olympic year competitions, the USOC will award $5,000 for first, $4,000 for second, $3,500 for third, $3,000 for fourth, and $2,500 for fifth through eighth. Before this new policy, the USOC had awarded $2,500 to any top eight finishers in all major competitions. Christine Brennan, "U.S. Athletes to Earn $15,000 for Each Olympic Gold Medal," *Washington Post*, 12 May 1993, pp. A1, A12.

101. Gutiérrez, conversation with Geralyn Pye. See also Brubaker, "Cuba's Renewed Mission," pp. D1, D6.

102. Dissatisfaction appears to be growing, especially among Cubans aged between fifteen and thirty. This discontent is expressed through public drunkenness, money changing, prostitution and pimping, and requests to tourists for gifts (Geralyn Pye, observations, Havana, 1988 and 1992). Crime was also a topic of some concern at the Fourth Congress of the PCC. The link between economic decline and rising crime seems evident: in 1990, 60 percent of crimes were property related (Reed, *Island in the Storm,* p. 96).

103. From 1987 to 1990, INDER budgets grew only slightly, from 112.3 million pesos to 117 million pesos. See González González et al., *Razones,* p. 152; also Vecsey, "Pins Are Toppling." Benjamin, "Things Fall Apart," p. 15; Gutiérrez, conversation with Geralyn Pye.

CHAPTER 7. CUBA TODAY AND TOMORROW:
A HOME RUN FOR SPORTS, A STRIKEOUT FOR THE ECONOMY?

1. M. Benjamin, J. Collins, and M. Scott, *No Free Lunch: Food and Revolution in Cuba Today* (San Francisco: Institute for Food and Development Policy, 1984), pp. 90, 96–97.

2. L. A. Pérez, Jr., *Cuba Between Reform and Revolution* (New York: Oxford University Press, 1988), p. 357; González González et al., *Razones,* p. 52.

3. Pickering, "Cuba," p. 164; Caminada, "Recuento," p. 5; González González et al., *Razones,* pp. 153, 8–9.

4. Riordan, *Sport Under Communism,* p. ix.

5. Gutiérrez, conversation with Geralyn Pye.

6. Imports from the former socialist bloc have stopped (González González et al., *Razones,* p. 52). The drop in sports participation after leaving school is not unique to Cuba. The problem has also been documented in Australia (see *Youth Sport,* p. 13). Padula and Smith, "Women in Socialist Cuba," p. 87; Caminada, "Recuento," p. 8.

7. *Marianismo* describes the attitude of women who accept the traditional gender stereotypes, roles, and the accompanying male attitudes prevalent in *machismo.*

8. J. Paz, "¿Se puede bajar el peso?" p. 29.

9. Some exiled Cubans claim they were excluded from baseball for political reasons. See J. Carson, in J. Feinstein, "Cuban Refugees Ache for Shot at 'American Great Leagues'," *Washington Post,* 25 May 1980, pp. F1, F14.

10. See Caminada, "Recuento."

11. "Champions Call for Sacking of Sports Committee," *Survey* 12, no. 9 (October 1989), p. 16. See this volume, chapter 6, on reduced privileges for baseball players.

12. Louie Estrada, "Death Verdicts in Cuba Spur Outcry," *Times of the Americas,* 22 January 1992, p. 1.

13. A. Juantorena, cited in Boswell, "Cuba's National Treasures," pp. D1, D3.

14. Juantorena has important positions both in INDER and on the Central Committee of the PCC, so he feels he takes a part in the building of his country. This feeling may be less strong among those who do not have so much power.

15. Books and articles typically point out the political as well as the sporting merits of athletes. See, for example, D. A. Alvarez Guerra et al., *El deporte universitario,* and F. Guiral, *María Caridad Colón.*

16. Boswell, "Idle Play," pp. D1, D7.

17. D. Kanin, *The Role of Sport in International Relations,* unpublished Ph.D. dissertation, Fletcher School of Law and Diplomacy, 1976, pp. 6–7, and Strenk, "The Thrill of Victory," p. 460.

18. Strenk, "The Thrill of Victory," pp. 453–69.

19. Pickering, in Riordan, *Sport Under Communism,* p. 147.

20. Castro quoted in Pickering, "Cuba," p. 150.

21. Casal and Hernández, "The Role of Cultural and Sports Events."

22. F. Mastrascusa, "Un honor para Cuba," *LPV* 707, 6 January 1976, pp. 14, 15.

23. Domínguez, *To Make a World Safe,* p. 171; M. Rolo, "Cuban Construction Workers Finish Sports Complex in Jamaica," *GWR,* 10 August 1980, p. 11.

24. Domínguez, *To Make a World Safe,* p. 171; González González et al., *Razones,* pp. 70, 71, 172–75, 237–38.

25. González González et al., *Razones,* p. 174. See "Resolución sobre el desarrollo económico del país," point 5, *Congreso del Partido Comunista de Cuba,* p. 10. "Sports Agreement Signed with Venezuela," Havana Radio Reloj Network, 13 October 1992, translated by Foreign Broadcast Information Services, 15 October 1992, p. 5.

26. Pickering, "Cuba," p. 147.

27. Brubaker, "Cuba's Renewed Mission."

28. Rhoden, "You Need an Olympic Coach?" pp. A1, B10.

29. Tom Knott, "Americans Overwhelm Cuba by 79" and "U.S. Came and Saw, and Cuba Was in Awe," *Washington Times,* 29 June 1992, pp. C1, C2. Also Michael Wilbon, "Savor Day, Dream On," *Washington Post,* 29 June 1992, pp. C1, C7.

30. All quotations from Knott, "Americans Overwhelm Cuba."

31. Boswell, "Sí, Cubans' Ajete Is Ace," pp. F1, F9. See also Steve Wulf, "Of Major Interest," *Sports Illustrated* 77, no. 7, 17 August 1992, p. 52. Much has been read into this quote. The translation was the first base umpire's (it was also reported as "I hope I will be able to watch you there someday"). The implication was (from the first translation) that the Cuban hoped to play in the major leagues as well, which put a political spin on the remark.

32. "Castro Raps U.S. for Its Dream Team," *Washington Post,* 12 August 1992, p. B5.

33. The most noteworthy example of Cuban–U.S. sporting ties are boxing matches between the two countries, which have been held with reasonable regularity in both countries in recent years. Alfonso, *Puños dorados,* pp. 214–17.

34. Strenk, "The Thrill of Victory," p. 457.

35. Douglas Farah, "Castro's Travels Connote a Tight Grip," *Washington Post*, 27 July 1992, p. A10.

36. Hart, "Will Cuba Follow Kremlin's Example?" p. 10, and Gunn, "Cuba in Crisis," p. 104.

Index

Equestrian sports, 145

ESBECs. *See* Basic Secondary Schools in the Countryside

Escuela de las Iniciación de Deportívas Escolares (EIDE). *See* School for the Initiation of Scholastic Sports

Escuela Provincial de Educación Física (EPEF). *See* Provincial School for Physical Education

Escuelas Secundarias Básicas en el Campo. *See* Basic Secondary Schools in the Countryside (ESBECs)

Escuela Superior de Educación Física. *See* Higher School of Physical Education (ESEF)

Escuela Superior de Perfeccionamiento Atletico. See Higher Institute of Athletic Perfection (ESPA)

ESPA. *See* Higher Institute of Athletic Perfection

Estadio Latinoamericano, 88, 89, 90, 182, 186: and bust of Dihigo, 32; and renovations by CDRs, 82, 89

Estalella, Roberto, 34, 37

Estefan, Gloria, 218

Exiles. *See* Cuban exiles

Fajardo, Comandante Manuel. *See* Higher School of Physical Education (ESEF)

Federation of Cuban Women (FMC), 81, 86: and adult physical culture, 107, 110; role of in Street Plan, 105; and study of students' free time, 104

Familia Cederista LPV. See Listos Para Vencer *(LPV)*

Federation of (High) School Students (FEEM), 86

FEEM. *See* Federation of (High) School Students

Fencing, 144–45: and foreign coaches, 149; participation of women in, 123; pre-revolution, 17, 53, 55. *See also* Fonst, Ramón

Fernandez Alvarez, José Ramón, 218

Figuerola, Enrique, 149

Florida International League, 36–37. *See also* Havana Cubans

FMC. *See* Federation of Cuban Women

Fonst, Ramón, 17, 42, 53. *See also* Fencing

Forbes, Irene, 125

Fordham University, 26

Fortún, Rafael, 55–56, 65, 126

France, 213

Freedom Now Committee, 217–18

Fuentes, José, 5, 170

Fuentes, Tito, 179–80

Fuerzas armadas revolucionario. See Revolutionary Armed Forces

Gálvez y Delmonte, Wenceslao, 28

Gambling, 16, 17, 22, 24, 45, 46–47 (table 3), 48, 61, 64, 176: and boxing, 43; and dog races, 22; and horse races, 22; and jai alai, 22, 50, 51, 252n103; and pelota vasca, 22, 252n103

Games of the Armed Forces. *See* Military games

Garbey, Barbaro, 176, 189

García Bango, Jorge, 85, 96, 148

García, Silvio, 33. *See also* Baseball, Negro leagues in; Baseball, and "color line"

General Directory of Sports (DGD), 25, 49, 69, 81, 85, 98: dissolution of, 70

Germany, East, 15, 135, 148, 153–54, 158, 205–06, 210–11, 216

Giants. *See* New York Giants

Gibson, Josh, 31. *See also* Baseball, Negro leagues in

Gil, Huberto, 119–20

Gómez, Pedro "Preston," 34, 184, 193

González, Manuel, 13, 102

González, Mike, 29, 179. *See also* Baseball, U.S. professional; Boston Braves

Goodwill Games, 213, 220, 224. *See also* Turner, Ted

Gosport. *See* Soviet Sports Ministry

Gotov k trudu i oborone (GTO), 11, 101, 257n31

Grandparents' groups. *See* Círculos de abuelos

Granma, 32

Great Leagues. *See* Baseball, U.S. professional

Pitt Latin American Series

James M. Malloy, Editor

ARGENTINA

Argentina Between the Great Powers, 1936–1946
Guido di Tella and D. Cameron Watt, Editors

Argentina in the Twentieth Century
David Rock, Editor

Argentina: Political Culture and Instability
Susan Calvert and Peter Calvert

Argentine Workers: Peronism and Contemporary Class Consciousness
Peter Ranis

Discreet Partners: Argentina and the USSR Since 1917
Aldo César Vacs

The Franco-Perón Alliance: Relations Between Spain and Argentina, 1946–1955
Raanan Rein, translated by Martha Grenzeback

The Life, Music, and Times of Carlos Gardel
Simon Collier

Institutions, Parties, and Coalitions in Argentine Politics
Luigi Manzetti

The Political Economy of Argentina, 1946–1983
Guido di Tella and Rudiger Dornbusch, Editors

BOLIVIA

Unsettling Statecraft: Neoliberalism in the Central Andes
Catherine M. Conaghan and James M. Malloy

The State and Capital Accumulation in Latin America. Vol. 1: Brazil, Chile, Mexico. Vol. 2: Argentina, Bolivia, Colombia, Ecuador, Peru, Uruguay, Venezuela
Christian Anglade and Carlos Fortin, Editors

BRAZIL

Capital Markets in the Development Process: The Case of Brazil
John W. Welch

External Constraints on Economic Policy in Brazil, 1899–1930
Winston Fritsch

The Film Industry in Brazil: Culture and the State
Randal Johnson

Sport in Cuba: The Diamond in the Rough
Paula J. Pettavino and Geralyn Pye

ECUADOR

Military Rule and Transition in Ecuador: Dancing with the People
Anita Isaacs

Unsettling Statecraft: Neoliberalism in the Central Andes
Catherine M. Conaghan and James M. Malloy

The State and Capital Accumulation in Latin America. Vol. 1: Brazil, Chile, Mexico. Vol. 2: Argentina, Bolivia, Colombia, Ecuador, Peru, Uruguay, Venezuela
Christian Anglade and Carlos Fortin, Editors

MEXICO

The Dynamics of Domination: State, Class, and Social Reform in Mexico, 1910–1990
Viviane Brachet-Márquez

The Expulsion of Mexico's Spaniards, 1821–1836
Harold Dana Sims

The Mexican Republic: The First Decade, 1823–1832
Stanley C. Green

Mexico Through Russian Eyes, 1806–1940
William Harrison Richardson

Oil and Mexican Foreign Policy
George W. Grayson

The Politics of Mexican Oil
George W. Grayson

Voices, Visions, and a New Reality: Mexican Fiction Since 1970
J. Ann Duncan

PERU

Domestic and Foreign Finance in Modern Peru, 1850–1950: Financing Visions of Development
Alfonso W. Quiroz

Economic Management and Economic Development in Peru and Colombia
Rosemary Thorp

The Origins of the Peruvian Labor Movement, 1883–1919
Peter Blanchard

Peru and the International Monetary Fund
Thomas Scheetz

Peru Under García: An Opportunity Lost
John Crabtree

Poverty and Peasantry in Peru's Southern Andes
R. F. Watters

Renaissance on the Right: Neoliberal Coalitions in the Central Andes
Catherine M. Conaghan and James M. Malloy

CARIBBEAN

The Last Cacique: Leadership and Politics in a Puerto Rican City
Jorge Heine

A Revolution Aborted: The Lessons of Grenada
Jorge Heine, Editor

To Hell with Paradise: A History of the Jamaican Tourist Industry
Frank Fonda Taylor

The Meaning of Freedom: Economics, Politics and Culture After Slavery
Frank McGlynn and Seymour Drescher, Editors

CENTRAL AMERICA

At the Fall of Somoza
Lawrence Pezzullo and Ralph Pezzullo

Black Labor on a White Canal: Panama, 1904–1981
Michael L. Conniff

The Catholic Church and Politics in Nicaragua and Costa Rica
Philip J. Williams

Perspectives on the Agro-Export Economy in Central America
Wim Pelupessy, Editor

OTHER NATIONAL STUDIES

The Overthrow of Allende and the Politics of Chile, 1964–1976
Paul E. Sigmund

Military Rule and Transition in Ecuador: Dancing with the People
Anita Isaacs

Primary Medical Care in Chile: Accessibility Under Military Rule
Joseph L. Scarpaci

Rebirth of the Paraguayan Republic: The First Colorado Era, 1878–1904
Harris G. Warren

Restructuring Domination: Industrialists and the State in Ecuador
Catherine M. Conaghan

U.S. POLICIES

The Hovering Giant: U.S. Responses to Revolutionary Change in Latin America
Cole Blasier

Illusions of Conflict: Anglo-American Diplomacy Toward Latin America
Joseph Smith

Images and Intervention: U.S. Policies in Latin America
Martha L. Cottam

Unsettling Statecraft: Neoliberalism in the Central Andes
Catherine M. Conaghan and James M. Malloy

Selected Latin American One-Act Plays
Francesca Colecchia and Julio Matas, Editors and Translators

The Social Documentary in Latin America
Julianne Burton, Editor

The State and Capital Accumulation in Latin America. Vol. 1: Brazil, Chile, Mexico, Vol. 2: Argentina, Bolivia, Colombia, Ecuador, Peru, Uruguay, Venezuela
Christian Anglade and Carlos Fortin, Editors

Transnational Corporations and the Latin American Automobile Industry
Rhys Jenkins